Steps for Critical Thinking

Recognize the Argument
- ▲ Count the claims
- ▲ Look for reasons
- ▲ Identify the purpose

Analyze the Argument
- ▲ Pay attention to inference indicators
- ▲ Identify the premises and conclusion
- ▲ Determine the issue
- ▲ Analyze any subarguments
- ▲ Diagram the argument

Evaluate the Argument
- ▲ Determine the reasoning style
- ▲ Identify the argument kind
- ▲ Use appropriate terminology and tools

Deductive Reasoning

Categorical Arguments
- ▲ Translate into standard form
- ▲ Check validity using a Venn diagram

Truth-Functional Arguments
- ▲ Translate into symbolic form
- ▲ Check validity using a truth table

Inductive Reasoning

Inductive Generalizations
- ▲ Present in general form
- ▲ Assess how well the sample represents the target

Analogical Arguments
- ▲ Present in general form
- ▲ Assess the analogy

Causal Arguments
- ▲ Present in general form
- ▲ Determine the method
- ▲ Assess the causal evidence

Common Fallacies

Begging the Question	The conclusion of an argument is assumed by the argument's premises.
Appeal to Ignorance	The arguer illegitimately shifts the burden of proof to his or her opponent.
Appeal to Illegitimate Authority	The arguer uses a source that is not an authority on the subject in question to support a conclusion.
Ad Hominem	The arguer rejects an opposing argument based on the characteristics of its author.
Strawman	The arguer mischaracterizes the conclusion of his or her opponent's argument and then attacks the argument in its distorted form.
Red Herring	The arguer distracts the reader from the issue by using irrelevant premises.

Argumentative Essay Structure

Introduction	Identify the issue, conclusion, and premises.
Body	Provide reasons, evidence, and/or examples that support each premise.
Objection/Reply	State the strongest objection to your conclusion, and effectively respond to it.
Conclusion	Restate your conclusion and premises.
Citations	Give full and detailed credit for others' ideas.

Critical Thinking

A USER'S MANUAL
Second Edition

DEBRA JACKSON

&

PAUL NEWBERRY

California State University, Bakersfield

CENGAGE
Learning·

Australia • Brazil • Mexico • Singapore • United Kingdom • United States

**Critical Thinking: A User's Manual,
Second Edition**
Debra Jackson and Paul Newberry

Product Manager: Debra Matteson

Content Developer: Florence Kilgo

Associate Content Developer: Joshua Duncan

Product Assistant: Abigail Hess

Intellectual Property Analyst: Alexandra
Ricciardi

Marketing Manager: Christine Sosa

Manufacturing Planner: Sandee Milewski

Art and Design Direction, Production
Management, and Composition: Cenveo®
Publisher Services

Cover Image: ©www.gettyimages.com

Cover design: Evgeni Dinev Photography/
Moment Open/Getty images

For product information and technology assistance, contact us at
Cengage Learning Customer & Sales Support, 1-800-354-9706

For permission to use material from this text or product,
submit all requests online at **www.cengage.com/permissions**.
Further permissions questions can be emailed to
permissionrequest@cengage.com.

Library of Congress Control Number: 2014947910

ISBN: 978-1-285-19684-8

Cengage Learning
200 First Stamford Place, 4th Floor
Stamford CT 06902
USA

Cengage Learning is a leading provider of customized learning solutions with
office locations around the globe, including Singapore, the United Kingdom,
Australia, Mexico, Brazil and Japan. Locate your local office at **www.cengage
.com/global.**

Cengage Learning products are represented in Canada by
Nelson Education, Ltd.

For your course and learning solutions, visit **www.cengage.com**.

Purchase any of our products at your local college store or at our preferred
online store **www.cengagebrain.com**.

Instructors: Please visit **login.cengage.com** and log in to access instructor-
specific resources.

Printed at CLDPC, USA, 03-19

Brief Contents

Brief Contents

Contents

Supplementary Chapters

Preface

As college instructors, we know that critical thinking changes lives. Learning to recognize, analyze, evaluate, and construct arguments can provide students with the foundation to successfully complete college, pursue their future careers, and become more discerning citizens. To provide the best opportunities for our students to acquire these vital skills, we created a genuinely different kind of text, one that is

- ▶ accessible, yet challenging, to both beginning and advanced students;
- ▶ focused on building foundational skills in a step-by-step fashion;
- ▶ committed to integrated, active learning strategies;
- ▶ packed with clear examples and exercises that epitomize the skills learned; and
- ▶ structured to ensure that students transfer critical thinking skills beyond the classroom.

Why do we call this text *A User's Manual*? User's manuals are written for the beginner and the do-it-yourselfer. We have taken the same approach here. We focus on four essential skills—argument recognition, analysis, evaluation, and construction—and break each down into its basic components. In this way, students learn to think critically in a step-by-step fashion, as they would learn to master any skill, be it speaking Japanese, playing basketball, or painting a portrait. In addition, like any good user's manual, this text is easy to follow. We provide clear examples and explanations, and we integrate workbook-style writing and thinking exercises that promote active learning.

Step-by-Step Approach—IMPROVED!

We continue to treat the acquisition of critical thinking skills as a process and make every effort to present our exposition in the clearest way possible, maintaining as much exactness as the topic or skill warrants without making it overly complex for the novice. For example, in Chapter 3 (Analyzing Arguments), we begin by analyzing very simple arguments containing inference indicators. Next, we introduce, one by one, arguments without inference indicators, arguments with extra claims, and arguments with implied claims. Only then do students encounter arguments with multiple conclusions and chain arguments. This process is repeated in Chapter 4 (Diagramming Arguments) as students learn to draw argument diagrams, again in a step-by-step manner. By the end of Chapter 4, students are able to recognize, analyze, and diagram complex chain arguments containing extra and implied claims.

In this second edition, we have not only incorporated suggestions given by reviewers and users of our first edition, but also have made changes based on our own teaching experience to make our unique step-by-step method more seamless throughout the text. For example, we significantly changed Chapters 2 and 5. In Chapter 2, we more explicitly emphasize the step-by-step method to demystify the distinctions between arguments and nonarguments, and introduce the analysis of nonarguments in a Critical Précis (the new name for our previous Basic Analysis). In Chapter 5 (Preparing to Evaluate Arguments), we have expanded the discussion of the five types of arguments that are the focus of the succeeding five chapters and added exercises to help strengthen students' ability to differentiate these argument types and use the appropriate terminology in evaluating them.

"Your Turn!"

By reading actively, with a pencil in hand, students are more likely to apply what they learn in the context of their own experiences. It can be difficult to get students to read this way, so we provide frequent, workbook-style "Your Turn!" exercises to help students focus their reading, check their understanding of new content immediately, and integrate earlier skills with later ones. This feature can be incorporated into lectures, utilized in group activities, or included with homework assignments.

Abundant, Integrated Exercises—IMPROVED!

This text includes over 1,100 exercises, designed to provide students with immediate practice of individual skills as they are learned. These exercises are progressive, so that students have time to absorb the basics before encountering tougher problems, and cumulative exercises are provided for additional reinforcement. Those of you who have used our first edition will find many refreshed exercises and examples. We believe it is important to show students how to apply critical thinking skills to current issues and controversies, which requires eliminating those that have gone stale. As in the first edition, answers to selected exercises are provided in the back of the book as a self-check for students.

"Putting It All Together"—IMPROVED!

As a means to improve critical thinking through writing, we provide comprehensive writing exercises at the end of Chapters 3 through 11. In these highly structured assignments, students integrate previously learned skills with those presented in the current chapter. Each "Putting It All Together" section includes clear instructions and examples of the proper way for students to complete the assignments. In addition, to facilitate student awareness of the transferability of the skills beyond the critical thinking classroom, the examples are mined from a wide variety of sourced material—books, magazine and newspaper articles, advertisements, websites, and so on—and from a broad range of topics relevant to both their academic and their extracurricular lives.

"One Step Further"—NEW!

In response to reviewer requests that the second edition include a vehicle for students to apply each skill outside of textbook exercises, we have added "One Step Further" activities at the end of each chapter. These exercises allow instructors to move beyond the text in many innovative ways. They can be used as in-class or homework assignments, as discussion starters, or as a place where you can add your own variations to what we have suggested. Each chapter's "One Step Further" relates specifically to that chapter's skill set.

Flexibility—IMPROVED!

Although we expect and allow for some instructor choice about which topics are covered and in which order they are covered, the material is most effective when Chapters 1 through 5 are taught in order. By doing so, you can best take advantage of the step-by-step progression built into the text. However, the remaining chapters may be chosen according to instructor preference, depending on course time and needs.

To further enhance the flexibility of the text, we have made two significant changes. First, we relocated the chapter on fallacy recognition from the middle of the text, as Chapter 5, to near the end of the text, as Chapter 11. This change makes it clearer to students and instructors that our text includes discussions and examples of more fallacies than the six central ones included in that chapter. Chapters 8, 9, and 10, for example, integrate fallacies into the discussions of inductive generalizations, analogical arguments, and causal arguments, respectively. Additionally, since fallacious arguments are no longer sprinkled throughout "Putting It All Together" exercises, instructors can skip fallacies altogether or include them at almost any stage after Chapter 5.

The second significant change is to the chapters on evaluating deductive arguments—Chapter 6 (Evaluating Categorical Arguments) and Chapter 7 (Evaluating Truth-Functional Arguments). In the first edition, these chapters were lengthy, in part because they introduced multiple methods for evaluating these arguments. In the second edition, we selected one method of evaluation for each chapter and created supplemental chapters for instructors who wish to allot more time and delve more deeply into the evaluation of these deductive arguments. You may wish to assign both the chapter and the supplement or limit your instruction to the primary chapter.

Learning and Teaching Aids

Critical Thinking: A User's Manual, Second Edition, is available with Aplia™, an online interactive homework solution that improves comprehension and outcomes by increasing student effort and engagement. Founded by a professor to enhance his own courses, Aplia™ provides automatically graded assignments with detailed, immediate explanations on every question as well as innovative teaching materials. This easy-to-use system has benefited more than 1,000,000 students at over 1,800 institutions.

Instructor materials are available on the Instructor Companion website. This website offers instructors an all-in-one resource for class preparation, presentation, and testing. Accessible through Cengage.com/login with your faculty account, the website provides prepared lecture slides and the complete *Instructor's Manual*, which includes teaching suggestions for each chapter and answers to all exercises. Finally, Cengage Learning Testing, powered by Cognero®, is available for *Critical Thinking: A User's Manual*, Second Edition, and is accessible through Cengage.com/login with your faculty account. This test bank contains multiple-choice and essay questions for each chapter. Cognero® is a flexible online system that allows you to author, edit, and manage test bank content for *Critical Thinking: A User's Manual*, Second Edition. Create multiple test versions instantly and deliver them through your Learning Management System (LMS) from your classroom or wherever you may be, with no special installs or downloads required. The following format types are available for download from the Instructor Companion site: Blackboard, Angel, Moodle, Canvas, and Desire2Learn. You can import these files directly into your LMS to edit and manage questions and to create tests. The test bank is also available in PDF format from this site.

Acknowledgments

We are grateful for all the assistance, advice, and inspiration from our Wadsworth/ Cengage team, especially to Joann Kozyrev, our former managing editor, for championing our second edition early on in the process, and to Debra Matteson, our current managing editor, for enthusiastically endorsing the project. We also want to give special thanks to Florence Kilgo, our development editor, whose meticulous edits and suggestions for every chapter have significantly improved this text.

The book was also improved by the comments of the following reviewers:

Stephen Brown, Briar Cliff University; Charles Cardwell, Pellissippi State; Denise Chambers, Normandale Community College; Gloria Cockerell, Collin College; Jeff Davis, Stevens-Henager College; Dawn Gale, Johnson County Community College; Emily Isaacson, Chowan University; Sandra McClammy, Cape Fear Community College; Peter Murphy, University of Indianapolis; N. Mark Rauls, College of Southern Nevada; Gary Russell, Spoon River Community College; Dennis Ryan, Edgewood College; Bonnie Sarnoff, Limestone College; Patrick Smith, San Francisco State University; Ed Teall, Mount St. Mary College; and Lori Underwood, Christopher Newport University.

For their reviews and suggestions contributing to the first edition, we wish to express our continued thanks to:

Robert Abele, Diablo Valley College; Ralph Acampora, Hofstra University; Minerva Ahumada, Northeastern Illinois University; Patricia Allen, MassBay Community College; James Anderson, San Diego State University; Robin Arneson, Normandale Community College; Julie M. Aultman, Northeastern Ohio University Colleges of Medicine and Pharmacy and Youngstown State University; Claudia Basha, Victor Valley College; Michael Bishop, Florida State University; Diana C. Blauvelt, Passaic County Community College; Daniel R. Boisvert, University of North Carolina at Charlotte; Michael Boring, Estrella Mountain Community College; Craig Bradley, Grossmont College; William Brunson, University of Nevada, Las Vegas; Leslie Burkholder, University of British Colombia; Christopher Caldwell, Virginia State University; Delilah Caldwell, Virginia State University; Charles E. Cardwell, Pellissippi State Community College; Barbara Carlson, Clark University; Jennifer Caseldine-Bracht, Indiana University-Purdue University Fort Wayne; Denise Chambers, Normandale Community College; Dobin Choi, SUNY–Buffalo; Doug Clouatre, Mid-Plains Community College; Alan Clune, Sam Houston State University; Marlys Cordoba, College of the Siskiyous; Judy Covington, Trident Technical College; Sharon Crasnow, Riverside Community College; Marcel Daguerre, CSU–Chico; Michelle Darnell, Fayetteville State University; William Davenport, Lakeland Community College; Theresa Dolan, Los Angeles Trade Technical College; Tom Duran, Labette Community College; Joe Emeka, Quincy University; Frank Fair, Sam Houston State University; Stephen Findley, Webster University; Galen Foresman, North Carolina A&T State University; David Foster, University of Findlay; LaVerne S. Fox, CSU–Long Beach; Matthew Freytag, University of Maine at Farmington; Amy Garcia, Fullerton College; Kristen Gerdes, Cerritos Community College; William Gifford, Truckee Meadows Community College; Nuria Giralt, CSU–Long Beach; Cynthia Gobatie, Riverside City College; Nathan Griffith, Belmont University; Shahrokh Haghighi, CSU–Long Beach; Courtney Hammons, Cuyamaca College; Mara Harrell, Carnegie Mellon University; William J. Hawk, James Madison University; Kenneth Hochstetter, College of Southern Nevada; Sharon M. Hope, Maria College; Steven A. Jauss, University of Arkansas–Little Rock; Joseph Jedwab,

Kutztown University; Doris Jones, The American University in Cairo; Veronica C. Jones, Southeast Community College–Lincoln; Andrew Jones-Cathcart, College of the Canyons; Allyn Kahn, Champlain College; David Kite, Champlain College; Rory Kraft, York College of Pennsylvania; Michael LaBossiere, Florida A&M University; Carole Mackewich, Clark College; Terrance MacMullan, Eastern Washington University; Ivan Nikolaeff, Everest College; Susan Nylander, Victor Valley College; John Orr, Fullerton College; Slobodan Perovic, Carleton University; Jamie Phillips, Clarion University of Pennsylvania; Susan Priest, Western Nevada College; Michael Principe, Middle Tennessee State University; N. Mark Rauls, College of Southern Nevada; Andrea Reynolds, Ventura College; Dennis Ryan, Edgewood College; Paula Sabin, CSU–Long Beach; Leah Savion, Indiana University; Suzette Schlapkohl, Scottsdale Community College; Michael Schroeder, Savannah State University; Janet Simpson, Suffolk County Community College; Robert Skipper, St. Mary's University–San Antonio; Dennis Slivinski, CSU–Channel Islands; Richard Smith, University of Findlay; Cindy Stern, CSU–Northridge; Lou Suarez, Lorain County Community College; Patricia Jo Teel, Victor Valley College; Susan Vineberg, Wayne State University; Susan Weaver, University of the Cumberlands; James Wilson, Victor Valley College; and James Woolever, Foothill College.

Special Thanks

We are grateful for support and constructive feedback from our CSUB colleagues Jacquelyn Kegley, Steven Gamboa, Maria Paleolgou, and Senem Saner and for our numerous Logical Reasoning students who inspire us. In addition, Paul wishes to thank his wife, Joanne Newberry, for her continual support, helpful suggestions, and careful edits; and Debra gives special thanks to her partner, Michael Tann, for his loving encouragement and incredible patience throughout the development of this book.

Thinking Critically

Imagine that you check your Facebook account and see that your friend Sara has posted a new status update encouraging everyone to join a campaign to make your campus smoke-free. You also see that a number of people have commented on her post, some supporting the campaign and others opposing it.

 Sara says Hey people! Check out this link! We should definitely start this campaign on our campus…

 Smoke-Free Campus The Smoke-Free Campus Initiative aims to promote a clean, safe, and healthy campus environment by eliminating smoking from college campuses…

 James says I don't smoke, but I don't think it's a good idea to ban smoking on campus. Since when does completely banning something work? Alcohol and drugs are illegal on campus, so no one uses them, right? Wrong!

 Davion says If you want to subject yourself to the health risks of smoking, that's fine. But smoking in public places should be banned. Why? It's simple. Smoking poses a health risk to others, and anything that does that should be outlawed. Period.

 Veronica says Are we living in a fascist state now??? The only people who would support this are uptight nonsmokers who want to take away my freedom to express myself and enjoy life. I know smoking is bad for me, but it's my choice!

EXERCISE 1.1

Your Turn!   Which of these arguments do you find the most persuasive? Which is the least persuasive? Explain why.

You have probably encountered exchanges similar to this one on social networking sites like Facebook, in blogs, or in the comments sections following Internet news and video posts. Like James, people often encourage others to approach problems by appealing to similar cases. But what exactly are we to accept from such comparisons? Davion's comment offers compelling reasons for banning smoking, but only if he's right about the extent of the dangers from secondhand smoke. How do we go about evaluating the credibility of his claims? Responses like Veronica's are very common (and usually much more brutal). Personal attacks and rhetoric quickly get out of hand, and the conversation veers away from the original topic. Should you respond to attacks of this sort by engaging in some name-calling of your own, replying with more reasonable arguments, or just ignoring them?

EXERCISE 1.2

Your Turn!   What is your response to the discussion about the campaign for a smoke-free campus?

Each of the posts is trying to persuade you, but not all should succeed. In this text, you will learn to recognize that:

- Sara doesn't offer an argument at all. She merely states her opinion.
- James's and Davion's responses employ different styles of reasoning. In order to determine whether their arguments are convincing, you need to utilize different criteria.
- Veronica's reply commits a common mistake in reasoning called a fallacy. She attacks the people who support the smoking ban rather than their reasons for doing so.

This book will provide you with the critical thinking tools necessary for constructively engaging in conversations like these. It will do so by teaching you when you should be persuaded and when you should not. But here we can make an important distinction to help you better understand the focus of this text. Often thought of as "the art of persuasion," *rhetoric* typically includes every device one might use to persuade others—from rational argumentation to other, nonrational means of persuasion. These nonrational devices include a variety of recognizable techniques, such as emotional appeals, assertions made without any supporting evidence, the use of words and phrases with powerful connotations, and even the use of powerful, persuasive images. Our interest in this text is to focus on rational persuasion and separate it from that which is not.

This focus is grounded on a couple of reasons. First, we humans are rational creatures. So when people try to convince us using logic and reasoning, they are treating us as self-directed, responsible human beings. They provide us with the materials we need to decide for ourselves where we stand on an issue. Rational arguers do not manipulate, trick, pander, or force us to believe or do what they want. Thus, reason is the best means of persuasion to use in any society that values tolerance and civil discourse. We demonstrate respect for one another when we are willing to let reasons do the convincing.

Second, even though we live in a world with plenty of rational argumentation and respect, too much public discourse is manipulative, cynical, and mean-spirited. With the skills you will acquire from studying this book, you will learn to recognize the kinds of discourse that you should take seriously and those that you should set aside or be skeptical of. By focusing on rational means of persuasion—that is, arguments—you will be better positioned to turn away from the nonsense and put your good mind to work to improve your life and the lives of those around you.

So what do we mean by "thinking critically"? When we talk about critical thinking, the term doesn't describe thinking that is severe, negative, or harsh; instead, **critical thinking** refers to thinking that uses reason to decide what to do and what to believe. Since arguments provide reasons that support their claims, the fundamental critical thinking skills are the recognition, analysis, evaluation, and construction of arguments. Others may conceive of critical thinking somewhat differently, but the skills of argumentation you will study here are basic to any and all conceptions of critical thinking.

LEARNING OUTCOMES

In this chapter, you will learn how to:

▶ Define *critical thinking*,
▶ Identify the four major skills that constitute critical thinking, and
▶ Describe four broad contexts in which critical thinking will be useful to you.

As a way to begin the building of critical thinking skills, we will describe how their usefulness extends beyond the fun of participating in online conversations about controversial issues. In fact, the skills you will learn as you study this text will help you do well in your college classes, be more successful in your career, avoid being manipulated by people who want your money or your support, and live a deeper, more meaningful life. That's quite a lot for any book to claim, so let us provide some evidence to back it up.

Using Critical Thinking in the Classroom

Over the years, our fellow educators in various disciplines—business management, criminal justice, nursing, psychology, biology, and others—have repeatedly said how important it is for students in their classes to have strong critical thinking skills. Our colleagues are apparently in good company, according to a 1994 report by the Foundation for Critical Thinking (www.criticalthinking.org). In a survey of faculty at 38 public and 28 private California universities, nearly 90% of respondents claimed that critical thinking constitutes a primary objective of their teaching. Yet only a small minority (9%) clearly taught critical thinking skills on any given day. The first statistic shows just how important critical thinking is in the eyes of instructors, but the second indicates that you must acquire those vital skills *before* you get to the discipline-based courses.

Why do professors consider these skills—the most essential of which are taught in this text—so important to students in their disciplines? One reason is that in college you are expected not only to learn more advanced material than you learned in high school, but also to do things with that material that are more cognitively sophisticated and demanding than what has been expected of you up to this point. From elementary school through high school, your learning has focused on basic information such as the main characters and events in American history, the structure of a grammatically correct sentence, the proper procedures for a chemistry experiment, the rudiments of speaking another language, and so on. All of this is important knowledge. In college, however, you must go far beyond these basics both in content and in what you are asked to do with the information you learn. This is shown in a well-known pyramid of cognitive activities known as Bloom's Taxonomy.

Of course, in college you still must demonstrate knowledge and comprehension of subjects. However, you are also expected to employ Bloom's higher-order cognitive skills of application, analysis, evaluation, and creation. So instead of merely memorizing pertinent information to repeat back on exams or in written work, you must dismantle the parts, apply them in new ways and to new problems, and determine what works well and what doesn't. That is, you must use higher-order cognitive skills. For example, if your Economics instructor asks you, "Is Adam Smith's argument for the 'invisible hand' that guides economic interaction convincing or not?" he or she is asking you to utilize a higher-order cognitive skill—namely, *evaluation*. For such an assignment, you cannot simply recite the information provided to you, but instead must assess its

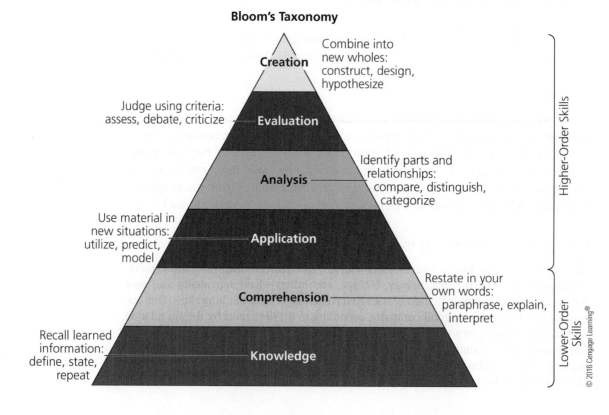

Bloom's Taxonomy

Creation — Combine into new wholes: construct, design, hypothesize

Judge using criteria: assess, debate, criticize — Evaluation

Analysis — Identify parts and relationships: compare, distinguish, categorize

Use material in new situations: utilize, predict, model — Application

Comprehension — Restate in your own words: paraphrase, explain, interpret

Recall learned information: define, state, repeat — Knowledge

Higher-Order Skills

Lower-Order Skills

worth. The major critical thinking skills taught in this book—recognizing, analyzing, evaluating, and constructing arguments—are all higher-order cognitive skills.

 EXERCISE 1.3

Your Turn!   If you are asked to *paraphrase* Adam Smith's argument, which cognitive skill is required? What if you are asked to *compare* Smith's argument to that of Karl Marx? Which of the two activities requires critical thinking? Why?

Critical thinking skills are useful in college courses for yet another reason. As you learn more about a subject, you move beyond the material everyone in the discipline accepts to ideas, theses, and formulations that experts in the field disagree about. For example, because you have been exposed to American history throughout your education, it might appear that all the "facts" about American history have already been discovered and agreed upon. But historians argue, sometimes vehemently, over the credibility of eye-witness testimony, the usefulness of recently acquired documents or artifacts, and the value of innovative research methods. In your college history courses, you are expected to analyze and evaluate these kinds of arguments.

Consider, for example, a debate between historians and a psychoanalyst over whether to accept an eyewitness report of an uprising of prisoners at the Auschwitz death camp in 1944. The historians argued that the woman's testimony was useless because she remembered four chimneys exploding, but only one chimney had been destroyed. The psychoanalyst who had interviewed her disagreed. Her testimony was valuable because it affirmed what had previously been thought impossible—that Jewish armed resistance had in fact occurred. How should we understand such disagreements? Strong critical thinking skills can help you understand what's at issue in controversies like these, understand the strengths and flaws in each side's reasoning, and reach your own conclusion.

Argumentation plays an important part in other disciplines, too. For example, public policy programs often must prepare students to choose a course of action by determining which of two opposing causal explanations is the more powerful. The aftermath of Hurricane Katrina provides one such example. According to a 2005 article from the *Washington Post*, two different agencies—the Army Corps of Engineers and the Louisiana State University (LSU) Hurricane Center—disagreed on the cause of the breaching of the flood walls that resulted in extensive damage to the city. The army blamed the flooding on surges that were too massive for the flood-protection system. However, the LSU Hurricane Center provided evidence that the storm surges never overtopped the flood-protection system. LSU placed the blame for flooding on poor design and/or construction of the flood walls. Students studying to become public policy analysts have to determine which argument is stronger in order to prevent future disasters.

 EXERCISE 1.4

Your Turn!   If you are asked to judge the strength of LSU's argument, which cognitive skill is required? Does this require critical thinking? Why or why not?

Aerial view of massive flooding and destruction in the aftermath of Hurricane Katrina, taken on September 1, 2005 in New Orleans, LA.

For courses in all disciplines—whether history, sociology, biology, business, or anything else—arguments play a large role in the college classroom. Having information, especially in the Internet era, is not sufficient in your advanced courses. You must be able to use that information as never before by applying it in novel situations and critically appraising the results of others doing the same. That is, you must be able to recognize, analyze, evaluate, and construct arguments in a variety of disciplines.

 EXERCISE 1.5

Using Bloom's Taxonomy, choose the highest-level skill required to address each of these sample course assignments. Indicate which assignments require critical thinking.

1. How long was the Hundred Years' War?
   a. Knowledge
   b. Application
   c. Creation
2. In a short paragraph, explain how a gang may serve as a substitute family.
   a. Comprehension
   b. Analysis
   c. Evaluation
3. Jones argues that the lessons learned from the English occupation of Calais and Bordeaux during the Hundred Years' War prevented a permanent peace. Determine whether she gives a persuasive argument, and justify your answer.
   a. Knowledge
   b. Analysis
   c. Evaluation

4. Write an essay in which you show how Joan of Arc's role as a military leader during the Hundred Years' War could give our military leaders a better understanding of religious mysticism among violent extremists in our own time.
   a. Comprehension
   b. Application
   c. Creation

5. What is the American Medical Association (AMA) definition of *mercy killing*?
   a. Knowledge
   b. Comprehension
   c. Analysis

6. In a five-paragraph essay, debate the pros and cons of the AMA definition of *mercy killing*.
   a. Application
   b. Creation
   c. Evaluation

7. Design a classroom activity to teach students about ratios.
   a. Comprehension
   b. Creation
   c. Evaluation

8. Using your own words, describe the purpose of an annual physical exam.
   a. Comprehension
   b. Analysis
   c. Evaluation

9. Compare the financial impacts of Hurricane Katrina and Hurricane Ivan on low-income residents of coastal communities in the United States.
   a. Knowledge
   b. Analysis
   c. Application

10. What did Socrates mean when he claimed, "The unexamined life is not worth living" (Plato, *Apology* 38a)?
    a. Comprehension
    b. Application
    c. Evaluation

Using Critical Thinking in the Workplace

Each year, the National Association of Colleges and Employers (NACE) asks employers which abilities they want college graduates to possess. At or near the top of that list each year is "analytical reasoning," the kind of critical thinking skills taught in this text. Yet accounting majors might ask, "Aren't mathematical and business skills more important for a career as an accountant?" Likewise, nursing majors might suggest that knowledge of medicine is more important for them. Although accountants and nurses obviously need these skills, they must also have a full complement of higher-order thinking skills. People in these kinds of careers must be prepared to solve difficult problems by applying their knowledge to new situations. In addition, they must be able to decide which new ideas they should accept or reject and be able to justify their decisions. On any given day, people in these careers, and most of the careers you may be considering after college, must be able to effectively use critical thinking skills.

For example, suppose at work, one of your employees asks to take a week off the following month and you respond like this:

> *A week off next month? Do you think that work is just somewhere to drop in once in a while? Some other employee will have to do your work in addition to his or her own, and that's certainly not fair. Sorry. Forget it!*

Does this seem like a reasoned response to the employee's request? Notice how you have distorted the request. Instead of objecting to the person being gone for a week, you have presented his or her position as thinking that "work is just somewhere to drop in once in a while." Is that a fair appraisal of the request? We don't think so.

Here is a more balanced response you can give:

> *A week off next month? I'm afraid that's not going to work out. February is our busiest month due to Valentine's Day, and we already have two people who will be gone for medical reasons. I'm afraid it will have to wait.*

Even though you have still turned down the request, by giving a fair and honest justification for your response, you have shown the employee both courtesy and respect.

 EXERCISE 1.6

Your Turn! Which skill from Bloom's Taxonomy is utilized in the example above? Why?

Finally, when you apply for a job in whatever career you follow, you will have to write a cover letter in which you make a case for your candidacy for the position. Imagine that you are an employer who receives a letter of application such as the following:

> *I am writing to apply for the entry-level accountant position currently open. Am I the person for you! I'm a can-do, proactive, think-outside-the-box kind of person who will be a terrific asset to your company. Seeing is believing! When can we schedule an interview?*

Does this letter convince you that you should interview this candidate? Probably not. What you are given is a list of empty, clichéd personal characteristics (can-do; proactive; think-outside-the-box) that actually tell you nothing about the applicant's credentials or skills. Do you know what any of those terms actually means? We sure don't. In addition, the applicant tries to make a favorable impression with a show of bravado (am I the person for you; terrific asset to your company; seeing is believing). This letter is long on mere rhetoric, but, sadly, much too short on argument.

Here's a better example of the kind of argument the applicant might make:

> *I am writing in response to your advertisement for an entry-level accountant in your tax division. I believe that I am a strong candidate for this position because I have a bachelor's degree in business and accounting, I completed two summer internships for a tax broker while in college, and I have experience preparing tax returns for a temp agency.*

Notice that this person is giving an argument to convince you that he or she is qualified for the position. When you want to convince someone to hire you, you will have to give him or her good reasons to do so.

EXERCISE 1.7

Divide into groups and discuss how you would convince someone at work to accept the following claims. Refer to your own experience in situations like these if possible.

1. I should be given a pay raise (or promotion).
2. I should be allowed to do my job differently.
3. One of my co-workers should be reprimanded (or fired).

Using Critical Thinking Skills in Civic Life

Not only are critical thinking skills useful in the classroom and workplace, but also they will serve you well as a consumer in the marketplace. Advertisements are notorious sources of nonrational means of persuasion.

Although most of us may be naturally wary whenever someone is trying to sell us a product, much advertising can be quite persuasive—perhaps at our expense. Good critical reasoning skills can prevent us from succumbing to persuasive appeals that are neither rational nor reasonable. People are emotional creatures, and descriptions of cozy fireplaces, sounds of sizzling steaks, and images of frosty beer mugs all tug at our minds powerfully. Sadly, the result is too often the purchase of a product that we don't really need, with a luster that fades all too quickly. With polished reasoning skills, such as the ability to detect fallacious reasoning, we are better able to assess the reasons we have been given to buy a particular product.

Let's look at an example of an ad you might encounter. Suppose you read this:

> *Why spend years earning a college degree? With AcademicDegree.com, you can earn a degree in as little as three months and begin earning the good salary you deserve. Visit our website to begin your new life today.*

At first glance, this might sound very appealing. After all, college is hard work, and it takes a long time. That's especially true these days when costs have risen and the majority of students have to hold down one or two part-time jobs in addition to their classes. Of course, it is tempting to think that you could get your degree in a much shorter time. But notice the qualifier "in as little as three months." What does this tell us? It will take three months, at the minimum, but it certainly could be much longer. Also, the ad mentions the good salary "you deserve." So everybody who reads this ad deserves this good salary? That's unlikely. The ad also doesn't mention the cost of this great education or the percentage of AcademicDegree.com graduates obtaining these "good" salaries. Finally, when you think about it, what can you learn in such a short time that will really be of use to you? You might be provided with some information, but you certainly will not have the time to develop the higher-order cognitive skills that employers demand.

The world of politics also tries to grab your attention, your support, and your dollars. In many cases, it might seem wiser to let your favorite political party decide for you about whether or not health-care reform, bank regulation, or additional money for a war is a good idea. However, if you want to think for yourself and make your own decisions about who and what warrant your support, you need to have critical thinking skills. With so very much at stake, politicians and partisans of all stripes will use whatever they can to persuade you to support them and their causes. However, to make a smart decision, you really must insist on looking at the evidence and making your own judgments.

Consider this example from an ad for presidential candidate Rick Santorum:

> *As President, I will protect America's moral foundation, empower American families and build America's economic freedom. And I won't compromise on my values to do it.*

Initially, we might think this describes the virtues of a candidate for public office. But notice the power of some of the words to move our feelings rather than our brains: *moral foundation, American families, economic freedom,* and *won't compromise.* These words are chosen for their ability to stir our emotions rather than engage our minds. And since this ad omits specific details about what this candidate means by any of these powerful terms, it is a slogan that could be endorsed by almost any candidate.

A final area of civic life in which critical thinking skills are vital concerns your potential responsibility as a juror at a trial. While the opposing attorneys will certainly give arguments in court, they are also likely to use persuasive techniques that are non-argumentative. The judge should be able to prevent their use of the most prejudicial techniques, but the attorney may nonetheless appeal to jurors' biases or emotions in an attempt to make their case appear stronger than it is. If you sit on a jury, the judge will instruct you to consider only the evidence presented, reminding you that such parts of the trial as the attorneys' closing statements are not evidence. At trial, the stakes are

During the 2013 trial of George Zimmerman for the shooting of Trayvon Martin, attorneys introduced evidence of yells for help audible in a recorded 911 call. The judge ruled that the analysts' testimony about the identity of the screamer was inadmissible because their techniques were not proven to be reliable. How hard would it have been for a juror to ignore that evidence?

Joe Burbank/Orlando Sentinel/McClatchy-Tribune Information Services/Alamy very high for the parties involved, and our legal system relies on peers who can accurately understand what is good evidence and what is not.

In 1924, Clarence Darrow successfully defended two young Chicago socialites, Nathan Leopold and Richard Loeb, and saved them from hanging for the sport killing of a 14-year-old neighbor and cousin of Loeb. Darrow persuaded the jury to spare the lives of these two killers through a number of powerful arguments, one of which still has broad implications today. He argued that the twisted characters of these two privileged young men were not their own creation, but instead were the product of their heritage and their childhoods. Here are some of his words to the jury:

> Your Honor, I am almost ashamed to talk about it. I can hardly imagine that we are in the 20th century. And yet there are men who seriously say that for what Nature has done, for what life has done, for what training has done, you should hang these boys.

Are these good reasons to vote "Not guilty"? This is a question that still resonates today when we seriously consider possible mitigating factors in crimes. In fact, the Leopold/Loeb case evokes the recent circumstances involving Ethan Couch, who killed four people while driving drunk in Texas. His lawyer is said to have used the "affluenza" defense, arguing the young man was a victim of his overindulged upbringing, and secured probation instead of a jail sentence for his client. No easy answer exists, but having good thinking skills will certainly be important if you ever have to determine guilt or innocence.

The critical thinking skills you will be taught in this book will help you decide when it makes sense to buy an advertised product, support a politician, and reach a guilty verdict. That is, you will learn how to distinguish mere rhetoric—nonargumentative persuasion—from legitimate reasoning. We like to think of these skills as special tools to help you avoid being a "sucker."

 EXERCISE 1.8

Your Turn! Which character traits and attitudes would you want jurors to possess if you were on trial? What traits should they not have? Why?

 EXERCISE 1.9

In small groups, identify the main point in each of the following passages. Then determine which offer relevant reasons as support, which appeal to your emotions, and which give no reasons at all. For those that appeal to your emotions, try to identify which emotions.

1. A picture of a beautiful woman appears beside the following words: "Zinn's Cosmetic Surgery Center. Now you can have the body nature *should* have given you."

2. I need your help to return me to Congress, where I can continue to work for the wonderful people of my district. I've become the target of an ultraconservative fascist who will say or do anything to bring her radical agenda to Washington. I'm counting on you!

3. Ladies and gentlemen of the jury, my client cannot be the person who embezzled money from the church because he would never steal money from a church. Please don't add to the misery he has already experienced. When you go into that jury room, acquit my client!

4. A vote for Governor Thomas is a vote for bipartisanship. Governor Thomas has won praise from both the environmental organizations and the energy industry by bringing together Republicans, Democrats, and Independents to update standards for new oil exploration. "Green Nevada" calls Governor Thomas "the best friend the environment has seen in three decades," and the Oil Producers' Council hailed the new agreement as "the most co-operative oil-related legislation in any state." Support Governor Thomas with your vote in November.

5. Did you enjoy your dinner tonight? We're glad. But millions of children in the Third World didn't eat dinner tonight. Nor did they have lunch or breakfast. Yet a mere 20 cents a day will feed a child three nutritious meals a day. You have so much—won't you share just a little with those who have nothing?

Living an Examined Life

One of the most celebrated critical thinkers in history is Socrates, the ancient Greek philosopher. He was executed because he questioned the wisdom of the authorities. Socrates famously declared at his trial, "The unexamined life is not worth living" (Plato, *Apology* 38a). The kind of life Socrates was advocating by this claim is one built on a sound foundation of knowledge, principles, and good habits. Rather than merely accepting what everyone else did and said, Socrates carefully examined the basis for his society's beliefs and practices. Although we hope that you never face the same fate as Socrates, we believe his life offers an important lesson: Critical thinking is essential for living in a democratic society. You are responsible for making decisions that affect both your own life and the lives of your fellow citizens, and you need to be able to think carefully about arguments so that you can make better choices.

 EXERCISE 1.10

Your Turn! Why might a totalitarian government want to prevent its citizens from acquiring critical thinking skills?

Developing the habit of critical thinking is an essential part of a worthwhile life. It is through argument that we can not only evaluate the claims others make about what is true and how we should act, but also test the wisdom of our own beliefs. By providing instruction and practice in argument recognition, analysis, evaluation, and construction, we hope to offer you a starting point for acquiring the skills needed for living an examined life of your own.

EXERCISE 1.11

Your Turn!   Here's a philosophical question to think about: Is an easier life a better life? Why or why not?

EXERCISE 1.12

What is the main point in each of the following passages? Which do you find most persuasive? Briefly state why.

1. Your mother and I think you should pursue a career that will allow you to live comfortably and support a family. Finding "meaning" is nice, but not what matters. You can find meaning on the weekends, and you'll have plenty of time for doing what you want when you retire.
2. The best career is one that you enjoy and that gives you satisfaction. Money is secondary; money will never provide the satisfaction of meaningful work.
3. The most important thing you have to do today is win this game because, as the great coach Vince Lombardi said, winning isn't the best thing—it's the *only* thing.
4. Son, either go to law school or forget about any inheritance from me.
5. Ignorance is bliss. Simple people with simple lives are better off than those who stress themselves out to learn everything about everything.

Developing Critical Thinking Skills

We hope that the evidence we've presented here has left you ready to begin improving your critical thinking abilities. However, you may wonder exactly how you will acquire these skills. In this book, you will learn to think critically about arguments by developing the skills of argument recognition, analysis, evaluation, and construction. Those four skills are composed of many narrower skills, and you will learn them one step at a time. As you work through this book, you can use the flowchart featured on the inside front cover of the book to see where you are in the process.

Acquiring skills is not like acquiring information. Rather, skill building is a matter of forming good habits. For example, if you want to master a musical instrument, a sport, or a new language, you must practice scales, drills, or conjugations. You must repeat the same skills until they become second nature. Think about a time you watched someone who is extraordinarily good at something. His or her performance seemed effortless, but we know that it was not. It took hours and hours of practice to get to that point. You learn critical thinking skills the same way you learn any other skill. To become a better thinker, you will need to commit yourself to a practice regimen.

Fortunately, you're not alone. With the help of your instructor, we will coach you through this process. Because this book is devoted entirely to helping you develop critical thinking skills in a progressive fashion, it includes the following features:

- A step-by-step explanation of each skill.
- Plenty of examples to demonstrate how you apply each skill.
- "Your Turn!" exercises, which provide opportunities for you to reflect on and apply a skill or concept immediately after it's described and explained.
- Lots and lots of exercises for you to practice on, progressing from easier to more challenging ones.
- Comprehensive exercises, "Putting It All Together," aimed at incorporating the acquired critical thinking skills into your writing.
- "One Step Further" activities at the end of each chapter to provide more challenging, real-world applications of critical thinking skills.
- Answers to selected problems at the back of the book so that you can check your progress along the way.

CHAPTER REVIEW QUESTIONS

1. Define *critical thinking*.
2. What are the four foundational skills of critical thinking taught in this text?
3. According to the text, what are the four situations in which the skills taught in this text will be most useful?

ONE STEP FURTHER

Martha Nussbaum, philosopher and professor at the University of Chicago School of Law, has argued throughout her career for the importance of philosophy as an instrument of social good. In the following passage from her book *Not for Profit: Why Democracy Needs the Humanities* (Princeton University Press, 2010), she outlines the benefits of critical thinking for a democracy.

I shall argue that cultivated capacities for critical thinking and reflection are crucial in keeping democracies alive and wide awake. The ability to think well about a wide range of cultures, groups, and nations in the context of a grasp of the global economy and of the history of many national and group interactions is crucial in order to enable democracies to deal responsibly with the problems we currently face as members of an interdependent world. And the ability to imagine the experience of another—a capacity almost all human beings possess in some form—needs to be greatly enhanced and refined if we are to have any hope of sustaining decent institutions across the many divisions that any modern society contains. (10)

1. Nussbaum is clearly trying to persuade us. Is she using a rational or a nonrational means of persuasion? Explain your answer.
2. Nussbaum sees value in critical thinking in part because it allows us to see the viewpoints of those different from ourselves. In what ways is that argument relevant to critical thinking's value in the classroom and workplace?
3. What value do you see in critical thinking?

Recognizing Arguments

Going to college is a great idea, but it costs a lot of money. According to the *Huffington Post*, the average college loan balance for a family with two college graduates is $53,000. Is college really worth it? Since your choice to pursue a college degree can affect the rest of your life, how should you decide? Perhaps you will ask some people you know for their opinion or read some news articles from experts on the subject. Here are some examples of the responses you might encounter.

> *Stay in college! You should definitely stay in college. Attending college is what you really should be doing.*—Your best friend

> *I left school because I didn't feel like school was an environment that left me free to learn.*—Dale Stephens, founder of Uncollege.org

> *Education is the key to a good life. Why? I can give you two great reasons. First, you'll have a much better chance of being employed if you graduate from college. College grads are twice as likely to have a job as those without a bachelor's. And besides, college is a great experience—you meet all kinds of different people from different cultures, and you take classes in so many different areas.*—Dr. Rick Wartzman, Executive Director of The Drucker Institute

Which of these responses, if any, should influence your decision? The speakers may be trying to persuade you, but not all of them provide you with good reasons to accept their advice. In fact, some of them don't offer you any reasons at all because not all of these responses are arguments. Why does that matter? Because whenever you allow yourself to be persuaded to do or to believe something without being given good reasons, you fail to think for yourself. Thinking for yourself doesn't mean that you should never listen to the advice of others; it means that you need to be discerning. You should consider following advice only when it's supported with good reasons—and this requires the ability to recognize arguments. In critical thinking, an **argument** is a set of claims that offers reasons as evidence for the truth of one of its claims. Recognizing arguments is an important first step to determining when you should allow someone to influence your beliefs and decisions.

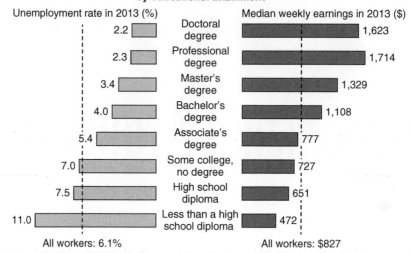

**Earnings and unemployment rates
by educational attainment**

Unemployment rate in 2013 (%)   Median weekly earnings in 2013 ($)

	Unemployment rate		Degree		Median weekly earnings
	2.2		Doctoral degree		1,623
	2.3		Professional degree		1,714
	3.4		Master's degree		1,329
	4.0		Bachelor's degree		1,108
	5.4		Associate's degree		777
	7.0		Some college, no degree		727
	7.5		High school diploma		651
	11.0		Less than a high school diploma		472

All workers: 6.1%   All workers: $827

Note: Data are for persons age 25 and over. Earnings are for full-time wage and salary workers.
Source: Current Population Survey, U.S. Bureau of Labor Statistics, U.S Department of Labor

> If someone pointed to data such as these in an effort to influence your decision, would that person be giving you a good reason to go to college?

LEARNING OUTCOMES

In this chapter, you will learn how to recognize arguments by:

▶ Distinguishing claims from non-claims,
▶ Counting the number of claims in a single passage,
▶ Deciding whether one claim offers a reason for another claim,
▶ Determining the purpose of any reasons given in a passage, and
▶ Writing a Critical Précis of a passage that is not an argument.

Identifying Claims

Accurately recognizing arguments requires knowing when a passage satisfies the definition of an argument, so it is to that definition we now turn. The definition makes clear that an argument must be *a set of claims*. Therefore, our first step in learning to recognize arguments is detecting when a passage contains a set of claims. A passage that does not contain a set of claims is not an argument. But before counting claims, we need to understand what a claim is so that we know what we are counting.

A **claim** is a statement that has **truth-value**; that is, it can be either true or false. Some examples of claims include the following:

> *The state of California is bordered on one side by the Pacific Ocean.*
> *The sun is in orbit around Earth.*
> *Marilyn Monroe liked to eat persimmons.*

Most Americans, at least, would recognize the claim in the first sentence as obviously true. Hopefully, everyone understands that the second claim is false. And it is unlikely that anyone reading this book knows whether or not the third claim is true. All three of these statements, however, are *claims* regardless of whether they are true, whether they are false, or whether you know their truth-value (their truth or falsity).

Although claims are expressed in sentences, not every sentence is a claim. For example, questions, commands, exclamations, and greetings are not claims. To illustrate, none of the following sentences is a claim because none of them could be true or false.

> *Was pilot error the cause of the plane crash?*
> *Brush your teeth after meals.*
> *Thank you for your consideration.*

One way to determine whether or not a sentence expresses a claim is to use the phrase *It is true that*... before the sentence. The ones that make sense are claims; the ones that don't are not. Notice that "*It is true that* Marilyn Monroe liked to eat persimmons" makes grammatical sense, but "*It is true that* thank you for your consideration" does not.

EXERCISE 2.1

Your Turn!   Use the phrase *It is true that*... to show that the other two sentences listed above are not claims.

When it comes to determining whether or not a sentence contains a claim, you may wonder how you should treat sentences that express subjective feelings such as personal attitudes or moral opinions. You may think that, unlike objective claims about the external world, expressions of internal feelings or beliefs aren't the sorts of things that can be true or false. Or you may believe that everyone is entitled to his or her own opinion, so all opinions, even contradictory ones, are equally true. Consider these examples.

> *I wish you would leave me alone!*
> *That movie was terrible.*

EXERCISE 2.2

Your Turn!   Use the phrase *It is true that*... to show that the two sentences above are claims.

Not only do these sentences pass the *It is true that*... test, but also they are debatable. The person speaking may in fact wish to be left alone, or her friend may think she is expressing her anger rather than her genuine desires. One person may think that the movie was terrible, and another may think that it was Oscar-worthy. Such disagreements can be dealt with in three distinct ways. One way is with mere **dogmatic assertion**: putting forward a judgment without providing reasons or justification. Another way to try to win people over to your view is by using nonrational means of persuasion, such as the kinds of emotional appeals that are used in advertisements and in way too much political discourse. A better way to deal with disagreements is to offer good reasons or justification in the form of arguments. As we discussed in Chapter 1, providing reasons to support your opinions treats those with whom you disagree as rational and responsible—the way we all certainly wish to be treated.

EXERCISE 2.3

Determine which of the following sentences express claims.

1. Please silence your cell phones during class.
2. Dogs are descended from wolves. ✓
3. The hypotenuse of a triangle is the longest leg of the triangle. ✓
4. What color are blackberries when they aren't ripe?
5. Good for you!
6. It's wrong to tell any kind of lie.
7. In the future, people will live several hundred years. ✓
8. It will rain today. ✓
9. I hope that we will get rain today.
10. The Seminoles are the best team in our region. ✓
11. What was the score of the last Phillies game?
12. It's hot!
13. The major cities of the western states will suffer from water shortages if the drought continues. ✓
14. Being unfaithful to your partner is the worst form of betrayal.
15. Newspapers should try to print more good news and focus less on tragedies. ✓
16. How much money did the newspaper lose this year?
17. Always do your schoolwork when you are rested and alert.
18. I *did* do my schoolwork when I was rested and alert!
19. Leticia believes that she is destined for greatness. ✓
20. Never spank your child when you are angry. ✓

Counting Claims

Now that we have defined what a claim is, we can focus on what the definition means by a *set* of claims. In this context, a *set of claims is at least two claims*. Thus, by definition, *an argument must contain a minimum of two claims*. So, to determine whether a passage contains an argument, you must first count its claims: If it contains fewer than two claims, it is not an argument.

When counting claims, you must keep four considerations in mind. First, a single claim can be represented by more than one sentence. This is because sentences can express the same meaning in different ways. Arguers will often present the conclusion at the beginning and at the end of the argument. Notice this technique in the following example.

> *You should vote against Proposition 8. It violates the equal protection rights of gay and lesbian citizens of California. Therefore, this proposition should be opposed.*

You may notice that each sentence in the above paragraph expresses a claim. How many claims are there in total? Although there are three sentences, there are only two claims. The sentences "You should vote against Proposition 8" and "Therefore, this proposition should be opposed" express the same claim. That is, they mean the same thing, and thus count as only one claim.

EXERCISE 2.4

Your Turn!   How do you know that the proposition referred to in the sentence "Therefore, this proposition should be opposed" is Proposition 8?

A second consideration to remember when counting claims is that a single sentence may refer to more than one claim. For example, the sentence "She is a writer" could refer to many different women. Perhaps the writer referred to is Virginia Woolf, in which case "She is a writer" means "Virginia Woolf is a writer." Or perhaps the sentence refers to Sue Grafton, in which case the claim would be "Sue Grafton is a writer." To count claims accurately, be sure to clearly and completely identify each claim in a passage. This means, for example, determining the referents of any pronouns.

EXERCISE 2.5

Your Turn!   Count the number of claims expressed in this passage.

Many important leaders majored in philosophy while in college. Pope John Paul II was an important leader, and he was a philosophy major. Thomas Jefferson was an important leader, and he was a philosophy major. Finally, Canadian Prime Minister Pierre Trudeau was an important leader, and he was a philosophy major.

Third, sometimes claims are combined in a way that creates a single claim. Two of these worth remembering are disjunctions and conditionals, both of which are single claims. A **disjunction** is an *either...or...* claim. Although disjunctions have two parts (called *disjuncts*) that would count as two separate claims if they were on their own, joining them together with the word *or* creates a single claim. For example, combining the two claims "The Dodgers will acquire a power hitter" and "The Dodgers will continue to be outscored" using *either...or...* creates one claim.

Either the Dodgers will acquire a power hitter or they will continue to be outscored.

This sentence expresses only one thing—namely, that one of the disjuncts is true. If you were to slice the claim into two parts, treating the sentence as making two claims, you would miss the point of the word *or*. And that would be a big mistake! The relation between the two parts is what the disjunction is informing us about. For that reason, a disjunction is only one claim.

> **Hint!**
> Not all disjunctions contain the word *either*. The word *or* is enough to signal a disjunction. Also, a sentence that negates a disjunction (*neither...nor...*) is a single claim.

The other single claim that should not be mistaken for two claims is a conditional. **Conditionals** (also called *hypothetical claims* or *implications*) are *if...then...* claims. Though they have two parts (called the *antecedent* and *consequent*), which can be expressed as two separate claims, conditional claims have only one truth-value, and thus are single claims. For example, although "You want to get into the nursing program" and "You must take two years of prerequisites" looked at by themselves would count as two claims, joining them in a sentence using *if...then...* creates a single claim.

> *If you want to get into the nursing program, then you must take two years of prerequisites.*

This sentence does not tell us that you do want to get into the nursing program, nor does it tell us that you must take two years of prerequisites. Instead, it tells us one thing—what you must do if you want to get in to the program. The sentence has one truth-value, and thus expresses only one claim.

> **Hint!**
> In some conditional claims, the *then* is only implied, or the order of the parts is reversed. For example, you can see that each of the following sentences expresses the same conditional claim by identifying the placement of the antecedent and consequent.
>
> *If you want to get into the nursing program, you must take the prerequisites.*
>   **antecedent**   **consequent**
>
> *You must take the prerequisites if you want to get into the nursing program.*
>   **consequent**   **antecedent**
>
> *You will get into the nursing program only if you take the prerequisites.*
>   **antecedent**   **consequent**
>
> Conditional claims will be discussed more thoroughly in Chapter 7. For now, the important point is that conditional claims are single claims.

A final consideration to keep in mind when counting claims is that multiple claims can be expressed in a single sentence. For example, the two claims "Pine trees are evergreen" and "Birch trees are deciduous" may be expressed in two separate sentences, or they may be expressed in a single sentence like this.

> *Pine trees are evergreen, and birch trees are deciduous.*   "and"

This is called a **conjunction** because it joins two claims (called *conjuncts*) using the word *and*. (Logically, *but* and *yet* work the same as *and*.) Although, in one sense, a conjunction makes one claim—namely, that both conjuncts are true (more on this point in Chapter 7)—for counting purposes, the sentence expresses two claims.

EXERCISE 2.6

Your Turn!   Why does the sentence "Sally owns a cat and Jim owns a dog" express two claims, whereas "Sally owns a cat or Jim owns a dog" expresses only one?

Is it possible to shave better? Yes, says our dermatologist.

Some of our guiding dermatologist's recommendations are quite practical: Use a face scrub to lift hairs. Lather up to reduce friction. Then the doctor goes deeper: Cleanse and exfoliate daily, and you can expect fewer ingrown hairs, less razor burn. Our formulas help you satisfy all the good doctor's advice. And guarantee great skin, great shaves.

Find your routine at clinique.co.uk

CLINIQUE

Allergy Tested. 100% Fragrance Free.

This advertisement contains both claims and non-claims. How many claims can you find?

Multiple claims can also be combined using pronouns, as in this example.

Dr. Newberry's class is held in room 106, which is located in the southern side of Dorothy Donahoe Hall.

At first glance, this sentence appears to contain only one claim. But in fact it contains two. The first claim is easy to identify: "Dr. Newberry's class is held in room 106." The second claim is trickier because it requires that we determine what noun is referred to by the word *which*. Does it refer to *Dr. Newberry's class* or *room 106*? Since *room 106* is the noun closest to the pronoun *which*, *room 106* is the referent. So the second claim is "Room 106 is located in the southern side of Dorothy Donahoe Hall."

 EXERCISE 2.7

Your Turn!   Identify the two claims expressed in the sentence "Carl, who won the outstanding senior award, plans to attend law school after college."

Multiple claims can also be combined in single sentences with terms such as *because*, *for*, *since*, *so*, and *therefore*. In critical thinking, these terms (called *inference indicators*) are valuable clues for recognizing and analyzing arguments. But initially our concern with inference indicators is to show how they indicate that a single sentence contains more than one claim. For example, consider this sentence.

Gary could not study more than two hours for his midterm because he was called in to work this weekend.

This sentence expresses two claims, "Gary could not study more than two hours for his midterm" and "Gary was called in to work this weekend." In this case, the first claim precedes *because*, and the second claim follows it.

Or consider this example.

Because Gary was called in to work this weekend, he could not study more than two hours for his midterm.

Notice that this sentence also contains two claims, "Gary was called in to work this weekend" and "Gary could not study more than two hours for his midterm." The inference indicator *because* at the beginning of the sentence reveals that one claim will follow immediately and that a separate claim will come after the comma. As you can see, each claim passes the *It is true that...* test: "*It is true that* Gary was called in to work this weekend" makes sense, and "*It is true that* Gary could not study more than two hours for his midterm" does also.

Whereas inference indicators are often used to join a set of claims, some indicator words have alternate meanings. In these cases, the sentences express one truth-value, not two, and thus are single claims. The most common example is the word *since*. Compare the following two sentences containing the word *since*.

You should vote for Jones, since she is honest.
I haven't tasted cake this good since the last time I ate at your house.

The most reliable way to see if *since* signals more than one claim is to substitute *because* in its place and see whether the sentence retains the same meaning. In the first example, it makes sense to say that "You should vote for Jones *because* she is honest." This shows that *since* combines two claims. In the second example, "I haven't tasted cake this good *because* the last time I ate at your house" does not make sense. The substitution demonstrates that in this sentence *since* has a temporal meaning, and consequently, the sentence is just one claim.

EXERCISE 2.8

Your Turn! The word *for*, like *since*, also has multiple meanings. Compare the two sentences below.

> *I haven't eaten for a long time.*
> *I haven't eaten for I am fasting.*

Which of these expresses two claims? How do you know?

Tips for Counting Claims

▶ A single claim can be represented by more than one sentence.
▶ A single sentence may refer to more than one claim.
▶ Multiple claims can be joined together to make a single claim.
▶ Multiple claims can be expressed in a single sentence.

EXERCISE 2.9

Identify the number of claims expressed by each of the following passages. Whenever multiple claims are present, clearly and completely state each claim, replacing all pronouns with the proper referent. Mark as "nonargument" those passages that do not contain the minimum number of claims required of arguments.

1. Human existence has meaning if God exists. nonargument
2. If a tree fell in the forest and no one was around to hear it, would it make a noise?
3. Last weekend I saw *Machete*, which is a film directed by Richard Rodriguez. I wonder if the sequel will be as enjoyable as the first movie.
4. Hermione Granger isn't dating Neville Longbottom because she only dates good Quidditch players.
5. When you repaint your house, be sure to avoid lead-based products. Nonargument
6. Lowering payroll taxes may provide people with bigger paychecks, but it will reduce Louisiana's ability to fund higher education.

7. Either Juan wants to go into the nursing program or he wants to become a psychologist.
8. Juan can become a psychologist only if he passes the statistical methods course.
9. Weevils are in the flour, we are out of salt, and the milk has turned sour.
10. Snakes have been considered evil since ancient times.
11. Bill went to the store for milk, eggs, and butter.
12. Be frugal with your paycheck. For the economy is awful, and there's little hope of improvement anytime soon.
13. You should upgrade your smartphone today because now is the time to do it!
14. If you get caught cheating on your exam, you will be reported to the dean for academic dishonesty. Since you were caught, you will be reported.
15. Given that the holiday shopping season now begins in October, busy retailers will most likely hire part-time employees for two months instead of one.
16. Jerry will consider the truck a business expense for tax purposes.
17. My older sister is majoring in modern languages at Vanderbilt, and she's learning a new language. My younger sister is studying abroad, so she's also learning a new language.
18. Jim works at the Guitar Center, yet he doesn't know how to play a guitar.
19. Anyone who gets the flu shot is unlikely to get the flu virus this winter. Therefore, you are unlikely to get it because you got the shot last week.
20. Brian's headaches were caused from using glasses with the wrong prescription. How do I know? Well, his eyeglasses had to be the problem, since his headaches went away after he got new glasses.

Looking for Reasons

When determining whether a passage contains an argument, you can classify any passages with fewer than two claims as nonarguments. But it doesn't follow that every passage containing a set of claims is an argument. The definition of argument has a further requirement. An argument, remember, is a set of claims that *offers reasons* as evidence for the truth of one of its claims.

So the second step in recognizing arguments is to see whether one of the claims offers a reason for another claim. Accurately making this determination can be challenging, but fortunately, many arguers utilize **inference indicators**—those words or phrases discussed above that signal that one claim is offered as a reason for another claim. Some inference indicators, such as the word *because*, signal that the claim following them is a reason. Other inference indicators, such as the word *therefore*, signal that a claim preceding them is a reason. (See the table below for commonly used inference indicators.)

Synonyms for *because*	Synonyms for *therefore*
since . . .	thus . . .
for . . .	consequently . . .
given . . .	so . . .
as . . .	hence . . .
follows from . . .	accordingly . . .

As discussed in the previous section, these terms sometimes are used with alternative meanings, as when the word *since* is used to indicate time. However, when they are being used as inference indicators, they make clear not only that the passage contains more than one claim, but also that one of the claims offers a reason for another.

Let's look at a few examples to see how inference indicators can help us find reasons. Consider this one.

> *The auto parts store was burglarized because the employees forgot to lock the back door.*

Notice that although there is only one sentence, there are two claims, which are combined with the word *because*. The inference indicator *because* signals that the claim following it is a reason.

> *The auto parts store was burglarized because <u>the employees forgot to lock the back door.</u>*   **reason**

The claim "The employees forgot to lock the back door" provides a reason for the claim "The auto parts store was burglarized."

Next, consider this one.

> *The burglar is armed, so he's dangerous.*

Again, notice that although there is only one sentence, there are two claims, which are combined with the word *so*. As you can see from the table above, *so* is a synonym for *therefore*; it signals that the claim preceding it is a reason.

> *<u>The burglar is armed</u>, so he's dangerous.*
>   **reason**

The claim "The burglar is armed" provides a reason for the claim "The burglar is dangerous."

Let's consider one more example.

> *A 9mm casing was found at the scene of the crime, and 9mm bullets are used only in pistols. Therefore, a pistol was the weapon used by the gunman.*

How many claims does this passage contain? Although there are two sentences, there are three claims presented. The inference indicator *therefore* signals that the two claims preceding it (separated by *and*) are both reasons. "A 9mm casing was found at the scene of the crime" and "9mm bullets are used only in pistols" provide reasons for the claim "A pistol was the weapon used by the gunman."

 EXERCISE 2.10

Your Turn!   Which claim in the following sentence is the reason? Write the claim so that it makes sense on its own.

Since she's on a diet, Jasmine better not order the cheeseburger.

When an author provides you with an inference indicator, you have a head start in your search for reasons. Unfortunately, not all arguments contain inference indicators. So, when inference indicators are not given, you must pay close attention to the context and the content of the passage to figure out whether one claim offers a reason for another. One way to do this is to insert the inference indicator *because* between the claims. If the passage makes sense, then you know that one claim is a reason for another. But if the passage does not make sense, then you know that one claim is not a reason for the other, and hence the passage cannot be an argument.

Let's try out this technique.

Infrastructure is extremely important. We must begin rebuilding it today.

Here we have two claims, but no inference indicator. We can test the passage to see if one claim offers a reason for another by inserting the inference indicator *because* between them. Does this work?

Infrastructure is extremely important because we must begin rebuilding it today.

No. This doesn't work. The second claim does not offer a reason for the first. Does the first claim support the second? Let's reverse the order of the claims and see.

We must begin rebuilding infrastructure today because it is extremely important.

Many people rely on charts like this one to decide which movies to watch. Do you think this is a reasonable decision? Why or why not?

© 2013 MCT

Staff/MCT/Newscom

Yes, this works! The author offers us a reason—namely, "Infrastructure is extremely important"—for the claim "We must begin rebuilding infrastructure today."

EXERCISE 2.11

Your Turn! Why did we reword the claims when we used the *because* test in the above example?

Now consider this example.

> *You should vote for Tom Allon for Mayor of New York City. Also, you should vote for John Liu as comptroller.*

Passages like this one may cause you trouble, since it contains at least two claims and it does appear that the author is trying to persuade you to vote for Allon and Liu. Let's try to insert the word *because* between the claims to see if one claim offers a reason for another.

> *You should vote for Tom Allon for Mayor of New York City* because *you should vote for John Liu as comptroller.*

No. This doesn't work. The second claim does not offer a reason supporting the first. Does the first claim support the second? Let's reverse the order of the claims and see.

> *You should vote for John Liu as comptroller* because *you should vote for Tom Allon for Mayor of New York City.*

No. This doesn't work either. The author doesn't offer us a reason to vote for either Allon or Liu. So the passage is merely a dogmatic assertion, not an argument.

EXERCISE 2.12

For each of the following passages, determine whether one claim offers a reason for another. If so, write the reason so that it makes sense on its own. Mark as "nonargument" those passages that do not contain a claim offering a reason for another claim.

1. You should buy your flowers from FTD florists because they consistently deliver on time.
2. Basketball is popular. Consequently, the recreation department added several new night leagues.
3. Bill went to the store, and Martha went swimming.
4. Capital punishment is not only cruel and unusual; it is also immoral.
5. Figs are sweet; therefore, Janie is sure to like them.
6. Dolores will be good at tennis, since she is good at playing the violin.

7. Given that all sailboats are expensive, a Hobie Cat will be an expensive purchase.
8. Cash is inconvenient. Hence, John seldom carries any.
9. Chocolate contains sugar. Thus, it's bad for your teeth.
10. Jean-Paul Sartre must have been a brave man, as he was a member of the French Resistance.
11. The National Rifle Association is a nonprofit organization with over 4.3 million politically active members. Politicians wanting to win elections stay on the NRA's good side.
12. Because a good dictionary is useful in every university course, it is a wise investment for all students.
13. For a change of pace, try doing your logic homework standing up. If that doesn't help, try lying down.
14. You should vote for Jones in the upcoming election for he promises to cut taxes.
15. I think that killing is always wrong. The Bible says so.
16. There have been no good-looking presidents since Kennedy. He was President of the United States from 1961 until 1963.
17. Given that the Roadrunners are the best team in our region, they are expected to beat the Bulldogs tonight.
18. If you do not begin saving for your retirement now, you will not have enough money to live on when you are older.
19. Mosquitos spread malaria and other diseases. Accordingly, a large number of international health organizations are devoted to eradicating them.
20. Malaria is a potentially fatal disease caused by a parasite, which is usually transmitted by a bite from an infected mosquito. Between one and three million people die each year from the disease.

Determining the Purpose of Reasons

By this point, you have some experience with the first two steps in recognizing arguments: counting claims and looking for reasons. Now, we must shift our attention to the third step. Recall the definition of an argument: It is a set of claims that offers reasons *as evidence for the truth of one of its claims*. This last part of the definition emphasizes the purpose of the reasons in an argument. Determining the purpose of the reasons is crucial for recognizing arguments because reasons can be used in explanations, which are easily confused with arguments.

Like arguments, explanations have at least two claims and often include words such as *because*, which signal that one claim is providing a reason for another. However, despite these similarities, the purpose of the reasons is different for arguments and explanations.

The reasons in an argument prove that some contested claim is true. The fact that a claim is contested means that arguments are attempts to resolve an issue; therefore, the reasons given must provide evidence to support one side of that issue. The reasons in an explanation, on the other hand, do not attempt to prove anything; they *explain* how or why some accepted claim is true. Since the speaker assumes that the claim is already accepted as true, there is no issue up for debate. As you can see, the only way to be sure that a passage is an argument is to determine the purpose of the reasons given. If the reasons offer evidence for the truth of another claim, then the passage is an argument. If the reasons do not offer such evidence, then the passage is an explanation, not an argument.

Let's look at some examples, beginning with an explanation.

Frank was late to class because his car wouldn't start.

In this sentence, the word *because* tells us, first, that the sentence consists of two claims—"Frank was late to class" and "Frank's car wouldn't start." Second, the word *because* tells us that the claim following it is a reason. That's just what *because* means.

Frank was late to class because <u>his car wouldn't start</u>.
reason

So far, this passage could be either an argument or a nonargument.

To determine whether this passage is an argument or not, you must ask yourself, What is the purpose of this reason? Does it provide evidence to prove something? No. "Frank's car wouldn't start" does not prove that "Frank was late to class." It gives a reason that *explains* the lateness. In this case, there is no controversy about whether Frank was late to class. Instead, the speaker assumes that we already accept the fact that Frank was late and perhaps want an account of why the tardiness occurred. Since the reason is not used as evidence to prove that a claim is true, the passage is not an argument.

Now, let's examine an argument.

Frank's car trouble can't be a battery problem because he just replaced the battery last month.

This passage is similar to the first in a couple of ways. For one thing, like the previous example, it presents two claims joined together by the word *because*. Also, what comes after the word *because* is a reason for what comes before it.

Frank's car trouble can't be a battery problem because <u>he just replaced the battery last month</u>.
reason

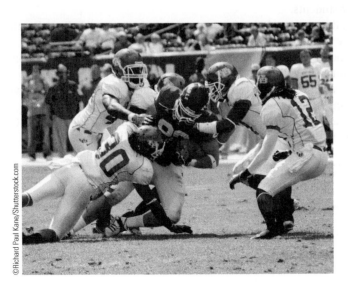

©Richard Paul Kane/Shutterstock.com

After a settlement agreed upon by the National Football League (NFL), its commissioner responded to public reactions by stating that NFL players live an average of three years longer than the average male. Can his statement be considered a reason that explains why repeated concussions don't necessarily lead to premature deaths, or does it provide support to prove that they don't?

What is the purpose of this reason? Does it provide evidence to prove something? Yes. "Frank just replaced the battery last month" provides evidence to prove that "Frank's car trouble can't be a battery problem." Notice that there is a controversy in this case. We do not already know the cause of Frank's car trouble. To resolve the issue, the speaker provides evidence to convince us that the battery is not to blame. As a result, this passage is an argument.

Hint!

Sometimes the reasons given by an arguer do not actually provide evidence to prove a claim because they are not good reasons. In these cases, the passage is still an argument because the arguer *intends* to use the reasons as evidence.

 EXERCISE 2.13

Identify and write out the reason given in each of the following passages. Then determine whether or not the passage is an argument by determining the purpose of that reason.

1. The Lakers will beat the Jazz tomorrow night, since they beat them the last five times they played.
2. The Lakers beat the Jazz the last five times they played, since the Lakers have more talented players.
3. I saw a new guy picking up a uniform at the personnel office yesterday, so we must have hired another member for the night shift.
4. The crew that is on now cannot keep up with the workload, so we hired another member for the night shift.
5. My professor hates me because I used to date his daughter.
6. My professor hates me because he constantly makes fun of me in front of other students.
7. Hawaii is a great choice for our vacation this summer given that the scenery is unlike anything we will see here in Iowa.
8. We chose Hawaii for our vacation this summer given that the scenery is unlike anything we will see here in Iowa.
9. The reason that the defendant's fingerprints were on the murder weapon is that she used it to kill the victim.
10. The defendant's fingerprints were found on the murder weapon. Consequently, she is the one who killed the victim.

Recognizing Arguments

In this chapter, you have learned to recognize arguments by counting claims and examining reasons. Let's review this step-by-step procedure.

How to Recognize an Argument

Step 1: Count the claims.
▶ If the passage has fewer than two claims, it is not an argument.
▶ If it has two or more claims, proceed to Step 2.

Step 2: Look for reasons.
▶ If no reason is offered, the passage is not an argument.
▶ If one or more reasons are offered, proceed to Step 3.

Step 3: Determine the purpose of the reasons.
▶ If the reasons do not offer evidence for the truth of a claim, then the passage is not an argument.
▶ If the reasons do offer evidence for the truth of a claim, then the passage is an argument.

Let's apply the decision procedure above to a few examples. Consider this one first.

Jack has exclusively eaten Dreyer's ice cream since he was 10 years old.

Step 1 of the decision procedure is to count the claims. To determine whether the sentence contains one claim or two, you should substitute the word *because* for the word *since*.

 EXERCISE 2.14

Your Turn! Rewrite the sentence above by replacing *since* with *because*. What does this tell you about the word *since* in this sentence?

Now consider this example.

Jack bought Dreyer's ice cream at Vons. Then he stopped at Chevron to buy gasoline.

This passage contains the required two claims—"Jack bought Dreyer's ice cream at Vons" and "Jack stopped at Chevron to buy gasoline"—so let's move to Step 2. Does one claim offer a reason for another? Since no inference indicators are present to guide us, let's insert the word *because* to check. Do either of these sentences work?

Jack bought Dreyer's ice cream at Vons because he stopped at Chevron to buy gasoline.

Jack stopped at Chevron to buy gasoline because he bought Dreyer's ice cream at Vons.

No. Neither version makes sense, so neither claim offers a reason to support the other. Thus, the passage is not an argument.

Here's another example.

Jack bought Dreyer's ice cream, since it was the cheapest they had.

This passage has two claims combined with the word *since*, and this time *since* signals that one claim offers a reason for the other. The second claim, "Dreyer's was the cheapest they had," is a reason for the first, "Jack bought Dreyer's ice cream." Now move to Step 3. Is this reason offered as evidence that "Jack bought Dreyer's ice cream"? Not at all. The author is not trying to convince us that Jack bought that particular brand of ice cream, but rather is explaining why he did. Thus, this passage is not an argument.

How about this one?

Jack should buy Dreyer's ice cream, since it is the best.

Like the example above, this one contains two claims combined with the word *since*, which signals that one claim offers a reason for the other. "Dreyer's ice cream is the best" is offered as a reason for the claim "Jack should buy Dreyer's ice cream." Now, determine the purpose of the reason. Does it offer evidence to convince you that Jack should buy Dreyer's ice cream? Yes—because it's the best! In this case, the passage is an argument.

EXERCISE 2.15

Your Turn! Look back at the various views about college presented at the start of this chapter. Which of the three passages gives an argument? For those that fail to give an argument, what features are they lacking?

EXERCISE 2.16

Using the above decision procedure for recognizing arguments, determine which of the following passages are arguments and which are not.

1. Gregg failed his psychology course because he missed too many classes.
2. The nearest gas station is four blocks away. Go left at the stop sign up ahead, and then you will see the Shell station on your right at the large intersection.
3. The weather has been cold and clear since last weekend. Therefore, the snow should be perfect for skiing tomorrow.
4. Physician-assisted suicide is always wrong. For it involves killing human beings and killing human beings is wrong.
5. Dark chocolate contains antioxidants, and it goes perfectly with cappuccinos.
6. Because you have exceeded your sales target for this quarter, the boss is recommending you for a raise. What great news!
7. I had orange juice for breakfast because I'm giving up coffee.
8. Mike is happy because he got a new Mustang.
9. Mustangs are the hottest cars on the road today.

10. The reason your patient has a fever is that she has an infection.
11. You should come to class for the exam next week.
12. You should come to class today, since the exam is next week and you want to do really well on it.
13. There are currently three major traffic delay areas in Spokane: Division Street, the corner of 3rd and Maple, and Sprague Avenue. The worst of these is Division Street, although, of course, traffic congestion is increasing all over the city.
14. Either Frankie has two older brothers or he is the middle child. I can never remember which it is.
15. This term there are eight offerings of English composition. The classes that meet three days per week last for 90 minutes, and those that meet two days per week last for two hours and 15 minutes.
16. If you have plenty of paint and plenty of rollers, then you are ready to start painting your house. Since you don't have enough paint, you aren't ready to begin.
17. The defendant should be acquitted insofar as the evidence is weak and the witness is unreliable.
18. Since I was throwing the javelin farther than I ever had, and since I do best at high altitude, I decided to see what I could do at the Olympic trials in Denver.
19. The number of miles driven per year on U.S. highways has risen every year since the statistics were first tracked in the 1950s.
20. Moving into a community that has basic services within walking distance makes good sense. You get good exercise by walking, you become acquainted with more of your neighbors, and you save money on gasoline.

PUTTING IT ALL TOGETHER: Writing a Critical Précis of a Nonargument

In this section, we introduce a writing exercise that will be employed for the remainder of the text. It's called a Critical Précis, and with it, you will be able to present in paragraph form an analysis and evaluation of any passage. Although you have not learned how to analyze or evaluate arguments at this point, you can begin a Critical Précis by identifying whether or not a passage contains an argument and, if not, by clarifying which feature of an argument is lacking.

Hint!
A précis (pronounced "PRAY-SEE") is a formal writing style typically used in various disciplines to summarize and assess a longer text. Its purpose is to concisely identify the essential elements of the original work.

Before trying a Critical Précis on your own, let's work through several examples, beginning with passages that are not arguments. Consider this one first.

It has been said that democracy is the worst form of government except all the others that have been tried.—Sir Winston Churchill

This passage contains only one claim. Since arguments require at least two claims, this passage is not an argument. Therefore, the Critical Précis should read as follows:

> **This passage from Sir Winston Churchill does not contain an argument. It contains only one claim, and arguments require at least two claims.**

> **Hint!**
> When the source of a passage is known, you must correctly identify the source, and that includes proper style. Typically, book titles are italicized when typed and underlined when handwritten, and article titles are placed in quotation marks. Be sure to check with your instructor to verify the formatting style that he or she prefers.

Now consider this one.

Generosity is giving more than you can, and pride is taking less than you need.—Kahlil Gibran

Unlike the first passage, this one has two claims, so you cannot immediately categorize it as a nonargument. Instead, you need to determine how the claims are related. Does one of the claims offer a reason for the other?

 EXERCISE 2.17

> **Your Turn!** For the Kahlil Gibran passage above, use *because* to see if one claim offers a reason for another.

Since neither claim offers a reason for the other, the passage cannot be an argument. Therefore, the Critical Précis should read as follows:

> **This passage from Kahlil Gibran does not contain an argument. It contains at least two claims, but neither claim provides a reason for the other, as is necessary in arguments.**

Now let's consider another passage that fails to be an argument.

Because they believe it infantilizes women, feminists condemn Zooey Deschanel's hair, clothes and her tweets about puppies, kittens, and cupcakes.—The Week, January 25, 2013

In this passage, there are two claims joined together with the word *because*. Thus, the first claim offers a reason for the second. But what kind of reason is given? Does it provide evidence that feminists condemn Zooey Deschanel's appearance and tweets? No, it does not try to prove that they condemn her. Instead, the author of this news item explains why they condemn her. Therefore, the Critical Précis should read as follows:

> **This passage from the January 25, 2013, issue of *The Week* does not contain an argument. It contains at least two claims, one of which offers a reason for the other, but the reason does not attempt to prove that the other claim is true.**

Notice that the Critical Précis for each of the three examples above not only identifies the passage as a nonargument, but also fully explains why the passage fails to be an argument.

Let's now turn to a passage that contains an argument.

> *Since few men are wise enough to rule themselves, even fewer are wise enough to rule others.*—Edward Abbey

Like the previous example, this sentence contains two claims, one of which offers a reason for the other. The word *since* tells us that the first claim offers a reason for the second. What is the purpose of this reason? Does it provide evidence to prove the second claim? Yes, it does! The claim "Few men are wise enough to rule themselves" offers evidence to convince us that "Few men are wise enough to rule others." Therefore, this passage contains an argument. Now you can begin your Critical Précis of the passage.

> **This passage from Edward Abbey contains an argument.**

In the next chapter, you will develop the skills necessary to analyze arguments by identifying the issue, conclusion, and premises. Once you do so, you will add this information to your Critical Précis.

    EXERCISE 2.18

Write a Critical Précis for each of the following passages.

1. Ethics generally starts with truth and fairness. In the case of advertising, truth and fairness go hand in hand. Lying about a product is unfair to customers, who are cheated and exploited by the dishonest claim. So the foundation of ethical advertising is that ads should tell the truth.—Dean A. Bredeson and Keith Goree, *Ethics in the Workplace*
2. Baseball is 90% mental, the other half is physical.—Yogi Berra
3. The foods you choose have cumulative effects on your body. Some of the foods you eat today become part of "you" tomorrow. The best food for you, then, is the kind that provides sufficient nutrients and water.—Frances Sizer and Ellie Whitney, *Nutrition: Concepts and Controversies*
4. I went to the woods because I wished to live deliberately, to front only the essential facts of life, and see if I could not learn what it had to teach, and not, when I came to die, discover that I had not lived.—Henry David Thoreau, *Walden*

5. I believe we find in the movement of revolt the common ground on which men can unite.—Albert Camus

6. An apology gains credibility as time passes without a relapse, and for this reason we can only finally judge the offender's commitment to reform over the duration of her life.—Nick Smith, *I Was Wrong: The Meaning of Apologies*

7. I agree that every household should add $5 to their taxes to help work the pumps to keep water in the Kern River during the summer, as long as the money goes to this purpose.—Letter to the editor, *The Bakersfield Californian*

8. You can rely on York. The Affinity Series air conditioners are always quiet, energy-efficient and dependable.—Ad for York Air Conditioners

9. The Cubs' only Type A free agent would have gained the club two draft picks if he had been offered arbitration and signed elsewhere. —*Chicago Tribune*

10. Court officials say a Birmingham, Alabama woman who changed her name to Jesus Christ was excused from jury service because she was disruptive and kept asking questions instead of answering them.—*StarTribune.com*

CHAPTER REVIEW QUESTIONS

1. Define *argument*.
2. How can you tell whether a sentence is a claim or not?
3. What are the four considerations to keep in mind when counting claims?
4. How can you determine whether one claim offers a reason for another claim?
5. What is the purpose of an argument?
6. What information do you need to include when you write a Critical Précis of a passage that is a nonargument?

ONE STEP FURTHER

On December 14, 2012, Adam Lanza shot and killed 26 people, including 20 children, at Sandy Hook Elementary School in Newtown, Connecticut. Across the country, Americans responded with expressions of grief and outrage, attempts to understand why the massacre occurred, and proposals for what should be done to prevent future tragedies. Consider these example letters to the editor, and then answer the questions that follow.

In the wake of the Sandy Hook tragedy, many people are asking, "Why did he do it?" Although we may never fully know the reason, I can venture a guess. Poor parenting, plain and simple.—Mother of three

An end to school shootings is possible only if we are willing to take self-defense seriously. First, teachers should be able to carry guns to protect the children in their classrooms. Second, parents should be allowed to carry and

patrol the halls as well. Finally, our kids should be encouraged to protect themselves and others.—NRA member

1. Which of the above passages offers reasons? What is the purpose of the reasons?
2. Brainstorm several reasons that could be given to support one of the solutions offered by the NRA member. Alternatively, brainstorm several reasons that could be given to defeat it.
3. Review the letters to the editor published by the *Lexington Herald-Leader* on December 23, 2012, at http://www.kentucky.com/2012/12/23/2453936/letters-to-editor-sandy-hook-massacre.html. Which of the letters present arguments? How can you tell?

Officer Rick Moore patrols Oakland Technical High School in Oakland, California.

CHAPTER

3

Analyzing Arguments

One of the important decisions in your life right now is which area of study you should choose as your major. At times, the answer may seem obvious. For example, if you want to become a chemist, then chemistry seems the best choice. But at other times, the best choice may not seem so obvious. Some careers may become obsolete in the coming decades, while others may have yet to emerge. Subjects you enjoy today may become boring, while those you currently dislike may become inspiring. How can you prepare for this uncertainty? You may seek out advice from your family members, friends, and teachers. You might even read articles outlining hiring trends or predicting future economic needs. Consider this advice from Dr. Dan Albert, Founding Director of the McPherson Eye Research Institute at the University of Wisconsin.

> *Many students preparing for a career in science believe that humanities classes are a waste of time. But how could they be? The humanities prepare you to fulfill your civic and cultural responsibilities, they strengthen your ability to communicate and work with others, and they help you understand the future scientific needs of society.*

This chart is based upon data from a PayScale Salary Survey of more than 1,000 colleges and universities across the United States. How would your choice of major change if you considered both data sets instead of only the starting salary data?

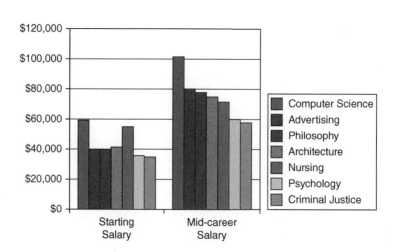

Chart using the data on Starting vs. Mid-career salaries by major from http://www.payscale.com/college-salary-report-2014/majors-that-pay-you-back. List a mix of high paying careers in science, business, and humanities.

Visit our website: academic.cengage.com/philosophy/Jackson

Using the argument recognition skills you learned from Chapter 2, you should be able to identify this passage as an argument. But what exactly does Dr. Albert want us to believe? And what reasons does he offer to convince us? In this chapter, you will learn how to answer these questions by acquiring the skills of argument analysis. To **analyze** something is to break it down into its most elementary parts. In the case of an argument, that means identifying the issue, conclusion, and premise(s). Analyzing arguments is a foundational skill, since you cannot begin to determine how good an argument is until you understand exactly how the argument works.

Identifying the parts of an argument can be a daunting task. Arguments often fail to be as clearly constructed as we might like. This lack of clarity may result from the arguer's writing style or may be due to the complexity of the argument. Arguers may or may not use inference indicators to assist you in argument analysis. Sometimes arguers give arguments that imply claims, making argument analysis more challenging. Other times arguers provide more than one argument, and you must sort out how, if at all, the arguments relate to one another. Ideally, an analysis will indicate how every claim in an argument contributes to convincing the reader of the truth of the conclusion. This involves both clarifying what the claims are and determining the role played by each claim in the argument.

LEARNING OUTCOMES

In this chapter, you will learn how to analyze arguments by:

▶ Stating the conclusion, premises, and issue of an argument;
▶ Excluding claims that are neither premises nor conclusions from your analysis;
▶ Articulating premises and conclusions that are implied by non-claims;
▶ Analyzing arguments with multiple conclusions;
▶ Analyzing chain arguments; and
▶ Writing a Critical Précis of an argument.

Analyzing Arguments with Inference Indicators

Recall from Chapter 2 that an **argument** is a set of claims that offers reasons as evidence for the truth of one of its claims. The claims offered as evidence are called the **premises**, and the claim supported by the evidence is called the **conclusion**. In order to determine which claim is a premise and which is a conclusion, you should take advantage of any clues provided by the author, such as inference indicators. **Inference indicators** are words or phrases that reveal the argument's structure. There are two kinds of inference indicators: premise indicators and conclusion indicators. A **premise indicator** signals that the claim following it is a premise, and a **conclusion indicator** signals that the claim following it is a conclusion. Inference indicators are your most valuable tools in argument analysis.

Let's look at some examples to see how to use inference indicators to analyze arguments. Consider the following:

> *Knowing how to apply first aid may help save someone's life some day; therefore, you should develop your ability to do so.*

First, notice that this passage contains two claims combined with the inference indicator *therefore*. This inference indicator signals that the claim following it is the conclusion. It also indicates that the previous claim is the premise.

_____; *therefore,* _____.

premise   **conclusion**

You can analyze the argument formally by stating the premise above a line and the conclusion below the line and by labeling each premise with the letter P and the conclusion with the symbol ∴, as done below. We call this technique a **Formal Analysis**.

P: Knowing how to apply first aid may help save someone's life some day.
∴   You should develop your ability to apply first aid.

Notice that in this Formal Analysis, the wording of the conclusion differs from that of the original. This is because the point of analysis is to clarify the meaning of each claim, as well as to determine the role each claim plays in the argument. When the passage states, "You should develop your ability to do so," what is actually claimed is "You should develop your ability to apply first aid."

After you have stated the premise(s) and the conclusion, you should then state the issue. The **issue** is what is up for debate or being questioned. Since the purpose of the reasons in an argument is to support a position on one side or the other, this means that the issue is the same regardless of which side of the issue the arguer defends. For example, the issue of the previous argument can be stated as follows, by placing the word *whether* in front of the conclusion.

Issue: Whether you should develop your ability to apply first aid

Even if the arguer concludes that you *should not* develop your ability to apply first aid, the issue is still the same. In other words, the issue should be stated positively, even when the conclusion is a negative claim.

 EXERCISE 3.1

Your Turn!   How does identifying the conclusion help you identify the issue?

If instead of a conclusion indicator the author utilizes a premise indicator, you can begin the analysis with the premise and then look to see what it supports. Here's an example.

You should buy Suave because it costs less than similar products from a salon.

Like the previous example, this passage contains two claims combined with an inference indicator. *Because* signals that the claim following it is a premise. In this case, it also tells you that the claim before it is the conclusion.

_____ *because* _____.

conclusion   **premise**

To analyze the argument formally, you should write the premise above a line and label it with the letter P and then write the conclusion below the line and label it with the conclusion symbol. The issue should be labeled and written underneath the argument.

P: Suave costs less than similar products from a salon.

∴   You should buy Suave.

Issue: Whether you should buy Suave

Like the previous example, the wording of the claims in the Formal Analysis differs from the original. When the arguer says, "it costs less than similar products from a salon," we need to know what *it* is. So the pronoun, *it*, is replaced with its referent, *Suave*.

Sometimes arguers utilize more than one inference indicator, as in the following example.

> *When oil prices start falling, oil producers usually begin to limit supply. Thus, we can expect that oil producers will begin limiting supply in the next month or two given that oil prices have been steadily falling for the past three months.*

This passage expresses three claims in these two sentences. The first claim is presented in the first sentence, and the second and third claims are presented in the second sentence. Notice that the second sentence contains two inference indicators. The first inference indicator, *thus*, signals that a conclusion follows and that the premise for that conclusion precedes it. The second inference indicator, *given that*, signals that a premise follows and that this premise supports the claim preceding it.

_____. Thus, _____, given that _____.
   premise   **conclusion**   **premise**

Since there are two premises, you should number them in your Formal Analysis and draw a line that separates the premises from the conclusion.

P1:   When oil prices start falling, oil producers usually begin to limit supply.

P2:   Oil prices have been steadily falling for the past three months.

∴   Oil producers will begin limiting supply in the next month or two.

Notice how the wording of the conclusion in the Formal Analysis differs from that in the original. Why not state the conclusion "We can expect that oil producers will begin limiting supply in the next month or two"? Because the point of the argument is what oil producers will do, not what we can expect. Rather than being part of the conclusion, the phrase "we can expect that" introduces it.

 EXERCISE 3.2

Your Turn!   Complete the Formal Analysis of the example above by identifying the issue of the argument.

> **Hint!**
> Accurately stating the premises and conclusions in your Formal Analysis can be challenging, but with practice, you can hone your skills. Be sure to omit phrases that introduce claims, but are not part of the claims. Some of the worst culprits include phrases like these.
>
> We can expect that . . .   I heard that . . .
> I'm certain that . . .   Studies show that . . .
> I think that . . .   We know that . . .
> They said that . . .   Some people believe that . . .

Not every claim in an argument will have an inference indicator signaling its role. In these cases, you can begin with the inference indicators given, and from there, you can determine the role of any remaining claims. Consider this example.

> *The last time her kitchen sink was draining more slowly than usual, Kim found that using a plunger fixed the problem. Since it is draining slowly again, it's probably a good idea to use the plunger once more.*

This passage contains three claims: The first sentence contains one claim, and the second sentence contains two. The word *since* signals that the claim following it is a premise. Placed at the beginning of the sentence like this, *since* also indicates that the second claim in that sentence is the conclusion.

_____. Since _____, _____.
                                premise   **conclusion**

Using this inference indicator, you can begin your argument analysis. Notice that the wording of the claims is once again altered from the original to clarify the meaning of the claims.

P: Kim's kitchen sink is draining slowly again. _____

∴   Kim should use the plunger to clear the drain in her kitchen sink.

What about the first sentence in the passage? Without an inference indicator, you must rely on the content of the claim to determine its role. This is a single claim referring to what happened in the past: Using the plunger cured the slowly draining sink. And since Kim's sink is clogged again, the arguer suggests that the previous solution be reapplied. Thus, the claim makes sense as another premise supporting the conclusion. Your Formal Analysis can now be completed.

P1:   The last time her kitchen sink was draining more slowly than usual, Kim found that using a plunger fixed the problem.

P2:   Kim's kitchen sink is draining slowly again. _____

∴   Kim should use the plunger to clear the drain in her kitchen sink.

Issue: Whether Kim should use the plunger to clear the drain in her kitchen sink

Accurately recognizing premise and conclusion indicator words is the best tool for successful argument analysis. You should make a list of indicator words you encounter and commit them to memory if you are having *any* trouble recognizing them, starting with the list from Chapter 2. These words and phrases may provide the only tangible clues to an argument's structure.

> **Hint!**
> When you come across an inference indicator, you may sometimes be unsure whether the word or phrase indicates a premise or a conclusion. The easiest way to check is to remember that all premise indicators are synonyms for *because* and all conclusion indicators are synonyms for *therefore*. This means that you can simply ask yourself, Does this word mean the same thing as *because* or *therefore*?

Also, remember that inference indicators reveal an argument's structure even if the content does not make sense. If a political candidate should say, "You should vote for me for governor because the moon is made of cheese," this loony arguer is giving a conclusion and a supporting premise, even though the reasoning makes no sense. Premise and conclusion indicators mean what they say—"Here is a premise" or "Here is a conclusion."

 EXERCISE 3.3

Identify each blank as a premise or conclusion using the given inference indicators. A dictionary may help you understand any terms that are unfamiliar to you.

1. _____ because _____.
2. _____. Thus, _____.
3. Since _____, _____.
4. Given that _____ and _____, _____.
5. _____. Consequently, _____, for _____.
6. _____. In conclusion, _____.
7. We can conclude that _____, based on _____.
8. _____ and _____, which imply that _____.
9. _____. As a result, _____ inasmuch as _____.
10. _____ is indicated by _____ and _____.
11. _____. This proves that _____.
12. _____ and _____. These show that _____.
13. _____ may be inferred from _____.
14. _____. We may infer that _____.
15. _____ in that _____ and _____.
16. _____ in view of the fact that _____.
17. _____. _____. _____. For all these reasons, _____.
18. _____ may be derived from _____.
19. _____, for the reason that _____.
20. _____. This entails that _____.
21. _____. This demonstrates that _____.
22. The reason that _____ is that _____.
23. Because _____ and _____, _____.
24. _____, as _____ and _____.
25. _____. Accordingly, _____.

Analyzing Arguments without Inference Indicators

Inference indicators, unfortunately, are not always supplied by arguers. Without them, it can sometimes be difficult to determine which claim in a passage is the conclusion and which is a premise. When that is the case, read the passage carefully, and ask yourself, What is the speaker trying to get me to do or believe? What reasons does the speaker supply to convince me?

Consider this example.

> *Gas prices have increased every year for the past decade. You can be sure they will continue to escalate.*

If it is not immediately obvious to you which claim is the conclusion and which is the premise, you should try inserting your own inference indicator to see which interpretation of the passage makes the better, more logical sense. Does this work?

> *Gas prices have increased every year for the past decade* because *you can be sure they will continue to escalate.*

No. This doesn't work. The second claim does not provide evidence that the first claim is true. Does the first claim support the second? Let's reverse the order of the claims and see.

> *You can be sure that gas prices will continue to escalate* because *they have increased every year for the past decade.*

Yes, this works! "Gas prices have increased every year for the past decade" provides evidence to prove that "Gas prices will continue to escalate."

Now, you can present your Formal Analysis of the argument.

P: Gas prices have increased every year for the past decade.

∴   Gas prices will continue to escalate.

Issue: Whether gas prices will continue to escalate

> **Hint!**
> Remember to verify that the purpose of the reasons is to prove that another claim is true. You don't want to mistake an explanation for an argument!

It can sometimes be more intimidating to analyze longer arguments without inference indicators, but the process works the same as in the shorter ones. Consider this example.

> *I don't think that we should buy Lawrence a car. He is not responsible enough to own a car. And we don't have enough money to pay for an extra car.*

 EXERCISE 3.4

> **Your Turn!**   Try inserting *because* between the claims to identify the conclusion of the argument.

Once you insert your own inference indicator, you can see that the author is try-ing to establish a conclusion—namely, that "We should not buy Lawrence a car." The remaining claims, then, make sense as two premises in support of it.

Here is the argument presented formally.

P1: Lawrence is not responsible enough to own a car.

P2: We don't have enough money to pay for an extra car.

∴ We should not buy Lawrence a car.

Issue: Whether we should buy Lawrence a car

Notice that the issue is stated positively even though the conclusion is a negative claim.

 EXERCISE 3.5

Write a Formal Analysis of each argument, making sure to present each claim so that it can stand alone.

1. Your gums are bleeding, and your tooth aches. So you should go to the dentist immediately.
2. The reason that hybrid cars are the most important development from the automotive industry since the 1970s is that gasoline will become increasingly scarce in the years ahead.
3. You should get your holiday shopping done early because many stores are not restocking their shelves this year.
4. The university trustees voted to raise student fees yet again. It follows that we can expect enrollment to drop, since many students cannot afford even a small increase in college costs.
5. Inasmuch as the military has had an increasingly difficult time meeting recruitment goals and veteran soldiers are retiring at an unusually high rate, it is likely that the military will soon be much smaller than it was five years ago.
6. Video piracy has reached unprecedented levels, and the cost to make a Hollywood movie continues to escalate. As a consequence, studios will be increasingly hesitant to invest in films that are unlikely to be box office hits.
7. Binge drinking is a serious problem for American women and girls. It increases the risk for breast cancer, heart disease, and sexually transmitted diseases.
8. The study of religion is vital for understanding our world. Religious differences have been the cause of war throughout history, and they continue to promote conflict in the international arena.
9. We hope you agree that our fraternity is the best on campus. The majority of students who responded to a campus survey said our fraternity would have been their number one pick. And that many people could not possibly be wrong.
10. Prohibition of alcohol didn't work. Prohibition of drugs hasn't worked. Prohibiting steroids and other performance enhancers won't work either.

Analyzing Arguments with Extra Claims

Most arguments are presented in a context with other types of discourse. In these cases, you must sort through which claims are part of the argument and which are not. Claims that are presented with an argument, but are neither conclusions nor premises, are extra claims. Arguers use extra claims in a variety of ways. The claims may provide background information about the topic, they may simply provide rhetorical flourish, or they may motivate the argument by presenting an opponent's viewpoint. Even though extra claims may concern the topic addressed by the argument, you should simply leave them out of your analysis because they do not play a role in the argument itself.

Let's look at a few examples of arguments combined with extra claims.

> *The next City Council election is on November 5. You should vote for Jocelyn Jones because she is committed to the well-being of all our city's residents.*

This passage contains three claims. The first claim is expressed in the first sentence, and the second and third claims are expressed in the second sentence. The inference indicator *because* signals that the second sentence contains two claims (one before and one after *because*). This inference indicator also signals that the second claim in the sentence is a reason for the first. In fact, this reason supports the first claim in the sentence, so the passage is an argument.

$$\underline{\hspace{3cm}}. \underline{\hspace{3cm}} \textit{because} \underline{\hspace{3cm}}.$$
$$\textbf{conclusion} \qquad \textbf{premise}$$

Notice that the analysis below rewords the premise from the original passage so that the meaning of the claim is clear.

P: Jocelyn Jones is committed to the well-being of all our city's residents.

∴ You should vote for Jocelyn Jones.

Issue: Whether you should vote for Jocelyn Jones

What about the first claim in the passage? Is it a premise or a conclusion? No. It is neither a conclusion nor a premise. None of the other claims proves that the next City Council election is on November 5, and when the next City Council election will be held doesn't provide evidence for how you should vote. Instead, the first claim is an extra claim; thus, it should be left out of your Formal Analysis.

Here's another example of an argument presented with an extra claim.

> *Since the population of Texas consists of both English- and Spanish-language speakers, elementary school education should be bilingual. That's not to say that making it so would be easy.*

 EXERCISE 3.6

Your Turn! Rewrite the above argument by substituting a blank for each claim. Then, using the remaining inference indicators, identify whether each blank represents a premise or a conclusion.

The first and second claims are presented in the first sentence, and the third claim is presented in the second sentence. The inference indicator *since* in the first sentence signals that what comes after it is the premise and that the claim following the comma is the conclusion.

EXERCISE 3.7

Your Turn!   Use the inference indicator *because* to test whether the first claim is a premise or a conclusion in the argument.

The third claim, "That's not to say that making it so would be easy," is related to the topic of the argument, since it suggests that there may be problems with enacting bilingual education. However, this claim is neither a premise nor a conclusion: It doesn't provide evidence for either of the other claims, and neither of the other claims provides evidence to prove it. Thus, the third claim is an extra claim and should be left out of your Formal Analysis.

P: The population of Texas consists of both English- and Spanish-language speakers.

∴   Elementary school education should be bilingual.

Issue: Whether elementary school education should be bilingual

Before moving on, let's examine a more complex use of extra claims.

Many people argue against large tax cuts. I disagree—we should enact large tax cuts because that is the best way to increase spending.

Phrases like "I disagree" can help you recognize arguments, as they signal a dispute or clash of ideas. In this case, the arguer is taking a stance against what is said by the "opponents" in the first sentence. Using the content of the first claim, we can see that, unlike "many people," the arguer *favors* large tax cuts.

EXERCISE 3.8

Your Turn!   Rewrite the above argument by substituting a blank for each claim. Then, using the remaining inference indicators, identify whether each blank represents a premise or a conclusion.

Although the second sentence in the passage might at first appear to contain three claims, it contains only two. Once we determine what the author means by "I disagree," we can see that he or she is expressing the claim "We should enact large tax cuts," and that's just what the claim following the dash states! Now we can analyze the argument.

The premise indicator *because* confirms that "we should enact large tax cuts" is the conclusion, and it also signals that what follows *because* is a premise. When the arguer writes "that is the best way to increase spending," we must determine what *that* refers to and then specify this referent in the Formal Analysis.

> **P:** Enacting large tax cuts is the best way to increase spending.
>
> ∴ We should enact large tax cuts.
>
> **Issue:** Whether we should enact large tax cuts

What about the first claim? The arguer includes the opponents' viewpoint in order to motivate his or her argument for the other side. Although the first claim is not part of the argument, it does engage the same issue. Recall that the issue is what is up for debate or being questioned. The arguer's conclusion is "We should enact large tax cuts," and the opponents' view is "We should *not* enact large tax cuts." The two positions disagree on the issue of whether we should enact large tax cuts. It may sometimes be challenging to sort out the arguments described by the arguer from those that he or she advocates, but with practice, doing so will get easier.

EXERCISE 3.9

Your Turn! How do you tell which claim in a passage is advocated by the author of the passage?

EXERCISE 3.10

Using a Formal Analysis, identify the premises, conclusion, and issue for each passage, excluding any claims that are not part of the argument.

1. Francisco is most likely good at math because he has an analytical mind. He is one of the students in my English composition class.
2. Last year you waited until the last minute to do your shopping. But this year you should get your holiday shopping done early because many stores are not restocking their shelves this year.
3. Conrad is running for reelection. You definitely should vote for him. Why? He's a visionary, that's why.
4. Because Andrea speaks three languages, she should look for work in international business. At least, that's what I think.
5. Schnauzers make the best family dogs. They are good with children, and they are naturally wary of strangers. You can get them as miniatures or standards.
6. Many political pundits believe that an increase in troop levels is the best means for fighting an insurgency. Not I. Increasing troop levels puts more of our troops at risk and increases the possibility of civilian casualties.
7. Aiding big industrial giants like General Motors and Chrysler is a form of tampering with the free markets. I agree that such tampering is usually a bad idea.

But right now, we should tamper with the market because otherwise the entire economy is liable to go into a disastrous free fall.

8. The district attorney has presented many interesting and persuasive arguments. However, the case against my client, members of the jury, is based on inadmissible evidence because it consists of hearsay.

9. It would be a welcome relief to have a rainy year. I bet this year will be rainier than most due to the fact that tropical oceans are warming.

10. There's been a lot of talk lately about reforming our health-care system. But we should resist doing so for two important reasons. First, it is unnecessary. Second, it would be too expensive.

Analyzing Arguments with Implied Claims

You may recall from Chapter 2 that questions, commands, and phrases are not claims, and for this reason, they are not part of arguments. However, some arguments are presented using non-claims such as questions and commands in a *rhetorical* fashion. When these non-claims are used rhetorically in arguments, they *imply* claims. Therefore, you must identify the claim that is implied when completing your analysis.

Consider the following example.

> *Don't move. You're about to step right on a rattlesnake.* ← claim

In this passage, the first sentence is a command, and the second is a claim. At first, you may think that this cannot be an argument because the passage contains only one claim. However, that doesn't mean that whoever is speaking isn't trying to convince you of a serious point. After all, the speaker provides a reason, "You're about to step right on a rattlesnake," to convince you of another claim. Although "Don't move" is not a claim, in this context it implies a claim—namely, "You should not move."

©Robert Landau/Corbis

This billboard does not contain any claims, nevertheless it tries to persuade you. What conclusion does it imply?

With this implied claim identified, you can analyze the argument as follows:

P: You're about to step right on a rattlesnake.

∴   You should not move.

Issue: Whether you should move

An implied claim can also serve as a premise in an argument. Consider the following example.

You should select Chapman for CEO. Don't you agree that Chapman is an innovative leader?

In this passage, the claim "You should select Chapman for CEO" is followed by a question: "Don't you agree that Chapman is an innovative leader?" However, when the author asks the question, he or she is not really looking for an answer. Instead, the question is *rhetorical*; the author is *implying* that Chapman is an innovative leader and, thus, giving a premise in support of the conclusion.

P: Chapman is an innovative leader.

∴   You should select Chapman for CEO.

Issue: Whether you should select Chapman for CEO

 EXERCISE 3.11

Your Turn!   How is it possible that a sentence that is not a claim can play a role in an argument?

In addition to rhetorical questions and commands, arguers may imply claims using other non-claims. Consider this example containing a command and three words.

Vote for Lopez. Experience; Honesty; Integrity.

During election years, this kind of message on yard signs and bumper stickers is common. In this case, no claims are given, and thus you may think that this cannot be an argument. Nonetheless, most people would easily recognize that the person who created this message wants the reader to be persuaded to do something—to vote for this candidate. Therefore, a conclusion, "You should vote for Lopez," is implied. What seem to act as reasons are three election-year buzzwords. By using these words, the arguer is implying that the candidate has these three attributes, and thus they serve as the reasons that you should vote for this candidate. So in this case, a command implies the conclusion, and three isolated words imply three separate premises.

P1:   Lopez has experience.

P2:   Lopez is honest.

P3:   Lopez has integrity.

∴   You should vote for Lopez.

Issue: Whether you should vote for Lopez

Before moving ahead, let's look at one more example.

The boss said yesterday that she would lay off anyone who has more than six unexcused days off this month. I see that yesterday was your eighth unexcused day off this month. You know what that means, don't you?

This passage contains two claims and a question. By asking "You know what that means, don't you?" the speaker is expecting you to draw the conclusion from the premises provided. All you have to do is consider the first claims as premises and the proper conclusion will be easy to see—especially if your job is at stake!

> **P1:** The boss said yesterday that she would lay off anyone who has more than six unexcused days off this month.
> **P2:** Yesterday was your eighth unexcused day off this month.
> ∴ You are going to be laid off.
>
> **Issue:** Whether you are going to be laid off

Hint!
We are not saying that rhetorical questions, commands, and so on are sometimes claims and sometimes not. These kinds of statements always remain non-claims. Instead, a non-claim can be used for rhetorical purposes to imply a claim in an argument, and this implied claim can be a premise or a conclusion.

 EXERCISE 3.12

Your Turn! Look back at the passage presented at the start of this chapter. Provide a Formal Analysis of the argument.

How to Write a Formal Analysis of an Argument

Step 1: Use inference indicators to identify the premises and conclusion of the argument.
▶ Write out each premise as a claim that can stand on its own.
▶ Underneath the premises, write out the conclusion as a claim that can stand on its own.
▶ Do not include any extra claims.

Step 2: Label the premises and conclusion as such.
▶ Label each premise with a P (P1, P2, P3, etc., for multiple premises).
▶ Label the conclusion with the symbol ∴.
▶ Draw a single line separating the premises from the conclusion.

Step 3: Identify the issue of the argument.
▶ Write out the issue of the argument underneath the conclusion, and label it "Issue."
▶ Make sure that the issue is stated positively and that it matches the conclusion of the argument.

EXERCISE 3.13

Using a Formal Analysis, identify the premises, conclusion, and issue of each argument, including any claims that are implied by non-claims.

1. Pay attention. If you don't, you might miss something important.
2. The car needs a safety inspection. Aren't you planning a long trip this summer?
3. The best man for the job is a woman. Vote Councilwoman Hagen for mayor.
4. The animal shelter needs to be modernized. How can we treat our animals humanely with outmoded facilities?
5. Vitality and poise. Power and elegance. The new Alturus just may be the best mid-size sedan on the market.
6. The university is sending a mixed message to the community. Aren't we trying to encourage all students to apply at the same time as we are limiting enrollment?
7. Help us! You're the only one we know who can understand the tax code language.
8. Study harder! Don't you want to pass?
9. Which program should you choose? The one that will make you happiest over the long haul. This is because no amount of money will make up for a boring, unsatisfying career.
10. The only people who can be hypnotized are those who are easily persuadable, and you aren't persuadable at all. You know what follows from that, don't you?

 EXERCISE 3.14

Using a Formal Analysis, identify the premises, conclusion, and issue for each passage, including any implied claims and excluding any claims that are not part of the argument.

1. Electricians make good money, and they are highly sought-after workers. Shouldn't you consider this fascinating career?
2. Don't you deserve a total makeover? Choose Sirius Professional Makeover Service. Open 9–5 daily.
3. Obviously, we don't want to ban all cell-phone use when driving: What if you need to report a drunk driver on the highway?
4. Some people claim that insider trading is inevitable. If that were true, then there wouldn't be laws against it. However, insider trading is illegal. Hence, they must be mistaken.
5. I've noticed that Anna's new espresso machine makes the worst coffee I've ever tasted. So don't even consider buying one.
6. Don't drive over the speed limit! What's to keep you from breaking other laws?
7. Bigger. Better. Barbie's Burgers.
8. Don't quit your job. Jobs are hard to come by, and you don't have a great résumé.

9. We must pass laws to curtail hate speech. Would you want someone to disparage *your* race?

10. Green. Inexpensive. American. Try corn-based ethanol.

11. The scale shows that you are 20 pounds overweight, and no one who is overweight can get into the Police Academy. You do understand what follows, don't you?

12. Will you stop being so squeamish? Surely, you have seen blood before, and besides that, you're wearing gloves.

13. Low fat. Inexpensive. Fun to eat. Why not take cottage cheese for lunch tomorrow?

14. Get new tires for your car right now. With those threadbare tires, you could have a blowout on the freeway.

15. Stop staying up late studying; it's ruining your health.

16. Move right now! Local realtors suggest that rents will climb as much as 25% next month.

17. Student fees have been raised every year for the past decade. You can figure out what's going to happen next year, can't you?

18. Stop whining! Dizziness is not a medical emergency.

19. Why should your children listen to you? Because you're the mom, that's why.

20. Persist! That's what successful people do.

Analyzing Multiple Arguments

So far, you have learned how to use inference indicators to identify the issue, conclusion, and premises of an argument; how to exclude claims that are neither premises nor conclusions from your analysis; and how to articulate premises and conclusions that are implied by non-claims. We now turn to the analysis of multiple arguments. There are two types of multiple arguments—arguments with multiple conclusions and chain arguments. You will know that a passage contains a multiple argument whenever there is more than one conclusion present.

Consider, first, this example.

> *Rafael was given greater responsibilities at work. Therefore, he deserves a raise, and he should also be given a promotion.*

This passage contains three claims. The first claim is presented in the first sentence, and the second and third claims are presented in the second sentence. The inference indicator *therefore* signals that the claim following it is a conclusion and the claim prior to it is a premise. What about the third claim? The word *and* tells us that the role played by the claim following it will be the same as that played by the claim prior to it. In other words, it is also a conclusion!

     _____. *Therefore,* _____, *and* _____.
       premise   **conclusion**   **conclusion**

Earlier you learned that every argument has exactly one conclusion and at least one premise. Since this passage contains two conclusions, that means the passage contains two arguments. Looking back at the structure of the passage, notice again that there are two claims combined with the word *and* following the inference indicator *therefore*. This structure signals that the conclusion indicator applies to both claims.

So the premise supporting the third claim is the same as the premise supporting the second one. Now, we can set out each conclusion with its supporting premise.

P: Rafael was given greater responsibilities at work.

∴   **Rafael deserves a pay raise.**

P: Rafael was given greater responsibilities at work.

∴   **Rafael should be given a promotion**

When a passage contains more than one conclusion following from the same premise(s), as in this case, it is known as an **argument with multiple conclusions**. And because there are two conclusions, there are two issues. The first is "whether Rafael deserves a pay raise," and the second is "whether Rafael should be given a promotion." Although we will talk about these kinds of arguments as if they are single arguments, they are actually two different, albeit related, arguments.

P: Rafael was given greater responsibilities at work.

∴   Rafael deserves a pay raise.

Issue: Whether Rafael deserves a pay raise

P: Rafael was given greater responsibilities at work.

∴   Rafael should be given a promotion.

Issue: Whether Rafael should be given a promotion

> **Hint!**
> When presenting arguments with multiple conclusions using a Formal Analysis, the order in which you present them does not matter. Just make sure that each argument is presented fully so that it can stand on its own.

The other kind of multiple argument—the **chain argument**—consists of a *chain* of reasoning, with some conclusions serving as premises for other conclusions. Those claims that do double duty as conclusions and premises are called **intermediate conclusions**. They stand between the initial premises and the ultimate conclusion. All chain arguments contain intermediate conclusions, and it is by recognizing intermediate conclusions that you will be able to identify chain arguments. Although we may informally speak of a chain argument as a single argument, it actually consists of two or more distinct

Although images by themselves are not arguments, they can be rhetorically persuasive. How might you construct an argument inspired by this image?

arguments forming a chain of reasoning leading to one main conclusion. The intermediate conclusions and the premises that support them are known as **subarguments**.

Consider this example.

> *This year is predicted to be warmer and drier than normal throughout most of the country, so the drought in the Southeast will most likely continue. Therefore, Georgia's farmers face another poor season.*

Like the previous example, this passage contains three claims. The first two claims are presented in the first sentence, and the third claim is presented in the second sentence. Also, notice that there are two inference indicators in the passage, *so* and *therefore*. These are both conclusion indictors! That means that this passage contains two conclusions, and, hence, there are two arguments presented.

_____, *so* _____. *Therefore,* _____.
    premise   **conclusion**   **conclusion**

The conclusion indicator *so* signals that the first claim is a premise and the second claim is its conclusion. We can analyze this argument as follows:

> **P:**   This year is predicted to be warmer and drier than normal throughout most of the country.
> _____
> ∴   The drought in the Southeast will most likely continue.

Unlike the previous example of an argument with multiple conclusions, here, the second conclusion is presented with its own conclusion indicator rather than being combined with the first conclusion using the word *and*. This signals that the claim that follows *therefore* is a further conclusion, not one supported by the same premise. But if the first claim is not its premise, which claim could be? It is supported by the preceding conclusion, the claim directly preceding the word *therefore*.

> **P:**   The drought in the Southeast will most likely continue.
> _____
> ∴   Georgia's farmers face another poor season.

Since these two conclusions do *not* share a premise, this is *not* an argument with multiple conclusions. Instead, this is a chain argument consisting of one argument and one subargument. Notice that the premise supporting the final conclusion is the same claim as the first conclusion.

 EXERCISE 3.15

Your Turn!   Which of the two conclusions above is the *intermediate* conclusion? Which is the final (or main) conclusion?

To continue with the analysis of this argument, you must identify the issue. The issue for a chain argument will be based on whatever is the main point, or main conclusion, of the argument. When presenting a Formal Analysis of a chain argument, you should always list the subargument first and state the issue, as usual, at the bottom of the analysis.

P:	This year is predicted to be warmer and drier than normal throughout most of the country.
∴	The drought in the Southeast will most likely continue.
P:	The drought in the Southeast will most likely continue.
∴	Georgia's farmers face another poor season.

Issue: Whether Georgia's farmers face another poor season

As you can see, there is no issue associated with the intermediate conclusion, since it also plays a role as a premise.

Intermediate conclusions sometimes occur with one or more other premises to support the main conclusion, as in the following example.

> *You should be a good candidate to win the essay contest. This is because you made a powerful argument due to the fact that you presented important evidence for your thesis. Furthermore, your essay was clearer than any of the others submitted.*

 EXERCISE 3.16

Your Turn!   Rewrite the argument above by substituting a blank for each claim. Then, using the remaining inference indicators, identify whether each blank represents a premise or a conclusion. How do the inference indicators help you determine that the passage contains a chain argument?

Here is the main argument.

P1:	You made a powerful argument.
P2:	Your essay was clearer than any of the others submitted.
∴	You should be a good candidate to win the essay contest.

The premise indicator *due to the fact that* signals that the third claim, "you presented important evidence for your thesis," supports the claim immediately preceding it. Since this supported claim already serves as a premise in an argument, it is part of the following subargument.

P:	You presented important evidence for your thesis.
∴	You made a powerful argument.

 EXERCISE 3.17

Your Turn!   Present the complete Formal Analysis of the chain argument above, including the issue.

Hint!

Subarguments can be thought of as a response to one who doubts, or may doubt, whether a supporting premise is true. So, imagining the question "Why should I believe your premise?" the arguer presents supporting evidence in the form of a subargument.

Once you have completed a Formal Analysis for a passage that contains multiple arguments, it should be easy to determine whether the passage is an argument with multiple conclusions or a chain argument. When the two conclusions share the same premise, the passage is an argument with multiple conclusions. When the conclusion of one argument serves as a premise for another argument, the passage is a chain argument.

EXERCISE 3.18

Using a Formal Analysis, identify the premises, conclusion, and issue for each argument in the following passages. Then determine whether the passage is a chain argument or an argument with multiple conclusions.

1. John graduated summa cum laude from a fine university. That means he should get a good job. In addition, won't he be more likely to get into a good grad school?
2. John graduated summa cum laude from a fine university, so he should get a good job. Thus, he should be quite successful.
3. Because Maria tore up all her credit cards, she will again be living within her means. Accordingly, she should be able to earn back an excellent credit rating. Her FICO score used to be over 700.
4. This winter has already been colder than normal. Thus, we can expect more snow, and we can expect more damage to our fruit trees.
5. You should move to Arizona, since it is much warmer. Therefore, you should give two weeks' notice at your office.
6. Prohibition of alcohol didn't work, so it's pointless to try to prohibit recreational drug use. It's equally pointless to try to prohibit steroids and other performance enhancers.
7. The recent study concerning the health consequences of diabetes drugs for young people is not to be believed. This is because the survey was flawed. Why? The sample size was too small.
8. Spiders are quite beneficial to the ecosystem. Accordingly, don't squash them, and don't spray poisons on them.
9. You and your family have paid a great deal of money for your college education. So you really must take your studies more seriously. Therefore, you should quit working 40 hours a week.
10. My brother thinks that the Seahawks will win the Super Bowl. But he's wrong. They are playing the Denver Broncos, and given that the Broncos have the highest-scoring offense in NFL history, they are sure to win.
11. Horatio took little care of his teeth when he was a teenager, so he will probably have dental problems when he gets older. Consequently, he should always buy dental insurance. Dental insurance typically costs less than $30 per month.

12. You should be frugal with your paycheck, and you should put more money in savings, for the economy is awful and there's little hope for improvement anytime soon.
13. Because a good dictionary is useful in every university course, it is not only a wise investment for all students, but also a wise investment for anybody wishing to be better educated.
14. Nearly six million American citizens, those with a felony conviction, are barred from voting and excluded from jury service. However, ex-felons should be allowed to vote, and they should be allowed to serve on a jury. This is because once a person has fully repaid his or her debt to society, that person should have his or her full citizenship rights reinstated.
15. Inasmuch as the military has had an increasingly difficult time meeting recruitment goals and veteran soldiers are retiring at an unusually high rate, it is likely that the military will soon be much smaller than it was five years ago and it will remain smaller for years to come.
16. The European Union has a bloated bureaucracy, so it needs to resist the urge to add new member states. Accordingly, the vote on adding Ukraine should be postponed.
17. Anderson will likely get a raise. This is because she will receive a promotion, since the Hamer project, which she directed, was a great success.
18. The city zoo is heavily in debt, and it is poorly managed. It follows that extreme measures must be taken. Thus, the town council should take charge right away.
19. Since Natalie wants to save more money, she should open a money market account at the bank, and she should cancel her credit cards.
20. Students who have internship experience are more attractive to employers. As a result, sophomores and juniors should not plan on spending their summer having a vacation. Instead, they should actively apply for internships related to their career goals.

PUTTING IT ALL TOGETHER: Writing a Critical Précis of an Argument

In Chapter 2, you learned how to write a Critical Précis of a nonargument. Now that you have learned how to analyze arguments with and without inference indicators and with extra claims and implied claims, as well as arguments with multiple conclusions and chain arguments, you can now write a Critical Précis of an argument.

How to Write a Critical Précis of an Argument
In *paragraph form*, use complete sentences and proper English grammar and spelling to do the following:

Step 1: Identify the passage.
▶ Completely and correctly identify the author and the source (whenever such information is given).
▶ If the passage contains an argument, identify it as such. Then complete Step 2.

> ▸ If the passage does not contain an argument, identify it as a nonargument. Then specify which feature of an argument is lacking.
>
> **Step 2:** Analyze the argument.
> ▸ Clearly and completely identify the issue, conclusion, and premise or premises *in that order.*
> ▸ If the passage is a *multiple argument,* write *separate paragraphs* to analyze each separate argument.

Before trying to write a Critical Précis of an argument on your own, let's work through several examples, beginning with this one.

> *Since few men are wise enough to rule themselves, even fewer are wise enough to rule others.*—Edward Abbey

At the end of Chapter 2, we recognized this passage as an argument. Although there is only one sentence, there are two claims. The inference indicator *since* tells us that the first claim offers a reason for the second. In fact, that reason offers evidence to prove the second claim. The Formal Analysis of the argument is as follows:

P: Few men are wise enough to rule themselves.

∴   Very few men are wise enough to rule others.

Issue: Whether very few men are wise enough to rule others

EXERCISE 3.19

Your Turn!   In the Formal Analysis of the passage, the wording of the conclusion is altered from the original. Why?

Once you have recognized the argument and identified its parts, you can present the analysis of the passage in paragraph form. In your first sentence, you must identify the passage as an argument, and since the passage is accompanied by its source, you should also include that information. In the subsequent sentences, you should identify the issue, conclusion, and premise.

> **This passage from Edward Abbey contains an argument. The issue is whether very few men are wise enough to rule others. The conclusion is that very few men are wise enough to rule others. The premise is that few men are wise enough to rule themselves.**

Notice that the Critical Précis presents the analysis of the argument in its logical order: The most important information is presented first—namely, the issue, then the conclusion, then the premises.

Let's now consider a passage from the director for the Washington Department of Corrections.

I started the Sustainability in Prisons Project in 2004. Inmates are ideal candidates for conservation projects since they can work in a controlled environment and have a lot of time to dedicate.—Dan Pacholke

EXERCISE 3.20

Your Turn! Rewrite the above argument by substituting a blank for each claim. Then, using the remaining inference indicators, identify whether each blank represents a premise or a conclusion.

The inference indicator *since* tells us that the two claims following it are premises for the claim that comes before it. But what about the first claim? Although it concerns the overall topic of the passage, it does not serve as a premise or a conclusion, so it is an extra claim. Here's the Formal Analysis of the argument.

P1: Inmates can work in a controlled environment.

P2: Inmates have a lot of time to dedicate to a project.

∴ Inmates are ideal candidates for conservation projects.

Issue: Whether inmates are ideal candidates for conservation projects

Just as extra claims are left out of the Formal Analysis, they are also left out of the Critical Précis.

> **This passage from Dan Pacholke contains an argument. The issue is whether inmates are ideal candidates for conservation projects. The conclusion is that inmates are ideal candidates for conservation projects. The first premise is that inmates can work in a controlled environment. The second premise is that inmates have a lot of time to dedicate to a project.**

Let's now consider an argument with an implied claim.

People who are physically active have low body fat, healthy skin tone, and a youthful appearance. Shouldn't you step up to claim these benefits?
—Frances Sizer and Ellie Whitney, Nutrition: Concepts and Controversies

This passage contains three claims in the first sentence and a question in the second sentence. Moreover, when the authors ask, "Shouldn't you step up to claim these benefits?" they aren't really asking you a question. Instead, they are implying that "You should step up to claim the benefits of physical activity," or, more simply, "You should become physically active."

P1: People who are physically active have low body fat.

P2: People who are physically active have healthy skin tone.

P3: People who are physically active have a youthful appearance.

∴ You should become physically active.

Issue: Whether you should become physically active

Now you can present this information in a Critical Précis.

> **This passage *from* Sizer and Whitney's book *Nutrition: Concepts and Controversies* contains an argument. The issue is whether you should become physically active. The implied conclusion is that you should become physically active. The first premise is that people who are physically active have low body fat. The second premise is that people who are physically active have healthy skin tone. The third premise is that people who are physically active have a youthful appearance.**

Notice that the implied conclusion is labeled as such.

What about arguments with multiple conclusions and chain arguments? Let's consider a couple of examples to see what a Critical Précis of a passage containing a multiple argument should look like.

> *Dreams give information about the secrets of the dreamer's inner life. As long as these are undiscovered, they disturb his waking life. This means that we cannot effectively treat the patient from the side of consciousness alone, but we must do so in and through the unconscious.—Carl Jung, Modern Man in Search of a Soul*

This passage contains four claims. The inference indicator *this means that* signals that the conclusion follows it, and the word *but* tells us that both the third and the fourth claims are conclusions. The Formal Analysis of the multiple argument is presented below.

P1: Dreams give information about the secrets of the dreamer's inner life.

P2: As long as the secrets of the dreamer's inner life are undiscovered, they disturb his waking life.

∴ We cannot effectively treat the patient from the side of consciousness alone.

Issue: Whether we can effectively treat the patient from the side of consciousness alone

P1: Dreams give information about the secrets of the dreamer's inner life.

P2: As long as the secrets of the dreamer's inner life are undiscovered, they disturb his waking life.

∴ We must treat the patient in and through the unconscious.

Issue: Whether we must treat the patient in and through the unconscious

Since we have an argument with multiple conclusions, the Critical Précis must contain multiple paragraphs.

> **This passage from Carl Jung's book *Modern Man in Search of a Soul* contains an argument. The issue is whether we can effectively treat the patient from the side of consciousness alone. The conclusion is that we cannot effectively treat the patient from the side of consciousness alone. The first premise is that dreams give information about the secrets of the dreamer's inner life. The second premise is that as long as the secrets of the dreamer's inner life are undiscovered, they disturb his waking life.**

> **This passage contains another argument. The issue is whether we must treat the patient in and through the unconscious. The conclusion is that we must treat the patient in and through the unconscious. The first premise is that dreams give information about the secrets of the dreamer's inner life. The second premise is that as long as the secrets of the dreamer's inner life are undiscovered, they disturb his waking life.**

Just as there are two arguments presented in the Formal Analysis, there are two arguments presented in the Critical Précis.

Consider this chain argument next.

> *Mondays are usually the busiest times for vets, because of pets that get sick over the weekend; therefore, the best time to take your pet to the vet is Tuesday at 9 am.—AARP Magazine*

This passage utilizes two inference indicators: *because* tells us that the second claim is a premise for the first, and *therefore* tells us that third claim is the overall conclusion.

P:	Pets often get sick over the weekend.
∴	Mondays are usually the busiest times for veterinarians.
P:	Mondays are usually the busiest times for veterinarians.
∴	The best time to take your pet to the veterinarian is Tuesday at 9 am.

Issue: Whether the best time to take your pet to the veterinarian is Tuesday at 9 am

 EXERCISE 3.21

Your Turn! Why is there only one issue in the above Formal Analysis?

As in the previous example, there are two arguments in this passage, so the Critical Précis will contain two paragraphs.

> **This passage from the *AARP Magazine* contains an argument. The issue is whether the best time to take your pet to the veterinarian is Tuesday at 9 am. The conclusion is that the best time to take your pet to the veterinarian is Tuesday at 9 am. The premise is that Mondays are usually the busiest times for veterinarians.**
>
> **This passage contains a subargument. The intermediate conclusion is that Mondays are usually the busiest times for veterinarians. The premise is that pets often get sick over the weekend.**

Notice that because the passage is a chain argument, there is only one issue, and it corresponds to the conclusion of the main argument.

Now that you have seen several examples, you are ready to try some on your own. Remember that a Critical Précis does not involve any new skills. You are only presenting what you have learned about recognizing and analyzing arguments in a new, written format.

Hint!

In your Critical Précis, remember the following rules.

▸ Your Critical Précis should be written in proper paragraph format.
▸ The content of each claim must make sense on its own. This means, for example, that each claim should be written in a complete sentence and that pronouns should be replaced with their referents.
▸ Inference indicators should not be included with the statement of any claim.
▸ The issue should be phrased positively, even when the conclusion is negative.
▸ Intermediate conclusions, implied conclusions, and implied premises should be labeled as such in your analysis.
▸ Extra claims should not be included in your analysis.
▸ Chain arguments have only one issue.

 EXERCISE 3.22

Write a Critical Précis for each of the following passages.

1. Changes are real. Now, changes are only possible in time, and therefore time must be something real.—Immanuel Kant, *Critique of Pure Reason*
2. Because the limbic system has a primary function in emotions such as pain, pleasure, anger, rage, fear, sorrow, sexual feelings, docility, and affection, it is sometimes called the "emotional" brain.—Gerard Tortora, *Principles of Human Anatomy*
3. School sponsorship of a religious message is impermissible because it sends the ancillary message to members of the audience who are nonadherents that they are outsiders, not full members of the political community, and an accompanying message to adherents that they are insiders, favored members of the political community.—U.S. Supreme Court, *Santa Fe v. Doe* (2000)
4. In the stratosphere the air temperature begins to increase with height, producing a temperature inversion. The reason for the inversion in the stratosphere is that the gas ozone plays a major part in heating the air at this altitude. —C. Donald Ahrens, *Essentials of Meteorology*
5. There is no need for a legal definition of death. There is no assurance that it would accomplish its intended purpose, and such legislation would lead directly to euthanasia.—The National Conference of Catholic Bishops, Committee for Pro-Life Activities
6. Will disconnecting a USB drive before ejecting it destroy my data? It can. Damage is rare but severe, ranging from permanent errors to a dead drive. Better safe than sorry. Always click Eject.—*Popular Science*
7. What the country needed, argued the Whigs, was improvement, vigorous federal support for economic development. No, countered the Democrats, what the country needed was expansion, vigorous federal action to buy more land.—Hine and Faracher, *The American West*
8. Belonging is a primary goal in life since all of us want to know we are important to family, friends, class, and school. When that goal is not reached, students tend either to withdraw or to misbehave, neither of which is good for the teacher, student, or class. Therefore, teachers should foster a sense

of belonging in every member of the class.—Charles and Senter, *Elementary Classroom Management*

9. *Drop Dead Diva* is a great show for women and a great show for women to watch with their daughters. It promotes beautiful images of different kinds of women and it also has this great heroine who really doesn't have to sell herself short in any way.—Margaret Cho, *Parade*

10. Jahi McMath has been labeled a "deceased" person. Yet, she retains all the functional attributes of a living person, despite her brain injury. This includes a beating heart, circulation and respiration, the ability to metabolize nutrition and more. Jahi is a living human being.—Terri Schiavo Life and Hope Network

CHAPTER REVIEW QUESTIONS

1. What are the three parts of an argument that must be identified in an analysis? How do you identify them?
2. What should you do with claims that are presented in a passage, but are not part of the argument?
3. How can a sentence that is not a claim be part of an argument?
4. What are the two types of multiple arguments? How can you tell the difference between them?
5. How do you write a Critical Précis of an argument?
6. How do you write a Critical Précis of a multiple argument?

ONE STEP FURTHER

Set in the antebellum era, the award-winning 2012 film *Django Unchained* features a freed slave (Jamie Foxx) who travels across the Deep South and Old West with a bounty hunter (Christoph Waltz) in order to rescue his wife (Kerry Washington) from a brutal Mississippi plantation owner (Leonardo DiCaprio). Like many of Quentin Tarantino's other films, *Django Unchained* elicited both accolades and criticism. Many critics objected to the film's use of violence and racial epithets. But there was also controversy over the film's promotional products—namely, action figures of the main characters in the film. Consider, for example, the following petition started by Brockton, Massachusetts, resident Geralyn Smith through the website www.change.org.

National Entertainment Collectibles Association (NECA): Stop the manufacture and sale of Django Unchained collector dolls

These dolls, while based on fictional characters, are slaves and remind many Black people of a painful past. This movie has no historical significance and was made solely for entertainment value. I don't see how NECA can, in good conscience, make a doll that represents a period in OUR history when Blacks were raped and hung and families destroyed just because of the color of our skin. Did you make Schindler's List *dolls when it came out? These dolls are disrespectful to the Black Americans who helped build this country. They are an insult to our heritage.*

1. What is the conclusion of the argument presented in this petition? What are the main premises supporting that conclusion? Are any of these claims implied? Specify how.
2. Would you consider signing this petition based solely on the argument presented? If so, why? If not, why not?
3. Visit www.change.org. Find a petition that you find particularly well-argued. What makes it a good argument? Alternatively, find a petition that you find well-intentioned, but poorly argued. How would you rewrite the petition?

National Entertainment Collectibles Association, Supplied by PacificCoastNews/Newscom

National Entertainment Collectibles discontinued the 10-doll collection of *Django Unchained* action figures after receiving complaints that they were offensive. Do you agree with this decision? Why or why not?

Diagramming Arguments

Imagine that you and your classmates are studying together for an upcoming criminal justice exam. One of your fellow students presents the following argument against capital punishment.

> *It's clear that we should eliminate the death penalty. First, the financial costs of it are significantly greater than those of keeping someone in prison for life. Second, the death penalty has no greater deterrent value than life in prison without parole.*

The Cost of Capital Cases

In Maryland, a death penalty case costs about three times more than a case in which the prosecutor does not seek the death penalty, according to a study by the Urban Institute. The study evaluated all 1,227 homicides that occurred in the state from 1978 to 1999 in which the defendant was eligible to receive the death sentence.

	DEATH SENTENCE NOT SOUGHT	DEATH SENTENCE UNSUCCESSFULLY SOUGHT	DEATH SENTENCE SUCCESSFULLY SOUGHT
Trial	$158,000	$601,000	$775,000
Penalty phase	0	$71,000	$263,000
State appeals	$83,000	$175,000	$565,000
Federal appeals	0	0	$96,000
Prison	$862,000	$946,000	$1,318,000*
Total	**$1,103,000**	**$1,793,000**	**$3,017,000**

*Defendants sentenced to death have higher prison costs because supervising them is more expensive and not all are actually executed.

You accept the first premise as true based on evidence presented in your course textbook. However, you are not convinced that the second premise is true. Should you, then, accept or reject the conclusion?

One factor in making your decision concerns whether the premises are dependent on or independent of each other. This chapter will provide you with the skills you need to make this decision by introducing you to a technique for identifying an argument's structure called an argument diagram. Sometimes referred to as an argument map or an argument tree, an **argument diagram** provides a visual representation of the argument's structure. It indicates whether the premises provide dependent or independent support for the conclusion and whether the argument contains one or more subarguments supporting the premise(s) of the main argument. After learning the basics of the diagramming technique, you will utilize the skills you learned in Chapter 3 to diagram a variety of arguments including those with extra claims and implied premises, as well as multiple arguments and extended arguments.

LEARNING OUTCOMES

In this chapter, you will learn how to diagram arguments by:

- ▶ Numbering and underlining the claims in a passage,
- ▶ Determining how premises in an argument are related,
- ▶ Excluding claims that are neither premises nor conclusions from your diagram,
- ▶ Incorporating implied claims into your diagram,
- ▶ Representing arguments with multiple conclusions and chain arguments in a single diagram,
- ▶ Diagramming extended arguments, and
- ▶ Including an argument diagram with a Critical Précis of an argument.

Underlining and Numbering Claims

The first step in diagramming an argument is to identify all the claims given in a passage by underlining and numbering them in the order in which they appear. This step relies on what you learned in Chapter 2 about identifying and counting claims: (1) Not every sentence is a claim, (2) a single claim can be represented by more than one sentence, (3) a single sentence may refer to more than one claim, (4) multiple claims can be combined to create a single claim, and (5) multiple claims can be expressed in a single sentence. Let's see how each of these lessons is relevant to diagramming arguments.

First, you learned that, although claims are expressed in sentences, not every sentence is a claim. Because the following sentence is not a claim, it would not be underlined or numbered.

What evidence can be provided for the defendant's guilt?

Moreover, when identifying a claim, do not include inference indicators or any other words that are not part of the claim. Notice that only the claim is underlined and that the indicator word is left out in the following example.

Consequently, ① the defendant is guilty of murder.

EXERCISE 4.1

Your Turn!   Underline and number the claim in the following sentence.

It is clear that the alibi witness cannot be trusted.

You also learned in Chapter 2 that a single claim can be represented by more than one sentence. Whenever you encounter a claim that is repeated in this way, you should underline each claim and assign the *same number* to each additional expression of the same claim. Although it may occur in other circumstances, a claim is most often repeated when the arguer presents the conclusion at both the beginning and the end of the argument. Since the first and third sentences in the following example express the same claim, they are underlined and given the same number.

① *The victim, Erika Silverman, was stabbed by the defendant, Joe Belser.*
② *Detective Stokes identified Mr. Belser's DNA on the weapon used to kill the victim.* Therefore, ① *it was Joe Belser who killed Ms. Silverman.*

The third lesson you learned about counting claims is that a single sentence may refer to more than one claim. The sentence "It counts as academic dishonesty" is used twice in the passage below. But in the first instance *it* refers to copying someone else's exam answer, while in the second instance *it* refers to plagiarism. Thus, rather than assigning the same number to each, you should assign different numbers because the sentences express different claims.

① *Copying someone else's exam answer is a form of cheating,* so ② *it counts as academic dishonesty.* ③ *Plagiarism is also a form of cheating,* so ④ *it counts as academic dishonesty,* too. Therefore, ⑤ *you should be careful to avoid both copying someone's exam and plagiarism.*

To ensure that you do not mistakenly apply the same number to different claims, verify the referents for any pronouns you encounter.

The fourth lesson about claims from Chapter 2 is that multiple claims can be combined in ways that create single claims. Whenever this occurs, be sure to treat the claim as a single claim rather than breaking it into parts. The following conditional claim is a single claim, and thus should be underlined and numbered as such.

① *If cocaine is a drug, then it is addictive.*

"Cocaine is a drug" and "It is addictive" would be separate claims if they appeared on their own. However, because they are combined to make a single claim, the resulting conditional claim should be underlined and numbered as a single claim.

EXERCISE 4.2

Your Turn!   Underline and number the claims in the following sentence.

Count Dracula was either killed by Jonathan Harker or killed by Professor Van Helsing. Either way, he is dead.

Finally, you learned that multiple claims are sometimes expressed in a single sentence. Whenever a sentence contains more than one claim, underline each claim, and assign each claim its own number. For example, the following sentence contains two claims, and thus they are each underlined and given different numbers.

① <u>Cocaine is a drug</u>, and ② <u>drugs are addictive</u>.

 EXERCISE 4.3

Your Turn!   Underline and number the claims in the following sentence.

Cocaine is a drug because it is addictive.

Recall that identifying multiple claims in a single sentence can be difficult when the claims are combined using pronouns or when one claim is buried inside another. Consider this example.

① <u>Your house must be infested with termites</u>. ② <u>There are mud tubes running from the soil into cracks of masonry on the house</u>, ③ <u>which could be caused only by termites</u>.

When underlining and numbering, you might think "which could be caused only by termites" isn't a complete claim, and thus shouldn't be numbered. But thinking more carefully, notice that the word *which* is a pronoun, referring to the mud tubes. The third claim would then be "The mud tubes on your house could be caused only by termites."

EXERCISE 4.4

Your Turn!   Underline and number the three claims in the following passage.

The realtor said that if your house is infested with termites—which it is— then you need to have it fumigated. That means, then, that you need to get the house fumigated.

Utilizing Inference Indicators

Once you have all the claims underlined and numbered, the next steps in diagramming an argument require that you utilize the argument analysis skills you learned in Chapter 3—namely, identifying the conclusion and the premises that support it. The number that corresponds to the conclusion should be placed at the bottom of your diagram, and the number(s) that correspond to the premise(s) for that conclusion should be placed above the conclusion with an arrow pointing to the conclusion from the premise(s). But how can you tell which claim is a conclusion and which is a premise? Recall that inference indicators are your best guide for identifying the argument's structure; they are like big signs exclaiming "Hey! Here is a premise!" or "This is a conclusion!" This means that you can often diagram an argument without examining the content of the claims. Consider the following examples.

①, *thus* ②.

```
①
↓
②
```

Here, *thus* indicates that ② is the conclusion and ① is the premise.

①, *because* ②.

```
②
↓
①
```

In this sentence, *because* indicates that ② is the premise for ①.

Inasmuch as ①, ②.

```
①
↓
②
```

Inasmuch as indicates that ① is a premise, but what about ②? The sentence states that since ① is true, ② is also true. That means that ② is the conclusion.

① *and* ②; *therefore,* ③.

```
        ③
```

Therefore indicates that ③ is the conclusion and that ① and ② are the premises.

 EXERCISE 4.5

> **Your Turn!** Underline and number the claims in the following sentence. Then draw a diagram of the argument.
>
> *The defendant must be the murderer, since his DNA was on the murder weapon.*

As you learned in Chapter 3, some authors do not utilize inference indicators in their arguments. Consider this example.

> *The Giants beat Florida last week. They'll most likely beat Houston when they play tomorrow.*

Without indicator words, you must determine which of the claims is the conclusion by examining their contents. If it is not immediately obvious to you which claim is the conclusion and which is the premise, remember that you can insert your own inference indicator to see which interpretation of the passage makes better, more logical sense, as you did in Chapter 3.

 EXERCISE 4.6

> **Your Turn!** Determine which claim is the premise and which is the conclusion in the above example by inserting your own inference indicator between the claims.

It should sound quite strange to say that what will happen tomorrow proves something about what happened last week. Instead, what happened last week offers evidence for what will happen tomorrow. The diagram, then, will look like this.

① *The Giants beat Florida last week*. ② *They'll most likely beat Houston when they play tomorrow.*

EXERCISE 4.7

Diagram each of the following arguments using the inference indicators as your guide.

1. ①. Thus, ②.
2. ① because ②.
3. Given that ①, ②.
4. ①. This proves that ②.
5. ① follows from the facts that ② and ③.
6. ①; accordingly, ②.
7. ①. It follows that ②.
8. ①, as ②. Besides, ③.
9. ①. Therefore, in view of the fact that ②, ③.
10. ① and ②. This means that ③.

Determining the Relationship between the Premises

As you already know, most arguments have more than one premise supporting the conclusion. For arguments of this sort, you will need to determine the relationship between those premises and then draw the diagram in a way that reflects this relationship. Some arguments have premises that independently support the conclusion, whereas others have premises that are dependent on each other to support the conclusion.

When premises are independent, we call them **convergent**. If one of the premises is missing, the conclusion is still supported because the remaining premise(s) provides independent support for the conclusion. The following argument has convergent premises.

> *Cocaine is addictive, and it is illegal. Consequently, you should not use cocaine.*

The conclusion of this argument is "You should not use cocaine." There are two premises given: "Cocaine is addictive" and "Cocaine is illegal." These premises provide independent support for the conclusion. If only one of the two premises was provided, the conclusion could still be supported by the remaining premise.

When premises depend on each other to support the conclusion, we call them **linked**. In arguments with dependent premises, all of the linked premises must be true in order to support the conclusion. That means that if one of the premises is missing, the conclusion is no longer supported. The following argument has linked premises.

> *Cocaine is a drug, and drugs are addictive. Therefore, cocaine is addictive.*

The conclusion of this argument is that "Cocaine is addictive." There are two premises given: "Cocaine is a drug" and "Drugs are addictive." These premises are dependent on each other to support the conclusion. If one of the premises was missing, then the conclusion would no longer follow because the remaining premise could not support the conclusion on its own.

 EXERCISE 4.8

Your Turn!   Look back at the argument about the death penalty presented at the start of this chapter. Did the student in the study group present an argument with linked or convergent premises? How do you know?

Once you have determined whether the premises are dependent or independent, you will signal this relationship in the way you draw your diagram. Convergent premises are indicated by drawing an arrow from each independent premise to the conclusion, whereas linked premises are indicated by using a " + " to join the dependent premises, underlining them, and drawing a single arrow from the group of linked premises to the conclusion.

Let's diagram the two arguments from above.

> ① *Cocaine is addictive*, and ② *it is illegal*. Consequently, ③ *you should not use cocaine*.

This diagram tells us that the third claim is the conclusion and that the first and second claims provide independent support for it. Notice how this diagram differs from the next one.

> ① *Cocaine is a drug*, and ② *drugs are addictive*. Therefore, ③ *cocaine is addictive*.

This diagram tells us that the third claim is the conclusion and that the first and second claims depend on each other to support it.

Hint!
Each of the claims in the previous example is a categorical claim because it relates two terms or concepts: cocaine/drug, drugs/addictive, and cocaine/addictive. Watch for categorical claims because they are usually linked together in arguments. Similarly, two kinds of claims you encountered in Chapters 2 and 3 will help you spot arguments with linked claims. *Conditional* claims (if . . . then claims) are commonly linked with another premise when they appear in arguments. *Disjunctive* claims (either . . . or claims) also typically link with another premise in arguments.

EXERCISE 4.9

Your Turn!   What has gone wrong with the following diagram?

The final step in diagramming an argument is to confirm that all claims that are part of the argument have been diagrammed and to check your work by presenting the argument to yourself using the diagram. In checking your work, begin with the conclusion, ensuring that the arrows leading to it provide the reasons for believing that it is true. For example, suppose you have arrived at the following diagram.

① *Hurricane season begins in June. Therefore,* ② *hurricane season will begin soon, since* ③ *it's the end of April.*

This diagram shows that claims ① and ③ offer independent support for the conclusion. To check this diagram, begin with the conclusion, and ask yourself whether the claim(s) pointing to it can independently support the conclusion. Since there are two arrows, you should do this twice.

② Hurricane season will begin soon because ① it's the end of April.
② Hurricane season will begin soon because ③ hurricane season begins in June.

You should be able to see that something is wrong with the diagram. The problem is that claims ① and ③ cannot support claim ② on their own; they depend on each other to support the conclusion. That means that the diagram must show that the premises are linked, not convergent.

EXERCISE 4.10

Your Turn! Draw the correct diagram for the previous argument.

Hint!
Although *and* cannot indicate whether premises are dependent or independent, a handful of indicators signals that a claim is independent from other claims in the passage. A few examples of these are *besides*, *furthermore*, and *additionally*. When followed by a premise, these indicators usually signal that the subsequent premise or premises provide support for the conclusion independently of any of the previous ones. Be sure to verify that your diagram is accurate by checking the content of the claims.

EXERCISE 4.11

Diagram each of the following arguments.

1. People have been smuggled into the United States since the slave trade was outlawed in the early 19th century. Therefore, smuggling of persons is not likely to be easily eliminated.
2. Because implanting a computer chip in the brain could vastly increase anyone's knowledge, cyborgs may be a reality in the not-so-distant future.
3. You should get your holiday shopping done early because many stores are not restocking their shelves this year.
4. All sportscasters are athletes, and no athletes are college professors. Accordingly, no sportscasters are college professors.
5. Inasmuch as the military has had an increasingly difficult time meeting recruitment goals and veteran soldiers are retiring at an unusually high rate, it is likely that the military will soon be much smaller than it was five years ago.
6. Tomlin would make the best mayor. She is honest, and she knows how to work with people who disagree with her.
7. You should vote to reelect Judge Wilson. She is tough on crime, and we really need a judge on the bench who will fully enforce the law. Besides, she is the candidate with the most experience.
8. There are several reasons why you should stop smoking cigarettes. First, cigarette smoking causes serious health problems. Also, cigarette smoke makes you stink, and it makes your teeth yellow. Finally, cigarettes are very expensive.
9. You clearly have a case of the fungal infection called ringworm. You have a red, elevated, ring-like sore on your arm, and only ringworm causes sores like that.
10. If the economic picture does not improve soon—and it won't—there will be large-scale unemployment within the next few months. So, many people will be out of work before the end of the year.

11. If the defendant has an alibi, then you should vote not guilty. Since the defense has not provided an alibi for the defendant, you must vote guilty.

12. The recent outbreak of food poisoning among CSUB students was caused by corndogs served at the Club Fair yesterday. The corndogs must have been the problem because corndogs were served at the Club Fair and all of the students who became ill ate lunch at the Club Fair yesterday.

13. Alberto Giacometti was one of the most splendid 20th-century sculptors, for his human figures captured an existential pessimism and his plastic technique influenced many subsequent sculptors.

14. The university trustees voted to raise student fees yet again. It follows that we can expect enrollment to drop, since many students cannot afford even a small increase in college costs.

15. No Republicans are Democrats, so no Republicans are big spenders, since all big spenders are Democrats.

16. *The War of the Worlds* can be considered the most enduring science fiction movie of all time. This is because only it and *King Kong* are contenders for that honor and *King Kong* has not lasted as well.

17. The First Amendment must not be seen as allowing total freedom to act. After all, violent protestors can be arrested. Furthermore, hate speech is against the law.

18. Young children have increasingly large amounts of money to spend, and they exert significant influence on their parents' buying. Accordingly, marketers will spend even more money in the coming years attempting to attract young consumers.

19. We should raise the speed limit on I-5 to 80 mph. The highway was designed for high-speed travel, and cars get better gas mileage at high speed. Besides, everyone drives that fast anyway. So let's raise the limit.

20. If you go to the party tonight, then you will end up on academic probation. Why? Well, if you go to the party tonight, you won't be able to finish writing your paper. And if you don't finish writing your paper, you will fail your English composition class. And if you fail your English composition class, you will be put on academic probation.

Diagramming Arguments with Extra Claims

In Chapter 3, you learned that sometimes an argument is given in a passage that contains claims that are not part of that argument. Since these claims are neither premises nor conclusions, you do not include them in your analysis. When diagramming such an argument, you will make a similar move. Let's look at a passage containing an extra claim. Notice that every claim, including the extra one, is underlined and given a number.

① *You should be frugal with your paycheck*, for ② *the economy is awful* and ③ *there's little hope for improvement anytime soon*. ④ *That's not to say that the economy was all that great the previous year*.

According to a Eurobarometer survey, many people would buy genetically modified food if they were given good reasons to do so. Using the two most influential reasons presented in this chart, develop an argument for buying genetically modified foods. Are your premises linked or convergent?

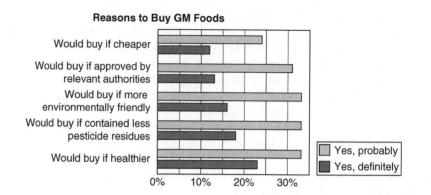

Reasons to Buy GM Foods

Would buy if cheaper
Would buy if approved by relevant authorities
Would buy if more environmentally friendly
Would buy if contained less pesticide residues
Would buy if healthier

Yes, probably
Yes, definitely

0% 10% 20% 30%

© 2016 Cengage Learning®

Although there are four claims in the passage, only three are included in our diagram. This is because the fourth claim is neither a conclusion nor a premise. Even though it is not part of the argument, it is still underlined and numbered in the passage because it is a claim.

Let's examine one more example.

① *Some people say that genetic engineering is a harmless solution to agricultural challenges*. But ② *they're wrong*. ③ *Genetically modified crops can hurt beneficial insects such as ladybugs, honeybees, and butterflies*. And ④ *cross-pollination of genetically modified crops with related weeds would require more toxic chemicals to get rid of them*.

There are four claims in the passage, but not all of them play a role in the argument. The first claim is an extra claim. Although it may seem to be part of the argument, it in fact makes a claim on the other side of the issue. Because it is neither a premise nor a conclusion, you should not include it in your argument diagram.

 EXERCISE 4.12

Your Turn!   Diagram the previous passage.

Diagramming Arguments with Implied Claims

You also learned in Chapter 3 that arguments can contain implied claims signaled by rhetorical questions, commands, or phrases. When analyzing such an argument, you identify the implied claim by utilizing the clues provided by the non-claim. Similarly, when diagramming the argument, you should identify the claims implied by any non-claims provided in the passage.

First, consider the following argument containing a command that indicates an implied claim.

Stop playing video games all night. Otherwise, you may develop carpal tunnel syndrome.

Although there is only one claim in the passage, the command given in the first sentence implies a claim—namely, "You should stop playing video games all night." To diagram this argument, then, you should treat the command as a placeholder for the claim it implies by underlining and numbering it along with the claim given in the argument. Then, for clarity, you should state the implied claim underneath the passage. Your argument diagram will look like this.

① _Stop playing video games all night_. ② _Otherwise, you may develop carpal tunnel syndrome_.
① You should stop playing video games all night.

Notice that the implied claim is given the same number as the one given to the non-claim in the passage.

Let's examine one more before you complete some on your own. Consider this argument with a claim implied by a rhetorical question.

> **We should keep the death penalty. How could a brutal murderer be allowed to live?**

Like the previous example, this argument offers only one claim. However, the second sentence is a rhetorical question implying a claim—namely, "Those who brutally murder others should not be allowed to live." Your underlining and numbering should appear as follows.

① _We should keep the death penalty_. ② _How could a brutal murderer be allowed to live?_
② Those who brutally murder others should not be allowed to live

EXERCISE 4.13

Your Turn!   Diagram the previous passage.

EXERCISE 4.14

Diagram each of the following arguments. Be sure to state and number any implied claims.

1. Why vote for Conrad? He's a visionary, that's why.
2. You should hire Elka Schmidt, since she is a hard worker.
3. Francisco is most likely good at math because he has an analytical mind.
4. Since you are having headaches, you ought to have your eyes tested.

5. The patient has post-traumatic stress disorder. She must begin hypnotherapy as soon as possible. Treatments typically require a year-long commitment to see results.

6. All sailboats are expensive to buy, and a Hobie Cat is a sailboat. You know what that means about Hobie Cats, right?

7. Since chocolate contains sugar, it's bad for your teeth.

8. Obviously, we don't want felons to have the right to vote: Would you want a convicted murderer to choose the next president?

9. There is clearly a health-care crisis in the United States. If there were people in need of health care who can't afford it, then the United States would have a health-care crisis. And aren't there lots of people who need health care, but can't afford it?

10. Some people blame violent video games for school shootings, increases in bullying, and violence toward women. But I'm not so sure. The majority of the research on the effects of video games on children is deeply flawed, and no causal relationship has been found between video games and social violence.

11. I heard that Toyota has recalled many of its 2009–2010 vehicles for mechanical problems. So you should bring your car to the dealership to fix the problem. Wasn't your car manufactured in 2010?

12. We hope you agree that our fraternity is the best on campus. The majority of students who responded to a campus survey said our fraternity would be their number one pick. How could they be wrong?

13. George would change parties only if Jones was elected. But there is no chance Jones is going to be elected. So you know what George is going to do.

14. Legalize marijuana now! There are important medical uses for it. Besides, most people smoke it anyway.

15. Video game players shouldn't become surgeons. Haven't you seen how many gamers have jittery nerves?

16. This cat has no tail, and the only kind of cat without a tail is a Manx. Don't you know what kind of cat this must be?

17. Don't get your children vaccinated! After all, I read on the Internet that some vaccines contain mercury, and mercury has been linked to autism. You surely don't want your child to develop autism, do you?

18. Which charity should you donate to? The one that supports projects in your community. This is because you will be able to see the benefits directly.

19. Don't cheat on your exam! What's to keep you from committing terrible violent crimes?

20. Maybe you think that ecotourism is cool, but I don't. Even when there are significant economic benefits to the area, the local communities are often harmed through forced relocation, human rights violations, and environmental hazards.

Diagramming Multiple Arguments

In Chapter 3, you learned how to analyze two kinds of passages that contain multiple arguments: arguments with multiple conclusions and chain arguments. Although such passages technically constitute two distinct arguments, they can be represented in a single diagram. Let's first look at an example of an argument with multiple conclusions.

*Nurse anesthetists are able to replace physicians in the operating room.
That means that they can demand higher salaries than the typical RN and
they can save hospitals money.*

If you rewrite the passage by replacing each claim with its number, you can more easily see that this passage contains more than one conclusion.

①. *That means that* ② *and* ③.

The indicator *that means that* signals to us that "They can demand higher salaries than the typical RN" and "They can save hospitals money" are both conclusions, and these two conclusions share the same premise—namely, "Nurse anesthetists are able to replace physicians in the operating room." Although you could diagram each of the arguments separately, you should use a single diagram to show that the one premise supports two different conclusions.

① <u>Nurse anesthetists are able to replace physicians in the operating room</u>.
That means that ② <u>they can demand higher salaries than the typical RN</u> *and*
③ <u>they can save hospitals money</u>.

More often, a passage has multiple arguments because there are one or more subarguments. Remember that a **subargument** is an argument whose premise(s) provide support for a premise of another argument. In such a case, the conclusion of the subargument is a premise of the main argument. Consider the following example.

*I studied more than 10 hours for my final exam; thus, I should do well on it.
Consequently, my semester grade will be up to passing level.*

When you rewrite the passage, you can more easily see that there are two conclusion indicators.

①; *thus,* ②. *Consequently,* ③.

Thus and *consequently* signal that both the second and the third claims are conclusions. Let's take up each separately.

What is the premise for the second claim, "I should do well on my final exam"? The indicator word *thus* tells us that the claim preceding it is the premise for what follows. The diagram for that argument will look like this.

① <u>I studied more than 10 hours for my final exam</u>; *thus,* ② <u>I should do well
on it</u>.

Now, what about the third claim, "My semester grade will be up to passing level"? The indicator word *consequently* signals that ③ is a conclusion.

Consequently, ③ *my semester grade will be up to passing level.*

Does the first or the second claim support ③? The indicator *consequently* signals that what comes before it is the premise. Since what comes before ③ is an argument, the premise for ③ will be the conclusion of that argument.

By putting the two preliminary diagrams together, you can show that the passage is a chain argument.

① *I studied more than 10 hours for my final exam;* thus, ② *I should do well on it.* Consequently, ③ *my semester grade will be up to passing level.*

Notice that the conclusion of the first argument is also the premise of the second argument. In Chapter 3, you learned that this is called an intermediate conclusion.

Let's look at one more example before moving ahead.

> *The Jones family will soon lose their house. This is because they won't be able to make their mortgage payments due to the fact that Mr. Jones was laid off from his job last month.*

There are three claims in the passage. When we rewrite the passage, we can focus on the inference indicators.

①. This is because ② due to the fact that ③.

This is because signals that the first claim is a conclusion and the second claim is its premise. *Due to the fact that* signals that the second claim is a conclusion and the third claim is its premise. How is it possible that the second claim can be both a premise and a conclusion? This is possible because the second claim is an intermediate conclusion! The passage, then, must contain a chain argument.

 EXERCISE 4.15

Your Turn!   Complete the diagram of the argument above.

Checking Your Work

When you were learning algebra, your instructor probably emphasized the importance of checking your work. Although doing so doesn't always tell you where your errors occur, it does help you determine if the steps you have followed led to the wrong answer. Similarly, checking your diagram will often help you identify possible mistakes. Reading the argument aloud using your diagram as a guide can help you hear when the connection between the premises and conclusion shown in your diagram doesn't work. The trick is, though, to make sure you understand exactly what the diagram means.

Let's compare the following diagrams containing three claims.

This diagram has convergent premises; the premises provide independent support for the conclusion. It states that claim ① is supported by claim ②, and that claim ① is supported by claim ③. Consider how this differs from the following argument with linked premises.

The premises in this diagram are dependent on one another. The diagram tells us that claim ① is supported by **both** claims ② and ③. Notice how, in the diagram with convergent premises, the conclusion still follows if one of the premises is missing, whereas in the diagram with linked premises both the premises must be present for the conclusion to be supported.

When first learning the diagramming technique, many people have difficulty distinguishing between an argument with linked premises and a chain argument. However, once you understand what an argument diagram says, the difference should become much clearer. Let's compare the previous argument with linked premises to the following chain argument.

This diagram tells us that there are two arguments. In the main argument, claim ① is supported by claim ②, and in the subargument, claim ② is supported by claim ③.

 EXERCISE 4.16

Your Turn!   Are chain arguments more like arguments with convergent premises or arguments with linked premises? Explain.

Notice that the chain argument contains two arguments—the main argument and a subargument—whereas the argument with linked premises is only one argument. Also notice that in the one with linked premises, claim ② cannot support claim ① on its own; it is dependent on claim ③. But in the chain argument, claim ② provides independent support for claim ①, and claim ③ provides support for claim ②, not for claim ①.

Before trying some exercises on your own, let's recap the steps for diagramming an argument.

How to Diagram an Argument

Step 1: Underline and number each claim.
▶ Do not include indicator words. Consider circling or highlighting them.
▶ Remember that more than one claim can appear in a single sentence.
▶ If a claim is repeated, assign it the same number each time.
▶ If a non-claim serves as a placeholder for a claim, underline and number the non-claim, and state the claim it implies after the passage, using the same number given to the non-claim in the passage.

Step 2: Pay attention to indicator words.
▶ Rewrite the passage by substituting the numbers for the claims, and identify the role played by any claim accompanied by an inference indicator.
▶ If there are no inference indicators given, try inserting some of your own to determine the structure of the argument.

Step 3: Identify the main conclusion of the argument.
▶ Place the main conclusion at the bottom of the diagram.
▶ Do not confuse an intermediate conclusion with the main conclusion.

Step 4: Identify the premise(s) that support the main conclusion.
▶ Place the premise(s) above the conclusion.
▶ For convergent premises, place an arrow from each premise to the conclusion. Linked premises should be underlined and connected by a "+" with a single arrow from them to the conclusion.

Step 5: Diagram any subarguments.
▶ Look for claims that support any premise of the main argument.

Step 6: Check your work.
▶ Confirm that all claims relevant to the argument have been diagrammed. Omit any extra claims from your argument diagram.
▶ Present the argument aloud to yourself, and listen for errors.

EXERCISE 4.17

Diagram each of the following arguments, using the inference indicators as your guide. *Note:* If you cannot tell whether the premises are linked or convergent, provide a diagram of each possibility.

1. ①; accordingly, ②. So ③.
2. ①, for ②. Consequently, ③.
3. Assuming that ①, ②. As a result, ③.
4. ①. Thus, ② and ③.

5. ①, ②, and ③. For all these reasons, ④.
6. ①, since ② and ③. Moreover, ④.
7. ①, as ②. We must then conclude that ③.
8. ① and ② given that ③.
9. ① due to the fact that ② and ③. Therefore, ④.
10. There are several reasons that ①. First, ②. Second, ③. Third, ④.

EXERCISE 4.18

Diagram each of the following arguments.

1. If this is a dinosaur, then it is extinct. Therefore, it must be a dinosaur inasmuch as it is extinct.
2. I'm certain that this tree is deciduous. First, it has leaves that don't look at all like pine needles, and, second, my botany professor said that we don't have evergreens around here.
3. It is important for university students to use their education to help people who never had the opportunity to go to school, since they have benefited from others who came before them. Also, making their community better will help students develop the wisdom necessary to apply their knowledge.
4. John graduated summa cum laude from a fine university, so he should get a good job. Thus, he should be quite successful.
5. Because Maria tore up all her credit cards, she will again be living within her means. Accordingly, she should be able to earn back an excellent credit rating.
6. You should move to Arizona, since it is much warmer. Therefore, you should give two weeks' notice at your office.
7. You should go into teaching, for you should go into teaching if you want to help your community, and you do want to help your community.
8. More and more people are becoming infected with HIV in underdeveloped countries, and the cost of the only effective drugs rises each year. Hence, the war on HIV/AIDS is unlikely to be won in the near future.
9. Prohibition of alcohol didn't work, so it's pointless to try to prohibit drug use, and it's equally pointless to try to prohibit the use of steroids and other performance enhancers.
10. Spiders are quite beneficial to the ecosystem. As a result, you should never squash them, and you shouldn't spray poisons on them.
11. You should consider working fewer hours while attending college full-time. Since you and your family have paid a great deal of money for your college education, you really must take your studies more seriously. Therefore, you should stop working so much.
12. Horatio took little care of his teeth when he was a teenager, so he will probably have dental problems when he gets older. Consequently, he should always buy dental insurance.
13. Only airplanes have wings, and everything that flies has wings, so all things that fly are airplanes.

14. I do more work than anybody else in the shipping department, and I haven't gotten a raise in five years. Thus, I should get a raise this year.

15. Anderson will soon be getting a raise. This is because she is likely to get a promotion, since she was so successful on the Hamer project.

16. The city zoo is heavily in debt, and it is poorly managed. It follows that extreme measures must be taken. Thus, the town council should take charge right away.

17. The European Union has a bloated bureaucracy, so it needs to resist the urge to add new member states. Hence, the vote on adding Ukraine should be postponed.

18. I got the new job! That means that I will be able to afford my mortgage payments and I can start replenishing my savings account.

19. Gay marriage? No way. If we allow gay marriage, then we will have to allow polygamy. And there's no way we can allow polygamy because it's just un-American.

20. If the Iranians really had perfected their long-range missiles, then they wouldn't have needed to alter the photos of their missile tests. Therefore, the Iranians couldn't have perfected their long-range missiles, since it's clear that the photos of their missile tests were altered.

Diagramming Extended Arguments

Thus far, you have considered relatively simple arguments. In this section, you will apply your diagramming skills to extended arguments. An **extended argument** contains several subarguments. Diagramming these longer arguments will not require learning any additional skills. Although these arguments may be intimidating to diagram, you will be successful if you take your time: Break the passage down into smaller, more manageable parts, and pay very close attention to indicator words. Let's start with one that is only slightly longer than the arguments that you have diagrammed thus far.

> *Look, if you don't get to the gate by 5:45, you will miss your flight. And, frankly, there's no way you will get to the gate by 5:45, since it's 5:40 and you haven't yet made your way through security. So you have to accept that you will miss your flight.*

The first step is to underline and number each claim in the passage. Next, write out the argument using the numbers to replace the claims in order to focus closely on the indicator words in each sentence.

> *Look, ①.*
> *And, frankly, ②, since ③ and ④.*
> *So you have to accept that ⑤.*

Notice that the passage utilizes two inference indicators, *since* and *so*. These indicators tell you a lot about the structure of the argument before you start to examine the content of the claims. You should diagram each sentence containing indicators, starting with "And, frankly, ②, since ③ and ④." *Since* tells us that claims ③ and ④ are premises and that they support claim ②. Because you do not yet know whether the premises are linked or convergent, you should consider both possibilities.

To decide which of these diagrams is correct, you must return to the content of the claims. One strategy is to imagine that one of these premises is missing and then see if the conclusion is still supported. If the conclusion follows from the remaining premise, then the premise is independent. However, if the conclusion doesn't follow, the premise is dependent. So imagine that ③ is missing. Does claim ④—"You haven't yet made your way through security"—provide independent support for concluding that "There's no way you will get to the gate by 5:45"? It does not. If the time is 5:00 instead of 5:40, you may still have plenty of time to get to the gate even if you haven't yet cleared security. This means, then, that ③ and ④ are linked premises.

 EXERCISE 4.19

Your Turn! Draw the correct diagram for claims ②, ③, and ④.

Now, turn to the other sentence in the passage with an inference indicator, "So you have to accept that ⑤." This indicator tells us that claim ⑤ is a conclusion. "But wait!" you might be thinking. "That means there are two conclusions!" Since there are two conclusions in the passage, ② and ⑤, one of them is likely a conclusion of a subargument and, hence, a premise of the main argument. Which of the two is the overall conclusion: "There's no way you will get to the gate by 5:45" or "You will miss your flight"? Generally, the main conclusion will appear after the intermediate conclusion in the passage. Let's check it. Does ② support ⑤? Yes. "You will miss your flight" is the overall conclusion of the argument, and "There's no way you will get to the gate by 5:45" offers support for this conclusion.

 EXERCISE 4.20

Your Turn! Draw the preliminary diagram for claims ②, and ⑤.

Now, you must consider whether ② offers independent support for ⑤ or whether it depends on another premise. What other premise is available? Since ③ and ④ are already premises for ②, they cannot be premises for ⑤. That leaves only ①. Is "There's no way you will get to the gate by 5:45" enough to support "You will miss your flight"? It is not. It depends on "If you don't get to the gate by 5:45, you will miss your flight." You can now complete the diagram of this argument.

The last steps are to put the two pieces together and then check your work. Your final diagram should look like this.

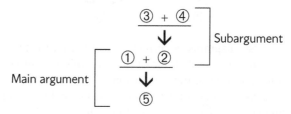

Notice that the diagram tells us that there are two arguments: a main argument and a subargument. To check the diagram, begin at the bottom of the diagram, and work your way up. First, start with the main argument.

⑤ *You will miss your flight* because ① *if you don't get to the gate by 5:45, you will miss your flight* and ② *there's no way you will get to the gate by 5:45*.

This works well. Next, check the subargument.

  EXERCISE 4.21

Your Turn!   Check the subargument by substituting the claims represented by the numbers. Does it work? Why or why not?

② because ③ and ④.

Let's now try a significantly longer argument. Although its length can be quite daunting, don't panic. Remind yourself that you already have all the tools you need to successfully diagram arguments of this size and even larger.

The Galaxy Corporation wants to build a casino in St. Louis, but we should not allow it to be built. First, gambling is immoral, since gambling is motivated by greed and greed is an immoral desire. Second, communities with casinos have higher crime rates. This is because casinos attract people who take risks and risk-takers are more likely to break the law. Finally, studies show that people living within 10 miles of a casino have a 90% increased risk of becoming pathological gamblers; thus, casinos encourage psychological problems for the people who live near them. For all these reasons, the proposed casino should be opposed.

  EXERCISE 4.22

Your Turn!   Highlight or circle all of the indicator words in the passage above. Then underline and number each claim in the passage.

Now you are likely wondering "How in the world am I ever going to tackle this? It has 10 separate claims!" The key is to pay close attention to the indicator words and to break down the argument into smaller, more manageable parts. The first step is to rewrite the argument by substituting the numbers assigned to the claims so that you can pay closer attention to the inference indicators.

①, *but* ②.
First, ③, *since* ④ *and* ⑤.
Second, ⑥.
This is because ⑦ *and* ⑧.
Finally, ⑨; *thus,* ⑩.
For all these reasons, ②.

Notice that the indicator words tell you a great deal about the structure of the argument before you even begin to examine its contents. For each sentence, you can draw a preliminary diagram using the inference indicators. Remember that whenever there are multiple premises given, you cannot tell immediately whether the premises are linked or convergent. For these preliminary sketches, you should consider all possibilities.

 EXERCISE 4.23

Your Turn! From the argument above, diagram the sentence that has been rewritten as:

First, ③, *since* ④ *and* ⑤.

 EXERCISE 4.24

Your Turn! From the argument above, diagram the sentences that have been rewritten as:

Second, ⑥. *This is because* ⑦ *and* ⑧.

 EXERCISE 4.25

Your Turn! From the argument above, diagram the sentence that has been rewritten as:

Finally, ⑨; *thus,* ⑩.

EXERCISE 4.26

Your Turn! From the argument above, diagram the sentence that has been rewritten as:

For all these reasons, ②.

Notice that there are four conclusions—a valuable clue that you are working with subarguments. Before trying to identify which of these four conclusions is the overall conclusion, first determine whether the premises that you have found for each conclusion are linked or convergent.

Starting with the first diagram above, do claims ④ and ⑤ work independently, or do they depend on each other to support claim ③? Now, move on to the second diagram. Do claims ⑦ and ⑧ work independently, or do they depend on each other to support claim ⑥? The third diagram has only one premise for the conclusion. Check to make sure that ⑨ can, by itself, provide support for ⑩. Your four diagrams should look like these.

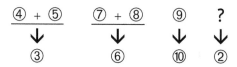

Which of our four conclusions, if any, is the overall conclusion of the argument? It should be clear to you that ② is the overall conclusion of the argument. The arguer wants to convince you that you should oppose the construction of a casino in St. Louis by Galaxy Corporation. What are the premises for this claim? To answer this question, you should identify which claims can possibly serve as premises for ② and which cannot.

EXERCISE 4.27

Your Turn! Why can't claims ④, ⑤, ⑦, ⑧, and ⑨ be premises for ②?

Claims ①, ③, ⑥, and ⑩ are the only possibilities as premises for our overall conclusion. Let's consider each of these individually. Does ① provide a reason to accept ②? It does not. What about ③? Does it provide independent support, or does it need to be linked with another claim? What about ⑥ and ⑩? Test each one separately. You can now draw the diagram for the fourth argument. It should look like this.

EXERCISE 4.28

> **Your Turn!** Put the four arguments together in a single diagram of the entire extended argument.

Finally, you can complete the last step of the diagramming technique—checking your work! First, check the main argument. There are three independent premises for the main conclusion, so you should treat each as a separate argument.

②　We should not allow the Galaxy Casino to be built in St. Louis because ③ gambling is immoral.

②　We should not allow the Galaxy Casino to be built in St. Louis because ⑥ communities with casinos have higher crime rates.

②　We should not allow the Galaxy Casino to be built in St. Louis because ⑩ casinos encourage psychological problems for the people that live near them.

After checking the diagram, you should be able to see that each of these premises does offer independent support for the conclusion. Now, you can check the subarguments.

 EXERCISE 4.29

> **Your Turn!** Rewrite each of the three subarguments by using the claims represented by the numbers.
>
> ③ because ④ and ⑤.
> ⑥ because ⑦ and ⑧.
> ⑩ because ⑨.

What about claim ①? We should not include it in the argument diagram. Why? Claim ① does not support any claim in the passage, and no other claim supports it; thus, it does not appear in the diagram, even though it is a claim.

 EXERCISE 4.30

Diagram each of the following arguments.

1. You are going to end up on academic probation. Why? Because you are going to the party tonight, and if you go to the party tonight, you will end up on academic probation, in that you won't have time to finish your term paper.

2. Without a tax increase, community college tuition will go up again. But the governor refuses to raise taxes inasmuch as he promised voters that he wouldn't when he ran for election. For these reasons, we'll be paying more to go to school next year.

3. You won't graduate this year unless you complete senior seminar. Accordingly, you won't graduate, since you can't complete senior seminar. After all, you didn't even enroll in it!

4. The Detroit Lions lost to the New Orleans Saints in 2010, they lost in 2011, and they lost in 2012. They will certainly lose when they play the Saints again in 2014.

5. The recent study concerning the health consequences of diabetes drugs for young people is not to be believed. This is because the survey was flawed given that the sample size was too small.

6. Look, Leila. Since you want to save more money, you should open a money market account at the bank, and you should cancel all of your credit cards.

7. Portugal is a country, and all countries are on a map. Hence, Portugal is on a map. Assuming that all things on a map can be identified by satellite, Portugal can be identified by satellite.

8. We won't have good government unless qualified people are elected. This proves that we won't have good government, for no good people are elected. If we don't have good government, then life will be harder, so it appears that life will be harder.

9. Given that clowns perform in rodeos, we can conclude that they get paid. This is because anyone who performs in a rodeo gets paid. This means that clowns should pay taxes, in view of the fact that, if clowns get paid, we should make them pay taxes.

10. Because Jack has started the Atkins diet and people on the Atkins diet lose lots of weight, it follows that Jack will lose lots of weight. And anyone who loses lots of weight is likely to get a date. So you know what that means for Jack, don't you?

11. If Jorge marries Sally, he will be ecstatic. Jorge will marry either Sally or Susanna. But there is no way he is going to marry Susanna. As a result, he will marry Sally, and we can conclude that he will be ecstatic.

12. All self-employed workers are professionals. Beauticians are self-employed; hence, they are professionals. Now, all professionals need licenses. This proves that beauticians need a license.

13. Severe hurricanes will not develop unless the ocean water is warm. Accordingly, severe hurricanes won't develop this season, as the ocean water is not expected to be warm. Consequently, those who live in a high-risk hurricane area will breathe easier this year.

14. Given that the Battle of the Somme took place during World War I, we can conclude that it occurred around the time of the Russian Revolution. This is because whatever took place in World War I occurred around the time of the Russian Revolution. Consequently, the Battle of the Somme took place in the 20th century, since if the Battle of the Somme occurred around the time of the Russian Revolution, then the Battle of the Somme took place in the 20th century.

15. Since Europeans were divided in the 1930s and anytime Europeans are divided it will become a "dishonest decade," we can conclude that the 1930s was a dishonest decade. And a dishonest decade is liable to cause trouble in the long run. Thus, the results of the 1930s are obvious.

16. Precipitation is not sunshine. This is due to the fact that if precipitation were sunshine, then humidity would be dry, and humidity isn't dry. So given that the autumnal equinox is in the fall, if precipitation is not sunshine, it must be that the autumnal equinox is in the fall.

17. Benzene is a hydrocarbon, and all hydrocarbons are volatile organic compounds. Therefore, benzene is a volatile organic compound. Because all volatile organic compounds can be harmful to human health when released into the atmosphere, benzene can be harmful to human health when released into the atmosphere.

18. If meteorites are the rarest materials found on Earth, then they are the oldest things humans have touched. Either meteorites are the rarest materials found on Earth or flawless diamonds are the rarest, and diamonds aren't the rarest things found on Earth. Therefore, meteorites are the rarest things found on Earth, and consequently are the oldest things humans have touched.

19. All opiates are pharmaceuticals. Vicodin is an opiate, so it is a pharmaceutical. All things that are pharmaceuticals require a prescription. So Vicodin requires a prescription.

20. Infants may be programmed for fear. Thus they will feel fear even without being taught about what is dangerous, because a programmed emotional response requires no teaching. And if infants feel fear even without being taught about what is dangerous, then parents need not be surprised when children express separation anxiety. Consequently, parents need not be surprised by children's separation anxiety.

 EXERCISE 4.31

Diagram each of the following arguments.

1. There are three strong reasons you should vote to reelect the governor in the next election. First, she has done an excellent job of balancing the state budget. Second, she is trustworthy due to the fact that the policies that she has recommended and supported are those she promised to support during her election campaign. Finally, you should vote for her because she has vowed to defeat any attempt by the legislature to increase university tuition costs.

2. Tomas will be left behind if he forgets to make reservations, and he probably will forget to make reservations. As a result, it's very likely Tomas will be left behind. Besides, he is always spacing out, and people who space out usually get left behind.

3. Tyrone won't be happy unless Jesse Ventura is elected. But Ventura won't get elected, since he is not on the ballot, so you can see for yourself what will follow from that. Now, if Tyrone is unhappy, then Grace will be unhappy, too. Thus, it is clear that Grace will be unhappy.

4. Otto von Bismarck will unite Germany if he can keep Prussia dominant, and he probably can keep Prussia dominant. Accordingly, it is very likely that Otto von Bismarck will unite Germany. Moreover, he will be able to promote trade and growth, and any leader able to promote trade and growth will be able to unite Germany.

5. If both parents carry a gene for a serious hereditary disorder, then it is likely that the child will develop that disorder. Since both my husband and I carry the gene for a serious hereditary disorder, our child is likely to develop this disorder. Given that genetic counseling helps people make decisions about what to do in cases where children are likely to inherit serious genetic disorders, we should consider getting genetic counseling.

6. If art is something that any person can learn to appreciate, then art must be able to be judged by an objective measure. Now it's unlikely that art can be judged by an objective measure, given that what is called art varies so widely, so art must not be something that any person can learn to appreciate. Besides, if only a few people get an emotional feeling from art, then art must not be something that people can learn to appreciate, and only a few people can get an emotional feeling from art.

7. All reasoning creatures have a self-concept, and children are reasoning creatures. You can see what follows from that, I'm sure. Now, since any creature with a self-concept has desires and preferences, it's clear that children must have desires and preferences.

8. The CEO of American Paper Products, Inc., said that his company would stop harvesting old growth forests only if doing so threatened the habitat of an endangered species. But harvesting old growth forests does not threaten the habitat of an endangered species. Of course, you know what that means. And if American Paper Products does not stop harvesting old growth forests, then environmental activists will sabotage its operations. From all of this, it follows that environmental activists will sabotage its operations.

9. Good afternoon, ladies and gentlemen of the jury. It is evident that my client, Janie Jacobson, is not guilty of kidnapping Baby Zack. Since Baby Zack was taken from his mansion in the Hamptons on December 20, 2010, Ms. Jacobson could not be guilty of kidnapping him if she was in Las Vegas at that time. And she was in Las Vegas on that day, as is evidenced by the casino surveillance footage.

10. Don't get Lonnie a dog! Look, he is not responsible, as he has shown by not caring for his things. And anyway, we don't have enough money to provide food and medical care for a dog in view of the fact that even now we have trouble making ends meet. This is true because last week you yourself complained about getting all the bills paid and you never complain without a really good reason.

11. We should legalize the sale of marijuana in Portland. Legalized marijuana sales will create new job prospects for many of our city's unemployed residents. Legalized marijuana sales will also generate new revenue for the city due to the fact that the sale of marijuana is currently illegal and the city cannot collect taxes on income that is earned illegally. Finally, legalizing the sale of marijuana can help stimulate the local economy in that tourists from neighboring cities will spend their money at local restaurants and other local businesses when they come to Portland to buy the drug.

12. If your children watch a lot of television, then they are more likely to believe in racial and gender stereotypes. You don't want your children to believe these harmful stereotypes, so you should turn off the television more often. Besides, if you limit the amount of television your children watch, then they are more likely to engage in constructive activities, and I know you want your children to engage in more constructive activities.

13. It was Maggie Simpson who shot Mr. Burns last night. How do I know? Well, obviously Mr. Burns was shot by one of the Simpsons—Homer, Marge, Bart, Lisa, or Maggie—because they are the only people that have a vendetta against Burns. And there's no way that Homer or Marge could have done it. After all, they were at a marriage retreat at Catfish Lake, and Catfish Lake is 200 miles from where the crime took place. It also could not have been Bart or Lisa, since they were visiting their aunts Patty and Selma last night. Besides, they were watching *The Itchy and Scratchy Show* at the time Burns was shot. That means that Maggie must have been the shooter.

14. It's clear that Miguel will be chosen for the lead in the upcoming musical production of *Cyrano de Bergerac* because only theater students are eligible for lead roles and there are currently only six theater students interested. But why must the role go to Miguel? Well, it can't be either of the two female theater students, since the lead is for a male role. It also can't be Nebo or Dudley in view of the fact that neither of them can dance and there's no way that they can learn to dance in time for the auditions. Finally, it can't be Rajit for the reason that he has a terrible voice. In conclusion, it must be Miguel who will be starring in *Cyrano*.

15. Who ate the last slice of cheesecake from the office workroom? Well, there's no doubt that it had to be one of the office workers, since only they have keys to the workroom. But it couldn't have been any of the secretaries. After all, they are all on low-fat diets. It also couldn't have been any of the custodians because they are on vacation this week. This all proves that the last slice of cheesecake must have been eaten by one of the members of the management team—CEO Saner or President Gamboa. But there's no way President Gamboa would have eaten the cheesecake, since he's diabetic. We can conclude that it had to be CEO Saner.

PUTTING IT ALL TOGETHER: A Critical Précis with Argument Diagram

In Chapter 3, you learned how to write a Critical Précis of an argument. Now that you also know how to diagram an argument, you can include an argument diagram with your Critical Précis when the passage you are analyzing is an argument. Of course, if the passage is not an argument, you will not include a diagram.

The most important thing for you to remember when including an argument diagram with your Critical Précis is that your written analysis must be consistent with your diagram. That means that if your diagram shows there are two premises for the conclusion, then there must be exactly two premises identified in your analysis. It also means that if your diagram shows there are two subarguments, your analysis must include three paragraphs: one for the main argument and one for each of the subarguments. Additionally, the premises in the subargument(s) should not be included in the first paragraph, since they are not premises for the main conclusion.

Let's look at a couple of examples before you try some on your own.

> *The suspect should be released from police custody immediately. There is no evidence that she committed a crime, and a person can be detained only if there is evidence that he or she committed a crime.*—Public defender

First, identify this passage as an argument or nonargument. The author attempts to prove that "The suspect should be released from police custody" and offers two premises to support this conclusion—namely, "There is no evidence that she committed a crime" and "A person can be detained only if there is evidence that he or she committed a crime." So it is an argument. Are these premises linked or convergent? Because the premises depend on each other to support the conclusion, the argument diagram and Critical Précis should appear as follows:

① *The suspect should be released from police custody immediately*.
② *There is no evidence that she committed a crime*, and ③ *a person can be detained only if there is evidence that he or she committed a crime*.

This passage from a public defender contains an argument. The issue is whether the suspect should be released from police custody immediately. The conclusion is that the suspect should be released from police custody immediately. The first premise is that there is no evidence that the suspect committed a crime. The second premise is that a person can be detained only if there is evidence that he or she committed a crime.

Notice that the diagram and analysis match exactly. The claim identified in the diagram as the conclusion is the same claim identified in the analysis as the conclusion, and the claims identified in the diagram as the premises are the same claims identified in the analysis as the premises.

> **Hint!**
> In each of the examples here, we have chosen to present the diagram before the written analysis of the argument. Although these elements need not be presented in this order, we find it easier to write the analysis after we have determined the structure of the argument.

Let's try another.

Your Honor, my client, Ms. Cromwell, should be released from police custody immediately. This is because there is no evidence that she committed a crime due to the fact that her DNA doesn't match the sample collected at the scene of the crime.—Defense attorney

This is an argument attempting to prove that "Ms. Cromwell should be released from police custody." What premise(s) are offered for this conclusion? Notice that the second sentence contains two premise indicators: *this is because* and *due to the fact that*. They signal that there is a subargument. The argument diagram and Critical Précis should appear as follows:

Your Honor, ① *my client, Ms. Cromwell, should be released from police custody immediately*. This is because ② *there is no evidence that* she committed a crime *due to the fact that* ③ her DNA doesn't match the sample collected at the scene of the crime.

This passage from a defense attorney contains an argument. The issue is whether Ms. Cromwell should be released from police custody immediately. The conclusion is that Ms. Cromwell should be released from police custody immediately. The premise is that there is no evidence that Ms. Cromwell committed a crime.

This passage contains a subargument. The intermediate conclusion is that there is no evidence that Ms. Cromwell committed a crime. The premise is that Ms. Cromwell's DNA doesn't match the sample collected at the scene of the crime.

Notice that the diagram and analysis match perfectly. The diagram shows that there are two arguments, and the analysis provides two paragraphs, each analyzing one of the arguments. Also notice that the premise of the subargument is identified only in the analysis of the subargument; it is not included in the first paragraph, since it is not a premise for the main conclusion.

 EXERCISE 4.32

Write a Critical Précis for each of the following passages. Include an argument diagram when appropriate.

1. Silence is more important than ever, as life today is full of noise.—Andrea Bocelli
2. Exercise fights obesity two ways. First, it burns calories. Second, it builds muscle, and muscle burns more calories than fat.—Pamela Peeke, MD
3. Physics is *the* fundamental science. It explains how the universe behaves and gives us an extraordinary power over the world. Professor Richard Wolfson's lectures introduce you to scores of fundamental ideas related to Newtonian mechanics, oscillations and waves, thermodynamics, electricity and magnetism, optics quantum theory, and more.—Ad for *Physics and Our Universe: How It All Works*
4. It is interesting to note that the number of children with severe disabilities is on the rise. Some screening and early intervention have led to a reduction in causes, but the number of children being born exposed to drugs and alcohol is increasing. In addition, medical advances have also resulted in more high-risk and low-birth-weight babies surviving and living longer.—Vaughn, Bos, and Schumm, *Teaching Exceptional, Diverse, and At-Risk Students*

5. Gestational diabetes is a form of diabetes that appears in pregnant women, but goes away after delivery. It has increased over the past few decades because more women have problems with obesity prior to becoming pregnant.—Mark Landon, Professor of Obstetrics and Gynecology at Ohio State University College of Medicine

6. Energy-drink consumption is a rising public health problem. More than 20,000 people were admitted to emergency rooms in 2011 with anxiety, rapid heartbeat, seizures, or heart attacks after downing energy drinks. In addition, many consumers combine the drinks with alcohol or prescription drugs, making the drinks even more dangerous.—U.S. Food and Drug Administration

7. Many people say they aren't very good with shape or that they have poor spatial sense. The typical belief is that you are either born with spatial sense or you are not. This simply is not true! We now know that rich experiences with shape and spatial relationships, when provided consistently over time, can and do develop spatial sense.—John A. Van De Walle, *Elementary and Middle School Mathematics*

8. If we want to produce excuses for lying to someone, these excuses should be capable of persuading reasonable persons, not merely some particular public locked in hostility to a particular group.—Sisela Bok, *Lying*

9. Violence as a way of achieving racial justice is impractical. It is impractical because it is a descending spiral ending in destruction for all. The old law of an eye for an eye leaves everybody blind.—Martin Luther King, Jr.

10. Some children are *mastery oriented*: they attribute their successes to their high ability but tend to externalize the blame for their failures ("That test was unfair"), or attribute them to unstable causes that they can easily overcome ("I'll do better if I try harder"). These students are called "mastery oriented" because they persist in the face of failure, believing that their increased effort will allow them to succeed.—Schaffer and Kipp, *Developmental Psychology: Children and Adolescents*

CHAPTER REVIEW QUESTIONS

1. What lessons from Chapter 2 do you need to remember when numbering claims?
2. How can you tell the difference between premises that are independent and those that are dependent on one another?
3. What should you do with extra claims (those that are neither premises nor conclusions)?
4. How do you include implied claims in an argument diagram?
5. How does a diagram of an argument with multiple conclusions differ from that of a chain argument?
6. How do you diagram an extended argument?
7. When do you include an argument diagram with a Critical Précis?

ONE STEP FURTHER

Controversy over the use of the death penalty has recently reignited. On January 16, 2014, 53-year-old Dennis McGuire, who was sentenced to death for raping and fatally stabbing a young pregnant woman in 1989, took 26 minutes to die by lethal injection, gasping repeatedly as he lay on a gurney with his mouth opening and closing. The state of Ohio used a previously untried drug combination because European and American manufacturers of the previously used drugs banned sales to the U.S. penal system on legal and ethical grounds. Five years earlier, in *Baze v. Rees* (2008), the U.S. Supreme Court considered whether Kentucky's lethal injection protocol violated the Eighth Amendment. Chief Justice Roberts wrote the opinion of the Court.

Petitioners in this case—each convicted of a double homicide—acknowledge that the lethal injection procedure, if applied as intended, will result in a humane death. They nevertheless contend that the lethal injection protocol is unconstitutional under the Eighth Amendment's ban on "cruel and unusual punishments," because of the risk that the protocol's terms might not be properly followed, resulting in significant pain. Petitioners contend that there is a risk of improper administration of thiopental because the doses are difficult to mix into solution form and load into syringes; because the protocol fails to establish a rate of injection, which could lead to a failure of the IV; because it is possible that the IV catheters will infiltrate into surrounding tissue, causing an inadequate dose to be delivered to the vein; because of inadequate facilities and training; and because Kentucky has no reliable means of monitoring the anesthetic depth of the prisoner after the sodium thiopental has been administered. In light of expert testimony regarding safeguards to protect against the maladministration of the procedure, we cannot say that the risks identified by petitioners are so substantial or imminent as to amount to an Eighth Amendment violation.

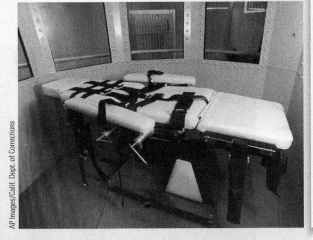

AP Images/Calif. Dept. of Corrections

Lethal injection is the practice of injecting a person with a lethal dose of drugs for the purpose of causing immediate death. It is the most commonly used method of execution in the United States. The European Union's recent ban on the export of any product used in an execution has caused a shortage of lethal injection drugs in many American jurisdictions.

1. The passage above presents two arguments, one from the petitioners and one from the Court. How can you tell the difference between them?
2. Diagram Justice Roberts's argument.
3. Browse the information presented at http://deathpenalty.procon.org/. Write an argument for or against the death penalty that offers three convergent premises.

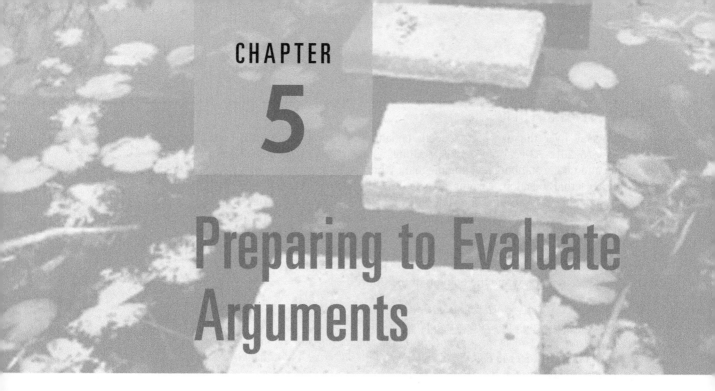

Preparing to Evaluate Arguments

Imagine that in your political science class you read this argument:

> *If the government of the United States is really built on the notion that all people are fundamentally equal, then every person will be equally treated under the law. But it's clear that not everyone is treated equally because crimes committed by wealthier individuals result in much lighter sentences than those committed by poor people. So we must conclude that the government of the United States is not really built on the idea of fundamental equality among persons.*

Socialite Nicole Richie leaves court in 2007 after being sentenced to 90 hours in jail, fined $2,048, and ordered to serve three years' probation for driving the wrong way on the freeway while under the influence of drugs.

ROBYN BECK/AFP/Getty Images

Many people would find this conclusion—that the United States is not reall[y] built on the idea of equality—deeply troubling. But since the goal of an argument is t[o] convince you of something using good reasons, maybe this conclusion really does fo[l]low. How can you decide? When you judge whether an argument's conclusion follow[s] or not, you are **evaluating** the argument.

In order to successfully accomplish any task, you must choose the right tool[s], and that choice depends on the kind of task you face. If, for example, you have a plumbing problem, it is not likely that a hammer will help—because hammers are typically useless for plumbing troubles. Similarly, when evaluating arguments, you must choose the proper tools, and this will depend on the kind of argument you are evaluating. In this chapter, you will learn how to recognize different argument types so that you can pair them with the appropriate evaluative tools. To do this, you will first learn to distinguish two different styles of reasoning: deductive reasoning and inductive reasoning. Once you understand the differences between these, you will learn to distinguish two kinds of arguments that utilize deductive reasoning and three kinds of arguments that utilize inductive reasoning. By the end of the chapter, then, you should be able to recognize five kinds of arguments. Although this chapter is not comprehensive in its presentation of argument types, it does offer a sampling of some of the most common arguments you will encounter. Chapters 6–10 will provide you with the specific tools needed to evaluate each of these five argument types.

LEARNING OUTCOMES

In this chapter, you will prepare for evaluating arguments by:

▶ Distinguishing deductive from inductive reasoning;
▶ Differentiating categorical arguments and truth-functional arguments;
▶ Differentiating inductive generalizations, analogical arguments, and causal arguments;
▶ Naming the appropriate terminology for evaluating deductive arguments;
▶ Naming the appropriate terminology for evaluating inductive arguments; and
▶ Adding argument identification to a Critical Précis.

Distinguishing Two Styles of Reasoning

The first step in preparing to evaluate an argument is determining what kind of support the arguer intends to provide for the conclusion. Premises can be used to support a conclusion in one of two ways. They can be used to *guarantee* a conclusion, or, alternatively, they can make a conclusion look very *likely*. These two ways of supporting a conclusion constitute two fundamental styles of reasoning: deductive reasoning and inductive reasoning. These terms, *deductive* and *inductive*, are probably familiar to you, but in critical thinking, they have technical meanings that may differ from the way you have previously learned to use them.

The key to understanding these two styles of reasoning lies in their distinct (yet similar-sounding) definitions. You'll need to give these careful thought. A **deductive**

argument is one in which the arguer attempts to demonstrate that the truth of the conclusion *necessarily* follows from the premises. When a deductive argument is properly constructed, the premises logically *entail* the conclusion. An **inductive argument**, on the other hand, is one in which the arguer attempts to demonstrate that the truth of the conclusion *probably* follows from the premises. This is because the conclusion of an inductive argument is a *projection* based on the premises. When you consider these two definitions together, you see that the only difference lies in the relationship between the premises and conclusion. Conclusions of deductive arguments are intended to follow by *necessity*, whereas conclusions of inductive arguments are intended to follow by *probability*.

Distinguishing between deductive and inductive arguments will take some practice. Let's consider some examples.

> *All U.S. Presidents are over the age of 35. Barack Obama is a U.S. President. Therefore, Barack Obama is over the age of 35.*

First, identify the premises, conclusion, and issue.

P1:	All U.S. Presidents are over the age of 35.
P2:	Barack Obama is a U.S. President.
∴	Barack Obama is over the age of 35.

Issue: Whether Barack Obama is over the age of 35

Assuming that the premises are true, does the conclusion follow necessarily or only probably? The conclusion follows from the premises *necessarily*. If every U.S. President is over the age of 35 and Barack Obama is a U.S. President, then he *must* be over the age of 35. The argument, then, utilizes deductive reasoning.

Notice how that argument differs from this one.

> *Most U.S. Presidents attended college. Barack Obama is a U.S. President. Therefore, Barack Obama attended college.*

Here the argument is presented with the premises and conclusion identified formally.

P1:	Most U.S. Presidents attended college.
P2:	Barack Obama is a U.S. President.
∴	Barack Obama attended college.

Issue: Whether Barack Obama attended college

Assuming that the premises are true, does the conclusion follow necessarily or only probably? In this case, it is only *probable* that the conclusion is true. Even if 42 of the 43 U.S. Presidents up to and including Barack Obama attended college, he may be that one who did not attend college. You *cannot be certain* that the conclusion is true given the premises that you are provided. Thus, the argument utilizes inductive reasoning.

Oftentimes arguers will include indicator words to signal whether an argument is deductive or inductive. Words such as *certainly, absolutely,* and *definitely* typically indicate that a conclusion *necessarily* follows from the premises, and therefore the argument is deductive. In contrast, words such as *likely, plausibly,* and *possibly* indicate that a conclusion *probably* follows from the premises, and therefore the argument is inductive.

However, deductive argument indicators are sometimes used improperly in everyday speech or inserted merely to make an argument appear more powerful than it is.

Consider this example.

> *Most U.S. Presidents attended college. Barack Obama is a U.S. President. Therefore, Barack Obama certainly attended college.*

Notice that the inclusion of the word *certainly* might be rhetorically persuasive, but it does not make the conclusion any more likely. The argument is still inductive because the premises offer only probable support for the conclusion, even though the argument includes a deductive argument indicator.

 EXERCISE 5.1

Your Turn! How can you tell whether or not an argument with a deductive argument indicator is really a deductive argument?

When evaluating an argument, it is important to remember that the truth or falsity of the premises has no bearing on whether the argument is deductive or inductive. Instead, you should consider what kind of support the premises provide for the conclusion by assuming that the premises are true. Consider the following example.

P1: Either Earth orbits the sun or Copernicus was mistaken.

P2: Earth does not orbit the sun.

∴ Copernicus was mistaken.

Issue: Whether Copernicus was mistaken

Assuming that both premises are true, does the conclusion follow necessarily or only probably? The conclusion necessarily follows from the premises, even though one of the premises—namely, "Earth does not orbit the sun"—is false. This is because *if* it were true that either Earth orbits the sun or Copernicus was mistaken, and *if* it were also true that Earth does not orbit the sun, then it would *have to be true* that Copernicus was mistaken. In the argument, the disjunction offers us two options, and the second premise takes one choice away, so only one option for the conclusion remains.

 EXERCISE 5.2

Your Turn! Why is the truth or falsity of the premises irrelevant to whether the argument is deductive or inductive?

In Chapters 3 and 4, you learned how to analyze and diagram multiple arguments. When authors present multiple arguments, they may not exclusively use one or the other style of reasoning. Instead, they may combine them, as in this example.

The Boilermakers will make it to the Final Four only if they win their next game. But the Boilermakers will not win their next game, since their best players are all hospitalized for swine flu. So the Boilermakers will not make it to the Final Four.

This passage contains two arguments: the main argument and a subargument. Here is the main argument presented formally.

P1: The Boilermakers will make it to the Final Four only if they win their next game.

P2: The Boilermakers will not win their next game.

∴ The Boilermakers will not make it to the Final Four.

Issue: Whether the Boilermakers will make it to the Final Four

Assuming that the premises are true, does the conclusion follow necessarily or only probably? The conclusion cannot fail to be true if the premises are true. So the conclusion follows by necessity. Now, what about the subargument?

EXERCISE 5.3

Your Turn! Provide a Formal Analysis of the subargument in the previous passage.

Notice that, although the conclusion of the main argument is necessarily true if its premises are true, the conclusion of the subargument is only probable given the premise. This means that the main argument is deductive and the subargument is inductive. Whenever you are asked to determine whether an argument is deductive or inductive, your answer should always refer to the main argument, even when the subargument utilizes a different style of reasoning.

EXERCISE 5.4

Your Turn! Look at the argument that began this chapter. Does it use deductive or inductive reasoning? How can you tell?

EXERCISE 5.5

Write a Formal Analysis of the following arguments. Then indicate whether the argument is deductive or inductive.

1. You are attracted to Matthew and Fouad. Since Bryant is like them in that they all are tall, dark, and handsome, you are probably attracted to Bryant as well.
2. Jamie fell off the roof three times, and she got hurt each time. As a result, she is sure to get hurt every time she falls off the roof.

3. Mitchell's roommate has seen the *Lord of the Rings* trilogy four times. Rita has never seen the *Lord of the Rings* trilogy. Accordingly, Rita cannot be Mitchell's roommate.

4. If the laws of physics are always correct, then what goes up must come down. And the laws of physics are always correct. So what goes up must come down.

5. The bad food in the dining commons can be attributed to the new cook. This is because the food started tasting bad as soon as the new cook arrived and nothing else changed. He's not very friendly either.

6. Either Waterman is older than Jackman or he's older than Bootman. Waterman is not older than Jackman, since Jackman was born four months later. Consequently, Waterman is older than Bootman.

7. Cows are carnivores, and all carnivores are rational beings. Thus, cows are rational beings.

8. People who have computer addictions will likely benefit from psychological counseling services. This is because computer addictions are like drug addictions and people with drug addictions often benefit from psychological counseling.

9. The airbag in Jose's car failed to deploy when he crashed, and anyone whose airbag fails to deploy in an accident gets hurt. So Jose's sure to have been hurt.

10. Nearly three-quarters of university students work at least 20 hours per week. This is the conclusion from a recent opinion poll done by the *New York Times*. It showed that 75% of the nearly 1,500 university students under the age of 25 they polled said they work at least 20 hours per week.

11. I've been trying to figure out why I do well on some of my exams and not well on others, and I think that I've found the cause. Over the last year, each time I did well on a test, I had gotten plenty of sleep the night before. Since a good night's sleep was the only thing the good performances had in common, it is likely that getting a good night's sleep helped me on my tests.

12. Given that *The Adventures of Tom Sawyer* and *Huckleberry Finn* were written by the same author and have similar stories and that *Huckleberry Finn* won the Nobel Prize for Literature, *The Adventures of Tom Sawyer* probably also won the Nobel Prize for Literature.

13. All calico cats are female, and your cat is a calico. You know what that means, don't you?

14. Haven't you had four different roommates? And hasn't each of them become a good friend? Clearly, you will become friends with whomever you get as a roommate. And if you become friends with whomever you get as a roommate, then you will be a happy person. Thus, you are sure to be a happy person.

15. If you join the soccer team, you will have to attend practice every afternoon. Since you work every afternoon, you cannot attend soccer practice. Looks like you won't be joining the team.

Distinguishing Two Kinds of Deductive Arguments

Now that you have some experience distinguishing deductive from inductive arguments, we'll make some further distinctions within each style of reasoning, beginning with deduction. Two of the most common types of deductive arguments are categorical arguments and truth-functional arguments. The difference between the two lies in what kinds of claims are presented in the argument. Although you will learn the details about how to evaluate these two kinds of deductive arguments in later chapters, for now the important skill you need to acquire is how to distinguish between them.

A **categorical argument** is a deductive argument that contains categorical claims. **Categorical claims** are claims that relate two categories of things. Although categorical claims can be expressed in many different ways, all categorical claims can be presented as one of only four formal sentence types: universal affirmative, universal negative, particular affirmative, and particular negative sentences.

A **universal affirmative** claim expresses a positive claim about the relation of an *entire* category of things to another category of things. For example,

> *All houses are buildings.*

A **universal negative** claim expresses a negative claim about the relation of an *entire* category of things to another category of things. For example,

> *No fish are vegetables.*

A **particular affirmative** claim expresses a positive claim about the relation of a *portion* of a category of things to another category of things. For example,

> *Some cars are Mustangs.*

Finally, a **particular negative** claim expresses a negative claim about the relation of a *portion* of a category of things to another category of things. For example,

> *Some Americans are not truck drivers.*

Notice that each of these examples expresses a claim that relates two categories of things—that *all, none,* or *some* members of a particular category of things are or are not members of another category of things. Note that this is true even when the words *all* and *none* are left out, as in the following examples.

> *Houses are buildings.*
> *Fish are not vegetables.*

The first sentence could be formally restated as "All houses are buildings" and the second sentence as "No fish are vegetables." At this point, don't worry about being able to distinguish between these four types of categorical claims. What's more important is that you can identify when an argument contains categorical claims.

 **EXERCISE 5.6**

Your Turn!   Provide your own example of each kind of categorical claim.

A **truth-functional argument** is a deductive argument that contains truth-functional claims. **Truth-functional claims** are claims that are composed of simple claims and logical operators. A **simple claim** is a claim that does not contain any other claim as a component. For example,

> Craig lives in Madison, Wisconsin.

When one or more simple claims are combined with a logical operator, the resulting truth-functional claim is called a **compound claim**. Although they can be expressed in many different ways, all compound claims can be presented as one of only four types: negation, conjunction, disjunction, and conditional. In ordinary language, these are claims containing the words *not*, *and*, *or*, and *if . . . then . . .*, or their equivalents.

A **negation** modifies a claim with the operator *not*. For example,

> *Anne is not enrolled in this class.*

In this example, the simple claim "Anne is enrolled in this class" is modified by the operator *not*. A **conjunction** modifies two other claims with the operator *and*. For example,

> *I have a job interview tomorrow, and I can't find a babysitter.*

This sentence combines the simple claims "I have a job interview tomorrow" and "I can't find a babysitter" with the operator *and*. A **disjunction** modifies two other claims with the operator *or*, as in this example.

> *Either we can go see* Clash of the Titans *or we can go see* Iron Man 2.

Here the two simple claims, "We can go see *Clash of the Titans*" and "We can go see *Iron Man 2*," are modified with the operator *or*.

> **Hint!**
> Notice that the term *simple claim* refers to the components of a truth-functional claim, not to the number of claims expressed by the sentence. Thus, the claim "Either we can go see *Clash of the Titans* or we can go see *Iron Man 2*" contains two simple claims, but these two parts are combined with the operator *or* to form one compound claim.

Finally, a **conditional**, sometimes referred to as a material implication, modifies two other claims with the operator *if . . . then. . . .* For example,

> *If you overdraw your account, then the bank will charge you a fee.*

Here the two simple claims, "You overdraw your account" and "The bank will charge you a fee," are modified by the operator *if . . . then. . . .* Remember from Chapter 2 that conditional claims do not always appear in standard *if . . . then . . .* format, as in the following examples.

> *The bank will charge you a fee if you overdraw your account.*
> *I will make it to my job interview tomorrow only if I find a babysitter.*
> *If we go see* Clash of the Titans, *we can't go see* Iron Man 2.

EXERCISE 5.7

Your Turn!   Provide your own examples of the five kinds of truth-functional claims.

 EXERCISE 5.8

For each of the following, determine whether it is a categorical claim or a truth-functional claim.

1. No libraries are office buildings.
2. Some clowns are not comedians.
3. If you have a full-time job, then you should take fewer courses.
4. Either the ministry or counseling would be a good career for Henri.
5. All freedom lovers are patriots.
6. Inert gases are noble gases.
7. If you do not have an alibi for the night of September 10, then you will be considered a suspect in our investigation.
8. Some of the best novelists are young women.
9. The word *rake* can refer to a garden tool or a man of dissolute habits.
10. Email messages are not private messages.

Determining whether a deductive argument is a categorical argument or a truth-functional argument is simply a matter of recognizing whether the argument contains categorical claims or truth-functional claims. Claims that relate two categories of things using words equivalent to *all*, *none*, or *some* signal a categorical argument. Truth-functional claims—those that combine simple claims using logical operators—signal truth-functional arguments. However, since categorical arguments may contain the words *and* and *not*, identifying truth-functional arguments requires that you look for disjunctions and conditional claims—that is, claims containing the words *or* and *if . . . then . . .*, or their equivalents. These operators are not found in categorical arguments.

 EXERCISE 5.9

Your Turn!   Identify the following as a categorical or a truth-functional claim, and explain your answer.

If all cats are mammals, then no cats are reptiles.

Let's examine a few arguments before you try some on your own. Consider the following argument.

All snakes are reptiles. Some snakes are venomous. Therefore, some reptiles are venomous.

Here is the argument in a Formal Analysis:

P1: All snakes are reptiles.

P2: Some snakes are venomous.

∴ Some reptiles are venomous.

Issue: Whether some reptiles are venomous

The first thing to notice about this argument is that it is deductive. If the premises are true, then the conclusion must be true. If all snakes are reptiles and some snakes are venomous, then some reptiles *must be* venomous. Next, we must determine whether the argument is categorical or truth-functional. Notice that both the premises and the conclusion express claims about categories of things. The first premise relates snakes and reptiles, the second premise relates snakes and venomous animals, and the conclusion relates reptiles to venomous animals. It is, then, a categorical deductive argument.

Next, consider this argument.

Some defendants are not felons. This is because felons are criminals and some defendants are not criminals.

Let's write this in a Formal Analysis:

P1: Felons are criminals.

P2: Some defendants are not criminals.

∴ Some defendants are not felons.

Issue: Whether some defendants are felons

First, we can tell that the argument is deductive. The conclusion could not be false if both premises were true. We also see that each claim of the argument relates two categories. The first premise relates felons and criminals, the second premise relates defendants and criminals, and the conclusion relates defendants and felons. Since the claims are categorical, the argument is categorical.

Compare those arguments to the next one.

If a snake has a rattle on its tail, then it is venomous. Since that snake has a rattle on its tail, it is venomous.

When we analyze this argument formally, we get the following:

P1: If a snake has a rattle on its tail, then it is venomous.

P2: That snake has a rattle on its tail.

∴ That snake is venomous.

Issue: Whether that snake is venomous

Again, notice that this is a deductive argument. If the premises are true, then the conclusion must be true. Next, is this argument categorical or truth-functional? This argument doesn't contain claims about categories of things. Instead, it includes truth-functional claims, the most noticeable of which is the *if . . . then . . .* claim in the first premise. Thus, this is a truth-functional argument.

Here is a final example.

> *The public will continue to disapprove of NSA phone surveillance, since either the phone surveillance program will be seriously restricted or the public will continue to disapprove of the NSA program, and clearly the NSA program will not be seriously restricted.*

Here is this argument in a Formal Analysis:

> **P1:** Either the NSA phone surveillance program will be seriously restricted or the public will continue to disapprove of the NSA program.
>
> **P2:** The NSA phone surveillance program will not be seriously restricted.
>
> ∴ The public will continue to disapprove of the NSA program.
>
> **Issue:** Whether the public will continue to disapprove of the NSA phone surveillance program

The argument is certainly deductive. If the premises are correct that only two actions are open as possibilities and one of those is eliminated, then the other action *has to be* what happens. What kind of claim is premise one? It's a disjunction, one of the compound claims you can recognize as truth-functional. Further, none of the claims relates categories. Therefore, this deductive argument is a truth-functional argument.

Hint!

Sometimes categorical claims can be expressed as truth-functional claims, and vice versa. For example, the categorical claim "All birds are mammals" could be expressed as the truth-functional claim "If it is a bird, then it is a mammal." For now, decide whether the argument is categorical or truth-functional based on the way that it is presented to you.

Of course, there are many deductive arguments that contain neither categorical claims nor truth-functional claims, such as arguments from mathematics and arguments from definition. In these cases, the rules of categorical logic and truth-functional logic will not apply. However, you should still be able to identify an argument as deductive rather than inductive whenever the arguer uses the truth of the premises to guarantee the truth of the conclusion.

How to Distinguish Kinds of Deductive Arguments

Step 1: Determine whether the passage is an argument.

▶ Does the passage contain at least two claims? If not, the passage is not an argument.

▶ Does one of the claims offer a reason for another? If not, the passage is not an argument.

▶ Do the reasons provide evidence to establish the truth of another claim? If not, the passage is not an argument.

Step 2: Determine whether the argument is deductive or inductive.

▶ Does the arguer attempt to demonstrate that the truth of the conclusion *necessarily* follows from the premises? If so, then proceed to Step 3.

▶ Does the arguer attempt to demonstrate that the truth of the conclusion *probably* follows from the premises? If so, then the argument is inductive, not deductive.

Step 3: Determine whether the argument includes categorical claims or truth-functional claims.

▶ Does the argument relate *all*, *none*, or *some* members of a category to another category of things? If so, then the argument is categorical.

▶ Does the argument include claims using the operator *or* or *if . . . then . . . ?* If so, then the argument is truth-functional.

EXERCISE 5.10

Your Turn! Look back to the argument at the start of the chapter. Is it a categorical or a truth-functional argument? How can you tell?

EXERCISE 5.11

Determine whether each of the following deductive arguments is a categorical argument or a truth-functional argument. Indicate which claim provides the clue.

1. If the laws of physics are always correct, then nothing can travel faster than light. And the laws of physics are always correct. So nothing can travel faster than light.
2. Soccer players are baseball players. And baseball players aren't accordion players. Consequently, soccer players aren't accordion players.
3. Either Naomi goes bowling or Miguel studies. Miguel does not study, and Naomi goes bowling. It follows that, if Miguel does not study, then Naomi goes bowling.
4. Some ants are insects. Thus, no ants are caterpillars given that some caterpillars are not insects.
5. No television commentators are accurate economic forecasters. This is because no television commentators are trained economists and only trained economists are accurate economic forecasters.
6. If you passed geology, then you passed a science class. And if you passed a science class, then you have qualified for honors. Consequently, if you passed geology, then you have qualified for honors.
7. Every student takes critical thinking, and some students are math majors. So, many people who take critical thinking are math majors.
8. Anyone who reads philosophy books will immediately get smarter. Everyone who gets smarter will change the world. So anyone who reads philosophy books will change the world.

9. The defendant must be found not guilty. A defendant is guilty of murder only if he intended to kill the victim, and my client, the defendant, had no such intention.

10. The mail carrier is the one who stole my package! I never received my package, and if the mail carrier stole my package, then I wouldn't have received it.

Distinguishing Three Kinds of Inductive Arguments

Recall that an inductive argument is one in which the arguer attempts to prove that the truth of the conclusion *probably* follows from the premises. Three of the most common kinds of arguments utilizing inductive reasoning are inductive generalizations, analogical arguments, and causal arguments. Although you will learn the details about how to evaluate these three varieties of inductive arguments in later chapters, for now the important lesson is that you can recognize and identify each of them based on their unique features.

An **inductive generalization** concludes that some, most, or all of a particular group have some feature based on evidence that a portion of that group has the feature. The conclusion of an inductive generalization will, then, be a general claim because a **general claim** makes a statement about all, most, or many members of a group or set. Since recognizing general claims is vital for recognizing inductive generalizations, let's first look at some examples of general claims. Each of the following is a general claim.

All swans are white.

One-third of college students smoke cigarettes.

Junk food is high in calories.

 EXERCISE 5.12

Your Turn! Provide your own example of a general claim.

An **analogical argument** is an inductive argument that uses an analogy to conclude that because one case has some feature, the other case should, too. As you can see by this definition, analogical arguments include analogies among their premises. An **analogy** is a claim that compares two (or more) things. Each of the following claims draws an analogy.

Learning is like rowing upstream.

My love is like a red, red rose.

Life is a roller coaster.

 EXERCISE 5.13

Your Turn! Provide your own example of an analogy.

A **causal argument** is an inductive argument that provides evidence to conclude that some causal claim is true. So being able to properly identify a causal claim is necessary for being able to identify a causal argument. A **causal claim** is a claim identifying the cause of some event. For example, each of the following expresses a causal claim.

> *Smoking causes cancer.*
>
> *Civil unrest results from political repression.*
>
> *The root of sexual violence is pornography.*

The first sentence expresses the claim that cancer is *caused* by smoking, the second sentence expresses the claim that civil unrest is *caused* by political repression, and the third sentence expresses the claim that sexual violence is *caused* by pornography. Notice that even though the second and third examples do not utilize the word *cause*, nonetheless each makes a causal claim. In causal arguments, the conclusion is always a causal claim.

EXERCISE 5.14

Your Turn!   Provide two examples of causal claims, one using the word *cause* and the other not using it.

EXERCISE 5.15

Determine whether each of the following is a general claim, an analogical claim, or a causal claim.

1. The cause of my dog's hair loss is a vitamin deficiency.
2. Every business major will be attending the job fair on Friday.
3. Recent DNA studies show that a genetic change caused dogs to be able to eat starches such as wheat and potatoes.
4. Being a literature major is similar to being a philosophy major.
5. Seetha is just like her mother.
6. Most new cars are overpriced and bad for the environment.
7. Cats are wise.
8. Having wet gloves can result in frostbite.
9. My dog's hair loss is like your dog's hair loss.
10. Political science majors are naturals for embassy jobs.

Determining whether an inductive argument is an inductive generalization, an analogical argument, or a causal argument is simply a matter of recognizing whether the argument contains a general claim as the conclusion, an analogy among the premises, or a causal claim as the conclusion. After you analyze the argument, examine the premises. Is there an analogy? If not, then examine the conclusion. Does it contain a general claim or a causal claim? Let's work through several examples before you try some on your own.

Consider this one.

I have suffered an allergic reaction to every cat I've ever encountered. I bet I'm allergic to all cats.

First, analyze the argument.

> **P:** <u>I have suffered an allergic reaction to every cat I've encountered.</u>
>
> ∴ I am allergic to all cats.

Issue: Whether I am allergic to all cats

You should recognize this as an inductive argument. If the premises are true, the conclusion is only probably true. It is likely that I am allergic to all cats, but there may be some cats that will not trigger an allergic reaction. Next, what kind of inductive argument is this? Let's look at the premise. Does it contain an analogy? No. The premise does not compare two (or more) things. What about the conclusion? Does it present a general claim or a causal claim? Notice that it does not state that one thing causes another. Instead, it makes a general claim, one about *all* cats, based on a claim about a portion of that same group—namely, the cats I have encountered. So this argument is an inductive generalization.

> **Hint!**
> Sometimes you may be unsure whether an argument containing claims about *all*, *some*, or *none* of a group is an inductive generalization or a categorical argument. In these cases, remember that inductive generalizations are inductive arguments and categorical arguments are deductive arguments. If you first determine whether the argument is deductive or inductive, you will avoid this confusion.

Here's another example.

About half of the people in Ukraine support a political agreement with the European Union. This is shown by a poll in which 45% favored the association agreement with the EU.

 EXERCISE 5.16

> **Your Turn!** Write a Formal Analysis of the argument above.

Again, this argument is inductive. The fact that 45% of the people who were polled supported this political agreement provides evidence that a similar portion of the entire population of Ukraine supports the agreement, but it doesn't have to be true. Next, examine the premise. Is there an analogy? No. There is no comparison made. What about the conclusion? Does it offer a general claim or a causal claim? There is no causal claim, but there is a general claim. The conclusion makes a statement about some—namely, *about half*—of the people in Ukraine. So this argument is an inductive generalization.

Now, let's identify other kinds of inductive arguments, starting with this one.

Dogs are a lot like cats. Since I am allergic to cats, I am probably also allergic to dogs.

Here is the argument presented in a Formal Analysis:

P1: Dogs are a lot like cats.

P2: I am allergic to cats.

∴ I am allergic to dogs.

Issue: Whether I am allergic to dogs

The first thing to notice about this argument is that it is inductive. The argument's use of the inductive indicator word *probably* is a helpful clue. If the premises are true, the conclusion is at best probably true. Next, examine the premises. Is there an analogy? Yes! The first premise compares dogs to cats. So this is an analogical argument.

Here's another example to consider.

Hernando was excited about the three music courses he took last year. Therefore, he'll probably be excited about the music class he is going to take in the spring, since the spring music class is quite similar to his previous music classes.

 EXERCISE 5.17

Your Turn! Write a Formal Analysis of the argument above.

This argument is inductive because, although it may be likely that Hernando will be excited by the spring music class given that he was excited by the three previous courses, he might not be. Is one of the premises an analogy? Yes! The arguer compares the music class Hernando will take in the spring to the ones he took before.

Let's now consider a few more examples of inductive arguments.

When my mother visited me this year, she experienced classic symptoms of an allergic reaction, including sneezing, itchy eyes, and congestion. Since the only thing different between this visit and her previous visits is that I now have an indoor cat, my mom's allergies must have been caused by the cat.

Here is the argument formally analyzed:

P1: When my mother visited me this year, she experienced classic symptoms of an allergic reaction, including sneezing, itchy eyes, and congestion.

P2: The only thing different between my mother's visit this year and the others is that I now have an indoor cat.

∴ My mom's allergies were caused by my new cat.

Issue: Whether my mom's allergies were caused by my new cat

The first thing to notice about this example is that it is an inductive argument. If the premises are all true, the conclusion is at best probable. Next, examine the premises. Is there an analogy? No, there is no comparison made. What about the conclusion? Is there a general claim or a causal claim? The conclusion of the argument is a causal claim. The arguer concludes that his or her mom's allergy symptoms were caused by being near a cat.

Here is a final example.

> *In a recent experiment, rats were found to have increased anxiety in stressful situations, and these rats had been given a popular antidepressant drug as adolescents. It seems likely that the rats become anxious as a result of ingesting antidepressant drugs.*

 EXERCISE 5.18

Your Turn!   Write a Formal Analysis of the argument above.

Again, we can see that the conclusion does not have to be true even if the premises are true, so this argument is inductive. What kind is it? Since there is no analogy in the premises, let's look at the conclusion. Notice that when it states that the rats' anxiety resulted from ingesting antidepressant drugs, it is claiming that the antidepressant drugs *caused* the rats to become anxious. So this is a causal argument.

Of course, there are inductive arguments other than inductive generalizations, analogical arguments, and causal arguments. In these cases, the evaluative tools you will learn will not apply. However, you should still be able to identify an argument as inductive rather than deductive whenever the arguer uses the truth of the premises to make the truth of the conclusion seem very likely.

How to Distinguish Kinds of Inductive Arguments

Step 1: Determine whether the passage is an argument.
▸ Does the passage contain at least two claims? If not, the passage is not an argument.
▸ Does one of the claims offer a reason for another? If not, the passage is not an argument.
▸ Do the reasons provide evidence to establish the truth of another claim? If not, the passage is not an argument.

Step 2: Determine whether the argument is deductive or inductive.
▸ Does the arguer attempt to demonstrate that the truth of the conclusion *necessarily* follows from the premises? If so, then the argument is deductive, not inductive.
▸ Does the arguer attempt to demonstrate that the truth of the conclusion *probably* follows from the premises? If so, then proceed to Step 3.

Step 3: Determine whether the argument contains a general claim, an analogy, or a causal claim.
▸ Do the premises include a claim comparing one thing to one or more others? If so, then the passage is an analogical argument.

> ► Does the conclusion make a general claim about all, most, or many of a group or set? If so, then the passage is an inductive generalization.
> ► Does the conclusion make a causal claim? If so, then the passage is a causal argument.

EXERCISE 5.19

Determine whether each of the following inductive arguments is an inductive generalization, an analogical argument, or a causal argument. Indicate which claim provides the clue.

1. You like spaghetti, and you like pizza. Since lasagna is similar to spaghetti and pizza, you should also like lasagna.
2. You like spaghetti and pizza, and they are both Italian foods. You probably like all Italian foods.
3. Bill, Juan, and Franklin work in the IT department, and they are really bright. Thus, it's likely that all members of the IT department are really bright.
4. In a study on tooth decay, the subjects who developed the most cavities were those who had both bacteria and food in their mouths. Thus, the tooth decay was caused by a combination of those two factors.
5. The bugs that were eating the spinach in my garden have disappeared. Given that I surrounded my garden with marigolds, the marigolds must have caused the bugs to disappear.
6. Each of my five classes at the University of North Carolina at Chapel Hill has been held in a large lecture hall. I expect that all of my classes here will be in large lecture halls.
7. In a small study in New York, half the members of a university choir were given three cigarettes to smoke. The other half of the choir did not smoke any cigarettes. Afterward, all were tested on their ability to hit a variety of notes. The "smokers" did not do well on the test, demonstrating that smoking hurt their vocal cords.
8. Horses, dogs, and cats all can be taught tricks by using positive reinforcement and lots of food treats. Thus, birds are probably trainable in the same way, since they are like horses, dogs, and cats.
9. Blair, Roscoe, Fatima, and Tin are all poets, and they all smoke cigarettes. Therefore, all poets probably smoke cigarettes.
10. Since Indianapolis, Fort Wayne, and Lafayette all have wild animal zoos, Bloomington likely also has a wild animal zoo. After all, Bloomington is a lot like the other three cities.
11. On August 23, 2009, Desiree Jennings, a healthy, vibrant woman, was administered the seasonal flu shot at a local grocery store. Ten days later, she came down with the flu and began having seizures. She now has difficulty speaking, walking, and eating. Doctors have diagnosed Ms. Jennings with a neurological condition called dystonia. Given that Desiree Jennings was perfectly healthy before getting the flu shot, it looks like her dystonia was caused by a severe reaction to the seasonal flu vaccine.
12. The two Democratic senators who supported abortion rights and same-sex marriage were opposed for reelection last year by the Committee for Family Values. Since Senator Brown and those two senators are alike in that they

both support abortion rights and same-sex marriage, we can expect the CFV to oppose Senator Brown, too.

13. There's been a lot of controversy over whether or not life on other planets is possible. Well, Mars is like Earth. Since Earth can support life, Mars is likely able to support life as well.

14. A recent survey of the residents of Macon, Georgia, found that 45% of the adult population uses tobacco. It's reasonable to conclude, then, that 45% of the adult population of the entire state uses tobacco.

15. Does poverty cause crime? Most definitely. Last year, unemployment rates rose from 15% to 25%, and crime rates rose in a similar fashion.

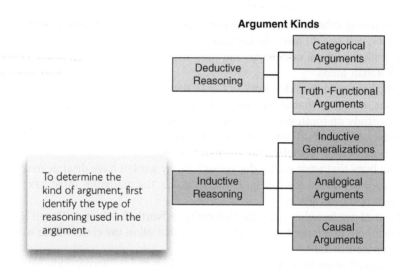

Argument Kinds

To determine the kind of argument, first identify the type of reasoning used in the argument.

EXERCISE 5.20

Determine whether each of the following arguments is a categorical argument, a truth-functional argument, an inductive generalization, an analogical argument, or a causal argument.

1. You can expect to see most states offering drug treatment programs as an alternative to jail or prison sentences for first-time drug offenders. This is because eight states now offer drug treatment. These states report that they have fewer repeat offenders and they save money.

2. Anand is the new chess grand master. This is because he beat Topalov, and if he beat Topalov, then Anand is the new chess grand master.

3. I developed a terrible case of laryngitis over the weekend. Since I don't have any cold symptoms, but did an unusual amount of yelling in the second half of the basketball game, my laryngitis must be the result of yelling so much.

4. All trumpet players are pianists. And some trumpet players are not guitar players. Consequently, some pianists are not guitar players.

5. The number of food recalls has increased in each of the last three years, and nothing seems to suggest that this trend will change. Thus, it is likely that the number of recalls will keep rising and rising.

6. Either Miles Davis or Louis Armstrong is the best jazz musician of all time. Since Louis Armstrong can't be the best jazz musician of all time, Miles Davis must be.

7. You clearly have a case of the fungal infection called ringworm. This is because you have a red, elevated, ring-like sore on your arm, and if you have ringworm, then you will have sores like those.

8. The number of students in criminology has increased each of the last three years. During this three-year period, more forensic crime series have been shown on television. The crime rate has been different for each year, the number of new jobs available has been different each year, and the recruiting has diminished each year. Thus, it is clear that the larger number of forensic crime programs on television has resulted in an increase in criminology majors.

9. The Louisiana State University football team beat Tulane in 2012, it beat Loyola in 2013, and it beat Northwestern in 2014. Since the University of New Orleans football team is a lot like the football teams at Tulane, Loyola, and Northwestern, LSU will certainly beat UNO in 2015.

10. If we don't have a tax increase, Stony Brook tuition will go up again. However, the governor refuses to raise taxes because he promised voters that he wouldn't when he ran for office. For these reasons, we'll be paying more to go to school next year.

11. Whenever I wear my team jersey while watching the Lions play, they win. And whenever I don't, they lose. The Lions' success in those games can, then, be attributed to my choice in apparel!

12. You should buy locally grown produce if you want to support small farmers in your region. Given that you don't buy locally grown produce, you must not care about small farmers.

13. There is no doubt that many pesticides are dangerous to human health. This follows from the fact that many pesticides are dangerous to the environment, and all things that are dangerous to the environment are also dangerous to human health.

14. A nickel is like a quarter. Since whenever I flipped a quarter it came up heads, when I flip a nickel it will also come up heads.

15. Lawyers have advanced degrees, and they make a much higher than average salary. High school teachers are akin to lawyers, so they, too, make a much higher than average salary.

16. I compared the cost of six different PCs, and each cost 20% more at The Discount Computer Store than at Electronics-R-Us. Since Macs are a lot like PCs, I bet their Mac prices are higher, too.

17. Some Macs are vulnerable to computer viruses, since all Macs are computers and most computers are vulnerable to viruses.

18. Most people nationwide would be pleased if their son or daughter became a registered nurse. Over 75% of respondents in a poll of 5,000 people nationwide said they would be pleased if their child became a registered nurse.

19. In a university study, 42 students were randomly chosen to be exposed to either sexually violent or sexually nonviolent materials. Afterward, the students' aggression was assessed, and no significant differences were found between the two groups. It is evident, then, that violent pornography did not make those viewers more violent.

20. Several fashion designers at a recent Paris exhibition made a point of using recycled materials in their fall lines of clothing. Therefore, we can expect most fashion designers to bring recycled materials into their collections.

Choosing Proper Evaluative Terms

When we evaluate any argument, we consider two questions. First, does the argument have a good structure? Second, are all of the premises true? How we go about answering these questions, however, depends on what kind of argument we are evaluating. Because the styles of reasoning differ, the terms used to evaluate deductive arguments differ from the terms used to evaluate inductive arguments. When evaluating deductive arguments, we use the language of *validity* and *soundness*; when evaluating inductive arguments, we use the language of *strength* and *cogency*. Let's explore what each of these terms means by examining how to evaluate deductive and inductive arguments.

The first step in evaluating an argument is to consider whether the premises support the conclusion as intended. Recall that a deductive argument is one in which the arguer attempts to demonstrate that the truth of the conclusion *necessarily* follows from the premises. When the arguer succeeds in this attempt, the argument is valid. A **valid deductive argument**, thus, is one in which, if the premises are true, then the conclusion must be true. In other words, it is impossible in a valid argument for true premises to produce a false conclusion. Deductive arguments that fail to support the conclusion as intended are called invalid arguments. Notice that whether the premises are in fact true or false is irrelevant to whether the argument is valid or invalid. The judgment of whether a deductive argument is valid or invalid is based entirely on the *structure* of the argument, not the truth-values of the argument's premises.

> **Hint!**
> When trying to decide whether a deductive argument is valid or invalid, assume that the premises are true. Ask yourself, If the premises are true, does the conclusion follow?

Once you have determined whether a deductive argument is valid or invalid, you can next judge whether it is sound or unsound. A **sound deductive argument** is a valid argument with all true premises. As you can see from this definition, there are two requirements for soundness: The argument must be valid, and the argument must contain all true premises. If an argument is invalid, then it is unsound, and if a valid argument has any false premises, it, too, is unsound.

  EXERCISE 5.21

> **Your Turn!**   Which of the five kinds of arguments that you learned to identify in this chapter are evaluated using the language of validity and soundness?

You can evaluate deductive arguments at two different levels. The first level—concerning an argument's validity—focuses on the *structure* of the argument. The *truth* of the premises is evaluated at the second level. This means that a deductive argument can have a good structure and yet still be unsuccessful because it contains one or more false premises. Additionally, a deductive argument can have all true premises and yet still be an unsuccessful argument because it does not have a good structure.

Evaluating Deductive Arguments

```
        Do the premises support
           the conclusion?
          ┌───────────┴───────────┐
        Yes                        No
          │                         │
    Are all the              Invalid and
   premises true?             unsound
   ┌──────┴──────┐
  Yes            No
   │              │
Valid and     Valid and
 sound         unsound
```

This flow chart illustrates how to evaluate deductive arguments.

 EXERCISE 5.22

Your Turn! For both columns, valid and invalid, circle the proper term for the conditions on the left.

	Valid	**Invalid**
True Premises **True Conclusion**	Sound or unsound?	Sound or unsound?
True Premises **False Conclusion**	**Impossible**	Sound or unsound?
At Least One False Premise **True Conclusion**	Sound or unsound?	Sound or unsound?
At Least One False Premise **False Conclusion**	Sound or unsound?	Sound or unsound?

 EXERCISE 5.23

Choose the best answer for each of the following questions by utilizing the definitions of validity and soundness.

1. If a deductive argument has all true premises, then
   a. The conclusion must be true
   b. The argument must be valid
   c. The argument must be sound
   d. None of the above

2. If a deductive argument is valid and all of its premises are true, then
   a. The conclusion must be true
   b. The conclusion is probably true
   c. The argument must be sound
   d. None of the above
3. If a deductive argument has a false premise, then
   a. The conclusion must be false
   b. The argument must be invalid
   c. The argument must be unsound
   d. None of the above
4. If a deductive argument has a false conclusion, then
   a. The argument must have a false premise
   b. The argument must be invalid
   c. The argument must be unsound
   d. None of the above
5. If a deductive argument has all true premises and a false conclusion, then
   a. The argument must be invalid
   b. The argument must be unsound
   c. Both a and b
   d. None of the above

The first step in evaluating an inductive argument, as in evaluating a deductive argument, is to consider whether the premises support the conclusion as intended. However, although the answer is "yes" or "no" when it comes to determining whether a deductive argument has good structure, for inductive arguments the answer will range on a continuum from better to worse. Recall that an inductive argument is one in which the arguer attempts to demonstrate that the truth of the conclusion *probably* follows from the premises. The likelihood that a conclusion of an inductive argument is true depends on how well the premises support the conclusion. **Strong inductive arguments** have premises that, if true, make the conclusion probable. Inductive arguments in which the premises, if true, do not make the conclusion probable are weak inductive arguments. Notice that whether the premises are in fact true or false is irrelevant to the strength of the argument. The judgment of whether an inductive argument is strong or weak is based entirely on the structure of the argument, not the truth-values of the argument's premises.

Hint!
When trying to decide whether an inductive argument is strong or weak, assume that the premises are true. Ask yourself, If the premises are true, does the conclusion probably follow?

Once you have assessed the strength of an inductive argument, you can next judge whether it is cogent or uncogent. A **cogent inductive argument** is a strong argument with all true premises. That means that there are two requirements for cogency just as there are two requirements for soundness. The argument must be strong, and the argument must contain all true premises. If an argument is weak, then it is uncogent, and if a strong argument has any false premises, then it is uncogent.

EXERCISE 5.24

Your Turn!   Which of the five kinds of arguments that you learned to identify in this chapter are evaluated using the language of strength and cogency?

You can evaluate inductive arguments at two different levels. The first level focuses on the *structure* of the argument. The *truth* of the premises is evaluated at the second level. This means that an inductive argument can have a good structure and yet still be an unsuccessful argument because it contains one or more false premises. Additionally, an inductive argument can have all true premises and yet still be an unsuccessful argument because it does not have good structure.

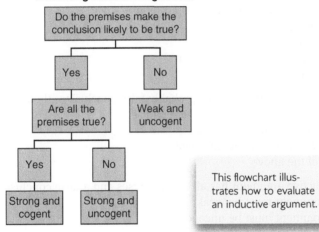

This flowchart illustrates how to evaluate an inductive argument.

EXERCISE 5.25

Your Turn!   For both columns, strong and weak, circle the proper term for the conditions on the left.

	Strong	Weak
True Premises (Probably) True Conclusion	Cogent or uncogent?	Cogent or uncogent?
True Premises (Probably) False Conclusion	Impossible	Cogent or uncogent?
At Least One False Premise (Probably) True Conclusion	Cogent or uncogent?	Cogent or uncogent?
At Least One False Premise (Probably) False Conclusion	Cogent or uncogent?	Cogent or uncogent?

🖎 **EXERCISE 5.26**

Choose the best answer for each of the following questions by utilizing the definitions of strength and cogency.

1. If an inductive argument has all true premises, then
   a. The conclusion must be true
   b. The argument must be strong
   c. The argument must be cogent
   d. None of the above

2. If an inductive argument is strong and all of its premises are true, then
   a. The conclusion must be true
   b. The conclusion is probably true
   c. The argument must be cogent
   d. None of the above

3. If an inductive argument has a false premise, then
   a. The conclusion must be false
   b. The argument must be weak
   c. The argument must be uncogent
   d. None of the above

4. If an inductive argument has a probably false conclusion, then
   a. The argument must have a false premise
   b. The argument must be weak
   c. The argument must be uncogent
   d. None of the above

5. If an inductive argument has all true premises and a false conclusion, then
   a. The argument must be weak
   b. The argument must be uncogent
   c. Both a and b
   d. None of the above

PUTTING IT ALL TOGETHER: Preparing to Evaluate

In Chapter 3, you learned how write a Critical Précis of an argument, and in Chapter 4, you learned how to include an argument diagram with your written analysis. Although you have not learned how to evaluate arguments at this point, you can now prepare to do so by identifying the kind of argument in your Critical Précis. Of course, if the passage is not an argument, you should specify which feature of an argument is lacking instead of writing an analysis.

Let's consider a couple of examples before you try some on your own.

Seawater can be mined for commercially valuable metals. This is shown by the fact that seawater is mined for magnesium, which is a commercially valuable metal.—Tom Garrison, Oceanography

First, decide whether or not the passage is an argument. There are three claims: one in the first sentence and two in the second. The inference indicator *this is shown by the fact that* signals that the first claim is a conclusion and that the second two claims are the premises. Thus, the passage is an argument.

Since this is an argument, we can diagram it.

① <u>Seawater can be mined for commercially valuable metals</u>. This is shown by the fact that ② <u>seawater is mined for magnesium</u>, ③ <u>which is a commercially valuable metal</u>.

Is this argument deductive or inductive? If the premises are both true, the conclusion must be true. So this is a deductive argument. Does it contain categorical claims or truth-functional claims? While there are no disjunctions or conditional claims, there are categorical claims. The first claim, for example, can be understood as relating two categories of things: seawater and things that can be mined for commercially valuable metals. Thus, this is a categorical argument.

 EXERCISE 5.27

Your Turn!   What two categories of things are related in the second claim? What about the third claim?

Now, you can write the Critical Précis. In the first paragraph, you should identify the passage as an argument and then analyze it. Then, in a separate paragraph, you should identify the kind of argument. Once you learn how to evaluate the argument, you will be able to include the evaluation in this final paragraph.

> **This passage from Tom Garrison's *Oceanography* contains an argument. The issue is whether seawater can be mined for commercially valuable metals. The conclusion is that seawater can be mined for commercially valuable metals. The first premise is that seawater is mined for magnesium. The second premise is that magnesium is a commercially valuable metal.**
> **The argument is a deductive categorical argument.**

Remember to ensure that your Critical Précis matches the diagram. The argument has two premises, claims ② and ③, so these should appear as the premises in the written analysis.

Let's work through one more example.

I stopped serving my family any foods produced with pesticides, and afterward my formerly noncompliant daughter became compliant and better able to focus at school. Therefore, my daughter's ADHD (Attention Deficit Hyperactivity Disorder) was likely a result of the pesticides.—Faye Elahi, nutritionist

First, determine whether or not the passage contains an argument. Given that the passage contains a set of claims that offer reasons as evidence for the truth of one of its claims, the passage is an argument.

The diagram should look as follows.

① I stopped serving my family any foods produced with pesticides, and
② afterward my formerly noncompliant daughter became compliant
and better able to focus at school. Therefore, ③ my daughter's ADHD
(Attention Deficit Hyperactivity Disorder) was likely a result of the pesticides.

$$\frac{① + ②}{}$$
$$\downarrow$$
$$③$$

To complete the analysis, you must determine the kind of argument. Notice the conclusion states that her daughter's ADHD is *likely* a result of the pesticides. This signals that the argument is inductive. Is the argument an inductive generalization, an analogical argument, or a causal argument? To decide, we should first examine the premises. Do they include an analogy? No, there is no comparison made between two or more things. Next, let's examine the conclusion. Is it a general claim or a causal claim? When the conclusion suggests that the daughter's ADHD is a result of the pesticides, it means that eating foods produced with pesticides *caused* her daughter to have ADHD symptoms. Thus, this is a causal argument.

Your Critical Précis should, then, read as follows.

> **This passage by the nutritionist Faye Elahi contains an argument. The issue is whether Faye Elahi's daughter's ADHD (Attention Deficit Hyperactivity Disorder) was a result of eating foods produced with pesticides. The conclusion is that Faye Elahi's daughter's ADHD (Attention Deficit Hyperactivity Disorder) was a result of eating foods produced with pesticides. The first premise is that Faye Elahi stopped serving her family any foods produced with pesticides. The second premise is that, after Faye Elahi stopped serving her family food produced with pesticides, her formerly noncompliant daughter became compliant and better able to focus at school.**
> **The argument is an inductive causal argument.**

The remainder of this textbook will guide you through the evaluation of each of the five kinds of arguments you have learned to identify. Chapters 6 and 7 instruct you on evaluating categorical arguments and truth-functional arguments, respectively, and Chapters 8, 9, and 10 teach you how to evaluate inductive generalizations, analogical arguments, and causal arguments, respectively. Once you have learned these evaluative skills, you can add your evaluation of these kinds of arguments to your Critical Précis.

EXERCISE 2.28

For each of the following, write a Critical Précis of the passage. Include an argument diagram and an identification of the argument type when appropriate.

1. Nearly 70% of married men and 60% of married women have had affairs, and, among my clients, 8 out of 10 who have committed adultery regret having done so. It's reasonable to conclude, then, that about 80% of all adulterers regret having cheated.—Holly Hein, *Sexual Detours*

2. If you're interested in protecting the planet, you have to look at what you're eating.—Alicia Silverstone

3. Hospital officials say conjoined boys born in Dallas have been safely separated and are doing well. The boys weighed a combined 11 pounds, 15 ounces at birth. Owen and Emmett were born joined from the breastbone to the belly button. The babies shared a liver and bowels. They also had a birth defect that left their intestines outside of their bodies and covered by a thin layer of tissue.—Associated Press

4. Reasoning with a drunkard is like going under water with a torch to seek for a drowning man.—Thiruvalluvar

5. Human tissue tears all too easily; spider silk is stronger than steel. So at Utah State, researchers are spinning spider silk into a fix for damaged shoulders and knees.—*Popular Science*

6. Why wouldn't a woman consider herself a feminist? Even my husband calls himself a feminist. If he can call himself that, then every woman should be able to call herself that.—Mary Elizabeth Winstead

7. Veganism is not merely a social philosophy or dietary preference. It may be entitled to legal protection. This is because the U.S. Equal Employment Opportunity Commission regulations protect religious practices, and a commitment to veganism is similar to traditional religious views in that it is based on moral or ethical beliefs on right and wrong that are sincerely held.—U.S. District Judge S. Arthur Spiegel, *Sakile S. Chenzira v. Cincinnati Children's Hospital Medical Center*

8. Americans want to cut their ties to dirty fuels and instead power their country with 100% clean energy. This is evidenced by a national survey of 1,000 registered voters conducted by Greenberg Quinlan Rosner, in which 61% of respondents think the country should be investing more in clean energy sources and energy efficiency rather than in fossil fuels like coal, oil and gas.—Sierra Club Executive Director Michael Brune

9. Some sediment-laden rivers do not have a broad continental shelf to provide a platform for sediment to accumulate, and all deltas require a broad continental shelf to provide a platform for sediment to accumulate. As a result, some sediment-laden rivers do not have deltas.—Tom Garrison, *Oceanography*

10. In 2010, an oil drilling rig leased by British Petroleum (BP) was damaged from an explosion, and oil began gushing out of a broken pipe into the Gulf of Mexico. In the six months after the accident, more than 600 sea turtles have been found dead along the Gulf Coast. Since this is a much higher amount than what is typical for the season, it is reasonable to conclude that the sea turtle deaths are a result of the oil spill.—National Wildlife Federation

CHAPTER REVIEW QUESTIONS

1. How can you tell whether an argument is using inductive reasoning or deductive reasoning?
2. How can you distinguish between categorical arguments and truth-functional arguments?
3. How can you distinguish among analogical arguments, inductive generalizations, and causal arguments?
4. What terms are used in evaluating deductive arguments?
5. What terms are used in evaluating inductive arguments?
6. How do you write a Critical Précis of a deductive argument?
7. How do you write a Critical Précis of an inductive argument?

ONE STEP FURTHER

The area along the Mississippi River between New Orleans and Baton Rouge, populated by hundreds of chemical plants, plastic plants, fertilizer manufacturers, electrical power plants, and oil refineries, is popularly known as "Cancer Alley." Environmental activists have drawn attention to the dangers to domestic animals, wildlife, and fish, as well as the unusually high rates of stillbirths, asthma, miscarriages, neurological disease, and cancer among the area's largely African-American and low-income residents. Corporate representatives, on the other hand, have rejected these claims. Consider this argument from a peer-reviewed study by scientists at the Shell Oil Company, for example.

A man cuts the grass at a cemetery in an area along the Mississippi River known as Cancer Alley.

JOEL SARTORE/National Geographic Creative

All-cause mortality and all cancer combined for white males in the Industrial Corridor were significantly lower than the corresponding Louisiana population. Similar patterns were observed for white females. The mortality for non-white males and females in the Industrial Corridor was generally similar to the corresponding populations in Louisiana. Therefore, contrary to prior public perceptions, mortality due to cancer in the Industrial Corridor does not exceed that for the State of Louisiana.

1. Determine whether the argument is deductive or inductive and which argument type or types it contains.
2. Discuss the persuasiveness of this argument. Does it matter to you that the study was conducted by researchers employed by Shell Oil Company? Why or why not?
3. Images, like written texts, can express values, an ideology, or a set of social and political beliefs. When you view them, you can interpret what their producers stand for, what they believe in, and what view of the world they are trying to present to you. Consider, for example, the work of internationally acclaimed American photographer Robert Misrach at http://fraenkelgallery.com/portfolios/petrochemical-america. How might you reconstruct the arguments he is presenting with his artwork?

CHAPTER 6
Evaluating Categorical Arguments

Imagine that you run into the residence hall director on your way to class and he mentions that he's been concerned about your roommate, Tony. He presents the following argument.

> *I'm certain that Tony is taking drugs. His eyes are always red, and we all know that people on drugs have red eyes.*

You may have already recognized this as a categorical argument, since you learned how to distinguish among different kinds of arguments in Chapter 5. A categorical argument is a kind of deductive argument often presented in the form of a syllogism. A **syllogism** is a formal argument containing two premises and a conclusion. In categorical syllogisms, all three claims (the two premises and the conclusion) are categorical claims. How convincing is the reasoning in the categorical argument presented above? Suppose the premises really are true: Yes, Tony's eyes are always red, and yes, people on drugs have red eyes. But does this conclusion follow from these premises?

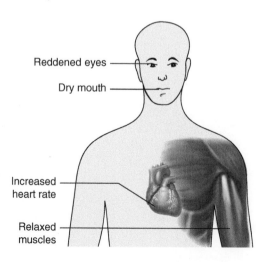

Reddened eyes

Dry mouth

Increased heart rate

Relaxed muscles

Physical effects of Cannabis use.

Visit our website: academic.cengage.com/philosophy/Jackson

In this chapter, you will learn how to evaluate categorical arguments by determining whether the premises support the conclusion. But to do so, you must first learn how to translate categorical claims into standard form, how to transform a categorical argument into a standard form syllogism, how to draw a Venn diagram, and how to use a Venn diagram to determine whether a categorical argument is valid or invalid.

LEARNING OUTCOMES

In this chapter, you will learn how to evaluate categorical arguments by:

▸ Translating categorical claims into standard form,
▸ Transforming categorical arguments into standard form syllogisms,
▸ Using a Venn diagram to determine whether a categorical argument is valid, and
▸ Writing a Critical Précis of a categorical argument.

Translating Categorical Claims

In Chapter 5, you learned that **categorical arguments** are deductive arguments containing categorical claims and that **categorical claims** relate two categories of things. Although you can express the content of a categorical claim in a great number of different ways, all claims in categorical logic are expressed by using one of four types of formal sentences. When claims follow the formal rules of expression in one of those four types, they are in **standard form.** ←————

Here are the four kinds of standard form claims with an example of each.

(1) All S are P.   *All cats are mammals.*
(2) No S are P.   *No turnips are apples.*
(3) Some S are P.   *Some violins are musical instruments.*
(4) Some S are not P.   *Some root beer floats are not desserts.*

Each part of sentences (1)–(4) has a name and a function. In each sentence, S (or, in the examples, *cats, turnips, violins,* and *root beer floats*) is called the **subject term**. Since the subject term identifies a class, group, or set, in formal language it is always expressed as a plural noun. In each sentence, the letter P (or *mammals, apples, musical instruments,* and *desserts*) must also be stated as a plural noun and is called the **predicate term**. The verbs that link the subject and predicate terms together, *are* and *are not*, are known as the **copula**. In standard form, the subject term precedes the copula, and the predicate term comes after it.

 EXERCISE 6.1

Your Turn!   Identify the subject term, the predicate term, and the copula for the following claim.

No dogs are fish.

The term that begins each of the four previous sentences is the most difficult to understand. This term is called the **quantifier**, and it has two different functions. It identifies both the *quantity* and the *quality* of the claim. First, the *quantity* is either universal or particular. A claim has a universal quantity if it refers to every member of the subject group. A claim has a particular quantity if it refers to some amount less than every member of the subject group. Since claim (1) has the quantifier *all*, it refers to each and every member of the group *cats*. The quantity of claim (1) is thus universal. Claim (3) is particular because the word *some* means *at least one*, but not necessarily all.

The *quality* of the claim is determined by whether the quantifier includes or excludes the members of the subject class as members of the predicate class. When the members of the subject class are *included* in the predicate class—as in claims (1) and (3)—then the quality is affirmative. When they are *excluded*—as they are in claims (2) and (4)—the quality is negative.

Each categorical claim is distinguished and identified by its quantifier and copula—that is, by its quantity and quality. Thus, claim (1) is known as a **universal affirmative**, or an A claim; claim (2) is an E claim—a **universal negative**; claim (3) is a **particular affirmative**, an I claim; and claim (4) is a **particular negative**, an O claim. It's thought that the letters—introduced in the Middle Ages—come from the first two vowels in the Latin words *affirmo* (I affirm) and *nego* (I deny). These four claims often use the letters S and P (for subject term and predicate term, respectively) to represent the plural nouns.

Kind of Claim	Quantity	Quality	Standard Form
A	Universal	Affirmative	All S are P.
E	Universal	Negative	No S are P.
I	Particular	Affirmative	Some S are P.
O	Particular	Negative	Some S are not P.

 EXERCISE 6.2

To get practice using the new terminology, try applying it in these ways.

Example: Take a standard form A claim. Change the *quality*, but not the *quantity*.

Procedure: The standard form A claim is "All S are P." The quantity is universal, and the quality is affirmative. So, keeping the quantity universal, change the quality from affirmative to negative. Thus, you now have an E claim.

Answer: No S are P.

1. Take a standard form E claim. Change the quality, but not the quantity.
2. Take a standard form O claim. Change the quality, but not the quantity.
3. Take a standard form A claim. Change the quantity, but not the quality.
4. Take a standard form I claim. Change the quantity, but not the quality.
5. Take a standard form O claim. Change both the quantity and the quality.
6. Take a standard form E claim. Change both the quantity and the quality.
7. "All violins are musical instruments." Change the quality, but not the quantity.
8. "No oranges are vegetables." Change the quantity, but not the quality.
9. "All rhinos are pterodactyls." Change both the quality and the quantity.
10. "Some books are not logic texts." Change both the quality and the quantity.

Now that you've learned the basics of standard form, you can turn your attention to arguments in ordinary English. Many arguments expressed in everyday English are actually categorical syllogisms even though they do not appear in standard form. In order to analyze and evaluate these arguments, each claim must first be translated into standard form. Translating these claims from English into standard form is just like translating from one language into another. In either case, the translator must take care to use the proper grammar so the translated sentence makes sense. The translated claim must also retain the exact meaning of the original. In this chapter, you will find a number of tools to assist you in translating categorical claims, but first we must clarify the requirements of the standard form.

All standard form claims must have plural nouns as subject and predicate terms. Sometimes claims already use plural nouns, so when translating these into standard form, you may just retain what has been given. However, you will also encounter categorical claims that don't have subject and predicate terms given as plural nouns. For these kinds of claims, you will have to determine how you can retain the original meaning while providing plural nouns for both the subject and the predicate terms. Fortunately, some common examples will provide basic rules for you to follow.

Universal claims sometimes use the adverbs *whoever*, *whatever*, *wherever*, and *whenever*. These words can be readily translated into standard form by replacing them with the general terms, respectively, *people*, *things*, *places*, and *times*. Let's translate an example of each of these. Notice that each adverb indicates that the claim is universal and the subject term is the term immediately following it.

Whoever studies seriously will do well on the test.
Translation: All people who study seriously are people who will do well on the test.

Whatever can be done should be done.
Translation: All things that can be done are things that should be done.

She goes wherever the wind blows her.
Translation: All places the wind blows her are places she goes.

Whenever the alarm rings, James wakes up.
Translation: All times the alarm rings are times James wakes up.

EXERCISE 6.3

Your Turn! Translate the claim "Wherever extreme poverty exists, life expectancy is low" into standard form, following the rules provided above.

Since subject and predicate terms in standard form are translated as plural nouns, adjectives, prepositional phrases, and other modifying terms must be accompanied by a suitable plural noun that may be missing in the original. For example, in English someone might make this kind of claim.

All apples are red.

Initially, this claim looks to be already in standard form. It has a proper quantifier and copula. Also, *apples* is already a plural noun, so that doesn't need changing. However, *red* is an adjective, not a noun. In order for this claim to be a proper categorical claim—that is, to have the proper *grammatical* form—you must make the predicate term a plural noun modified by the adjective *red*. One way to do that is to again employ the appropriate general noun.

Translation: *All apples are red* things.

The predicate term is now *red things*.

Here's another kind of claim in ordinary English.

No Americans are in combat.

Again, the quantifier is appropriate, as is the copula. The subject term is already a plural noun, so you need not change it. However, since *in combat* is a prepositional phrase and not a plural noun, you must add a plural noun for *in combat* to modify. The noun must make sense not only with the modifying phrase, but also with *Americans*, since the sentence is relating the subject and predicate terms. The best translation again uses the general noun that fits the prepositional phrase.

Translation: *No Americans are* people *in combat.*

By using a general noun, you avoid a problem that can occur in this kind of sentence. Since the quantity is *all*, if you translate the predicate as *Americans in combat* you have turned the predicate group into a mere subset of the subject group. That is, if you translated the claim as "No Americans are Americans in combat," then the members of the predicate group are all members of the subject group. As a result, the claim would not relate two categories of things as it must do. You can avoid that potential problem by using a noun that is more general, or broader, than the subject term. In this case, *people* is more general than *Americans*.

 EXERCISE 6.4

Your Turn! For the claim "All zebras are living on the African continent," provide two different plural nouns that are *more general than* the subject term.

Guidelines for Translating Categorical Claims

▶ *Whoever* introduces the subject of an A claim. The subject and predicate terms should be expressed in terms of *people*.
▶ *Whatever* introduces the subject of an A claim. The subject and predicate terms should be expressed in terms of *things*.
▶ *Wherever* introduces the subject of an A claim. The subject and predicate terms should be expressed in terms of *places*.
▶ *Whenever* introduces the subject of an A claim. The subject and predicate terms should be expressed in terms of *times*.
▶ Subject and predicate terms must be plural nouns.
▶ The predicate category cannot be a subset of the subject category.

 EXERCISE 6.5

Determine whether the subject and predicate terms are in standard form. For those that are not, translate them into standard form.

1. No fish are reptilian.
2. Wherever there's smoke there is fire.
3. Some violins are expensive.
4. Whoever makes the mess should clean it up.
5. Some contemporary music is terrible.
6. All physicians are in the military.
7. Whatever goes up must go down.
8. Some people who want a second chance are out of luck.
9. No businesses are charities.
10. I feel a pain in my heart whenever I hear her voice.
11. All peanut butter candies are wrapped individually.
12. All of the stagehands are in the cast.
13. Some tsunamis are not hazardous to coastal cities.
14. All students study in the library.
15. Some tunes are songs.

Another problem that will arise in translating ordinary language claims into standard form occurs in sentences referring to individuals or using proper names. This is because they refer to an individual, but categorical subjects and predicates must be classes or groups. The solution is to treat an individual as the lone member of a group of one. So, as odd as it may sound, translate individuals by using the words *identical to*, as shown in the following examples.

Quincy is a fine student.
Translation: All people identical to Quincy are fine students.

King Kong *is a classic monster movie.*
Translation: All movies identical to *King Kong* are classic monster movies.

> *My ticket was not expensive.*
> **Translation:** No tickets identical to my ticket were expensive purchases.

EXERCISE 6.6

Your Turn!   Using the translation rules provided above, translate the claim "General Motors is in the Fortune 500" into standard form.

The terms *only* and *the only* merit special attention. The reason is each has a logical meaning that is not readily apparent, but rather easily forgotten or ignored during translation. To get the correct meaning, you must remember that *only* introduces the *predicate* term of an A claim. *The only* introduces the *subject* term of an A claim. These rules hold wherever these terms are located in the sentence. You must learn how to translate these two terms accurately, for they are very important and their meaning is not always intuitively clear.

> *Only horses are mares.*
> **Translation:** All mares are horses.

The word *only* introduces the predicate term. That means *horses* is the predicate term, so *mares* must be the subject term.

> *The only integers are whole numbers.*
> **Translation:** All integers are whole numbers.

The only introduces the subject term. Thus, *integers* is the subject term of an A claim, and *whole numbers* must be the predicate term.

> *Dogs are the only pets.*
> **Translation:** All pets are dogs.

Even though *the only* appears midsentence, what follows—*pets*—is the subject term of the A claim.

Additionally, conditional claims can be expressed as categorical claims. The antecedent of the conditional (following *if*) is the subject term of an A claim. The consequent (following *then*) is the predicate term. Consider the following example.

> *If this animal is a cat, then it is a mammal.*
> **Translation:** All cats are mammals.

The antecedent is *this animal is a cat*, and *it is a mammal* is the consequent.

Conditionals are sometimes negative. These can be translated as categorical claims, except the subject and predicate terms need to be made affirmative, not negative. You do this by making the positive version of the consequent the subject term and making the positive version of the antecedent the predicate term. Consider the following example.

If this is not a mammal, then it is not a cat.
Translation: All cats are mammals.

Take the consequent, *it is not a cat*; get rid of the negative; and translate it as the subject term of an A claim, like this: *All cats....* Then take the antecedent, *this is not a mammal*; get rid of the negative; and translate it as the predicate term of the claim.

Finally, claims that use the phrase *not all* and *not every* can be particularly tricky to translate. Take this example.

Not all vehicles are cars.
Translation: Some vehicles are not cars.

Not all signals that the quantity is particular, so we use *some*. However, *not* signals that the quality is negative. Therefore, it should be translated as an O claim.

Additional Guidelines for Translating Categorical Claims
▶ Claims about individuals should be translated using the phrase *identical to*.
▶ *Only* or *none but* introduces the predicate of an A claim.
▶ *The only* introduces the subject of an A claim.
▶ *If...then...* translates as an A claim where the antecedent is the subject term.
▶ *If* not X, *then* not Y translates as an A claim. However, negate both the antecedent and the consequent, and then switch their positions to obtain the following: All Y are X.
▶ *Not all* and *not every* should be translated as *Some...are not....*

EXERCISE 6.7

Translate the following claims into standard form.

1. Only the studious are successful.
2. Firs are the only evergreen trees.
3. Theodore Roosevelt fought in the Spanish-American War.
4. Not all calderas are the result of a single cataclysmic eruption.
5. If you are over five feet tall, then you can ride on the Ferris wheel.
6. Only the good die young.
7. Ducks are the only birds in the pond.
8. My biology professor is my cousin.
9. Not all pigeons are dirty.
10. If this is a cow, then it is a mammal.
11. Only cows are mammals.
12. The only mammals are cows.
13. If this is a campaign contribution, then it is tax-deductible.
14. Aristotle systematized the rules of categorical logic.
15. You can't enter the movie theater if you are not over the age of 17.

EXERCISE 6.8

Translate the following claims into standard form.

1. Some lizards are brown.
2. Some lizards are in the woodpile.
3. A few bears are not mammals.
4. Bears are dangerous.
5. Whoever gets the job gets a paycheck.
6. Whatever is made of wood is flammable.
7. All basketballs are spherical.
8. A couple of students are history majors.
9. None of the children is in class.
10. Nobody on campus favors an increase in parking fees.
11. Every cow is a mammal.
12. There's a cow wherever there's a bull.
13. Not all final exams are multiple choice.
14. Few chemists fear mathematics.
15. Duct tape is the only universal tool.
16. Only tomatoes are vegetables.
17. The only renewable energy source is garbage.
18. None of the interns is getting paid.
19. Not one person listened to my explanation.
20. Peonies are flowers.
21. Some shirts are clothes.
22. All soups are served in bowls.
23. Every current criminal justice major is a sophomore.
24. Not every calf is a Holstein.
25. Only the foolish cut class.

Forming Categorical Syllogisms

A common form of argument that uses categorical claims is called a **categorical syllogism**. As mentioned above, a syllogism contains two premises and a conclusion, and in a categorical syllogism, all three claims are categorical claims. These claims will relate two categories, each of which is shared with one of the other two claims. Thus, all valid syllogisms will contain exactly three categories altogether, with each of the three appearing exactly twice in the argument. For example,

> *All cats are mammals.*
> *All mammals are animals.*
> *All cats are animals.*

Categorical syllogisms are typically represented like this, with two premises above the line and the conclusion below it. This syllogism contains three plural nouns, or categories: *cats*, *mammals*, and *animals*. Each of those three occurs exactly twice: *Cats* is the subject term in premise one and in the conclusion; *mammals* is the predicate term in premise one and the subject term in premise two; *animals* is the predicate term in premise two and in the conclusion.

The three terms in a categorical syllogism are identified by a name that indicates their role in the argument. The **major term** is the predicate term of the conclusion, and it will also appear in one of the premises. The **minor term** is the subject term of the conclusion, and it will always appear in the other premise. **The middle term** of the argument is the category that occurs in both premises, but is absent from the conclusion. Thus, the three terms for the preceding example are:

> Major term: animals
> Minor term: cats
> Middle term: mammals

EXERCISE 6.9

Your Turn!   Using *dogs* as the major term, *mammals* as the minor term, and *animals* as the middle term, properly insert the terms for the following categorical syllogism.

> All ___ are ___.
> All ___ are ___.
> All ___ are ___.

EXERCISE 6.10

Identify the major, the minor, and the middle terms in the following syllogisms.

1. All S are M.
   All P are M.
   All S are P.

2. All tomatoes are fruits.
   Some tomatoes are red foods.
   Some red foods are fruits.

3. No barn owls are pets.
   All pets are animals.
   No animals are barn owls.

4. No emeralds are gems.
   Some rubies are gems.
   Some rubies are not emeralds.

5. Some pumpkins are legumes.
   Some legumes are squash.
   Some pumpkins are squash.

6. All executives are workaholics.
   No workaholics can relax.
   No executives can relax.

7. All carrots are nutritious snacks.
   No fast food is a carrot.
   No fast food is a nutritious snack.

8. All quintuplets are hungry mouths to feed.
   All hungry mouths to feed are things to be avoided.
   All quintuplets are things to be avoided.

9. Not all bread slices are heels, and not all crusts are heels. Thus, some crusts are not bread slices.

10. All majors are officers. Since no majors are lieutenants, no lieutenants are officers.

Categorical syllogisms all have two linked premises. Consider the following example.

No animal products are allowed in a vegetarian diet, and eggs are animal products. Thus, eggs are not allowed in a vegetarian diet.

To diagram the argument, first underline and number the claims.

① *No animal products are allowed in a vegetarian diet*, and ② *eggs are animal products*. Thus, ③ *eggs are not allowed in a vegetarian diet*.

Then identify the premises and the conclusion. In this case, *thus* indicates that the conclusion is the final claim and that the two prior claims are premises.

Placed in standard form, the argument would appear like this:

No animal products are foods allowed in a vegetarian diet.
All eggs are animal products.
No eggs are foods allowed in a vegetarian diet.

Of course, the conclusion and the premises may be presented in any order. Consider the following example.

Registered nurses need state licenses because registered nurses are medical professionals and all medical professionals need state licenses.

First, underline and number the claims.

① *Registered nurses need state licenses* because ② *registered nurses are medical professionals* and ③ *all medical professionals need state licenses*.

Then identify the premises and conclusion. *Because* signals that the conclusion is the claim prior to that premise indicator and the premises are the two claims following. Notice that, again, the premises are linked.

In standard form, the argument would appear like this.

> All registered nurses are medical professionals.
> <u>All medical professionals are workers who need state licenses.</u>
> All registered nurses are workers who need state licenses.

 EXERCISE 6.11

Your Turn! Why are the premises in a categorical syllogism always linked?

Categorical syllogisms may also be part of a chain argument. For example,

Preschool teachers need patience, and everyone who needs patience would benefit from studying yoga. Thus, preschool teachers would benefit from studying yoga. Since people who would benefit from yoga are people who would benefit from massage therapy, preschool teachers would benefit from massage therapy.

Again, underline and number the claims.

> ① *Preschool teachers need patience, and* ② *everyone who needs patience would benefit from studying yoga*. Thus, ③ *preschool teachers would benefit from studying yoga*. Since ④ *people who would benefit from yoga are people who would benefit from massage therapy,* ⑤ *preschool teachers would benefit from massage therapy*.

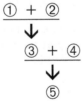

In standard form, the categorical syllogisms would be expressed in the following two arguments. Notice that, as always, the subargument is presented first.

> All preschool teachers are people who need patience.
> <u>All people who need patience are people who would benefit from studying yoga.</u>
> All preschool teachers are people who would benefit from studying yoga.

> All preschool teachers are people who would benefit from studying yoga.
> All people who would benefit from yoga are people who would benefit from
> <u>massage therapy.</u>
> All preschool teachers are people who would benefit from massage therapy.

EXERCISE 6.12

Diagram each argument. Then rewrite the argument as a standard form categorical syllogism.

1. All S are P. This is because no S are M and all M are P.
2. Since all bread slices are heels and not all crusts are heels, some crusts are bread slices.
3. Jack-o-lanterns are pumpkins, for jack-o-lanterns are Halloween objects, and some Halloween objects are pumpkins.
4. Given that some electronics engineers do satellite research and some who do satellite research are federal employees, most electronics engineers are federal employees.
5. If this is a campaign contribution, then it is tax-deductible, and if it is tax-deductible, then it's an economic investment. So, if this is a campaign contribution, then it's an economic investment.
6. Not every metaphysician is a rationalist. Since every rationalist is a Platonist, some metaphysicians are not Platonists.
7. Every member of student government is a student. Since the student body president is a member of student government, he or she must be a student. Since this is true and since every student can freely criticize campus administration, the student body president can freely criticize campus administration.
8. Brick layers are skilled workers because they have an apprenticeship. And every trade that has an apprenticeship consists of skilled workers.
9. All languages that are not spoken regularly are dead languages, and Latin is not spoken regularly. Consequently, Latin is a dead language. Given that Greek is also a dead language, Greek is Latin.
10. All majors are officers because all officers are enlisted, and majors are enlisted. Since no majors are squad leaders, no squad leaders are officers.

Evaluating Categorical Arguments Using Venn Diagrams

As you recall from Chapter 5, the structure of a deductive argument can be evaluated according to whether the premises support the conclusion. In a valid deductive argument, the premises support the conclusion in such a way that, if the premises are true, the conclusion must be true. Invalid arguments, by contrast, are deductive arguments in which it is possible to have a false conclusion when all premises are true. When evaluating categorical syllogisms in this chapter, we will be concerned solely with the structure of the argument, not with the actual truth or falsity of the premises. Our evaluation will determine whether the argument is valid or invalid, not whether it is sound or unsound. Here you will learn to determine the validity of categorical syllogisms using Venn diagrams. A second method for determining the validity of categorical syllogisms—namely, using rules—is presented in Chapter 13, which your instructor may or may not choose to utilize.

Both categorical claims and categorical syllogisms can be expressed in words, but their content can also be represented by overlapping circles known as **Venn diagrams**. Each of the four standard form claims—A, E, I, and O—can be represented in a unique Venn diagram, as shown on the next page:

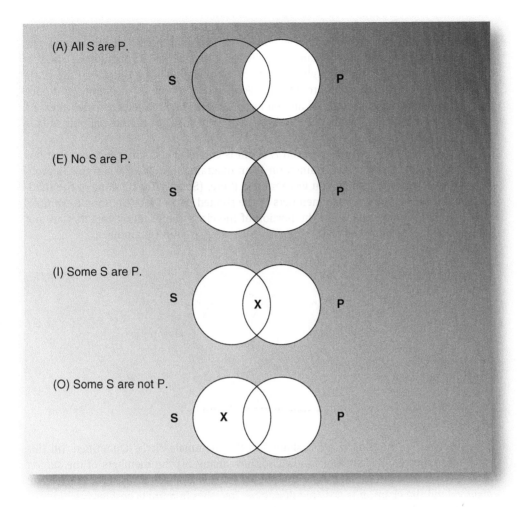

(A) All S are P.

(E) No S are P.

(I) Some S are P.

(O) Some S are not P.

Let's consider examples of each of these four types of Venn diagrams, beginning with an A claim.

(A) *All cats are mammals.*

The circle on the left represents the entire class of cats. Whatever is a cat is inside that circle. The circle on the right represents the predicate term—in this case, it is the class of mammals. Every mammal is inside that circle.

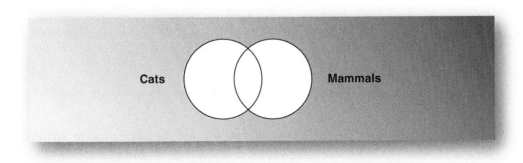

You'll notice that the circles intersect. Their intersection creates three areas with different members assigned to each. The section of the circle on the far left consists of cats that are outside of the circle of mammals—that is, cats that are not mammals. The section of the diagram on the far right consists of mammals that are outside of the circle of cats—that is, mammals that are not cats. So dogs, deer, rabbits, elephants, and mice (and many, many other mammals) are out here. The area where the two circles intersect contains those that are members of both groups. Everything in the overlapping area is both a cat and a mammal.

Now, the unique diagram for an A claim is created by *shading* the area that has no members. For those of you trained on Venn diagrams in math classes, this is probably just the opposite of how you were trained there. (Sorry!) Try thinking of the shading as eliminating any possible members in the shaded part of a circle. In our example, the A claim diagram shades out the portion of the circle representing cats that are not mammals. According to the claim, there are no cats that aren't mammals.

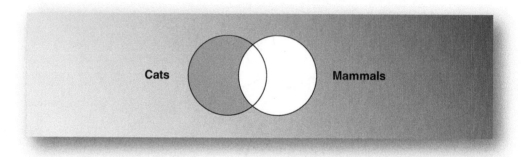

Notice that nothing at all is shaded in the mammals circle. Quantifiers (in this case, *all*) indicate only whether (and, if so, how many of) the members of the *subject* class are included or excluded from the predicate class. So, according to both the Venn diagram and the claim, it is possible that there are other mammals besides cats, but we don't know if they are more than merely logically possible. When you read this sentence back from the diagram, the shaded circle indicates the subject term. The claim is about all cats, not about all mammals. Thus, an A claim can be read back in only one direction.

Now, let's look at an example of an E claim.

(E) *No turnips are apples.*

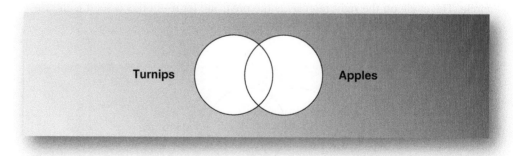

These two circles represent the subject term (on the left) and the predicate term (on the right) in the same way as the previous example. Thus, the section of the circle to the far left represents turnips that are not apples. In the middle are turnips that are also apples (since whatever is in here is inside both circles, and thus a member of both sets). The section on the far right represents apples that are not turnips. According to the claim, nothing is both turnip and apple, so shade (eliminate) that part of the diagram where the two circles overlap—right there in the middle. Two open areas remain—on the left, where turnips are not apples, and on the right, where apples are not turnips.

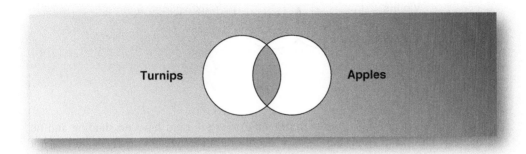

Notice that you can read this sentence back from the Venn diagram in *either* direction. You can correctly read either "No turnips are apples" or "No apples are turnips." As you saw in the first example, A claims don't work that way. They can be read in only one direction because the shaded circle has to be the subject term. E claims such as this one can be read from either direction. This distinction will be important later.

Here is the third example, an I claim.

(I) *Some violins are musical instruments.*

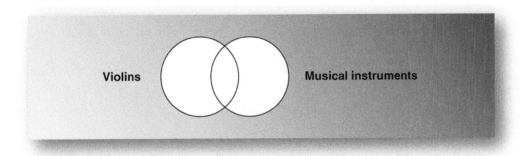

In logic, the word *some* means "at least one." Venn diagrams use an X to represent "at least one" for both particular claims—the I claim and the O claim.

 EXERCISE 6.13

Your Turn! What does the far left section of the circles represent? The middle section? The far right section?

Now, the I claim states that at least one member of the violin set is also a member of the musical instrument set. Therefore, place an X in the overlapped section.

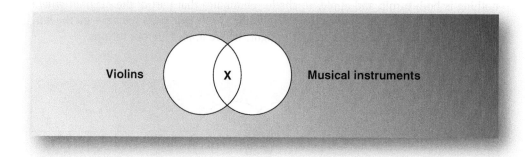

In this Venn diagram, the sections to the left and to the right have no shading and no X in them. This means that the sentence does not indicate whether there are or are not violins that exist that are not musical instruments. It also does not tell us whether there are or are not other kinds of musical instruments. Once you have determined that a categorical claim is an I claim, its Venn diagram will always look exactly the same as this one. Notice that, just as with E claims, you can read I claims back in either direction. In this case, from the diagram you can read that "Some violins are musical instruments" or that "Some musical instruments are violins." Again, this information will be important later.

EXERCISE 6.14

Your Turn! Why can the Venn diagram for "Some violins are musical instruments" also be read as "Some musical instruments are violins"?

Finally, here's an example of an O claim.

(O) *Some root beer floats are not desserts.*

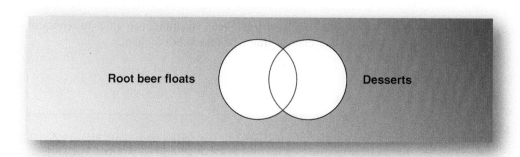

Root beer floats that are not desserts are represented in the section to the left. In the middle are root beer floats that are desserts. The section to the far right represents desserts other than root beer floats (pies, cakes, puddings, etc.). According to the claim, at least one member of the root beer float category exists that is *not* a dessert. Thus, you must place an X in the section to the far left.

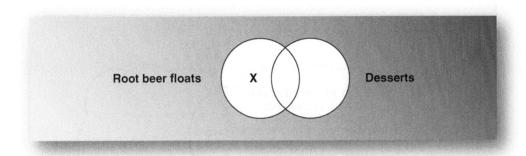

The diagram shows that at least one member of the class of root beer floats is not a member of the class of desserts. It does *not* show that there is a member of the root beer floats class that is a member of the desserts class. Thus, you have to be a bit careful with particular claims (I and O) to avoid inadvertently misrepresenting them in the Venn diagram. Since you are working with a formal language with specific meanings for each claim, your diagram must represent exactly what the claim asserts, not what you think it might imply. So here the O claim asserts only that some root beer floats are *not* desserts. It *does not imply* that some root beer floats *are* desserts. This rule applies also to I claims.

 EXERCISE 6.15

Your Turn! Explain why the Venn diagram for an O claim can be read back in only one direction.

 EXERCISE 6.16

Draw Venn diagrams for the following claims. Be sure to label the circles as plural nouns.

1. Some dining halls are not private businesses.
2. No figs are vegetables.
3. Some vegetables are not tomatoes.
4. No cell phones are GPS devices.

5. All phantoms are ghosts.
6. Some supernovae are cosmic explosions.
7. Some professors are not academic advisors.
8. No lilac bushes are presidential historians.
9. All long-haired male cats are troublesome house pets.
10. Some admissions costs are tax-deductible expenses.

Now that you have had some practice with Venn diagrams of claims, you are ready to learn how they can be used to determine the validity of a categorical syllogism. A Venn diagram for a categorical syllogism is derived from the Venn diagrams for categorical claims. However, because the argument has three categories, or classes, altogether, the Venn diagram will have three overlapping circles, one for each category.

Draw all of your Venn diagrams using the following format: The circle at the top represents the middle term of the argument; the bottom left circle represents the minor term; the bottom right circle represents the major term. To help explain what the diagram represents, we have inserted numbers into each section; however, Venn diagrams themselves do not use numbers. Let's look again at the earlier example.

> *All cats are mammals.*
> <u>*All mammals are animals.*</u>
> *All cats are animals.*

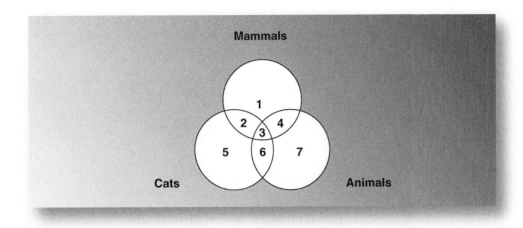

First, what does each section represent? Section 1 represents mammals that are not cats and not animals; section 2 represents cats that are mammals, but not animals.

 EXERCISE 6.17

Your Turn!   Determine what is represented in each of the remaining sections.

Section 3: _____ that are _____ and _____.
Section 4: _____ that are _____, but not _____.
Section 5: _____ that are not _____ and not _____.
Section 6: _____ that are _____, but not _____.
Section 7: _____ that are not _____ and not _____.

To test a categorical syllogism for validity, first draw the Venn diagram for each of the two premises, one at a time. If the argument is valid, the conclusion will already be shown in the Venn diagrams for the premises. You don't need to shade or place an X for the conclusion; just shade or show X's for premises. Since the shading may influence where X's are located, always begin with a premise that is universal, when one exists.

In our example, both premises are A claims (as is the conclusion), so you will only be shading. In that case, begin with the first premise. At first, you should focus solely on the two circles representing the two categories from this premise. In the first premise, because *cats* is the subject term, you will shade that circle exactly as you would for any standard A claim.

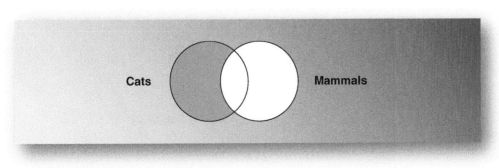

The shaded area above corresponds to sections 5 and 6 in the Venn diagram of the argument. Note that, since *three* circles are intersecting, you will always shade *two* sections. The result will be identical to the standard A claim Venn diagram.

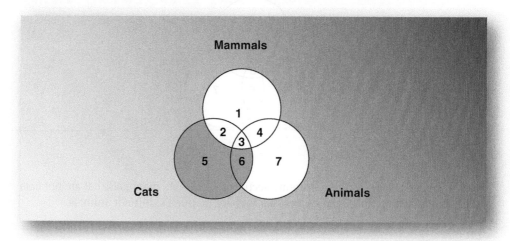

Next, draw the second premise: All mammals are animals. Since this, too, is an A claim, the subject term circle is again shaded.

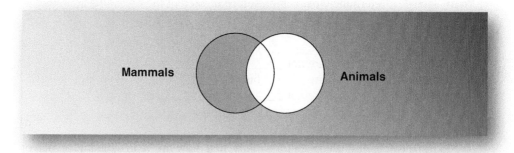

Now, however, the two circles involved are the top one (showing *mammals*) and the bottom right one (showing *animals*). So, since the circle for *mammals* is the subject term of this A claim, shade sections 1 and 2. Compare that drawing with the standard form A claim of those two terms. Here is the second premise combined with the first.

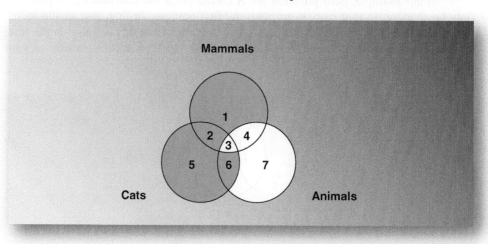

That's all the drawing you do. If the argument is valid, the conclusion will already be represented in the diagram. So, in this case, are all cats within the circle of animals? The answer is yes, since the only area of the cats circle not shaded is section 3, which is also part of the animal circle. Thus, the conclusion was necessitated by the premises, and that means the argument is *valid*. So long as the argument retains this formal structure, it will be impossible for both premises to be true and the conclusion to be false—no matter what specific terms occupy the major, minor, and middle term positions.

Let's try another example, this time involving a particular claim among the premises.

Some P are M.
All M are S.
Some S are P.

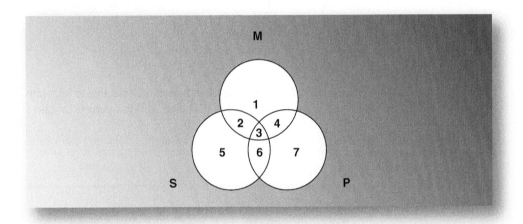

Since the first premise is particular, not universal, begin diagramming the second premise. *Shading always goes first.* When you apply the shading for the second premise, you shade all of the M circle outside of S. That would be sections 1 and 4.

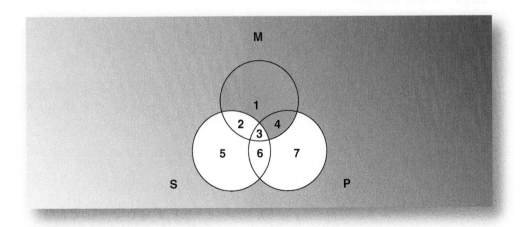

Look next at the first premise. Since this is a particular affirmative claim, you will be applying an X to the area where P and M overlap. Originally, before you shaded the

M circle in sections 1 and 4, two areas were overlapping P and M—sections 3 and 4. But now that 4 is shaded, that section is eliminated. Nothing can occupy that section. The only overlapping area remaining is section 3. Place an X inside that section, and check the argument for validity.

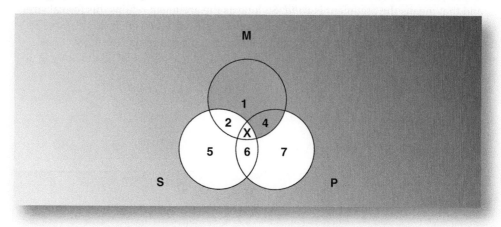

Is the conclusion already shown? Yes, because the conclusion claims that at least one S is also in P. And the X in section 3 is both in S and in P. Therefore, this argument is valid.

 EXERCISE 6.18

Your Turn!   Look back at the argument presented at the start of this chapter. Use a Venn diagram to determine whether the argument is valid or invalid.

Determining where to place an X in your diagram can often be challenging. Let's consider another example.

No P are M.
Some S are not M.
Some S are not P.

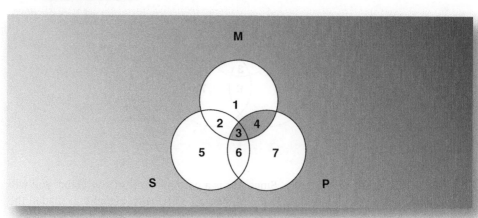

Do the shading first—sections 3 and 4 are shaded from the first premise. The shading must match the Venn diagram for the universal negative, an E claim. Next, diagram the second premise, a particular negative, by placing an X *inside* the S circle, but *outside* of the M circle. Two sections are available—5 and 6. Since the claim doesn't indicate whether the X belongs in 5 exclusively or in 6 exclusively, you must show it *between* the two sections. That is, draw the X *on the line* that separates sections 5 and 6.

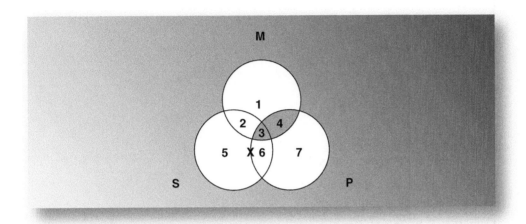

With the diagramming complete, check whether the conclusion is already represented in the drawing. In this case, an X is inside S (there *is* an S), but with the X on the line, it's unclear whether it is outside of P or not. According to this diagram, some S might be P or might not be P; you cannot tell. To be valid, the X would have to be *in* section 2 or 5. Since it isn't in either of those sections, the conclusion is *not* demonstrated in the drawing, and, thus, the argument is invalid.

How to Draw Venn Diagrams

Step 1: State the argument as a standard form categorical syllogism.

Step 2: Draw and label three intersecting circles.

Step 3: Shade the sections to represent the universal premises.

Step 4: Place an X in the section or on the line to represent any particular premises.

Step 5: Determine validity by checking whether the conclusion is represented in the diagram.

 **EXERCISE 6.19**

Draw Venn diagrams and determine the validity of the following arguments.

1. All S are M.
   All P are M.
   All S are P.

2. No S are M.
   <u>All P are M.</u>
   No S are P.

3. All S are M.
   <u>All M are P.</u>
   All S are P.

4. Some P are M.
   <u>All M are S.</u>
   Some S are P.

5. No M are P.
   <u>Some M are not S.</u>
   Some S are not P.

6. No emeralds are gems.
   <u>Some rubies are gems.</u>
   Some rubies are not emeralds.

7. Some legumes are pumpkins.
   <u>Some legumes are squash.</u>
   Some pumpkins are squash.

8. All executives are workaholics.
   <u>No workaholics can relax.</u>
   No executives can relax.

9. All carrots are nutritious snacks.
   <u>No fast food is a carrot.</u>
   No fast food is a nutritious snack.

10. All quintuplets are hungry mouths to feed.
    <u>All hungry mouths to feed are things to be avoided.</u>
    All quintuplets are things to be avoided.

11. Some lizards are poisonous.
    <u>Anything that is poisonous should be avoided.</u>
    Some lizards should be avoided.

12. All vine-ripened tomatoes require extra care at the store.
    <u>Some things that require extra care at the store need to be expensive.</u>
    Some vine-ripened tomatoes need to be expensive.

13. Some squirrels are not animals.
    <u>Some penguins are not animals.</u>
    No squirrels are penguins.

14. All squirrels are animals.
    <u>No penguins are animals.</u>
    No penguins are squirrels.

15. All kangaroos are Australian.
    <u>Some turtles are not Australian.</u>
    Some turtles are not kangaroos.

16. All kangaroos are Australian.
    Some turtles are not kangaroos.
    Some turtles are not Australian.

17. Some Danes speak English.
    All Northern Europeans speak English.
    All Northern Europeans are Danes.

18. No principals are teachers.
    No teachers are fifth-graders.
    No principals are fifth-graders.

19. All joules are units of work.
    No units of work are measurements.
    No joules are measurements.

20. All computer hackers who cause damage deserve to be prosecuted.
    Some who deserve to be prosecuted must be punished.
    Some computer hackers who cause damage must be punished.

EXERCISE 6.20

Rewrite each argument as a standard form categorical syllogism. Then draw a
Venn diagram, and determine the validity of the argument.

1. All presidents are farmers, and no farmers are senators. Thus, some presidents
   are not senators.
2. Since all reliefs are sculptures and a few reliefs are art forms, some art forms
   are sculptures.
3. All soccer players are athletes, since all athletes are baseball players and no
   baseball players are soccer players.
4. Some ants are insects. Thus, no ants are caterpillars given that some caterpillars are not insects.
5. Only vegetarians are farmers because no vegetarians are animal breeders and
   the only farmers are animal breeders.
6. If you passed geology, then you passed a science class. And if you passed a
   science class, then you have qualified for honors. Consequently, if you passed
   geology, then you qualified for honors.
7. Wherever there are turtles there are toads. Accordingly, since toads exist wherever there are snails, wherever there are snails there are turtles.
8. Because Socrates is not a man and only mortals are men, Socrates is not
   mortal.
9. Any senator is corruptible. So no senators are liars, as some liars are
   corruptible.
10. Some students take critical thinking, and some students are math majors. So
    some people who take critical thinking are math majors.
11. Anyone who reads philosophy books will immediately get smarter. Some
    people who get smarter will become President of the United States. So anyone
    who reads philosophy books will become President of the United States.

12. Mascots are the only animals allowed in the gym. Thus, only mascots are nuisances, since the only animals allowed in the gym are nuisances.

13. This is not the best omelet ever cooked because the best omelet ever cooked would not contain anchovies and this omelet contains anchovies.

14. No dog trainers are small business owners. This is because no small business owners are graduates of engineering programs at MIT and no dog trainers are graduates of engineering programs at MIT.

15. Every war crime is beyond any kind of moral justification. It demeans innocent humans, and anything that demeans innocent humans is beyond any kind of moral justification.

16. None of the summer camps on campus are accepting new students, and some of the summer camps at the high schools are not accepting new students either. So some of the summer camps at the high schools are also summer camps on campus.

17. Given that everybody on stage is an understudy, and all understudies are tap dancers, everyone on stage dances tap.

18. Avatars are sacred figures, and shamans are, too. So avatars are shamans.

19. Each stoic is a skeptic, and no stoic is a professor. Therefore, no skeptic is a professor.

20. Every bike racer is a competitor, and no competitor takes steroids, since that would be illegal. Therefore, no bike racers take steroids.

PUTTING IT ALL TOGETHER: Writing a Critical Précis of a Categorical Argument

In Chapters 2, 3, and 4, you learned how to recognize and analyze arguments and to present a Critical Précis with an argument diagram. In Chapter 5, you also learned how to distinguish among different kinds of arguments. Now that you can analyze and evaluate categorical syllogisms, you can put all of these skills together by adding categorical argument evaluation to the Critical Précis assignments.

Directions for a Critical Précis of a Categorical Argument
In *paragraph form*, use complete sentences and proper English grammar and spelling to do the following:

Step 1: Identify the passage.
▶ Completely and correctly identify the author and the source (whenever such information is given).
▶ If the passage contains an argument, identify it as such. Then move to Step 2.
▶ If the passage does not contain an argument, identify it as a nonargument. Then specify which feature of an argument is lacking.

Step 2: Analyze the argument.
▶ Clearly and completely identify the issue, conclusion, and premise or premises *in that order*.
▶ If the passage is a *multiple argument*, write *separate paragraphs* to analyze each separate argument.

Step 3: Diagram the argument.
▶ Verify that the diagram is consistent with your Critical Précis.

Step 4: Identify the kind of argument.
▶ If the argument is deductive, identify it as a categorical argument or a truth-functional argument.
▶ If the argument is inductive, identify it as an inductive generalization, an analogical argument, or a causal argument.

Step 5: Evaluate the argument.
▶ If the argument is categorical, state the syllogism in standard form, and *demonstrate* whether the argument is valid or invalid using a Venn diagram.

Let's work through a couple of examples to demonstrate a proper Critical Précis of a categorical argument. Consider the following passage.

> *Only that which science studies is real. Science cannot study consciousness. So consciousness is not real.*—Mary Midgley, *Science and Poetry*

The first step is to determine whether the passage contains an argument. Since the conclusion indicated by *so* is derived by making an inference from the two preceding claims, this passage contains an argument. Next, you should diagram the argument. Are the premises linked or convergent? Since the conclusion requires two terms, *consciousness* and *real thing*, the premises must be linked. Each premise delivers only one of the two required terms to the conclusion. Now, you can draw the argument diagram and write the analysis of the argument.

① *Only that which science studies is real*. ② *Science cannot study consciousness*. So ③ *consciousness is not real*.

This passage from Mary Midgley's book *Science and Poetry* contains an argument. The issue is whether consciousness is real. The conclusion is that consciousness is not real. The first premise is that only that which science studies is real. The second premise is that science cannot study consciousness.

All that remains is to evaluate the argument, something you do in a second paragraph. Since all of the claims are categorical claims and the argument is deductive, you should be able to recognize the argument as a categorical syllogism. That means that in the second paragraph you will need to identify the type of argument and prove it valid or invalid using a properly labeled Venn diagram. Remember, however, that you must first set up the argument in standard form.

This is a deductive categorical argument. The standard form of the argument is as follows:

All subjects that are real are subjects studied by science.
No subjects identical to consciousness are subjects studied by science.
No subjects identical to consciousness are subjects that are real.

The following Venn diagram demonstrates that the argument is valid:

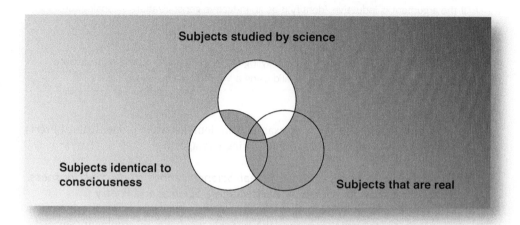

Let's consider a more complex example.

Given that sensitive people are self-reflective and all highly intelligent persons are sensitive, it's clear that all highly intelligent people are self-reflective. Thus, since some classical musicians are self-reflective, I'm moved to conclude that some classical musicians are highly intelligent.—Music critic

Again, our first task is to determine whether this passage contains an argument. Since it presents a conclusion drawn from premises, it is an argument. And since the argument relates categories of things to support the conclusion, it is a categorical argument. Moreover, given that one argument clearly precedes the conclusion indicator *thus* in the second sentence, this passage contains a chain argument.

The next step is to determine the structure of this multiple argument, and that is best done with an argument diagram.

 EXERCISE 6.21

Your Turn!   Underline and number each claim in the argument above.

Setting the indicator words out with the claim numbers, as you learned in Chapter 4, will make diagramming this argument much easier.

Given that ① *and* ②, *it's clear that* ③. *Thus, since* ④, *I'm moved to conclude* ⑤.

From this, we can see that claims ① and ② support claim ③. The argument then moves from claim ④ to support ⑤. Are ① and ② linked or convergent? Since the conclusion requires two terms and each premise contributes only one—namely, *highly intelligent people* and *self-reflective people*—the premises are linked. We can also determine that claim ④ must be linked with claim ③ to support the conclusion, claim ⑤, for the same reason.

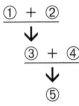

$$
\begin{array}{c}
① + ② \\
\downarrow \\
\underline{③ + ④} \\
\downarrow \\
⑤
\end{array}
$$

Now, you can write the analysis of the argument. The first paragraph will contain the main argument, and the subargument will be written in the second paragraph.

> **This passage from a music critic contains an argument. The issue is whether some classical musicians are highly intelligent. The conclusion is that some classical musicians are highly intelligent. The first premise is that all highly intelligent people are self-reflective. The second premise is that some classical musicians are self-reflective.**
> **This passage contains a subargument. The intermediate conclusion is that all highly intelligent people are self-reflective. The first premise is that sensitive people are self-reflective. The second premise is that all highly intelligent people are sensitive.**

The evaluation of the argument is all that remains to be done. Since each of the two arguments is deductive and all of the claims are categorical, this chain argument consists of two deductive categorical syllogisms. You will evaluate only the main argument, so that must be written in standard form.

> **This is a deductive categorical argument. The standard form of the argument is as follows:**
>
> **All highly intelligent people are self-reflective people.**
> **Some classical musicians are self-reflective people.**
> **Some classical musicians are highly intelligent people.**

The following Venn diagram demonstrates that the argument is invalid.

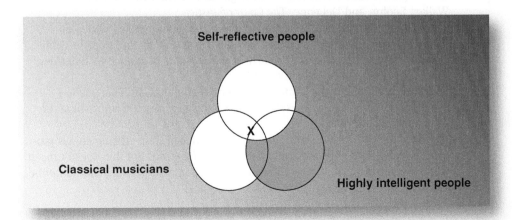

EXERCISE 6.22

Write a Critical Précis for the following passages. Include an argument diagram and an identification of the argument type when appropriate, and evaluate any categorical arguments using a Venn diagram.

1. Anything that is built on conjecture shouldn't be called a "science," because conjecture can't produce knowledge, and science properly so-called should consist entirely of knowledge.—Thomas Reid, *Essays on the Intellectual Powers of Man*

2. If an engaged couple knows or suspects that there may be diseases, such as hemophilia, cystic fibrosis, sickle-cell anemia, Down syndrome, fragile X syndrome, or Tay-Sachs disease in their family genetic makeup, they can seek genetic counseling before marriage.—Rosalind Charlesworth, *Understanding Child Development*

3. You can be certain that some assignments that reinforce writing skills involve laboratory experiments. This is because some of the homework assignments in physics reinforce writing skills, and some homework assignments in physics involve laboratory experiments.—Physics instructor

4. Coastal area cat owners flushing parasite-laden cat feces down the toilet has resulted in a decrease in the number of California's sea otters. This is because the number of otters has been decreasing in recent years, and the amount of parasites in the ocean water near the coast has increased—Miller and Spoolman, *Living in the Environment*

5. We must be familiar with the kinds of rocks in Earth's crust, what they are composed of, how they form, and what they tell us about prehistoric events. As a starting point, we can say that rocks are composed of minerals, which are naturally occurring, inorganic, crystalline solids, with a narrowly defined chemical composition and distinctive physical properties. So rocks are made up of naturally occurring, inorganic, crystalline solids.—Wicander and Monroe, *Historical Geology: Evolution of Earth and Life Through Time*

6. The authors of *The Bell Curve* argue that there are basic inherited differences in intelligence between races. We reject that argument. If there are no scientifically valid racial differences, the basic argument of *The Bell Curve* falls apart. And there are no scientifically valid racial differences, for the vast majority of anthropologists and sociologists reject the idea of separate races as biological entities. Thus, the basic argument of *The Bell Curve* falls apart.—Walker, Spohn, and DeLeone, *The Color of Justice*

7. All indefinite pronouns refer to unnamed or unknown people, places, or things. *Everyone* refers to unnamed people, because *everyone* is used to indicate any group of people. So it clearly is an indefinite pronoun.—VanderMey, Meyer, Van Rys, and Sebranek, *COMP*

8. I think of good writing being done in a very deliberate way. That's why I use a dip pen. It's to slow myself down and to keep myself from rushing the writing.—Shelby Foote

9. Defenders of advertising claim that, despite criticisms, advertising enjoys protection under the First Amendment as a form of speech. But this doesn't mean that all advertising should be allowed. Indeed, some advertising should *not* be

allowed because no allowable speech has bad social consequences, and some advertising has bad social consequences.—Shaw and Berry, *Moral Issues in Business*

10. When a 1989 Gallup Poll asked 1,249 adults to compare contemporary youth to those of 20 years ago, topping the list were the words "Selfish" (81 percent), "Materialistic" (79 percent), and "Reckless" (73 percent). These descriptors and the other data cited in the study are diametrically opposed to how teens actually view themselves. A survey of 1,015 high school students cited in the study found that the values teens hold dear are "being honest" (8.6 on a 10-point scale), "working hard" (8.4), "being a good student" (7.9), and "giving time to help others" (7.6).—Kent Baxter, "(Re)inventing Adolescence"

CHAPTER REVIEW QUESTIONS

1. What are the four types of standard form categorical claims?
2. How do you determine the quality and quantity of a categorical claim?
3. How do you translate a categorical claim into standard form?
4. How do you find the major, minor, and middle terms in a categorical syllogism?
5. When drawing a Venn diagram for a syllogism that has one particular premise and one universal premise, which do you draw first? Why?
6. How does a Venn diagram show that an argument is valid or invalid?

ONE STEP FURTHER

Violent and abusive behavior in intimate relationships may gain societal acceptance when glamorized and normalized in popular culture. For example, according to an article in the *Journal of Women's Health*, the best-selling novel *Fifty Shades of Grey* condones intimate partner violence by romanticizing and eroticizing an abusive relationship. Researchers from The Ohio State University analyzed the novel to look for patterns consistent with definitions of interpersonal violence and associated reactions known to occur in abused women. Consider the following summary of their findings.

The relationship between Anastasia and Christian fits the Centers for Disease Control and Prevention's definition of "intimate partner violence." Their interactions include stalking, intimidation, and isolation, and each of these characteristics meets the CDC's definition of intimate partner violence.

1. Convert the above argument into a standard form syllogism.
2. Then use a Venn diagram to evaluate the argument.

3. Review the Centers for Disease Control and Prevention's definition of intimate partner violence at http://www.cdc.gov/violenceprevention/intimatepartnerviolence/definitions.html. Can you think of other examples from popular culture that normalize or romanticize violence in relationships? Do you think that such representations are harmful or harmless? Why?

This advertisement is trying to influence you. What messages are communicated by the image?

Image Courtesy of The Advertising Archives

Evaluating Truth–Functional Arguments

Suppose that you are studying for an astronomy exam with your classmates and a debate ensues over how many planets are in our solar system: Some of your peers insist that there are nine planets, while others insist that there are only eight. One of the latter presents the following argument.

> *Look, everyone. Pluto is* not *a planet! There are three main conditions for an object to be considered a "planet": The object must be in orbit around the sun,*

This illustration shows the Pluto system from the surface of a moon-like object. Pluto is the large body at center right. Charon, the system's only confirmed moon, is the smaller round mass to the right of Pluto.

the object must be massive enough to be a sphere by its own gravitational force, and it must have "cleared the neighborhood" around its orbit. Since Pluto has not "cleared the neighborhood" around its orbit, Pluto can't be a planet.

You may have already recognized this as a deductive truth-functional argument, since you learned how to distinguish among different kinds of arguments in Chapter 5. But is it a *good* argument? Recall from Chapter 5 that the first step in evaluating an argument is to consider whether the premises support the conclusion as intended. Since this is a deductive argument, you should use the language of validity to evaluate its structure. A **valid deductive argument** is one in which the conclusion must be true if the premises are true. Deductive arguments that fail to support the conclusion as intended are called invalid arguments. In this chapter, you will learn a special technique for evaluating the validity of truth-functional arguments called the Truth Table Method. This technique allows you to present a table of all the possible truth-value outcomes for each premise and conclusion in the argument so that you can determine whether the truth of the premises guarantees the truth of the conclusion. To use this method, you must first learn how to translate truth-functional claims into symbolic form and how to determine the truth-values of these claims.

LEARNING OUTCOMES

In this chapter, you will learn how to evaluate truth-functional arguments by:

▶ Translating truth-functional claims into symbolic form,
▶ Applying truth-functional definitions to claims,
▶ Using a truth table to determine whether a truth-functional argument is valid, and
▶ Writing a Critical Précis of a truth-functional argument.

Translating Truth-Functional Claims

In Chapter 5, you learned that **truth-functional arguments** are deductive arguments containing truth-functional claims. You also learned that there are five types of truth-functional claims: simple claims, negations, conjunctions, disjunctions, and conditionals. To translate these claims into symbolic form, you should use a capital letter to represent each simple claim and a symbol to represent each of the four operators—*not, and, or, if… then…*—that can join simple claims.

A claim, you should remember from Chapter 2, is a statement that has truth-value; that is, it may be true or false. In truth-functional logic, the smallest unit having truth-value is called a **simple claim**. The following two sentences express the same simple claim because they express the same meaning.

> *The Mona Lisa was painted by Rembrandt.*
> *Rembrandt painted the Mona Lisa.*

Although you can use any symbol you wish, it is general practice to translate each simple claim by using a letter of the alphabet related to the content of the claim. For example, you might translate both of the above claims as R. When translating simple claims, make sure that whatever symbol you assign to a simple claim is used consistently to represent that claim and that no single symbol is used to represent more than one simple claim in a given passage.

> **Hint!**
> At a later point in the chapter, we will use the letters X and Y to represent simple claims with unknown content.

When simple claims are combined with a logical operator, they form compound claims. Logical operators should be translated using agreed-upon symbols. Although there are several in common usage, the following are used in this book.

Compound Claim	Operator	Symbol
Negation	not	~
Conjunction	and	•
Disjunction	or	∨
Conditional	if…then…	⊃

A **negation** is a compound claim which modifies another claim with the word *not* or its equivalent. For example, the following negations express the same compound claim.

> *The lightbulb was not invented by Henry Ford.*
> *It is not the case that the lightbulb was invented by Henry Ford.*

In both cases, the simple claim is "The lightbulb was invented by Henry Ford," which is modified by the logical operator *not*. To translate the negation above, you should first choose a letter to symbolize the simple claim and then apply the operator for *not* to that simple claim. Using the letter I to represent "The lightbulb was invented by Henry Ford," the negation would then be translated as follows:

~ I

> **Hint!**
> Whenever you encounter a claim that denies a negation, as in "It is not the case that the lightbulb was not invented by Henry Ford," you may translate the claim as either ~ (~ I) or I. The two translations are equivalent.

A **conjunction** joins together two claims with the word *and* or its logical equivalent (such as *but* or *yet*) to form a compound claim. Thus, the following conjunctions express the same compound claim.

The strawberries are organic, and the blueberries are overpriced.
The strawberries are organic, but the blueberries are overpriced.
The strawberries are organic, yet the blueberries are overpriced.

In these sentences, the two simple claims are "The strawberries are organic" and "The blueberries are overpriced," and they are modified by the logical operator *and*. To translate the conjunction above, you should first choose a letter to symbolize each simple claim and then apply the operator for *and* to join them. Using the letter S to represent "The strawberries are organic" and B to represent "The blueberries are overpriced," the conjunction would then be translated as follows:

S • B

EXERCISE 7.1

Your Turn!   Does the following sentence express the same meaning as the above conjunction? If so, why? If not, why not?

The blueberries are overpriced, and the strawberries are organic.

A **disjunction** is a compound claim that joins together two claims with the word *or* or its equivalent. The following disjunctions express the same compound claim.

Baton Rouge is located in Louisiana or Arkansas.
Either Baton Rouge is located in Louisiana, or Baton Rouge is located in Arkansas.
Baton Rouge is located in Arkansas, or Baton Rouge is located in Louisiana.

Notice that the meaning of the disjunction is not changed when the order of the simple claims is reversed. To translate the disjunction above, you should first choose a letter to symbolize each simple claim and then apply the operator for *or* to join them. Using the letter A to represent "Baton Rouge is located in Arkansas" and L to represent "Baton Rouge is located in Louisiana," the disjunction would then be translated as follows:

A ∨ L

EXERCISE 7.2

Your Turn!   Why shouldn't you translate the compound claim "Baton Rouge is located in Arkansas, or Baton Rouge is located in Louisiana" as B ∨ B?

A **conditional** joins together two claims with the phrase *if...then...* or its equivalent. For example, each of the following compound claims is a conditional.

If you are a nurse, then you passed an anatomy course.
You are a nurse only if you passed an anatomy course.
You passed an anatomy course if you are a nurse.

The translation of conditionals deserves special attention because the two simple claims composing the conditional play different roles. In what we will call standard form—*if...then...*—the claim following the word *if* is called the **antecedent**, and the claim following the word *then* is called the **consequent**.

If _____, then _____.
     antecedent   **consequent**

EXERCISE 7.3

To translate a conditional, you should first choose a letter to symbolize each simple claim and then use the symbol ⊃ to join them. Moreover, the antecedent in the conditional should always be placed before the ⊃, and the consequent should always be place after it. So, using N to represent "You are a nurse" and P to represent "You passed an anatomy course," the conditional "If you are a nurse, then you passed an anatomy course" would be translated as follows:

N ⊃ P

simple claims in conditionals does. Notice that the two conditional claims below do not express the same claim; the first is true, but the second is false.

If you are a chemistry major, then you are a college student.
If you are a college student, then you are a chemistry major.

As you learned previously, not every conditional is presented in standard form. Conditional claims may be expressed using the phrases *...only if...* and *...if...* rather than using the *if...then...* form. To translate these claims properly, you must determine which simple claim is the antecedent and which is the consequent. The easiest way to do that is to commit their structures to memory.

_____ *only if* _____.
antecedent   **consequent**

_____ *if* _____.
consequent   **antecedent**

 EXERCISE 7.4

Your Turn!   Underline each simple claim in the following conditionals. Then properly label the antecedent and consequent in each claim.

You are a nurse only if you passed an anatomy course.
You passed an anatomy course if you are a nurse.

Although the antecedent comes first when the conditional claim is in the *if...then...* or the *...only if...* sentence structure, it does not come first in the *...if...* structure. Nevertheless, when translating the conditional into symbolic form, the symbol for the antecedent must always be placed before the ⊃, and the symbol for the consequent must always be placed after it. For example, using N to represent "You are a nurse" and P to represent "You passed an anatomy course," the conditional "You passed an anatomy course if you are a nurse" would be translated as follows:

N ⊃ P

Notice that, although the consequent appears before the antecedent in the sentence, the symbol for the antecedent is presented before the ⊃, not after it.

EXERCISE 7.5

Your Turn!   Why should the conditionals "It is raining (R) only if there are clouds in the sky (C)" and "There are clouds in the sky (C) if it is raining (R)" both be translated as R ⊃ C?

Hint!
Do not confuse conditional claims with causal claims. Although causal claims may be expressed as conditional claims, not all conditional claims express a causal connection between two events. Instead, conditional claims express a *logical relationship* between the antecedent and consequent.

EXERCISE 7.6

Designate a letter to represent each simple claim. Then translate each of the following truth-functional claims into symbolic form.

1. People often think that all claims are either facts or opinions.
2. If John continues to look haggard, then someone must arrange to take him to the University Health Center to find out what's wrong.
3. The player on the field appears to be injured, and the team doctor has been called to the scene.
4. Kestrels are not common in this part of the country.
5. In an automobile accident, the insurance companies are interested in discovering who is liable or who has the money to pay.
6. Loose clothing is more comfortable in hot weather, but I have trouble finding loose clothing that is attractive.
7. All students on campus have access to either a desktop computer or a laptop computer.
8. The movie is unsuitable for children unless it has a G rating.
9. If a bear is in the house, then a crocodile is in the yard.
10. Either the car decelerates, or the motor is getting enough gasoline.
11. The car does not decelerate.
12. You definitely do not have a bronchial infection.
13. Llamas are South American ruminants, and bison are North American bovine mammals.
14. If the President declares these prairies a national park, then it will be clear that he is committed to preserving the habitat of the creatures that live here.
15. Primroses are hearty in our climate only if they are protected from the gophers.
16. Liu isn't usually considered an opportunist, yet he took advantage of his opponent's injury to win.
17. You can graduate from this university only if you pass the logical reasoning class.
18. If the regiment is split into two battalions, it will be more flexible.
19. An appraisal is required for tax purposes if a single donated item is valued at $500.
20. The flight will be smooth unless we encounter turbulence.

Compound claims often contain more than one operator, and when they do, your translation must specify which operations apply to which claims in order to retain the original claim's meaning. Parentheses signal that an operator located inside them combines only those claims that accompany it. Other punctuation symbols such as brackets and braces work similarly, indicating that the operator modifies only the claims located inside them. An operator outside of any punctuation symbols is the **main operator**. The key to using proper punctuation is identifying the main operator of the compound claim; it applies to the entire claim, not just to some of the parts of the claim.

Consider the following example.

If you do not go to the party with me, then I will find someone else who will.

To translate this claim, let's use G to symbolize the simple claim "You go to the party with me" and F to symbolize the simple claim "I will find someone else who will go to the party with me." Because the claim contains two operators—*not* and *if...then...*—we will use ~ and ⊃ to translate it.

Which of the following two translations accurately reflects the meaning of the compound claim?

~ G ⊃ F
~ (G ⊃ F)

In the first translation above, the main operator is the conditional; the antecedent is ~ G, and the consequent is F. In the second translation, the main operator is the negation; the conditional inside the parentheses, G ⊃ F, is negated. Only the first accurately translates the original compound claim. Notice that the operator *not* is located within the antecedent.

If <u>you do not go to the party with me</u>, then <u>I will find someone else who will</u>.
    antecedent   **consequent**

The second translation would represent the following sentence.

*It's not the case that, if <u>you go to the party with me</u>, then <u>I will find some-
one else who will</u>.*   **antecedent**   **consequent**

When the operator *not* is located outside the conditional, it modifies the entire conditional, not just the antecedent.

 EXERCISE 7.7

Your Turn!   Translate the following compound claim into symbolic form.

It is not the case that we live in Canada and we live in South America.

Let's look at another example of a sentence with multiple operators.

*If the defendant is an "enemy combatant," then he is either an enemy
soldier or a terrorist.*

To translate this claim, first choose a symbol for each simple claim. Let's make D represent "The defendant is an 'enemy combatant,'" S represent "The defendant is an enemy soldier," and T represent "The defendant is a terrorist." Next, translate the parts of the sentence.

D ⊃ S ∨ T

Since we have multiple operators, we must use parentheses to indicate whether the main operator is the conditional or the disjunction. Look back at the original sentence. Notice that the disjunction is contained within the consequent because it appears following the word *then*.

> If <u>the defendant is an "enemy combatant,"</u> then <u>he is either an enemy soldier or a terrorist</u>.
>   **antecedent**   **consequent**

The proper translation of the sentence is as follows:

D ⊃ (S ∨ T)

This translation shows that the disjunction applies only to the claims inside the parentheses and that the main operator of the compound claim is the conditional.

 EXERCISE 7.8

Your Turn! How would you translate the following compound claim?

Either the defendant is an "enemy combatant" only if he is an enemy soldier, or the defendant is a terrorist.

Some of the trickiest claims to translate are *neither...nor...* claims. For example,

Your new pet is neither a llama nor a bison.

Part of what is tricky about claims like these is that they can be translated in two ways depending on how you use the parentheses: They can be translated as a conjunction modifying two negations, and they can be translated as a negation modifying a disjunction.

~ L • ~ B
~ (L ∨ B)

The first translation can be expressed as follows:

Your new pet is not a llama, and your new pet is not a bison.

The second translation can be expressed as follows:

It is not true that your new pet is either a llama or a bison.

Although these may seem, at first, to be different claims, they express the same claim. What makes this possible is a rule called **DeMorgan's Law**, symbolized as:

$$\sim (X \vee Y) = \sim X \bullet \sim Y$$

Notice that when the negation is assigned to each simple claim, the claim must be translated as a conjunction. This is because when you say, "It is false that X or Y," you mean that both are false. Similarly, when a conjunction is denied, as in "It is false that X and Y," what is meant is that at least one of them is false. In other words, DeMorgan's Law also tells us that:

$$\sim (X \bullet Y) = \sim X \vee \sim Y$$

 EXERCISE 7.9

Your Turn! Apply DeMorgan's Law to the claim in Exercise 7.7.

 EXERCISE 7.10

Identify the main operator of each of the following compound claims.

1. $A \vee \sim B$
2. $\sim (C \bullet D)$
3. $E \vee (F \bullet G)$
4. $\sim (H \supset I) \vee J$
5. $(\sim K \bullet L) \supset M$
6. $N \supset \sim (O \vee P)$
7. $(Q \bullet R) \vee \sim S$
8. $T \bullet (U \supset V)$
9. $(W \vee \sim X) \bullet (Y \vee Z)$
10. $\sim [A \bullet (B \supset C)]$

 EXERCISE 7.11

Designate a letter to represent each simple claim. Then translate each of the following compound claims into symbolic form using proper punctuation. Finally, identify the main operator of the compound claim.

1. You do not feel safe in the dark, yet your mission is to go into that cave.
2. It is not the case that, if Earth is the center of the universe, then all professional astronomers are totally mistaken.

3. If the pet owner is not extremely consistent, housebreaking a new kitten can be difficult.
4. It is not the case that my car will start after a rainstorm only if I dry off the battery connections.
5. Toyota's new hybrid car gets excellent gas mileage and is available with either an automatic or a manual transmission.
6. You can't register your car if you don't pass the smog inspection.
7. It is not the case that you can have a successful business and you can hire dishonest employees.
8. You won't have a successful business unless you hire hard-working employees.
9. We can either go out to dinner or go to the movies if you want to go out tonight.
10. A crocodile is neither in the yard nor in the house.
11. Children are strong readers and have good math skills only if they attend preschool.
12. It's not the case that lawyers are ethical only if their firms are highly regulated.
13. If the drought continues, then farmers will lose their crops, and food prices will rise.
14. If you finish all of your dinner, then you won't have room for dessert.
15. Either limits must be placed on health-care costs, or health care will become more expensive and insurance premiums will rise.

© Tom Grundy/Shutterstock.com

Without punctuation, the meaning of this sign could be misinterpreted.

Applying Truth-Functional Definitions

In the remaining sections of this chapter, you will learn how to determine whether a truth-functional argument is valid or invalid using the Truth Table Method. A second method for evaluating truth-functional arguments, the Short-Cut Method, is presented in Chapter 14, which your instructor may or may not choose to utilize. To use either of these techniques, you must commit to memory the following **truth-functional definitions** for negation, conjunction, disjunction, and conditional. These definitions specify when a particular compound claim is true and when it is false. We will discuss each definition individually, starting with negation.

When any claim is negated, the truth-value of the negation will be the opposite value of the simple claim. We can represent this definition of negation in the truth table below, using X to refer to any simple claim and ~ to refer to the operation of negation.

$$\begin{array}{c c}
\sim & X \\
\hline
\mathbf{F} & T \\
\mathbf{T} & F
\end{array}$$

Since a negation contains one simple claim, there are two possible truth-value combinations for negation: Either X is true, or it is false. These possible values are placed in a column directly below the X. When that simple claim, X, is negated, its truth-value changes to its opposite value. That is, when X is true, ~ X is false, and when X is false, ~ X is true. These truth-values are placed directly below the ~ to indicate the truth-value once the operation has been performed. We can apply this definition to any negation to determine its truth-value. Consider this one, for example.

Venus is not a planet.

We know that this negation is false, but how? Because the simple claim, "Venus is a planet," is true. When this simple claim is negated, the truth-value of the negation changes to its opposite value. We can see this in the truth-functional definition for negation above by looking at the first row: When the simple claim is true, the negation will be false.

What about a conjunction? When any two claims are combined with *and*, the conjunction will be true only when both of the simple claims that compose it are true. The following is the truth-functional definition for a conjunction.

$$\begin{array}{c c c}
X & \bullet & Y \\
\hline
T & \mathbf{T} & T \\
T & \mathbf{F} & F \\
F & \mathbf{F} & T \\
F & \mathbf{F} & F
\end{array}$$

First, notice that there are twice as many possible truth-value combinations in a conjunction as in a negation. This is because a negation involves only one simple claim, whereas a conjunction involves two simple claims. Although X and Y have only two possible truth-values each, together there are four possible truth-value combinations. When X is true, Y could be true, or it could be false; when X is false, Y could be true, or it could be false. These possibilities are placed below the X and the Y in the table. When the conjunctive operation is performed, the truth-value of the conjunction is placed directly below the •. Notice that the only instance in which the conjunction is true is when both of the simple claims are true; otherwise, the claim is false.

We can apply this definition to any conjunction to determine its truth-value. Consider this one, for example.

Venus is a planet, and Neptune is an asteroid.

We know that this conjunction is false, but how? Because although the first simple claim, "Venus is a planet," is true, the second simple claim, "Neptune is an asteroid," is false. We can use the truth-functional definition for conjunction to see that this claim must be false by looking at the second row: When the first conjunct is true and the second conjunct is false, the conjunction will be false.

Next, let's look at the truth-functional definition for disjunction.

$$\frac{X \vee Y}{}$$
T **T** T
T **T** F
F **T** T
F **F** F

Like a conjunction, a disjunction involves two simple claims; hence, there are four possible truth-value combinations, and these possibilities are placed below the X and the Y in the table. When the disjunctive operation is performed, the truth-value of the disjunction is placed directly below the ∨. Notice that, unlike the conjunction, there are three possible instances in which a disjunction is true, and only one in which it is false.

This kind of disjunction is sometimes referred to as an inclusive disjunction in order to distinguish it from what is called an exclusive disjunction. The difference between these two kinds of disjunctions lies in how the term *or* is understood. For an **inclusive disjunction** to be true, *at least* one of the simple claims is true, whereas for an **exclusive disjunction** to be true, *exactly* one of the simple claims is true. Unfortunately, our ordinary usage of the term *or* sometimes treats the disjunction as exclusive and other times treats it as inclusive. For the purposes of this text, you should treat all disjunctions in the inclusive sense, as meaning *at least* one of the simple claims is true.

 EXERCISE 7.12

Your Turn!   What possibilities would be eliminated if you treated the following disjunction as exclusive rather than inclusive?

The Opportunity Award is a scholarship intended for those students who either face financial hardships or are first-generation college students.

We can apply this definition to any disjunction to determine its truth-value. Consider this one, for example.

Venus is a planet, or Neptune is an asteroid.

We know that this disjunction is true, but how? Because the first simple claim, "Venus is a planet," is true, even though the second simple claim, "Neptune is an asteroid," is false. We can use the truth-functional definition for disjunction to see that this claim must be true by looking at the second row: When the first disjunct is true and the second disjunct is false, the disjunction will be true.

Finally, let's examine the truth-functional definition for conditional claims.

$$
\begin{array}{ccc}
X & \supset & Y \\
\hline
\text{T} & \textbf{T} & \text{T} \\
\text{T} & \textbf{F} & \text{F} \\
\text{F} & \textbf{T} & \text{T} \\
\text{F} & \textbf{T} & \text{F}
\end{array}
$$

Our starting place is the same as for a conjunction or disjunction: Because there are two simple claims involved in the conditional, there will be four possible truth-value combinations to consider. When the conditional operation is performed, the truth-value of the conditional is placed directly below the $\supset$.

Like a disjunction, there are three possible instances in which a conditional is true, and only one in which it is false. To understand why, we need to think carefully about the differing roles played by the antecedent and consequent in a conditional claim. Every conditional claim expresses a particular relationship between the antecedent and consequent—namely, that *the truth of the antecedent is a sufficient condition for the truth of the consequent* and that that *the truth of the consequent is a necessary condition for the truth of the antecedent.*

Let's see how this applies to each row in the truth-functional definition for conditionals, starting with the first row. In this case, when the antecedent is true and the consequent is true, the conditional claim must be true. This is because the truth of the antecedent *guarantees* the truth of the consequent. That's just what it means for the antecedent to be a sufficient condition for the consequent. Now, what about the second row of the definition for conditionals? In this case, when the antecedent is true and the consequent is false, the conditional claim must be false. Why? Because the truth of the antecedent did *not* guarantee the truth of the consequent—the consequent is false even though the antecedent is true. What about the third and fourth rows? In both of these cases, the conditional is true when the antecedent is false. But why? Although the antecedent is a sufficient condition for the consequent, it is not a necessary one. The conditional claim tells us what must follow if the antecedent is true, but it doesn't tell us anything about what must follow if the antecedent isn't true. So, regardless of whether the consequent is true or false, the conditional claim will be true any time that the antecedent is false.

Hint!

You may find it strange to say that every conditional is true whenever the antecedent is false. Consider the following example.

If California is a planet, then there are intelligent life forms in other galaxies.

According to the truth-functional definition for conditionals, this claim is true because the antecedent is in fact false. It may seem difficult to accept this, since the antecedent and consequent have nothing at all to do with each other! In our everyday language, the antecedents and consequents in conditional claims typically have some kind of causal or logical relationship with each other. But truth-functional logic is not restricted to these everyday uses of conditional claims. The important thing to remember here is that the truth-functional definition of conditional is capturing the *logical structure* of the conditional claim. If the antecedent of a conditional claim is false, then the truth or falsity of the consequent simply doesn't matter. The conditional will always be true.

Truth-functional Definitions

Negation	Conjunction	Disjunction	Conditional
~ X	X • Y	X ∨ Y	X ⊃ Y
F T	T T T	T T T	T T T
T F	T F F	T T F	T F F
	F F T	F T T	F T T
	F F F	F F F	F T F

 EXERCISE 7.13

Translate each compound claim into symbolic form. Then determine the truth-value of each compound claim, using your own knowledge of the truth-value of each simple claim.

1. Soccer is not played on ice.
2. Either cowboys wear ballet slippers, or they wear boots.
3. Africa is a country, and ketchup is a vegetable.
4. If golf is a sport, then soccer is played on ice.
5. Bananas are yellow, and either apples are purple or carrots are green.
6. It is not the case that either apples are purple or carrots are green.
7. Either bananas are yellow or apples are purple only if carrots are green.
8. The sun rises in the east, but it does not set in the east.
9. Either Africa is a country, or Lima is not the capital of Peru.
10. If Africa is not a country, then the sun sets in the east.
11. Either horses neigh and pigs squeal, or puppies meow.
12. It is not the case that both horses have hooves and puppies can fly.
13. Giraffes have long necks and elephants are fish unless pelicans are not birds.
14. Ballerinas wear roller skates, yet if soccer is played on grass, then golf is not a sport.
15. Either golf is a sport if cowboys wear ballet slippers, or Christmas is in July.
16. If golf is not a sport, then cowboys wear boots.
17. If ketchup is a vegetable, then Marilyn Monroe liked lima beans.
18. If Queen Latifah has visited the Grand Canyon, then Africa is not a country.
19. Ballerinas wear ballet slippers, or Elvis liked to sing zydeco music.
20. Ketchup is a vegetable, and James Dean enjoyed painting landscapes.

Using the Truth Table Method to Determine Validity

Now that you have learned some basic truth-functional definitions, you can apply them to determine whether a deductive argument is valid or invalid, utilizing the Truth Table Method. A truth table provides a listing of all possible truth-value combinations for an argument. That is, it identifies the conditions under which each of the claims in the argument is true and the conditions under which each is false. With this information, you can then identify whether the argument in question is valid or invalid.

The first step in utilizing the Truth Table Method is translating the argument into symbolic form. Consider this example.

It must be raining. This is because either there are clouds in the sky or it is not raining, and there are clouds in the sky.

EXERCISE 7.14

Your Turn! Complete a Formal Analysis of the argument above.

Using C for "There are clouds in the sky," R for "It is raining," and the proper symbols for each operation, the argument would be translated as follows. Notice that the premises are listed above the line, and the conclusion is listed below it.

$$C \vee \sim R$$
$$\underline{C}$$
$$R$$

Hint!
When translating truth-functional arguments into symbolic form, you must use the argument analysis skills that you learned in Chapters 3 and 4. Remember that the conclusion of the argument may not appear as the last claim in the passage and that passages may contain extra claims or multiple arguments. You may find it useful to diagram the argument first to ensure that you put the premises and conclusion in their proper places and that you do not mistakenly include extra claims or premises from a subargument in your translation.

Next, create the table. To do so, write out the argument utilizing the symbol / to signal the start of a new premise and // to signal the conclusion.

$$C \vee \sim R / C // R$$

Then determine the possible truth-value combinations for the argument. First, count the number of simple claims in the argument. Remembering that each simple claim has two possible truth-values, determine the number of combinations for the argument with the following formula: $R = 2^n$. R represents the number of rows in the truth table (i.e., the number of possible combinations); 2 represents the number of truth-values for any given claim (i.e., true and false); and n represents the number of simple claims in the argument. Thus, an argument containing two simple claims will have 4 rows, one with three simple claims will have 8 rows, one with four simple claims will have 16 rows, and so on.

 EXERCISE 7.15

Your Turn! How many simple claims are in the argument on page 176? How many rows will your truth table have then?

Although randomly assigning truth-value combinations to the simple claims would be okay so long as all combinations were represented, having a consistent format for assigning those values makes your truth table more readable, gives you confidence that you haven't overlooked something, and assures that your truth tables will look like those of your classmates and instructor. The plan we use is to take the first simple claim (in this case, C), divide the number of rows in half, and assign *true* to the first half and *false* to the second half. Then move to the second claim (in this case, R). Divide the number of rows in the truth table in quarters, assigning *true* to the first quarter, *false* to the second, *true* to the third, and *false* to the fourth. This procedure is repeated for each additional simple claim. Your last assignment of truth-values should alternate *true* and *false* for all rows. Observe this pattern below.

C R	C v ~ R / C // R
T T	
T F	
F T	
F F	

The next step is to assign the possible truth-values to each of the simple claims in the argument, using the values assigned in the left-hand columns.

C R	C	v	~	R	/	C	//	R
T T	T			T		T		T
T F	T		F	T		T		F
F T	F		T	F		F		T
F F	F		F	F		F		F

Since you have the truth-values assigned to each simple claim, you can next apply the operators in the argument. Let's start with the first claim. Notice that there are two operators, v and ~. Since the main operator is v, you will apply it to the entire claim. That means that you must begin by applying ~ to R. Whenever R is true, ~ R will be false, and whenever R is false, ~ R will be true.

C R	C ∨ ~ R / C // R
T T	T **F** T T T
T F	T **T** F T F
F T	F **F** T F T
F F	F **T** F F F

Now, you can apply the main operator in the first claim. Notice that the disjuncts are C and ~ R, not C and R. Whenever one of the disjuncts is true, the disjunction is true; otherwise, it is false. Since there are no operators to apply in the second premise or the conclusion, your truth table is now complete.

C R	C ∨ ~ R / C // R
T T	T **T** F T **T** **T**
T F	T **T** T F **T** **F**
F T	F **T** F T **F** **T**
F F	F **T** T F **F** **F**

The final step is to interpret the table. Does it show that the argument is valid or invalid? Recall from Chapter 5 what it means for an argument to be valid: The truth of the premises *guarantees* the truth of the conclusion. That means that, in order for a deductive argument to be valid, *whenever all the premises are true, the conclusion must also be true*. So is this argument valid or invalid? As you can see in the second row, it is possible to have all true premises and a false conclusion. Thus, the argument is invalid. Here is the completed truth table, with the final truth-values assigned for each premise and conclusion indicated by the bold font and the second row highlighted to show that the argument is invalid.

C R	C ∨ ~ R / C // R
T T	T T F T **T** **T**
T F	T **T** T F **T** **F**
F T	F **T** F T **F** **T**
F F	F T T F **F** **F**

Hint!

Notice that the previous argument is invalid even though the first row of the truth table shows that all premises are true and the conclusion is true (when C is true and R is true). This is because an argument is valid only when the truth of the premises *guarantees* the truth of the conclusion. Since the second row shows that the premises are true and the conclusion is false (when C is true and R is false), the argument does not guarantee that the conclusion is true whenever all premises are true. In other words, it takes only *one* row of true premises with a false conclusion to show that the argument is invalid.

Let's walk through one more example before you try some on your own.

If your car won't start, then either it is out of gas, or the battery is dead. But your car can't be out of gas, in that you filled the tank this morning. Thus, either the car will start, or the battery is dead.

EXERCISE 7.16

Your Turn!   Diagram the above argument.

The first step is to translate the argument into symbolic form. Using S to represent "Your car will start," G to represent "Your car is out of gas," and B to represent "Your car's battery is dead," the argument should be translated as follows:

$\sim S \supset (G \vee B)$
$\underline{\sim G}$
$S \vee B$

EXERCISE 7.17

Your Turn!   Why isn't the claim "You filled the tank this morning" translated?

Next, create the table by writing out the argument horizontally. Then determine how many rows will be in the truth table, and assign truth values to each simple claim. Notice that there are eight rows because there are three simple claims in the argument. For the first simple claim, we have assigned *true* to the first half and *false* to the second half. For the second simple claim, we have assigned *true* to the first and third quarters and *false* to the second and third quarters. And for the third simple claim, we have alternated *true* and *false*. This procedure ensures that all possible truth-value combinations are represented in the table.

S G B	$\sim S \supset (G \vee B) / \sim G // S \vee B$
T T T	
T T F	
T F T	
T F F	
F T T	
F T F	
F F T	
F F F	

EXERCISE 7.18

Your Turn!   Transfer the truth-values for each simple claim in the argument, using the values assigned in the left-hand columns.

Once you have assigned truth-values to each simple claim in the argument, you can then determine the truth value of each premise by applying the operators in the claims. Since the first premise contains three operators, you must be sure to apply each operator in its proper order. This will take multiple steps. First, determine the values for the antecedent and consequent.

```
S G B       ~ S ⊃ (G ∨ B) / ~ G // S ∨ B
T T T       F T    T T T      T    T   T
T T F       F T    T T F      T    T   F
T F T       F T    F T T      F    T   T
T F F       F T    F F F      F    T   F
F T T       T F    T T T      T    F   T
F T F       T F    T T F      T    F   F
F F T       T F    F T T      F    F   T
F F F       T F    F F F      F    F   F
```

Now you can determine the value of the entire conditional.

```
S G B       ~ S ⊃ (G ∨ B) / ~ G // S ∨ B
T T T       F T T  T T T      T    T   T
T T F       F T T  T T F      T    T   F
T F T       F T T  F T T      F    T   T
T F F       F T T  F F F      F    T   F
F T T       F F T  T T T      T    F   T
F T F       T F T  T T F      T    F   F
F F T       T F T  F T T      F    F   T
F F F       T F F  F F F      F    F   F
```

The second premise and conclusion have only one operator each, so only one calculation is needed. The final truth-values assigned for each premise and conclusion are indicated by the bold font.

```
S G B       ~ S ⊃ (G ∨ B) / ~ G // S ∨ B
T T T       F T T  T T T      F T    T T T
T T F       F T T  T T F      F T    T T F
T F T       F T T  F T T      T F    T T T
T F F       F T T  F F F      T F    T T F
F T T       T F T  T T T      F T    F T T
F T F       T F T  T T F      F T    F F F
F F T       T F T  F T T      T F    F T T
F F F       T F F  F F F      T F    F F F
```

Your truth table is now complete. The final step is to interpret the table. Does it show that the argument is valid or invalid? In order for the argument to be valid, the conclusion must be true whenever all the premises are true. Since there is no row in which all premises are true while the conclusion is false, the argument must be valid.

How to Determine Validity Using the Truth Table Method

Step 1: Translate the argument into symbolic form.

Step 2: Write the argument horizontally, using / to separate premises and // in front of the conclusion.

Step 3: Calculate the number of rows in the truth table, using the formula $R = 2^n$.

Step 4: Assign a truth-value to each simple claim in the argument.

Step 5: Determine the truth-value of each premise and conclusion, using the appropriate truth-functional definitions. You may find it helpful to highlight or draw a box around these final values.

Step 6: Evaluate whether the argument is valid or invalid by looking for any row with all true premises and a false conclusion. If you find such a row, then the argument is invalid. If you do not, the argument is valid.

E X E R C I S E 7.19

Your Turn! Look back at the argument presented at the start of this chapter. Translate the argument into symbolic form, and then use a truth table to determine whether the argument is valid or invalid.

E X E R C I S E 7.20

Determine whether each of the following arguments is valid or invalid, using the Truth Table Method.

1. $M \supset K$
   $\underline{M}$
   K

2. $P \supset Q$
   $\underline{Q}$
   P

3. $S \supset C$
   $\underline{\sim S}$
   $\sim C$

4. $L \supset T$
   $\underline{\sim T}$
   $\sim L$

5. $\sim S \supset \sim C$
   $\underline{S}$
   C

6. $\sim A \supset B$
   $\underline{\sim A}$
   B

7. $\sim C \supset D$
   $\underline{D}$
   C

8. $\sim E \supset \sim F$
   $\underline{\sim F}$
   $\sim E$

9. Q
   $\underline{P \supset Q}$
   P

10. $\sim C$
    $\underline{S \supset C}$
    $\sim S$

11. A ∨ B
    <u>~ B</u>
    A

12. C ∨ D
    <u>C </u>
    ~ D

13. E ⊃ F
    <u>F ⊃ G</u>
    E ⊃ G

14. H ⊃ I
    <u>J ⊃ I</u>
    H ⊃ J

15. K ∨ L
    K ⊃ M
    <u>L ⊃ M</u>
    M

16. <u>N • ~ O</u>
    N

17. P ⊃ Q
    <u>R • Q</u>
    R ⊃ P

18. S ⊃ (T • R)
    <u>~ S</u>
    ~ (T • R)

19. Z ∨ W
    <u>W • ~ X </u>
    Z ⊃ (W • X)

20. ~ A
    B • C
    <u>A ⊃ (C ∨ ~ C)</u>
    ~ S

 EXERCISE 7.21

Diagram each argument. Then translate each argument into symbolic form, and determine whether the argument is valid or invalid, using the Truth Table Method.

1. The story you wrote is not a fairy tale. Accordingly, it is not for children because if a story is for children, then it is a fairy tale.

2. The mail carrier is the one who stole my package! I never received my package, and if the mail carrier stole my package, then I wouldn't have received it.

3. Anis's mother said that he will go to Disneyland only if he finishes all his homework. I guess he's going to Disneyland, then, because he finished all his homework.

4. If the defendant's fingerprints were on the murder weapon, then the defendant is guilty of murder. Therefore, the defendant is guilty of murder, since the forensics expert testified that the defendant's fingerprints were found on the murder weapon.

5. We won't have good government unless qualified people are elected. This means that we won't have good government. Haven't you seen who got elected?

6. Gay marriage? Why not? If we allow infertile heterosexual couples to marry, then we should allow same-sex couples to marry, and, of course, we should allow infertile heterosexual couples to marry.

7. If you spray pre-emergent on your lawn in the spring, then you don't water your lawn enough if it has weeds. Given that you did not spray your lawn with pre-emergent this spring, it is not the case that you don't water your lawn enough if it has weeds.

8. Without a tax increase, social services will be cut. But the governor refuses to raise taxes, since he promised voters that he wouldn't when he ran for election. Thus, we can expect more social service cuts.

9. If Paula is a grandmother, then either her son or her daughter has a child. Paula is not a grandmother, since neither her son nor her daughter has a child.

10. Your car should run just fine. This is because you change your oil regularly, and if you don't change your oil regularly, then your car won't run well. Besides, a car should run just fine if it is new, and your car is new—you just bought it last year.

11. Recently, the U.S. Consumer Product Safety Commission recalled a number of cribs due to strangulation and suffocation hazards. You might worry whether the crib you bought last year poses this kind of danger. But keep in mind that, if a child's crib is either a strangulation hazard or a suffocation hazard, then the U.S. Consumer Product Safety Commission will issue a recall of the item. Thus, you can trust that your child's crib is neither a strangulation hazard nor a suffocation hazard because it has not been recalled.

12. Those strawberries are labeled "certified organic" only if they are grown without the use of pesticides. Since the strawberries are either labeled "certified organic" or they are grown with the use of pesticides, that means that, if they are grown without the use of pesticides, then they will be labeled "certified organic."

13. Either federal prosecutors don't believe that they can win a criminal case against AIG (American International Group, Inc.), or they have been bribed to not prosecute. Accordingly, they must not have been bribed, as federal prosecutors don't believe they can win the case.

14. There's a great deal of controversy on the issue of global warming. However, either global warming is a reality, or leading climatologists are delusional. Thus, global warming is a reality because leading climatologists are not delusional.

15. There will be more traffic accidents unless people stop using their cell phones while driving. But people won't stop using their cell phones while driving because they do not realize how dangerous it is. As a result, traffic accidents will increase.

16. Should the judge remove herself from the case? I don't think so. This is because she should remove herself only if she has a conflict of interest or she is ill, and this judge both has a conflict of interest and is ill.

17. If the Eyjafjallajökull volcano erupts, then the Katla volcano will also erupt. And if the Katla volcano erupts, Iceland will be devastated. Consequently, Iceland will be devastated given that the Eyjafjallajökull volcano erupted.

18. Cinderella can go to the royal ball if she finishes all of her chores and finds something suitable to wear. Given that her stepsisters will sabotage her efforts, neither will Cinderella finish all of her chores, nor will she have something suitable to wear. Therefore, Cinderella won't go to the ball.

19. If the criminal justice major prepares graduates to work as CSIs and prison guards, then the number of criminal justice majors must exceed the number of job openings. Yet, oddly, the number of graduates does not exceed the number of job openings. So either criminal justice majors are not prepared to work as CSIs, or they are not prepared to work as prison guards. I find this just amazing.

20. If the first set of experiments conducted with the Large Hadron Collider (LHC) was not successful, then physicists would not be able to explain the prevalence of dark matter in the universe, and they would not be able to explain why gravity is so much stronger than other forces. Since physicists can explain neither the prevalence of dark matter nor why gravity is so strong, it's clear that the LHC experiments did not work.

PUTTING IT ALL TOGETHER: Writing a Critical Précis of a Truth-Functional Argument

In Chapters 2, 3, and 4, you learned how to recognize and analyze arguments and to present a Critical Précis with an argument diagram. In Chapter 5, you also learned how to distinguish among different kinds of arguments. Now that you can analyze and evaluate truth-functional arguments, you can put all of these skills together by adding truth-functional argument evaluation to the Critical Précis assignments.

Directions for a Critical Précis of a Truth-Functional Argument

In *paragraph form*, use complete sentences and proper English grammar and spelling to do the following:

Step 1: Identify the passage.
▶ Completely and correctly identify the author and the source (whenever such information is given).
▶ If the passage contains an argument, identify it as such. Then move to Step 2.
▶ If the passage does not contain an argument, identify it as a nonargument. Then specify which feature of an argument is lacking.

Step 2: Analyze the argument.
▶ Clearly and completely identify the issue, conclusion, and premise or premises *in that order*.
▶ If the passage is a *multiple argument*, write *separate paragraphs* to analyze each separate argument.

Step 3: Diagram the argument.
▶ Verify that the diagram is consistent with your Critical Précis.

Step 4: Identify the kind of argument.
▶ If the argument is deductive, identify it as a categorical argument or a truth-functional argument.
▶ If the argument is inductive, identify it as an inductive generalization, an analogical argument, or a causal argument.

Step 5: Evaluate the argument.
▶ If the argument is truth-functional, translate the argument, and *demonstrate* whether the argument is valid or invalid, using the Truth Table Method.

The most important thing for you to remember when writing a Critical Précis is that your evaluation should be directed to the main argument only. Since the premises of any subarguments support the premises, not the conclusion, of the main argument, they should be excluded in the evaluative process. However, the entire argument should be analyzed. Let's walk through an example before you try some on your own.

> *An employee commits "asset misappropriation" if he or she steals or misuses an organization's assets. And if the employee commits "asset misappropriation," then he or she commits fraud given that asset misappropriation*

is intentional embezzlement, and intentional embezzlement is fraud. As a consequence, an employee commits fraud if he or she steals or misuses an organization's assets.—Auditing: A Business Risk Approach

You should first identify the passage an argument. Then you can analyze and diagram it. Since the passage contains multiple arguments, the analysis must contain multiple paragraphs, one for each argument. Notice that the diagram is consistent with the analysis.

① *An employee commits "asset misappropriation" if he or she steals or misuses an organization's assets*. And ② *if the employee commits "asset misappropriation," then he or she commits fraud given that* ③ *asset misappropriation is intentional embezzlement*, and ④ *intentional embezzlement is fraud*. As a consequence, ⑤ *an employee commits fraud if he or she steals or misuses an organization's assets*.

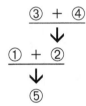

This passage from the book *Auditing: A Business Risk Approach* contains an argument. The issue is whether an employee commits fraud if he or she steals or misuses an organization's assets. The conclusion is that an employee commits fraud if he or she steals or misuses an organization's assets. The first premise is that an employee commits "asset misappropriation" if he or she steals or misuses an organization's assets. The second premise is that, if an employee commits "asset misappropriation," then he or she commits fraud.

This passage contains a subargument. The intermediate conclusion is that, if an employee commits "asset misappropriation," then he or she commits fraud. The first premise is that asset misappropriation is intentional embezzlement. The second premise is that intentional embezzlement is fraud.

Finally, after identifying the argument as a deductive truth-functional argument, you should evaluate it using a truth table. Notice that only the main argument is evaluated.

This is a deductive truth-functional argument. The truth table below demonstrates that the argument is valid because it is impossible for the conclusion to be false when both premises are true.

S = An employee steals an organization's assets.
M = An employee misuses an organization's assets.

A = *An employee commits "asset misappropriation."*
F = *An employee is guilty of fraud.*

(S ∨ M) ⊃ A	/	A ⊃ F	//	(S ∨ M) ⊃ F
T T T **T** T		**T** T T		T T T **T** T
T T T **T** T		T **F** F		T T T **F** F
T T T **F** F		**F** T T		T T T **T** T
T T T **F** F		**F** T F		T T T **F** F
T T F **T** T		**T** T T		T T F **T** T
T T F **T** T		T **F** F		T T F **F** F
T T F **F** F		**F** T T		T T F **T** T
T T F **F** F		**F** T F		T T F **F** F
F T T **T** T		**T** T T		F T T **T** T
F T T **T** T		T **F** F		F T T **F** F
F T T **F** F		**F** T T		F T T **T** T
F T T **F** F		**F** T F		F T T **F** F
F F F **T** T		**T** T T		F F F **T** T
F F F **T** T		T **F** F		F F F **T** F
F F F **T** F		**F** T T		F F F **T** T
F F F **T** F		**F** T F		F F F **T** F

Hint!

When diagramming truth-functional arguments, you may have noticed that the premises are always linked. This is because conditionals and disjunctions must be combined with at least one other claim for a conclusion to follow.

EXERCISE 7.22

Write a Critical Précis for the following passages. Include an argument diagram, and identify the argument type when appropriate. Additionally, evaluate any truth-functional arguments using a truth table.

1. The "man the hunter" theory—the view that early human ancestors were hunters and possessed a killer instinct—is the generally accepted paradigm of human evolution. But this theory is not supported by the fossil evidence. Early humans simply couldn't eat meat since they did not have sharp shearing blades necessary to retain and cut such foods. If they couldn't eat meat, why would they hunt?—Robert Sussman, *Man the Hunted*

2. African Americans are similar to other groups of people who have a country of origin outside the United States. We routinely refer to Irish Americans, Polish

Americans, and Chinese Americans, for instance, using the country of origin as the primary descriptor. Therefore, we should designate people whose country of origin is in Africa as African Americans.—Walker, Spohn, and DeLeone, *The Color of Justice*

3. Which physics laws should be taught first? We can either teach the correct, but unfamiliar, law or we can teach the approximate, but familiar law. We shouldn't teach the unfamiliar law first since it can't be understood unless the student knows the familiar law. So, it is with the familiar law that physics instruction should begin.—Richard Feynman, *Six Easy Pieces*

4. Remember the two benefits of failure. First, if you do fail, you learn what doesn't work; and second, the failure gives you the opportunity to try a new approach.—Roger von Oech

5. The Food and Drug Administration (FDA) does not have the authority to require that a food's label say that it is genetically modified if there is no material difference between a genetically modified (GM) food and its traditional counterpart. Since the methods used in the development of a new plant variety do not constitute material information, there is no material difference between genetically modified food and its traditional counterpart. Therefore, the FDA cannot require that GM foods be labeled as such.—Fred Degnan, "Biotechnology and the Food Label"

6. If parents permit their children to hold other people in contempt, and take pleasure in their antics, the children will lose a sense of distinction between good and evil and will not shed their bad habits even after they become adults.—Kaibara Ekken

7. Mr. Darden asked Mr. Simpson to try on those gloves and the gloves didn't fit. If it doesn't fit, you must acquit. He is then entitled to an acquittal.—Johnnie Cochran

8. Young Mr. Wansborough is the vestry clerk, and the vestry clerk is a sort of appointment that lawyers get. So, you know what follows from that, don't you? Young Mr. Wansborough *is* a lawyer.—Wilkie Collins, *The Woman in White*

9. If student researchers want to interview, survey, systematically observe, or collect other data from human subjects, the project must be authorized by the University's Institutional Review Board (IRB). Moreover, in order to get authorization from the IRB, all key personnel in the research project must be certified in Human Subjects Protection Training (HSPT). Therefore, if student researchers want to interview, survey, systematically observe, or collect other data from human subjects, all key personnel in the research project must be certified in HSPT.—University policy on human subject research

10. There has been a lot of controversy over who is to blame for the Deepwater Horizon oil spill. It is clear that BP, the well's owner, is ultimately responsible for the accident. This is because BP is responsible for the accident if their employees deliberately took "shortcuts," and there is evidence that they did take shortcuts.—Bureau of Ocean Energy Management, Regulation and Enforcement

CHAPTER REVIEW QUESTIONS

1. How do you translate a simple claim? A negation? A disjunction? A conjunction? A conditional?
2. How do you identify the antecedent and consequent of a conditional claim?
3. What is the purpose of a truth-functional definition?
4. How do you use a truth table to determine whether a truth-functional argument is valid or invalid?

ONE STEP FURTHER

First introduced in the U.S. Senate in 2001, the Development, Relief, and Education for Alien Minors Act, also called the DREAM Act, aims to give those individuals who meet certain requirements an opportunity to enlist in the military or go to college. Supporters of the act argue that it would provide a path to citizenship for many undocumented immigrants who have been living in the United States since they were young. Opponents argue that the DREAM Act encourages and rewards illegal immigration, acting as a "magnet" attracting more illegal immigrants and creating a chain migration by family members. Consider this commonly expressed view.

If a person is not in the United States legally, then that person is a criminal. Anyone who is undocumented is in this country illegally. Thus, that person is a criminal.

1. Evaluate this argument using a truth table. Does the conclusion follow from the premises?

In early 2014, the California Supreme Court granted a law license to Sergio Garcia despite the fact that his 1994 petition for U.S. citizenship is still pending. It remains unclear whether he can appear in federal court or in the courts of other states. Federal law makes it illegal for law firms to hire him.

Max Whittaker/Reuters/Corbis

2. Are the premises true? Consider this statement from a 2006 report by the Congressional Research Service (CRS).

> The INA [Immigration and Nationality Act] includes both criminal and civil components, providing both for criminal charges (e.g., alien smuggling, which is prosecuted in the federal courts) and for civil violations (e.g., lack of legal status, which may lead to removal through a separate administrative system in the Department of Justice). Being illegally present in the U.S. has always been a civil, not criminal, violation of the INA, and subsequent deportation and associated administrative processes are civil proceedings. For instance, a lawfully admitted nonimmigrant alien may become deportable if his visitor's visa expires or if his student status changes. Criminal violations of the INA, on the other hand, include felonies and misdemeanors and are prosecuted in federal district courts. These types of violations include the bringing in and harboring of certain undocumented aliens, the illegal entry of aliens, and the reentry of aliens previously excluded or deported. (Full report available at http://www.fas.org/sgp/crs/misc/RL33351.pdf)

3. Does it matter whether a person is referred to as an "undocumented immigrant" or an "illegal alien"? If so, how? If not, why not?

CHAPTER
8
Evaluating Inductive Generalizations

If you have ever taken an introductory psychology course, you were likely required to participate in one or more psychological "studies." These are behavioral science experiments in which a researcher tests a hypothesis by performing some kind of "experiment" on a number of subjects. Most of these are not at all harmful—many are merely questionnaires. Yet they are an important way in which the discipline of psychology develops a more complete understanding of what makes people tick. In these studies, the information gathered is typically generalized to a larger group than just those college students who took part. Here's an example.

> *Men have more confidence in their scientific abilities than women have in theirs. A recent study of nearly 400 students analyzed the attitudes toward science of students enrolled in entry-level general education courses at the University of Wisconsin–La Crosse in the areas of personal confidence, usefulness of the subject, perception of the subject as a male domain, and perception of the teacher's attitude. Males in the study were found to have more confidence than females, and females perceived science as a male domain more than men. Expected achievement and attitude toward science were shown to be strongly related.* —UW-L Journal of Undergraduate Research IX (2006)

From what you learned in Chapter 5, you should recognize this argument as an inductive generalization. **Inductive generalizations**, you may recall, conclude that some, most, or all members of a particular group have some feature based on evidence that a portion of that group has the feature. In this chapter, you will learn how to evaluate arguments like these according to their strength, from strong to weak. In order to determine the strength of an inductive argument, however, you must first learn to perform an additional analysis of the argument's parts by identifying the sample, target, and feature in the argument. Once you can do that, you will learn to apply the proper criteria for consistent and accurate argument evaluation.

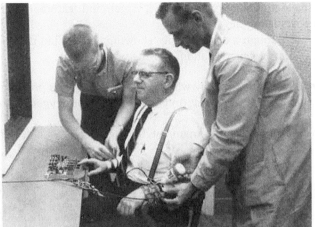

From the film Obedience © 1968 by Stanley Milgram. © Renewed 1993 by Alexandra Milgram and distributed by Alexander Street Press

One of the most famous and controversial psychological studies, the Milgram experiments, measured the willingness of study participants to obey an authority figure who instructed them to harm another person. Critics consider these experiments unethical and abusive. Today, many institutions and policies exist to ensure that human subject research is ethical and legal.

LEARNING OUTCOMES

In this chapter, you will learn how to evaluate inductive generalizations by:

▶ Identifying the sample, target, and feature of an inductive generalization;
▶ Determining whether the sample represents the target; and
▶ Writing a Critical Précis of an inductive generalization.

Analyzing Inductive Generalizations

Because inductive generalizations conclude that some, most, or all members of a group have a feature based on the evidence that some portion of that group has that feature, all inductive generalizations have the same basic structure. That is, even though you will encounter them in a wide variety of differing formats, all of them can be translated into a general form for inductive generalizations.

P: A sample (of the target) has a particular feature.

∴ All (or many or most) members of the target have the feature.

As you can readily see, inductive generalizations contain a sample (S), a target (T), and a feature (F). The **sample** is a portion of an entire class or group, and it appears in the single premise. The entire group or class represented by the sample is called the **target**; it appears in the conclusion. Thus, the sample *is a part* of the target. The argument works by citing the fact that the sample has a particular feature and making the inference that the target will have the feature, too. Thus, the feature appears in both the premise and the conclusion. When analyzing inductive generalizations, you must learn

---

to properly isolate and identify the sample, target, and feature, each of which plays a critical role in evaluating the arguments.

Let's work through a few examples showing how to find the sample, target, and feature in an inductive generalization, starting with this one.

> *Life on Earth can exist only when sufficient oxygen is present. Therefore, all life in the universe can exist only when sufficient oxygen is present.*

Here's the Formal Analysis of the argument, highlighting the sample, target, and feature.

> **P:**   Life on Earth can exist only when sufficient oxygen is present.
>
> ∴   All life in the universe can exist only when sufficient oxygen is present.
>
> **Issue:** Whether all life in the universe can exist only when sufficient oxygen is present

Because the feature is given as an attribute of both the sample and the target, it must be stated in such a way that the feature makes sense when attributed to the sample and also makes sense when attributed to the target. Here are the three parts as you should identify them.

> **Sample:** life on Earth
> **Target:** all life in the universe
> **Feature:** exists only when sufficient oxygen is present

Not all inductive generalizations appear in this general form, but they all should be translated to fit the pattern. They often contain extra claims, as in the following example.

> *During the summer, the university does not follow the same schedule as during the school year. This summer the library, the dining halls, and the recreation center are all closed on Fridays. Therefore, most buildings on campus are closed on Fridays during the summer months.*

First, diagram this argument.

> ① *During the summer, the university does not follow the same schedule as during the school year.* ② *This summer the library, the dining halls, and the recreation center are all closed on Fridays.* Therefore, ③ *most buildings on campus are closed on Fridays during the summer months.*

The first thing to notice is that claim ③ is the conclusion. Claim ② supports claim ③ but claim ① does not—it is an extra claim. The fact that the university does not follow the same schedule as during the school year is not evidence that most buildings on campus are closed on Fridays during the summer months. So in the diagram you would leave claim ① out.

> **Hint!**
> All inductive generalizations will contain only one premise and a conclusion.
> To make each claim in the argument make sense on its own, you often must
> rely on information presented in any extra claims that accompany the argu-
> ment. But remember that you should not include the extra claims in your
> analysis, since they are neither premises nor conclusions.

The Formal Analysis, then, looks like this:

P: This summer, the library, the dining halls, and the recreation center are all <u>closed on Fridays</u>.

∴   Most buildings on campus are closed on Fridays during the summer months.

Issue: Whether most buildings on campus are closed on Fridays during the summer months

S: the library, the dining halls, and the recreation center

T: all buildings on campus

F: closed on Fridays during the summer months

> **Hint!**
> Even though the conclusion is about *most buildings on campus*, as you can see,
> the target is still *all buildings on campus*. The target of all generalizations is always
> *all* of the members of that class. The claim is that *most* of them have the feature
> and the others don't—hence, the claim addresses all members of the target.

Here's another example of an inductive generalization, this one resulting from
an opinion poll.

> *An online survey in the* Journal of Computer-Mediated Communication
> *suggests that people who post comments of a personal nature on their
> blogs are likely to have gotten into trouble for things they've written. A total
> of 492 bloggers filled out the online surveys. Of these, some 70% reported
> that they had gotten into trouble with family and friends for something they
> had posted. Researchers point out that additional research is needed to
> better understand privacy concerns inherent in the practice of blogging.*

First, diagram the argument.

    ① <u>*An online survey in the* Journal of Computer-Mediated Communication *suggests that people who post comments of a personal nature on their blogs are likely to have gotten into trouble for things they've written.*</u> ② <u>*A total of 492 bloggers filled out the online surveys.*</u> ③ <u>*Of these,*</u>

some 70% reported that they had gotten into trouble with family and friends for something they had posted. ④ *Researchers point out that additional research is needed to better understand privacy concerns inherent in the practice of blogging.*

This argument contains two extra claims—claim ② and claim ④.

EXERCISE 8.1

Your Turn! Complete the diagram of the inductive generalization above.

Here is the argument, presented in a Formal Analysis.

P: Some 70% of the 492 bloggers who responded to an online survey in the *Journal of Computer-Mediated Communication* reported that they had gotten into trouble with family and friends for posting something of a personal nature.

∴ People who post comments of a personal nature on their blogs have gotten into trouble for posting something of a personal nature.

Issue: Whether people who post comments of a personal nature on their blogs have gotten into trouble for posting something of a personal nature

S: the 492 bloggers who responded to an online survey

T: all bloggers who post comments of a personal nature

F: gotten into trouble with family and friends for posting something of a personal nature

Notice that information from claim ②—the number of participants—must be included in the premise in order for that claim to make sense on its own. Many surveys include a number of extra claims whose information must be incorporated into the single premise and/or the conclusion.

EXERCISE 8.2

Diagram each of the following inductive generalizations. Then provide a Formal Analysis using the general form, and state the sample, target, and feature.

1. I've eaten lasagna and spaghetti. I thought both were delicious. Thus, I'll most likely find all Italian pasta dishes delicious.

2. Albuquerque is an arid region trying to create a stable economic base to fuel future growth. Restriction on urban sprawl helped Albuquerque become a more attractive place for business investment. So restrictions on urban sprawl will probably have the same results for every large community in the desert Southwest.

3. How do most Americans refer to a group of two or more people? They use the words *you guys*. This is the conclusion of an online survey of English usage conducted by Professor Bert Vaux of Harvard University that has had over 30,000 participants. When people were asked how they addressed a group of two or more people, the largest number (42.5%) said they used *you guys*. Interestingly, *y'all* was given by 14% of the respondents.

4. Since mice and rats are both rodents and they each make great pets, most rodents make great pets.

5. Hybrid cars are likely to get more than 40 miles per gallon. This is because both the Toyota Prius and the Ford Fusion get over 40 miles per gallon.

6. You sometimes hear it said that people who have good cognitive skills are just born with them. I disagree. Given that the cognitive skills required for computer programming, playing a musical instrument, and playing chess are acquired only after diligent and consistent practice, all cognitive skills must be acquired by the same means.

7. According to a *Salary.com* report, employees are dissatisfied with their jobs. The survey included over 7,000 employees, 65% of whom said they were actively looking for another job.

8. I have visited five small towns in southern Chile, and every one of them has had an old Spanish cathedral. It appears likely that the majority of small towns in southern Chile have old Spanish cathedrals.

9. Recently a team of archaeologists found a previously undiscovered Native American campsite in Michigan that contained hundreds of hunting implements. Five of the several hundred arrowheads and other hunting implements found at the site were carbon-dated. They were shown to be over 2,000 years old. So it's likely that the vast majority of the tools that were discovered at the site are a couple of thousand years old.

10. Salt marshes on the East Coast are among the most productive ecosystems in the country. The majority of them are in South Carolina. Unfortunately, these marshes are home to fewer birds and fish than in the recent past. It's a good bet that most salt marshes on the East Coast are having similar problems.

Evaluating Inductive Generalizations

In Chapter 5, you learned that the first step in evaluating inductive arguments is to examine the structure of the argument. That is, you must ask yourself, If the premises were true, would the conclusion likely be true? To do this, you must determine how well the sample *represents* the target. As the sample gets more representative, the argument gets stronger. Inductive generalizations lacking that kind of support from the premises are weak arguments.

> **Hint!**
> Recall from Chapter 5 that *strong* and *weak* are relative terms ranging from very strong to very weak. For this reason, the exercises in this section will instruct you to compare pairs of inductive generalizations to determine which argument is stronger.

The size of the sample is the most important factor in determining how well the sample represents the target in an inductive generalization. As a rule, the larger the sample is, the stronger the argument is. This is because larger samples tend to be more representative of the target. Of course, if an argument had the largest possible sample—that is, if all members of the target were in the sample—the premise would be identical to the conclusion. So in an inductive generalization, the sample will always be smaller than the target.

 EXERCISE 8.3

Your Turn! Why must the sample always be smaller than the target in an inductive generalization?

At the other extreme, when the sample is much too small to offer even minimal support for the conclusion, the argument commits a fallacy called **hasty generalization**. For example, if I argue that because my cousin, her husband, and I all think Proposition 22 should be defeated, a majority of voters believe the proposition should be defeated, then my argument is a hasty generalization. This is because the sample consists of only three voters (my cousin, her husband, and me). A sample of three people does not offer enough possible differences of viewpoint and opinion to provide evidence regarding all voters in any state.

In order to see how the size of the sample can be evaluated in an argument, we will consider a pair of generalizations. Examine the first one.

> *The student newspaper conducted a survey of its readers to determine which video games were most popular. Over 70% of the 175 who responded to the random survey said that* World of Warcraft *was their favorite. Thus,* World of Warcraft *must be the most popular video game among all readers.*

First, use a Formal Analysis to identify the sample, target, and feature.

P: Of the 175 respondents to the student newspaper survey, over 70% said that *World of Warcraft* was their favorite video game.

∴   *World of Warcraft* is the most popular video game among all readers.

Issue: Whether *World of Warcraft* is the most popular video game among all readers

S: the 175 respondents to the student newspaper survey

T: all readers of the student newspaper

F: said *World of Warcraft* was their favorite video game

Now, let's consider the second argument.

The student newspaper conducted a survey of its readers to determine which video games were most popular. Over 70% of the 545 who responded to the random survey said that World of Warcraft *was their favorite. Thus,* World of Warcraft *must be the most popular among all readers.*

Again, use a Formal Analysis to identify the sample, target, and feature.

P: Of the 545 respondents to the student newspaper survey, over 70% said that *World of Warcraft* was their favorite video game.

∴ *World of Warcraft* is the most popular video game among all readers.

Issue: Whether *World of Warcraft* is the most popular video game among all readers

S: the 545 respondents to the student newspaper survey

T: all readers of the student newspaper

F: said *World of Warcraft* was their favorite video game

Both arguments have the same target (all readers of the student newspaper) and the same feature (said *World of Warcraft* was their favorite video game). However, the size of the sample is different in each argument. The first contains a sample of 175 readers, whereas the second contains 545. A larger sample provides more evidence for the conclusion than a smaller one. So, if the respondents were chosen in the same manner, the second survey would be the stronger argument.

 EXERCISE 8.4

Your Turn! How do you use your identification of the sample, target, and feature to evaluate the strength of an inductive generalization?

 EXERCISE 8.5

For each of the following pairs of inductive generalizations, determine which is stronger and justify your evaluation.

1. **A.** I have visited 10 amusement parks, all of which had a wide selection of roller coasters. So I bet all amusement parks I visit will have a wide selection of roller coasters.

    B. I have visited two amusement parks, both of which had a wide selection of roller coasters. So I bet all amusement parks I visit will have a wide selection of roller coasters.

2. **A.** All professionals earn much higher than average salaries. This is because lawyers, doctors, engineers, and high school teachers all have advanced degrees, and all of them earn a much higher than average salary.

    B. All professionals earn much higher than average salaries. This is because lawyers and high school teachers have advanced degrees, and all of them earn a much higher than average salary.

3. **A.** I tasted three of the oranges from my tree, and all were sour. This tree must have very poor fruit.

    B. I tasted 10 of the oranges from my tree, and all were sour. This tree must have very poor fruit.

4. **A.** Grocery prices at a locally owned market are not much higher than those at one of the national supermarket chains. We bought an identical shopping basket of foods from the local market and from the chain market. The price of the basket of foods from the local market was higher by only 4%.

    B. Grocery prices at a locally owned market are not much higher than those at one of the national supermarket chains. We bought an identical shopping basket of foods once a week for a month from the local market and from the chain market. The price of the basket of foods from the local market was higher by only 4%.

5. **A.** The vast majority of students who eat in the dining commons think the food is quite good. A group of graduate students in sociology surveyed over 100 students who eat at least one meal a day in the dining commons, and 65% of them had no complaints about the quality of the food.

    B. The vast majority of students who eat in the dining commons think the food is quite good. A group of graduate students in sociology surveyed 30 students who eat at least one meal a day in the dining commons, and 65% of them had no complaints about the quality of the food.

Although the size of the sample is our first concern, in order for a sample to be representative of the target, it also must contain a similar degree of whatever relevant diversity exists in the target. So, if, for example, you want to draw a generalized conclusion about some group you belong to (such as a sports club, local political group, or college major) and the group has both male and female members, the sample needs to include both some men and some women in proportion to the make-up of the group in order to be representative of the entire group. Thus, when you choose your sample, you need to make sure that both men and women are among the ones chosen.

One way to evaluate whether an argument contains representative diversity is by considering whether the make-up of the sample is likely to emphasize or diminish the viewpoints favoring one kind of answer. For instance, if the sample at the sports club was created by choosing every fifth or tenth name on the membership list, we can assume that the position of a person's name on the list is unlikely to indicate how they would respond to your survey. So such a process should result in a strong argument. Another possibility for a strong argument like this would be to randomly interview people in a common meeting place. Of course, better and worse ways exist to create a random sample, but in each case, the aim is to ensure that the diversity of the target is reflected by the sample. What would not be a random sample is one that excludes part of the target. For example, a sample of sports club members chosen from those in the men's locker room would not include any women members.

> **Hint!**
> Professional pollsters ensure a representative sample by making the sample random. Interestingly, sample size does not always have to be huge if the sample is random. For instance, most nationwide surveys done by reputable polling companies use samples of only 1,000 to 1,200 respondents.

By comparing two similar examples, you can see the difference between an argument with a representative sample and one with a sample that is not representative of the target. Let's consider the first argument.

> *As part of a class project, I surveyed owners of a variety of businesses to see whether they expected to hire additional workers next year. Of the 36 owners, 20 said they had no plans to increase their workforce, 10 said they weren't sure, and 6 planned to add employees. Thus, the majority of local business owners probably will not be hiring more workers next year.*

First, use a Formal Analysis to identify the sample, target, and feature.

P: Of the 36 business owners from a variety of businesses I surveyed about their plans for the following year, 20 said they had no plans to increase their workforce, 10 said they weren't sure, and 6 planned to add employees.

∴ The majority of local business owners will not be hiring more workers next year.

Issue: Whether the majority of local business owners will be hiring more workers next year

S: the 36 business owners from a variety of businesses I surveyed

T: all local business owners

F: do not plan to hire more workers next year

Now, consider the second argument.

> *As part of a class project, I surveyed business owners who had filed for bankruptcy to see whether they expected to hire additional workers*

next year. Of the 36 owners, 20 said they had no plans to increase their workforce, 10 said they weren't sure, and 6 planned to add employees. Thus, the majority of local business owners will not be hiring more workers next year.

Again, use a Formal Analysis to identify the sample, target, and feature.

> **P:** Of the 36 business owners of bankrupt businesses I surveyed about their plans for the following fiscal year, 20 said they had no plans to increase their workforce, 10 said they weren't sure, and 6 planned to add employees.
>
> ∴ The majority of local business owners will not be hiring more workers next year.
>
> **Issue:** Whether the majority of local business owners will be hiring more workers next year
>
> **S:** the 36 business owners of bankrupt businesses I surveyed
> **T:** all local business owners
> **F:** do not plan to hire more workers next year

In these two arguments, the target is the same (all local business owners) and the feature is the same (do not plan to hire more workers next year). The same number of business owners was sampled in each argument. Even the conclusion is the same. What is different is the sample itself: The business owners in the first argument come from a variety of businesses, so the sample is representative. However, the business owners chosen for the second sample had all filed for bankruptcy and are, presumably, less likely to hire new workers. That means the sample is not representative. When an inductive generalization's sample misrepresents the target, the argument commits a fallacy called a **biased generalization**. So this second version of the argument is weak because it is a biased generalization.

> **Hint!**
> Because biased generalizations and hasty generalizations are common mistakes in reasoning that are often rhetorically persuasive, they are referred to as fallacies. You will learn about other common fallacies in Chapter 11.

Samples may also be biased when surveys require participants to initiate contact rather than using a survey taker to actively solicit responses. For example, surveys requiring that participants respond by sending a text message, going online, or phoning in their response are likely to get unrepresentative results, since the respondents are self-selected. Only people who are particularly interested in the issue are likely to respond to the survey. To make matters worse, unless surveys prevent respondents from contributing their answers more than once, the data are likely to be skewed by unscrupulous repeat respondents who are trying to influence the outcome.

Do you trust the media to deliver fair and unbiased news?

Click Here — **YES**

Click Here — **NO**

© iStockphoto.com/Pali Rao

Pop-up polls like this one are common on the Internet. In what ways might the results of this poll be biased?

EXERCISE 8.6

Your Turn! Which of the following sampling techniques for a voter survey would qualify as adequately representative? Defend your answer.

1. Choosing every tenth name on a list of registered voters.
2. Randomly dialing phone numbers.
3. Interviewing potential voters as they picked their children up from school.
4. Placing a survey on an Internet site and inviting whoever is interested to participate.

EXERCISE 8.7

For each of the following pairs of inductive generalizations, determine which is stronger, and justify your evaluation.

1. **A.** The majority of students on campus exercise regularly. I took a survey of students leaving the weight room, and the vast majority of the respondents said they exercised regularly.

   B. The majority of students on campus exercise regularly. I took a survey of students outside of the cafeteria, and the vast majority of the respondents said they exercised regularly.

2. **A.** The local newspaper conducted a survey of its readers to determine which comics were most popular. The majority of the 175 respondents said that *Bizzaro* was their favorite. Thus, *Bizarro* must be the most popular comic strip among all readers.

B. The local newspaper conducted a survey of its readers to determine which comics were most popular. The majority of the 175 respondents under the age of 21 said that *Bizarro* was their favorite. Thus, *Bizarro* must be the most popular comic strip among all readers.

3. **A.** How do most Americans refer to a group of two or more people? They use the words *you guys*. This is the conclusion of an online survey of English usage conducted by Professor Bert Vaux of Harvard University that has had over 30,000 participants. When people were asked how they addressed a group of two or more people, the largest number (42.5%) said they used *you guys*. Interestingly, *y'all* was given by 14% of the respondents.

B. How do most Americans refer to a group of two or more people? They use the words *y'all*. This is the conclusion of a survey of 30 people outside of the Opryland Hotel in Nashville, Tennessee. When they were asked how they addressed a group of two or more people, the majority said they used *y'all*.

4. **A.** The four literature courses I have taken assign one novel a week to read. Thus, most literature courses probably assign a novel a week to read.

B. The six literature courses I have taken assign one novel a week to read. Thus, most literature courses probably assign a novel a week to read.

5. **A.** To determine the water temperature at the lake, I set a thermometer in the top 6 inches of water and found the temperature to be 80°F. Thus, the water in the lake is probably around 80°F.

B. To determine the water temperature at the lake, I recorded the temperature in the top 6 inches of water, again at a depth of 10 feet, and once more at a depth of 30 feet. The average temperature was 58°F. Thus, the water in the lake is probably around 58°F.

 EXERCISE 8.8

For each inductive generalization, consider whether each listed adjustment to the argument makes the argument stronger or weaker than the original. Justify your evaluation.

1. Most of the customers of the West Lake Shopping Center would like to see a fitness center added to the complex. A survey of over 200 customers at the shopping center's main entrance showed that nearly 80% favored adding a fitness center to the complex.
   a. Suppose 450 customers at the shopping center were surveyed.
   b. Suppose 200 responses came from the comment card drop-box.
   c. Suppose 200 customers at the sporting goods store were surveyed.
   d. Suppose the members of one family were surveyed.

2. The food at the residence commons is not very good. I've eaten breakfast there twice, and I didn't like it at all.
   a. Suppose I've eaten breakfast, lunch, and dinner at the residence commons.
   b. Suppose I've eaten breakfast at the residence commons six times.
   c. Suppose I've eaten breakfast there twice, and my roommate has eaten lunch there three times.
   d. Suppose I've never eaten there, but have talked to 10 people who have.

3. What do Americans think about handgun waiting periods? Residents surveyed in three major high-crime metropolitan areas in the Northeast approved of waiting periods for handgun purchases. Therefore, it's clear that Americans approve of waiting periods for handgun purchases.
   a. Suppose residents were surveyed in three rural counties in the Northeast.
   b. Suppose residents were surveyed from states in the north, south, east, west, and middle parts of the country.
   c. Suppose residents from each of the 50 states were surveyed.
   d. Suppose victims of armed robbery were surveyed.
4. Laptop computers are likely to last at least three years. Our company purchased four identical new laptops three years ago, and all four are still working well.
   a. Suppose our company purchased two identical laptop computers three years ago.
   b. Suppose our company also purchased four desktop computers that lasted for three years.
   c. Suppose our company purchased four laptop computers from four different manufacturers three years ago.
   d. Suppose our company purchased two laptop computers and two desktop computers three years ago.
5. Whether or not to use designated hitters in professional baseball continues to be controversial. But sports fans approve of it. We distributed a survey in the sports section of the newspaper in 10 major league cities. More than 55% of respondents said they favored having a designated hitter.
   a. Suppose the survey was a random telephone survey in those 10 major league cities.
   b. Suppose we set up a website and asked people to voice their opinions.
   c. Suppose we announced the survey during a televised baseball game and asked respondents to text their answers.
   d. Suppose we surveyed fans leaving the stadium of the most recent World Series winner.
6. A survey of over 320 alumni from Selma Community College showed that a majority believed they received a good or very good education from SCC. Thus, it's likely that a majority of graduates of SCC are pleased with the education they received.
   a. Suppose the survey was of 510 alumni.
   b. Suppose alumni were asked in the alumni newsletter to text their opinion.
   c. Suppose 320 alumni who attended the most recent commencement were surveyed as they left the event.
   d. Suppose 320 successfully employed alumni were surveyed.
7. Golf on television is boring; I was bored silly watching golf on TV last weekend.
   a. Suppose I watched golf the last four weekends.
   b. Suppose last weekend I watched a local high school golf tournament on television and was bored.
   c. Suppose four of my friends watched golf with me, and all four of us were bored.
   d. Suppose I am also bored playing golf.

8. Few students in the residence halls like the new vegetarian options in the dining commons. The campus radio station conducted a survey where listeners could call in and register their opinions. Results showed that over 70% of the callers disliked the vegetarian options.
   a. Suppose a survey was handed out at the residence halls.
   b. Suppose the survey was of freshmen who attended a residence hall orientation.
   c. Suppose the survey was handed out by the dining commons staff during the dinner hour.
   d. Suppose the survey was of students at the campus Homecoming Dance.
9. What should the U.S. position be toward North Korea? The majority of respondents in a recent poll of nearly 1,100 registered voters in Wisconsin favored adopting a more lenient approach to the increasingly isolated nation. This shows that Americans would like to see the United States drop its traditional hard-line attitude toward this communist dictatorship.
   a. Suppose those surveyed also included voters from North Dakota, Florida, and California.
   b. Suppose only voters of Korean ancestry were surveyed.
   c. Suppose those surveyed were also asked about their attitudes toward Cuba.
   d. Suppose the survey was restricted to voters over 70 years old.
10. An online poll of attitudes toward national security asked visitors to its website to rate whether they favored or opposed the National Security Agency's continued global collection of cell-phone and Internet data. After nearly 100,000 responses, the answer is clear: Very few people favor the spy agency's data collection program.
    a. Suppose data were gathered by using random dialing techniques to contact 1,000 participants throughout the entire country.
    b. Suppose participants were freshmen at the University of California, Berkeley.
    c. Suppose the survey was of members of a libertarian political group.
    d. Suppose the participants were all convicted felons.

PUTTING IT ALL TOGETHER: Writing a Critical Précis of an Inductive Generalization

In Chapters 2, 3, and 4, you learned how to recognize and analyze arguments. In Chapter 5, you also learned how to distinguish among different kinds of arguments. Now that you can evaluate inductive generalizations, you can put all of these skills together by adding inductive generalization evaluation to your Critical Précis assignments.

Directions for a Critical Précis of an Inductive Generalization
In *paragraph form*, use complete sentences and proper English grammar and spelling to do the following:

Step 1: Identify the passage.
▶ Completely and correctly identify the author and the source (whenever such information is given).

- ▶ If the passage contains an argument, identify it as such. Then move to Step 2.
- ▶ If the passage does not contain an argument, identify it as a nonargument. Then specify which feature of an argument is lacking.

Step 2: Analyze the argument.

- ▶ Clearly and completely identify the issue, conclusion, and premise or premises *in that order*.
- ▶ If the passage is a *multiple argument*, write *separate paragraphs* to analyze each separate argument.

Step 3: Diagram the argument.

- ▶ Verify that the diagram is consistent with your Critical Précis.

Step 4: Identify the kind of argument.

- ▶ If the argument is deductive, identify it as a categorical argument or a truth-functional argument.
- ▶ If the argument is inductive, identify it as an inductive generalization, an analogical argument, or a causal argument.

Step 5: Evaluate the argument.

- ▶ If the argument is an inductive generalization, evaluate its strength by considering how well the sample represents the target.

Let's walk through a few examples of a Critical Précis before you try some on your own.

> *It appears that most of the teachers at East High School are very unhappy with the school district administration. We surveyed a dozen teachers who were recently laid off, and they complained about administrators.—The Telegraph*

This passage is an argument, since it contains at least two claims, one of which offers reasons as evidence for the truth of one of the other claims. So you should provide a Critical Précis and an argument diagram.

> *It appears that* ① *most of the teachers at East High School are very unhappy with the school district administration.* ② *We surveyed a dozen teachers who were recently laid off, and* ③ *they complained about administrators.*

③
↓
①

This passage from *The Telegraph* contains an argument. The issue is whether most of the teachers at East High School are happy with the school district administration. The conclusion is that most of the teachers at East High School are very unhappy with the school district administration. The premise is that the dozen laid-off teachers who were surveyed complained about administrators.

Notice that the extra claim is left out of the analysis and diagram. Because the passage is an inductive generalization, you must next evaluate the argument.

> **This argument is an inductive generalization. It is weak because the sample is biased and small. The sample is not random—it consists only of teachers who were recently laid off. Since they are more likely to be unhappy, they do not represent all of the teachers. The sample size is only a dozen teachers, so it is too small to make a strong argument.**

Here's another example, this one a survey of the kind that is readily available in newspapers, magazines, and websites.

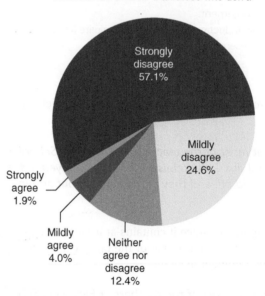

Large Twitter Following = Smart?

"People who have a large number of followers are smarter than those who don't."

- Strongly disagree 57.1%
- Mildly disagree 24.6%
- Neither agree nor disagree 12.4%
- Mildly agree 4.0%
- Strongly agree 1.9%

© Cengage Learning®

> *Twitter users don't think that people with more followers are smarter. This is the result of a survey of 432 highly involved Twitter users (who spend an average of 2¾ hours per day on Twitter). Over 80% of the respondents either mildly or strongly disagreed with the statement that "People who have a large number of followers are smarter than those who don't."—MarketProfs Twitter Survey*

This passage is an argument, since it contains at least two claims, one of which provides support for the other. So you should provide a Critical Précis and argument diagram.

① *Twitter users don't think that people with more followers are smarter*.
② *This is the result of a survey of 432 highly involved Twitter users*

(who spend an average of 2¾ hours per day on Twitter). ③ *Over 80% of the respondents either mildly or strongly disagreed with the statement that "People who have a large number of followers are smarter than those who don't."*

This passage from *MarketProfs Twitter Survey* contains an argument. The issue is whether Twitter users think that people with more followers are smarter. The conclusion is that Twitter users don't think that people with more followers are smarter. The premise is that, in a survey of 432 highly involved Twitter users, over 80% either mildly or strongly disagreed with the statement that "People who have a large number of followers are smarter than those who don't."

This argument is an inductive generalization. It is somewhat strong because the sample size is reasonably large. However, the sample is not random because it consists of "highly involved" Twitter users, and, thus, we must question whether those surveyed are more likely to have the feature than those left out of the survey.

EXERCISE 8.9

Write a Critical Précis for the following passages. Include an argument diagram, and identify the argument type when appropriate. Additionally, evaluate the strength of any inductive generalizations, and justify your evaluation.

1. In November of 2013, the first three women graduated from the Marine Corps infantry training camp. This suggests that women really are capable of becoming combat soldiers.—Political blog writer

2. No moral principle can be proved *a priori* because there can be no *a priori* proof that anything moves anything to act. And morals must move us to act.—David Hume, *A Treatise of Human Nature*

3. In 2008, several universities participated in a study in which 80 randomly selected new high school graduates were compared to another 82 students who served as the control group. The students who attended summer programs were more likely to attend a four-year school (41%, compared to 26% in the control group). This proves that the participants in the study are much more likely to enroll in college as a result of their participation in summer programs. Therefore, most students will benefit from summer programs run by their high schools that provide them with the information, skills, and support they need to succeed in college.—Karen Arnold, *Thought and Action*

4. If the Copernican and Darwinian theories are reasonable representatives of scientific revolutions, Sigmund Freud's theory of psychology is a candidate

for a revolution in thought. Thus, because both the Copernican and Darwinian theories are reasonable representatives of scientific revolutions, Freud's theory is a candidate for a revolution in thought.—Friedel Wienert, *Copernicus, Darwin, and Freud*

5. Infants can recognize human voices as early as 7 months of age. Researchers studied brain activity in 32 infants, half of whom were 4 months of age and the other half 7 months old. Researchers played different sounds, including human voices speaking nonsense languages, and brain activity suggested the 7-month-olds could distinguish the human voice from the other sounds, and the 4-month-olds could not.—*Neuron*

6. It seems that the high cost of private golf clubs prevents many minorities and women from joining. This is because few women and minorities belong to private clubs, and prices have remained high for years even though other barriers to membership have disappeared.—Kaser and Brooks, *Sports and Entertainment Management*

7. Among people who use multiple dietary supplements, fish oil/omega-3 supplements now top multivitamins in popularity. The conclusion is based on 6,012 responses collected in November from a sampling of subscribers to our free e-newsletter. Fish oil/omega-3 supplements were used by 74% of respondents, followed in popularity by multivitamins, which were used by 72%.—*ConsumerLab.com*

8. If any lies, like other sins, steal upon us, they should seek not to be justified but to be pardoned.—St. Augustine, "On Lying"

9. Since the sixteenth century, opium had been produced in India and carried by Dutch, and later, British traders. In fact, opium (derived from the poppy plant) was one of the very few commodities that Europeans could sell in China, and for this reason it became crucial to the balance of East-West trade.—Coffin and Stacey, *Western Civilizations*

10. For-profit hospices do not focus on the best interests of their patients. In one study assessing the impact of ownership status on care provided to patients, researchers found that patients receiving care from for-profit hospices received a narrower range of services than patients from non-profit hospices. The narrower range of services meant that patients with for-profit hospices were not receiving as much counseling services, medications, and personal care.—Carlson, Gallo, and Bradley, "Ownership Status and Patterns of Care in Hospice"

CHAPTER REVIEW QUESTIONS

1. How do you find the sample, target, and feature of an inductive generalization?
2. How do you determine whether the sample is representative of the target?
3. What is a hasty generalization?
4. What is a biased generalization?
5. How do you write a Critical Précis of an inductive generalization?

ONE STEP FURTHER

Stereotypes are generalizations about a group of people whereby we attribute a defined set of characteristics to this group. While stereotyping enables us to respond rapidly to situations, it often leads us make judgments about people that might not be true. For example, in the summer of 2011, a gunman killed 69 young people at a summer camp near Oslo, Norway. Terrorism experts initially proclaimed that this attack was the work of Al-Qaeda or another Muslim terrorist group. Who else, they initially thought, would be killing blond-haired, blue-eyed Norwegian children?

The reasoning of law enforcement officials seemed to follow something along these lines:

The most recent attacks on civilians in Western countries have been the work of Muslim terrorists. Thus, it is most likely that all attacks on civilians in Western countries are the work of Muslim terrorists.

1. Evaluate this argument. Is it strong or weak? Justify your evaluation.
2. The gunman, who later confessed, was a right-wing nationalist from Norway named Anders Breivik. Should knowing that fact change your evaluation of the argument's strength? Why or why not?
3. What attitudes, stereotypes, and other implicit biases influence your perception, judgment, and action? Find out by taking one (or more) of the Implicit Association Tests developed by Project Implicit at https://implicit.harvard.edu/implicit/research/. Did you discover anything surprising about yourself?

AP Images/Jonas Dahlberg Studio, NTB

Swedish artist Jonas Dahlberg was unanimously selected to be the designer of a public memorial to commemorate the victims of the Utoya massacre on July 22, 2011. He describes the project as "a wound or cut written within nature itself" and "an acknowledgment of what is forever irreplaceable."

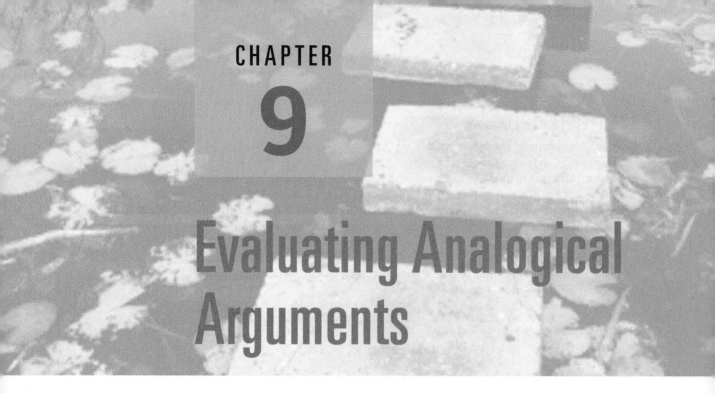

CHAPTER

9

Evaluating Analogical Arguments

Think back to the discussion about whether to support the Smoke-Free Campus Initiative in Chapter 1. Among the responses presented was the following:

James says I don't smoke, but I don't think it's a good idea to ban smoking on campus. Since when does completely banning something work? Alcohol and drugs are illegal on campus, so no one uses them, right? Wrong!

© iStockphoto.com/Joshua Hodge Photography

Using the skills you learned in Chapter 5, you should recognize this passage as containing an analogical argument. An **analogical argument**, you may recall, is an inductive argument that uses an analogy to conclude that, because one case has some feature, the other case should, too. In this example, James is comparing banning smoking on campus to banning alcohol and drug use on campus. When he asks his final question and answers it with "Wrong!" he implies that banning alcohol and drugs on campus has not stopped alcohol and drug consumption. From this, he concludes that banning smoking on campus will not stop smoking. In this chapter, you will discover that all analogical arguments, including this one, have the same basic structure and will practice identifying the core elements of that structure—namely, the source, target, and feature in the argument. You will then use that information to evaluate the strength of analogical arguments.

LEARNING OUTCOMES

In this chapter, you will learn how to evaluate analogical arguments by:

▸ Identifying the source, target, and feature in an analogical argument;
▸ Determining how many analogies are presented in the argument;
▸ Determining how many similarities are presented in the subargument;
▸ Determining how relevant the similarities are to the feature; and
▸ Writing a Critical Précis of an analogical argument.

Analyzing Analogical Arguments

Every analogical argument has the same basic structure. We will refer to this structure as the general form of analogical arguments. In its general form, each analogical argument contains two premises supporting the conclusion. One premise provides the analogy, and the other premise identifies the feature that the arguer concludes must be shared by the analogues. This general form for analogical arguments can be stated as follows:

> **P1:** The target is like the source.
>
> **P2:** The source has a particular feature.
>
> ∴   The target has the feature.

The first premise above presents the analogy. An **analogy** is a comparison of two (or more) things, typically called **analogues**. One of the analogues is called the source, and the other is called the target. The source (S) is the analogue that is given only among the premises. The target (T) is the analogue that the arguer is drawing a conclusion about; it will be found in both the analogy and the conclusion. The feature (F) is the characteristic of the source that the arguer is trying to prove is also a characteristic of the target.

Although some analogical arguments may be constructed differently, they can all be translated into this general form. Here's an example of an analogical argument, followed by a Formal Analysis of the argument highlighting the source, target, and feature.

> *Buying an energy-efficient washing machine should save you money in the long run. This is because energy-efficient washing machines are like energy-efficient dishwashers, and energy-efficient dishwashers save buyers money in the long run.*

> **P1:** Energy-efficient washing machines are like energy-efficient dishwashers.
>
> **P2:** Energy-efficient dishwashers save buyers money in the long run.
>
> ∴   Energy-efficient washing machines save buyers money in the long run.

> **Issue:** Whether energy-efficient washing machines save buyers money in the long run

Accurately identifying the source, target, and feature is critical for the evaluation of analogical arguments. Here is an example of the proper identification from the previous argument.

> **Source:**   energy-efficient dishwashers
> **Target:**   energy-efficient washing machines
> **Feature:** save buyers money in the long run

Some analogical arguments present the analogy with the source and target in a different order, as in this example.

> *Since my old laptop lasted over three years, it's reasonable to conclude that this new laptop will last over three years, too. This is likely because my old laptop is like my new laptop.*

EXERCISE 9.1

Your Turn! Write a Formal Analysis of the argument presented above. Then label the source, target, and feature.

Don't let the order of the analogues fool you into misidentifying them. The source will be found only in the premises of the argument, and the target will be found in both the analogy and the conclusion. Thus, the proper identification of the parts is:

Source: my old laptop
Target: my new laptop
Feature: will last over three years

EXERCISE 9.2

For each analogical argument, complete a Formal Analysis, and then state the source, target, and feature.

1. The new model of Avenger running shoes is like the past model of Avenger running shoes. The past model has a great deal of cushioning in the sole. Therefore, the new model probably has a great deal of cushioning in the sole.
2. Masking tape is similar to duct tape. Masking tape can be used on paper, so duct tape can probably be used on paper.
3. Beefsteak tomatoes are very juicy. Roma tomatoes are like Beefsteak tomatoes. Thus, Roma tomatoes are likely to be juicy.
4. The Spanish explorer Fernando Cortez was much like the English explorer Sir Francis Drake. Given that Cortez was eager to increase his country's influence in the New World, it seems probable that Drake was also eager to increase his country's influence in the New World.
5. A screwball is probably a very hard pitch to hit. This is because a screwball is like a curve ball, and a curve ball is a very hard pitch to hit.
6. The second chemistry exam is similar to the first chemistry exam. Because you did well on the first exam, it's likely that you will do well on the second exam.
7. Driving while under the influence of marijuana is a lot like driving under the influence of alcohol. Since you will lose your license if you are caught driving while under the influence of alcohol, you are also likely to lose your license if you are caught driving while under the influence of marijuana.
8. A Canadian porcupine is akin to an African porcupine. Therefore, a Canadian porcupine probably does not "throw" its quills because an African porcupine does not "throw" its quills.
9. The reason that the Hudson River is probably less polluted than it was a couple of decades ago is that the Hudson River is like the James River, and the James River is less polluted than it was a couple of decades ago.
10. Rats are similar to mice. Given that mice make great pets, rats probably also make great pets.

Understanding the general form of analogical arguments is important because many analogical arguments contain subarguments. These subarguments provide evidence to support the analogy (the claim that T is like S). In these cases, you must recognize that the evidence for the analogy constitutes the premises in the subargument, not in the main argument.

Consider the following example.

> *In April 2010, Arizona signed into law the toughest bill on illegal immigration in generations, making the failure to carry immigration documents a crime. We can expect that New Mexico will soon pass a similar law. After all, New Mexico is a lot like Arizona, given that both have a large population of immigrants and both are bordered by Mexico.*

Using the general form for analogical arguments, you can analyze the main argument formally. Notice that the first premise identifies the analogy (T is like S) and the second premise identifies the feature (S has F).

P1: New Mexico is a lot like Arizona.

P2: Arizona passed a law making the failure to carry immigration documents a crime.

∴ New Mexico will pass a law making the failure to carry immigration documents a crime.

Issue: Whether New Mexico will pass a law making the failure to carry immigration documents a crime

S: Arizona

T: New Mexico

F: passing a law making the failure to carry immigration documents a crime

What about the last two claims in the final sentence? Where do they fit? The inference indicator *given that* signals that they are premises for the first claim in that sentence. That is, they present evidence that New Mexico and Arizona are alike. Thus, the passage contains a subargument, as shown in the following Formal Analysis.

P1: New Mexico and Arizona have large populations of immigrants.

P2: New Mexico and Arizona are bordered by Mexico.

∴ New Mexico is like Arizona.

Now, we can diagram the argument.

In April 2010, ① Arizona signed into law the toughest bill on illegal immigration in generations, making the failure to carry immigration documents a crime. We can expect that ② New Mexico will soon pass a similar law. After all, ③ New Mexico is a lot like Arizona, given that

④ *both have a large population of immigrants* and ⑤ *both are bordered by Mexico*.

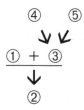

Notice that the main argument has the same structure as the other analogical arguments you have examined. There are two linked premises, one stating the analogy and the other identifying the feature as true of the source. The subargument offers the reasons for the claim that New Mexico really is like Arizona by identifying the ways in which the two analogues are similar.

> **Hint!**
> Analogies are often used for illustrative purposes; that is, a familiar concept is used to help someone understand an unfamiliar concept. Such uses of analogies do not prove any conclusion, and thus should not be confused with analogical arguments.

Understanding the general form for analogical arguments is also helpful when the arguer does not explicitly state the analogy. In these cases, the arguer provides

Protesters demonstrate against Arizona's tough new immigration laws at a large rally in Phoenix on May 29, 2010. What analogy is implied by the "Boycott Arizona" sign in the background?

MARK RALSTON/AFP/Getty Images

evidence for the analogy, but the analogy itself is missing. Part of the work, then, in analyzing analogical arguments includes identifying the analogy, even when it is not explicitly stated by the arguer.

Consider the following example.

> *The Nissan Leaf and the Chevy Volt are both new electric cars. Since the Chevy Volt can travel over 40 miles on electric power alone, the Nissan Leaf is likely to travel 40 miles on only electric power, too.*

At first, this analogical argument appears to have a different structure than the ones we have examined thus far. However, on closer inspection, the difference lies in the fact that the arguer has not stated the analogy explicitly, but has, instead, only offered evidence for an analogy. Your task, then, is to identify this unstated claim in your analysis.

 EXERCISE 9.3

Your Turn! What two things is the arguer comparing in the previous example?

Once you have identified the analogues, you can use the general form of analogical arguments to analyze the main argument. Notice that the first premise is the unstated analogy.

P1: The Nissan Leaf is like the Chevy Volt.
P2: <u>The Chevy Volt can travel over 40 miles on electric power alone.</u>
∴   The Nissan Leaf will travel 40 miles on only electric power.

Issue: Whether the Nissan Leaf will travel 40 miles on only electric power

S: the Chevy Volt
T: the Nissan Leaf
F: can travel over 40 miles on electric power alone

What, then, is the role of the first claim in the passage—namely, that the Chevy Volt and the Nissan Leaf are both new electric cars? It tells us what makes the two analogues similar. In other words, it is a premise for the subargument. You can analyze it as follows, adding in the unstated conclusion.

P: <u>The Nissan Leaf and the Chevy Volt are both new electric cars.</u>
∴   The Nissan Leaf is like the Chevy Volt.

Using the skills you learned from Chapter 4, you can now diagram the argument.

① *The Nissan Leaf and the Chevy Volt are both new electric cars*. Since
② *the Chevy Volt can travel over 40 miles on electric power alone,* ③ *the
Nissan Leaf is likely to travel 40 miles on only electric power, too.* ④ *The
Nissan Leaf is like the Chevy Volt.*

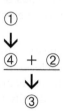

Notice that the diagram identifies the unstated analogy as an intermediate conclusion; it functions both as the conclusion of the subargument and as a premise of the main argument.

Before trying some on your own, let's examine James's response regarding banning smoking on campus presented at the beginning of this chapter.

*I don't smoke, but I don't think it's a good idea to ban smoking on campus.
Since when does completely banning something work? Alcohol and drugs
are illegal on campus, so no one uses them, right? Wrong!*

Analyzing this analogical argument is particularly challenging because neither the analogy nor the conclusion is explicitly stated. However, knowing the general form of analogical arguments can help. First, what is the analogy? James compares banning smoking on campus to banning alcohol and drug use on campus. Next, what feature does he conclude is true of banning smoking based on its being true of banning alcohol and drug use? When he says, "… no one uses them, right? Wrong!" he implies that banning alcohol and drug use on campus has not stopped their consumption. From this, he concludes that banning smoking on campus will not stop smoking. Let's set out this argument in a Formal Analysis.

P1: Banning smoking on campus is like banning alcohol and drug use on campus.

P2: Banning alcohol and drug use on campus does not stop alcohol and drug consumption.

∴ Banning smoking on campus will not stop smoking.

Issue: Whether banning smoking on campus will stop smoking

EXERCISE 9.4

Your Turn! Identify the source, target, and feature of the argument above.

EXERCISE 9.5

Provide a Formal Analysis and diagram of each of the following analogical arguments. Then state the source, target, and feature.

1. Lasagna and spaghetti both have pasta and tomato sauce, so lasagna is like spaghetti. Since spaghetti is tasty, lasagna is probably tasty.
2. A catfish has gills, and a trout has gills. Consequently, catfish are like trout. Now, catfish are able to live only a short while out of water. So trout can probably live only a short while out of water.
3. A prince is the child of a king. A princess, too, is the child of a king. So a prince is like a princess. Also, a princess leads a sheltered life. Thus, a prince most likely leads a sheltered life.
4. Horses, dogs, and cats all can be taught tricks by using positive reinforcement and lots of food treats. Thus, birds are probably trainable in the same way.
5. A DVD is read by a laser beam. A CD is also read by a laser beam. Therefore, a DVD is like a CD. Because a CD must not be scratched, a DVD probably shouldn't be scratched, either.
6. Astrology studies the stars and has been around for hundreds of years. Astronomy also studies the stars and has been around for hundreds of years. We know that astronomy is worthy of being called a science. Therefore, astrology is likewise worthy of being called a science.
7. Both high school principals and high school counselors have advanced degrees in education. Thus, high school principals are paid more than teachers, since counselors receive more pay than teachers.
8. Since navel oranges have thick rinds, have an acidic core, and are protected by thick leaves and Valencia oranges have similar rinds, acidic cores, and leaf protection, navel oranges are like Valencia oranges. Given that Valencia oranges can withstand a light freeze, navel oranges can be expected to withstand a light freeze as well.
9. The Mississippi River, the Potomac River, and the Hudson River are all bodies of fresh water that flow toward the ocean. So the Nile River probably flows toward the ocean, since it, too, is a body of fresh water.
10. Chimpanzees are highly intelligent, social, and able to use rudimentary tools. Thus, chimpanzees are like mandrills because they, too, are highly intelligent, social, tool-using animals. Because mandrills are capable of learning a simple form of sign language, chimpanzees can probably learn a simple form of sign language, too.
11. Eyes are like ears because both eyes and ears are sensitive to outside stimulation and have nerves leading directly to the brain. Thus, since ears give incomplete information about the outside environment, eyes, too, probably give incomplete information about the outside world.
12. We can infer that Utah is much like California because Utah is dry, mountainous, and dependent on water from other states and California is dry, mountainous, and dependent on water from other states. Because California has profited from large-scale drip irrigation of agricultural land, Utah would probably also profit from large-scale drip irrigation of agricultural land.
13. The last three economic recessions were made less damaging to people after Congress passed a stimulus package that gave all taxpayers a few hundred

extra dollars to spend. It seems likely, then, that the current economic recession will be made less damaging to people after Congress passes a similar stimulus package.

14. Apple, apricot, and plum trees all need to be pruned after their leaves fall. It stands to reason that peach trees will need to be pruned after their leaves fall.

15. Comedies and musicals are both theatrical performances. Given that musicals incorporate dancing, comedies are likely to incorporate dancing also.

Evaluating Analogical Arguments

When evaluating analogical arguments, you should use the terms appropriate for evaluating inductive arguments. Recall that an inductive argument is *strong* when the premises make the conclusion very likely to be true. Unlike deductive arguments, which are either valid or invalid, the strength of inductive arguments varies across a continuum from very strong to very weak. This means that assessing the strength of analogical arguments will involve using different criteria than assessing the validity of deductive arguments. The strength of an analogical argument depends on how much and in what ways the target is like the source. So, to evaluate an analogical argument, you must consider three things: the quantity of similarities shared between the source and target, the number of analogies presented, and the relevance of the similarities to the feature.

First, how many similarities between the source and target does the arguer identify? The more relevant similarities shared by the source and target, the stronger the argument. This is because the more characteristics the analogues have in common, the more likely it is that they will have an additional characteristic in common. To see this, compare a pair of analogical arguments. First, consider this one.

> Ron and Brian both like the movie Shaun of the Dead. *Since Ron also likes the movie* Zombieland, *Brian will, too.*

Notice that this argument contains a subargument. Analyzed formally, with the subargument presented first, as always, the argument looks like this.

P:	Ron and Brian both like the movie *Shaun of the Dead.*
∴	Brian is like Ron.

P1:	Brian is like Ron.
P2:	Ron likes the movie *Zombieland.*
∴	Brian will like the movie *Zombieland.*

Issue: Whether Brian will like the movie *Zombieland*

Now identify the source, target, and feature.

S:	Ron
T:	Brian
F:	likes the movie *Zombieland.*

Compare that argument to this one.

Ron and Brian both like the movies Evil Dead 2, Day of the Dead, Army of Darkness, *and* Shaun of the Dead. *Since Ron also likes the movie* Zombieland, *Brian will, too.*

Notice that this argument also contains a subargument. Analyzed formally, the argument looks like this.

P: Ron and Brian both like the movies *Evil Dead 2, Day of the Dead, Army of Darkness,* and *Shaun of the Dead.*

∴   Brian is like Ron.

P1:   Brian is like Ron.
P2:   Ron likes the movie *Zombieland.*
∴   Brian will like the movie *Zombieland.*

Issue: Whether Brian will like the movie *Zombieland*

 EXERCISE 9.6

Your Turn!   Identify the source, target, and feature of the previous argument.

In both arguments, the source, target, and feature are identical because the main arguments are identical. What differs is the amount of evidence provided in the subargument to support the analogy. In the first argument, Ron is like Brian because they both like one movie, and in the second argument, Ron is like Brian because they both like four movies. This means that the second argument is stronger due to the fact that the target and the source share a larger quantity of similarities. It is more probable that Brian will like a particular movie that Ron likes if they both like four other movies than if they both like only one other movie. The more that the analogues have in common, the more probable it is that the conclusion of the argument is true.

Hint!
Be sure that you do not confuse the similarities with the feature. The similarities are those commonalities between the source and target that the arguer presents as reasons to support the analogy. Thus, the similarities are found only in the premises of the subargument. The feature is the characteristic of the source that the arguer concludes is also a characteristic of the target. Thus, the feature is found in one premise and the conclusion of the main argument.

Second, how many analogues does the arguer provide in the source? Generally speaking, the more analogues presented in the source, the stronger the argument.

This is because each analogy offers additional evidence to support the conclusion. To see this, compare another pair of analogical arguments. First, consider this one.

> *I have taken a course in black-and-white photography, and it was interesting and fun. Therefore, I am likely to find a course in fashion photography interesting and fun.*

Analyzed formally, the argument looks like this.

P1: The course in fashion photography is like the course in black-and-white photography.

P2: The course in black-and-white photography was interesting and fun.

∴ The course in fashion photography will be interesting and fun.

Issue: Whether the course in fashion photography will be interesting and fun

Now identify the source, target, and feature.

S: the course in black-and white-photography

T: the course in fashion photography

F: interesting and fun

Compare that argument to this one.

> *I have taken courses in black-and-white photography, color photography, and documentary photography and have found all of them interesting and fun. Therefore, I am likely to find a course in fashion photography interesting and fun.*

Analyzed formally, the argument looks like this.

P1: The course in fashion photography is like the courses in black-and-white photography, color photography, and documentary photography.

P2: The courses in black-and-white photography, color photography, and documentary photography were interesting and fun.

∴ The course in fashion photography will be interesting and fun.

Issue: Whether the course in fashion photography will be interesting and fun

Now identify the source, target, and feature.

S: the courses in black-and-white photography, color photography, and documentary photography

T: the course in fashion photography

F: interesting and fun

In both arguments, the target is *the course in fashion photography*, and the feature is *interesting and fun*. But notice the difference in the source. The first argument provides only one analogue in the source, whereas the second provides three. Of the two, then, the second is stronger because the source is larger. In the second argument, the speaker enjoyed a wider variety of photography courses, making it more likely that he or she would enjoy another kind of photography course.

EXERCISE 9.7

For each of the following pairs of analogical arguments, identify the source, target, and feature. Then determine which argument is stronger in each pair, and explain why.

1. **A.** My Scion xB gets at least 25 miles per gallon, so this Scion xD will also get at least 25 miles per gallon.
   B. The Scion xA gets at least 25 miles per gallon. The Scion xB gets at least 25 miles per gallon. And the Scion tC gets at least 25 miles per gallon. You can, then, expect the Scion xD to get at least 25 miles per gallon.
2. **A.** I have visited Six Flags, Hershey Park, Kings Island, Joyland, and Carowinds, all of which had a wide selection of roller coasters. So I bet Disney World also has a wide selection of roller coasters.
   B. I have visited Six Flags and Hershey Park, both of which had a wide selection of roller coasters. So I bet Disney World also has a wide selection of roller coasters.
3. **A.** Preparing for a final exam requires studying and skill. Preparing for a wrestling tournament also requires study and skill. Since wrestlers do better if they get a good night's sleep before a match, students taking final exams should also do better on a good night's sleep.
   B. Preparing for a final exam requires studying, skill, and discipline. Preparing for a wrestling tournament also requires study, skill, and discipline. Since wrestlers do better if they get a good night's sleep before a match, students taking final exams should also do better on a good night's sleep.
4. **A.** Gopher snakes have brown markings on their backs, and they are harmless to people. Rattlesnakes also have brown markings on their backs, so they, too, must be harmless to people.
   B. Gopher snakes, Great Plains rat snakes, and eastern hog-nosed snakes all have brown markings on their backs, and they are harmless to people. Rattlesnakes also have brown markings on their backs, so they, too, must be harmless to people.
5. **A.** Commercial airplane flights are long, boring, and cramped. Commercial space flights will also be long, boring, and cramped. People can endure long commercial airplane flights if they are offered movies, food breaks, and space to walk around. Therefore, these options will be useful for commercial space flights.
   B. Commercial airplane flights are long and boring. Commercial space flights will also be long and boring. People can endure long commercial airplane

flights if they are offered movies, food breaks, and space to walk around. Therefore, these options will be useful for commercial space flights.

6. **A.** Tigers have strong leg muscles, long legs, loose-fitting skin, and a strong predatory instinct. Cheetahs, too, have strong leg muscles, long legs, loose-fitting skin, and a strong predatory instinct. Since cheetahs are extremely fast runners, tigers are probably also fast runners.

B. Tigers have strong leg muscles, long legs, and a strong predatory instinct. Cheetahs also have strong leg muscles, long legs, and a strong predatory instinct. Since cheetahs are extremely fast runners, tigers are probably also fast runners.

7. **A.** Lawyers, doctors, engineers, and high school teachers all have advanced degrees. Therefore, high school teachers earn a much higher than average salary, since lawyers, doctors, and engineers earn a much higher than average salary.

B. Lawyers and high school teachers have advanced degrees. Therefore, high school teachers earn a much higher than average salary, since lawyers earn a much higher than average salary.

8. **A.** People can use email to write informally to close friends and to write formally to strangers. Regular mail also can be used to write informally to close friends and to write formally to strangers. Since using sarcasm in regular mail can lead to misunderstandings, using sarcasm in email can also lead to misunderstandings.

B. People can use email to write informally to close friends, to write formally to strangers, and to manage various business issues. Regular mail also can be used to write informally to close friends, to write formally to strangers, and to manage various business issues. Since using sarcasm in regular mail can lead to misunderstandings, using sarcasm in email can also lead to misunderstandings.

9. **A.** MySpace and Facebook are both social networking websites that allow users to send messages to one another. Because Facebook is free for all users, MySpace is likely also free for all users.

B. MySpace and Facebook are both social networking websites that allow users to share information and photographs, as well as to send messages to one another. Because Facebook is free for all users, MySpace is likely also free for all users.

10. **A.** Gwen and Charles are very similar: They are the same age, exercise regularly, eat a well-balanced diet, and have no family history of heart disease. Since Charles has healthy cholesterol levels, Gwen should also.

B. Gwen and Charles are both 47 years old. Since Charles has healthy cholesterol levels, Gwen should also.

When we discussed the quantity of similarities and analogues, we stated that an analogical argument is stronger when there are more similarities and when there are more analogues. While this is generally true, you must also attend to another criterion—namely, *relevance*. Why? For any given analogy, there will be numerous ways in which the analogues are similar, so you must consider whether these similarities are in fact *relevant* to the feature. Only when they are relevant is the conclusion more likely to be true.

Consider, for example, the following analogical argument.

> *Humans are a lot like rats. They are both mammals, and they both have the same basic physiology. Since rats that are exposed to secondhand smoke have a high risk of developing cancer, humans who are exposed to secondhand smoke have a high risk of developing cancer.*

Let's first analyze and diagram the argument to isolate the similarities from the source, target, and feature.

> ① *Humans are a lot like rats.* ② *They are both mammals,* and ③ *they both have the same basic physiology.* Since ④ *rats that are exposed to secondhand smoke have a high risk of developing cancer,* ⑤ *humans who are exposed to secondhand smoke have a high risk of developing cancer.*

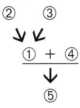

P1: Humans and rats are both mammals.

P2: Humans and rats have the same basic physiology.

∴ Humans are a lot like rats.

P1: Humans are a lot like rats.

P2: Rats that are exposed to secondhand smoke have a high risk of developing cancer.

∴ Humans who are exposed to secondhand smoke have a high risk of developing cancer.

Issue: Whether humans who are exposed to secondhand smoke have a high risk of developing cancer

In this example, the arguer compares humans to rats and identifies two ways in which they are similar: They are both mammals, and they have the same basic physiology. Then the arguer concludes that a feature that is true of rats—namely, those exposed to secondhand smoke have a high risk of developing cancer—is also true of humans. Are the similarities identified in the premises of the subargument relevant or irrelevant to this feature? They are relevant. It seems reasonable that mammals with the same basic physiology are likely to respond to environmental hazards in similar ways.

Now consider this argument.

> *Soccer is a lot like ice hockey: Both involve one team trying to outscore another, the teams each have one player guarding the goal, and players are penalized for being "offside." Given that ice hockey is played wearing ice skates, soccer must also be played wearing ice skates.*

EXERCISE 9.8

Your Turn! Diagram the analogical argument above. Then write a Formal Analysis of the argument.

For anyone who knows even a little bit about ice hockey and soccer, it should be clear that something has gone wrong in this argument. The arguer compares soccer to ice hockey, and, indeed, they do have these and many other similarities. Are the similarities relevant to the feature? Given that the issue is whether soccer is played wearing ice skates, the stated similarities are irrelevant; what kind of footwear players wear is not determined by the scoring and penalty rules of the game. Whenever the similarities between the source and target are irrelevant to the feature, we say that the argument commits a fallacy known as **faulty analogy**.

Hint!

To determine whether an argument uses a faulty analogy, you will need to identify the ways in which the analogues are different from each other. This will often require you to rely on information not presented in the argument, since arguers are unlikely to point out any relevant differences that might reveal the weaknesses of their argument. They are, after all, trying to convince you to accept their conclusion!

 EXERCISE 9.9

For each of the following, state the source, target, and feature. Then evaluate the analogy by identifying the similarities between the source and target and determining whether those similarities are relevant or irrelevant to the feature.

1. The University of Hawaii at Manoa is a lot like the University of Colorado at Denver. They are both public, coeducational universities located in the capital city of their state, and they both have student populations of approximately 20,000 students. Since 64% of the students at the University of Hawaii are of Asian or Pacific Island descent, approximately the same number of students at the University of Colorado at Denver are of Asian or Pacific Island descent.

2. Two years ago, my aunt had symptoms just like yours. She was tired all the time, experienced joint and muscle stiffness, and had swollen lymph nodes, and her limbs would often go numb, just like what has been happening to you. It turned out that she had Lyme disease, and I bet that's what you've got, too.

3. Director Tim Burton's next feature film is *Maleficent*, a retelling of Disney's *Sleeping Beauty* from the villain's perspective. There's little doubt this film will star Johnny Depp. This is because over the past five years, Burton has made four films—*Charlie and the Chocolate Factory*, *Corpse Bride*, *Sweeney Todd*, and *Alice in Wonderland*—all of which have starred Johnny Depp. So Burton will probably choose him again.

4. Workers in California are guaranteed by law six weeks of paid leave to care for their newborns, and workers in Washington are guaranteed by law five weeks of paid leave to care for their newborns. Therefore, since Texas is like California and Washington—they are all states located in the United States—workers in Texas are probably guaranteed by law several weeks of paid leave to care for their newborns.

5. Cars are four-wheeled vehicles and are used to transport people and goods from one place to another. Horse-drawn carriages are also four-wheeled vehicles and are used to transport people and goods from one place to another. Since cars can be safely driven on the freeway, horse-drawn carriages can probably be safely driven on the freeway.

EXERCISE 9.10

For each of the following analogical arguments, consider whether the listed adjustments to the argument would strengthen, weaken, or result in no change to the strength of the original argument.

1. Organic spinach from California was contaminated with *E. coli* bacteria. Thus, organic lettuce could also be contaminated with *E. coli* bacteria.
   a. Suppose the lettuce was from California.
   b. Suppose the lettuce was not organic.
   c. Suppose that chard and arugula were also contaminated with *E. coli* bacteria.
   d. Suppose it was broccoli, not lettuce, that had been contaminated with *E. coli* bacteria.

2. The new sports car Bob recently bought is equipped with a powerful V-8 engine, four-speed transmission, and racing clutch. The previous sports car Bob owned also had a V-8 engine, four-speed transmission, and racing clutch. So the new car is similar to the old one. Because Bob got several speeding tickets with his old car, he's probably going to get speeding tickets with the new one.
   a. Suppose Bob has owned six other sports cars and he has gotten a speeding ticket driving each of them.
   b. Suppose Bob's old car was turbocharged and so is his new one.
   c. Suppose Bob's new car has a four-cylinder engine.
   d. Suppose Bob's old car was black and his new one is red.

3. The stocks that Harold purchased are from Internet startups, are highly rated, and are selling for a low price. The stocks that Ashley bought are also from Internet startups, are highly rated, and are selling for a low price. Thus, Harold's stocks are similar to Ashley's stocks. Since Ashley's stocks made a 10% profit in the first year, Harold can expect his stocks to make at least a 10% profit, too.
   a. Suppose Gregg also purchased stocks from Internet startups that were highly rated and selling for a low price and they also made a 10% profit in the first year.

b. Suppose Harold bought stocks that were low-rated.

c. Suppose Harold bought stocks that were from a traditional brick-and-mortar business.

d. Suppose Harold bought his stocks from a broker.

4. Cleveland, Butte, and San Diego are three cities that have recently lost large numbers of factory jobs. However, all three cities have successfully developed a training program to teach ex-factory workers how to install and repair solar panels and other alternative energy devices. Detroit has also lost factory jobs. So, since the program worked well for Cleveland, Butte, and San Diego, it ought to work well here in Detroit.

a. Suppose the factory jobs in Cleveland, Butte, and San Diego were all high-skilled jobs and Detroit's factory jobs are high-skilled, too.

b. Suppose five cities that lost factory jobs had success with the training program.

c. Suppose Cleveland, Butte, and San Diego all had some solar energy companies and Detroit does not.

d. Suppose Detroit recently laid off a large number of city employees.

5. The Lions have won their last four home football games. Therefore, they will probably win when they play at home next Saturday.

a. Suppose the previous games were played in fair weather and rain is predicted for this Saturday's game.

b. Suppose the Lions' star receiver, who scored two touchdowns in each of the previous games, is out for the rest of the season.

c. Suppose the Lions won their last six home games.

d. Suppose the Lions have four players on the Dean's List for academic excellence.

PUTTING IT ALL TOGETHER: Writing a Critical Précis of an Analogical Argument

In Chapters 2, 3, and 4, you learned how to recognize and analyze arguments. In Chapter 5, you also learned how to distinguish among different kinds of arguments. Now that you can evaluate analogical arguments, you can put all of these skills together by adding analogical argument evaluation to your Critical Précis assignments.

Directions for a Critical Précis of an Analogical Argument

In *paragraph form*, use complete sentences and proper English grammar and spelling to do the following:

Step 1: Identify the passage.

▶ Completely and correctly identify the author and the source (whenever such information is given).

▶ If the passage contains an argument, identify it as such. Then move to Step 2.

▶ If the passage does not contain an argument, identify it as a nonargument. Then specify which feature of an argument is lacking.

Step 2: Analyze the argument.

▶ Clearly and completely identify the issue, conclusion, and premise or premises *in that order.*

▶ If the passage is a *multiple argument*, write *separate paragraphs* to analyze each separate argument.

Step 3: Diagram the argument.

▶ Verify that the diagram is consistent with your Critical Précis.

Step 4: Identify the kind of argument.

▶ If the argument is deductive, identify it as a categorical argument or a truth-functional argument.

▶ If the argument is inductive, identify it as an inductive generalization, an analogical argument, or a causal argument.

Step 5: Evaluate the argument.

▶ If the argument is an analogical argument, evaluate its strength by considering the quantity of similarities identified, the number of analogues presented, and how relevant the similarities are to the feature.

Let's consider a few examples before you try some on your own.

A woman without a man is like a fish without a bicycle.—Gloria Steinem

First, is this passage an argument? The author gives an analogy by comparing a woman without a man to a fish without a bicycle, presumably to counter assumptions that a woman needs a man. However, notice that there is only one claim here, so it cannot be an argument. The Critical Précis, then, should read as follows:

This passage by Gloria Steinem is not an argument. It contains only one claim, and arguments need at least two claims.

 EXERCISE 9.11

Your Turn!   Construct an analogical argument by using the analogy given by Gloria Steinem.

Next, consider this passage.

How do we know that animals can feel pain? Because animals are like human beings. The nervous systems of vertebrates, especially of birds and mammals, are fundamentally similar to that of human beings. And, both animals and humans behave in similar ways when injured: writhing, facial contortions, moaning, yelping, avoidance, etc. So, since we know that human beings can feel pain, we can conclude that animals can also.—Peter Singer

Unlike the previous example, this one contains an argument. The arguer uses an analogy (that animals are like humans) to draw a conclusion (that animals can feel pain). Let's start our analysis by diagramming the argument and then presenting the written analysis. Notice that the diagram and written analysis are consistent.

> *How do we know that animals can feel pain? Because* ① *animals are like human beings.* ② *The nervous systems of vertebrates, especially of birds and mammals, are fundamentally similar to that of human beings. And,* ③ *both animals and humans behave in similar ways when injured: writhing, facial contortions, moaning, yelping, avoidance, etc. So, since we know that* ④ *human beings can feel pain, we can conclude that* ⑤ *animals can also.*

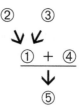

This passage from Peter Singer contains an argument. The issue is whether animals can feel pain. The conclusion is that animals can feel pain. The first premise is that animals are like humans. The second premise is that humans can feel pain.

The passage contains a subargument. The intermediate conclusion is that animals are like humans. The first premise is that the nervous systems of vertebrates, especially of birds and mammals, are fundamentally similar to that of human beings. The second premise is that both animals and humans behave in similar ways when they are injured: writhing, facial contortions, moaning, yelping, avoidance, etc.

To evaluate this argument, we must first identify the source, target, and feature. The source, recall, is the analogue mentioned only in the premises, the target is the analogue mentioned in the analogy and conclusion, and the feature is the characteristic that the arguer concludes is true of the target based on its being true of the source. In this argument, the source is humans, the target is animals, and the feature is can feel pain. What about the other claims about their nervous systems and behaviors? These are the similarities that support the claim that animals are like humans. Notice that those characteristics are mentioned only in the premises of the subargument. Now that we have completed this deeper analysis of the argument, we can evaluate it. How strong is the argument? As you can see in the paragraph below, each of the three criteria for evaluating analogical arguments is addressed.

This is an inductive analogical argument. There is one analogy presented. Since there are two similarities mentioned (similar nervous systems and similar behavioral responses to injury), there is good support for the analogy. And both similarities are relevant to the feature (can feel pain). Thus, this is a strong argument.

Hint!
Because the strength of analogical arguments will vary widely, it is essential that you explicitly discuss each of the three criteria for evaluation in your Critical Précis to support your judgment about the strength of the argument.

EXERCISE 9.12

Write a Critical Précis for the following passages. Include an argument diagram, and identify the argument type when appropriate. Additionally, evaluate the strength of any analogical arguments, and justify your evaluation.

1. Plants are a lot like animals, because they both transfer energy of one kind to energy of another. Since most plants get their energy directly or indirectly from sunlight, animals, too, must get their energy from sunlight.—Tom Garrison, *Oceanography*

2. It appears that the workers at the Downtown Assembly Plant are very unhappy with their working conditions. We surveyed one hundred of the workers, and they said the conditions were terrible.—*Des Moines Telegraph*

3. Just as the leader of an athletic team must have a management style that facilitates the group working together, so too the manager of a business must be able to help his or her employees to work well together. This is because a manager of a business is like an athletic team coach, given that each has to work well with people of all different backgrounds and personalities.—Les R. Deblay, James L. Burrow, and Brad A. Kleindl, *Principles of Business*

4. When studying the frontal lobe, the part of the brain that considers the consequences of actions, we made an insightful discovery about the adolescent brain. A major reason why adolescents often make poor decisions is because the nerve cells that connect their frontal lobes with the rest of their brains are sluggish.—Neuroscientist Francis Jensen

5. There is very great similitude between this earth which we inhabit, and the other planets, Saturn, Jupiter, Mars, Venus, and Mercury. They all revolve round the sun. They borrow all their light from the sun. They revolve round their axes like the earth. And, they are all subject to the same law of gravitation. From all this similitude, it is not unreasonable to think that those planets may, like our earth, be the habitation of various orders of living creatures.—Thomas Reid, *Essays on the Intellectual Powers of Man*

6. A Web poll reveals that the top feature iPod users would want on the next generation of the popular music player is an FM radio tuner. A recent online survey of more than 25,000 participants by Detroit-based rock radio consultants, Jacobs Media, found a full 43% of iPod owners want an FM radio integrated into the next version of the iPod. These participants are more than likely listeners to rock stations on the radio. Participation was solicited on 69 different rock radio stations.—*Infosyncworld.com*

7. University students are like customers in that they shop for the best deal they can afford, and they pay for a service that is delivered to them by employees.

Since the customer is "always right" in the business world, the student is "always right" at the university.—University student

8. When a candle was lit in a small glass chimney, something escaped through the top. It was either water or some other substance. It wasn't water, because what escaped had no moisture. So, it had to be the case that it was some other substance, one we found to be carbonic acid.—Michael Faraday, *The Chemical History of a Candle*

9. In 2010, a killer whale attacked and killed a trainer at Sea World in Florida as the audience watched in horror. According to officials, the 12,000-pound whale has killed three people in the past.—CBS News

10. In a study by Michelene Chi (1978), a group of graduate students were compared to a group of 10-year-old chess experts. The adults outperformed the children when it came to remembering strings of numbers, but the children clearly outperformed the adults when it came to remembering positions of pieces on a chess board. These findings indicate that having a detailed knowledge base for a particular domain (in this case chess) facilitates memory performance for information from that domain but not necessarily for information from other areas.—Schaffer and Kipp, *Developmental Psychology: Children and Adolescents*

CHAPTER REVIEW QUESTIONS

1. Where do you find the source, target, and feature of an analogical argument?
2. How can the quantity of similarities make an analogical argument stronger or weaker?
3. How can the number of analogies presented make an analogical argument stronger or weaker?
4. How do you determine whether the similarities are relevant in an analogical argument?
5. What specifically goes wrong in a faulty analogy?
6. How do you write a Critical Précis of an analogical argument?

ONE STEP FURTHER

Analogical arguments are commonly used in law. In the legal debate regarding same-sex marriage, for example, defenders of marriage equality often compare laws prohibiting same-sex marriage to past laws prohibiting interracial marriage. The court case they refer to is *Loving v. Virginia* (1967), in which the U.S. Supreme Court argued that antimiscegenation laws were ultimately an attempt to perpetuate racial inequality by maintaining racial segregation. Chief Justice Warren delivered the opinion of the Court, which affirmed the freedom to marry as a vital personal right:

Marriage is one of the "basic civil rights of man," fundamental to our very existence and survival. To deny this fundamental freedom on so unsupportable a basis as the racial classifications embodied in these statutes, classifications so directly subversive of the principle of equality at the heart of the Fourteenth Amendment, is surely to deprive all the State's citizens of liberty without due process of law. The Fourteenth Amendment requires that the freedom of choice to marry not be restricted by invidious racial discriminations. Under our Constitution, the freedom to marry, or not marry, a person of another race resides with the individual and cannot be infringed by the State.

1. How are laws prohibiting same-sex marriage similar to laws prohibiting interracial marriage? Which of these similarities are relevant? Why?
2. Construct an analogical argument incorporating the relevant similarities you identified in your answer to the above question.
3. How are laws prohibiting same-sex marriage different from laws prohibiting interracial marriage? Do these differences weaken the argument you constructed? Why or why not?

Bettmann/Corbis

In a 2007 interview, Mildred Loving (pictured here with her husband) stated: "I believe all Americans, no matter their race, no matter their sex, no matter their sexual orientation, should have that same freedom to marry. Government has no business imposing some people's religious beliefs over others. I support the freedom to marry for all. That's what *Loving*, and loving, are all about."

CHAPTER
10
Evaluating Causal Arguments

Causal arguments and the reasoning they employ are frequently used in everyday problem solving, as well as in scientific and legal reasoning. Suppose you come across an argument such as the following in your computers and society class:

> Students may believe that they are able to multi-task efficiently, but researchers are questioning that belief. In a recent study, researchers observed students studying. The students all had their computers on and the researchers recorded each time that one of the students switched tasks. Some of the students accessed their Facebook accounts at least once every fifteen minutes. Later, those students were found to have lower GPAs than those who stayed on task. This clearly shows that accessing Facebook while studying caused those students to earn lower grades.—Computers in Human Behavior

Using the skills you learned in Chapter 5, you can recognize this as an inductive **causal argument**: an argument that provides evidence that a causal claim is true. As an

© iko/Shutterstock.com

inductive argument, the premises, if true, prove that the conclusion is probably true. But how probable is the truth of the conclusion? Enough to make you reconsider your views about multitasking?

In this chapter, you will learn how to evaluate causal arguments like this one by assessing the argument's strength so you will be able to answer those questions. Just as with the other two types of inductive arguments you have learned about in this text—inductive generalizations and analogical arguments—you will discover that all causal arguments share a basic underlying structure, which you can use to identify the core features of a causal argument—namely, the resulting event, precipitating event, and method of causal reasoning. With that information, you will then learn how to determine which causal arguments should convince and which should not.

LEARNING OUTCOMES

In this chapter, you will learn how to evaluate causal arguments by:

▶ Identifying the resulting and precipitating events in a causal argument,
▶ Discerning which method of causal reasoning is used in the argument,
▶ Determining whether the precipitating event is the only possible cause of the resulting event, and
▶ Writing a Critical Précis of a causal argument.

Analyzing Causal Arguments

As you may remember from Chapter 5, the conclusion of a causal argument is a **causal claim**—that is, a statement expressing a causal relationship between one event and another. The following are some examples of causal claims.

> *The cause of Jacob's high fever was H1N1.*
> *Your sore back is the result of incorrect lifting.*
> *Increased regulation of banks will prevent future economic disasters.*

Even though these claims differ in content and style, they all are causal. The first claim states that Jacob's high fever was *caused* by H1N1. While we often speak about causes in this fashion, as if an object can cause something to happen, such language is actually inaccurate and misleading. Causes and effects are not objects, but *events*. Therefore, the first claim should be understood as expressing the claim that Jacob's *having* a high fever was *caused* by *contracting* H1N1. The second claim, then, states that your back's *being* sore was *caused* by *lifting* incorrectly. In the third claim, the causal relationship is stated in terms of one event being prevented by another, yet speaking about *prevention* is still a way of making a *causal* claim. So the third claim indicates that *avoiding* future economic disasters is *caused* by *increasing* bank regulation. When you analyze causal arguments, remember that your statement of the causal claim should always be phrased in terms of events.

Every causal argument can be analyzed to reveal the same basic structure. We call this causal argument pattern the general form of the argument. In its general form, a causal argument contains two premises supporting a conclusion. Although some causal arguments may appear to be somewhat different from these examples, every causal argument can be translated into this general form. This deeper analysis provides you with the means of identifying both the resulting and the precipitating events, key elements for determining the strength of the argument.

> **P1:** Some (resulting) event occurred.
> **P2:** Some (precipitating) event preceded it.
> ∴ The resulting event was caused by the precipitating event.

In this pattern, you can identify the two events that the arguer concludes are causally related. We identify these events as the *resulting event* and the *precipitating event*. The resulting event (R) is the event that the arguer knows has occurred and for which he or she infers the cause. The precipitating event (P) is the event that the arguer knows has occurred *prior* to the resulting event and that he or she suspects, or argues, is the cause of that resulting event.

> **Hint!**
> Although it might seem more natural to speak about these events as the effect and the cause, our analysis cannot assume what the argument is trying to prove—namely, that one is in fact the cause of the other. For this reason, we employ the terms *precipitating event* and *resulting event* rather than cause and effect.

Here's an example of an argument that shows the pattern.

I failed my geology midterm. My professor doesn't like me, so that must be the cause of my failing the test.

We'll set out the argument in a Formal Analysis to find the features of the general form of a causal argument.

> **P1:** I failed my geology midterm.
> **P2:** My professor doesn't like me.
> ∴ My failing the geology midterm was caused by my teacher not liking me.
>
> **Issue:** Whether my failing the geology midterm was caused by my teacher not liking me

In order to identify the resulting event and the precipitating event when the argument is translated into its general form, you should examine the conclusion, not the premises. The order of the premises is arbitrary in any argument, so looking there is unreliable. However, since both events will be in the conclusion, you should look to the verb or verb phrase there that will identify the events. In this example, the phrase *was caused by* indicates that the precipitating event is at the end of the sentence and the resulting event is at the beginning of the sentence.

Resulting event: failing the geology midterm

Precipitating event: being disliked

Consider another example of a causal argument, this one from a scientific study.

In a recent study, rats were fed bacon, sausage, cheesecake, frosting, and other fattening foods. Later, these rats became compulsive eaters. Therefore, the high-fat, high-calorie foods must have led to compulsive eating.

 EXERCISE 10.1

Your Turn! Diagram the argument above.

Next, we will set out the Formal Analysis.

P1: In a recent study, rats were fed bacon, sausage, cheesecake, frosting, and other fattening foods.

P2: The rats in a recent study became compulsive eaters.

∴ The high-fat, high-calorie foods led to the rats becoming compulsive eaters.

Issue: Whether the high-fat, high-calorie foods led to the rats becoming compulsive eaters

In this example, when the conclusion states that one thing led to another, it means that one event caused another. Notice how we alter the wording of the precipitating event and the resulting event to express them as events.

Resulting event: becoming compulsive eaters

Precipitating event: being fed bacon, sausage, cheesecake, frosting, and other fattening foods

 EXERCISE 10.2

Provide a Formal Analysis of each of the following causal arguments using the general form, and state the resulting event and the precipitating event.

1. You say you've had insomnia the last three nights and each of those three nights you drank coffee after dinner. It seems likely, then, that the coffee is what kept you awake.
2. I run the mile almost 10 seconds faster than my teammate. Since I do weight training every day and she doesn't, that is probably the reason I'm faster than she is.

3. The bugs that were eating the spinach in my garden have disappeared. Given that I surrounded my garden with marigolds, the marigolds must have caused the bugs to disappear.
4. Fewer fish are being caught in Miller Lake than used to be the case just a year ago. The likely cause is pollution from the nearby sewage treatment plant, which began operating just this last year.
5. Newspaper prices have gone up in Los Angeles, Salt Lake City, and Dallas. Because the common step taken by the major newspapers in all three cities is that they recently negotiated a higher salary package for their reporters and editors, the price increase must be caused by that extra cost to the papers.
6. It's likely that the clam chowder caused my two friends and me to get sick last night. This is because we all got sick after eating dinner together, and we all ate the clam chowder.
7. My dogs all started scratching yesterday morning. Their itching must be caused by fleas, since it's the only thing I can think of that would cause them all to itch so badly.
8. My car's battery was dead this morning. Since I had a car radio installed yesterday afternoon, the car radio installation must have caused the battery to die.
9. Tax increases last year led to an increased number of scofflaws, who don't pay taxes. The Internal Revenue Service reported a higher-than-usual number of people not paying their taxes last year, and this was the first year in a decade that taxes were increased.
10. Most of the small towns in the Owens Valley area have reported that their populations have decreased since the last census. Since seismic activity has been particularly heavy over that decade, it's likely that people are leaving the area for fear of earthquakes.

Although all causal arguments will identify a precipitating event among their premises, they can provide evidence that this event is the cause of the resulting event in many different ways. Nineteenth-century British philosopher John Stuart Mill identified and categorized five different methods of reasoning in causal arguments, collectively known as Mill's Methods. We will focus on two of the most commonly used of these methods: the method of agreement and the method of difference. When analyzing causal arguments, you should add the identification of the method to your identification of the resulting event and the precipitating event, since it is a vital piece of information for evaluating causal arguments.

First, consider an example of a causal argument that utilizes the method of agreement.

It's likely that the clam chowder caused my two friends and me to get sick last night. This is because we all got sick after eating dinner together, and we all ate clam chowder.

Here's the argument presented in the general form with the resulting event (R) and the precipitating event (P) identified.

P1: My two friends and I got sick after eating dinner together last night.
P2: My two friends and I ate clam chowder.

∴   My two friends and I getting sick after eating dinner together last night was caused by our eating clam chowder.

Issue: Whether my two friends and I getting sick after eating dinner together last night was caused by our eating clam chowder

Resulting event: being sick last night

Precipitating event: eating clam chowder

Next, you should identify the method the arguer uses to support the causal claim in the conclusion. To do this, consider why the arguer suspects that eating clam chowder is the cause of being sick. It is not only because it occurred prior to the resulting event, but also because eating clam chowder is an event *in common* among everyone who experienced the resulting event, being sick. This method of causal reasoning is called the **method of agreement**. We should add the identification of the method to our analysis, as shown.

M: agreement

A second way in which arguers may attempt to support a causal claim is by singling out the factor that is different between the occurrence and nonoccurrence of the resulting event. The reasoning here is that whatever factor is different between the times the resulting event happened and the times it did not is likely to be the cause of the resulting event. Let's look at an example of this method of causal reasoning from the previous exercise.

My car's battery was dead this morning. Since I had a car radio installed yesterday afternoon, the car radio installation must have caused the battery to die.

Here is the Formal Analysis of the argument with the resulting event and the precipitating event identified afterward.

P1:   The car battery was dead this morning.

P2:   I had a car radio installed yesterday afternoon.

∴   Installing a car radio yesterday afternoon caused the car battery to die.

Issue: Whether installing a car radio yesterday afternoon caused the car battery to die

R: being dead

P: installing a car radio

Notice that the premises in this causal argument support the conclusion in a different manner than in the previous example. Instead of having multiple instances of the resulting event as we saw in the previous argument, only one instance of the resulting event is given. This means that the resulting event is something different, possibly caused by the introduction of the precipitating event. Rather than identifying what all cases of the resulting event have in common, this argument identifies what is *different* between the time when the resulting event occurs and the times when it doesn't occur. In this example, the argument identifies the installation of the car radio as the difference between the occurrence of the resulting event (the car battery being dead) and its non-occurrence (the battery working). This method of causal reasoning is called the **method of difference,** and you should add it to your analysis.

M: difference

EXERCISE 10.3

Your Turn!   State the method used in each of the arguments in Exercise 10.2.

Knowing the general form of causal arguments can help you identify when causal arguments are presented with subarguments and/or extra claims. For example, causal arguments often contain subarguments to support the isolation of the precipitating event from other possible causes. Consider this one.

> *The Roadrunners finally beat the Bulldogs last night. Their victory must have been caused by the extra practice sessions this week, since that was the only thing they did differently. They used the same starting lineup, they ran the same plays, and their coach was the same.*

When you read this argument, you should readily see that it has more claims in it than the earlier causal arguments. Since constructing an argument diagram is the most direct way to set out an argument's structure, that is where we should begin our analysis. First, number and underline all of the claims.

> ① *The Roadrunners finally beat the Bulldogs last night.* ② *Their victory must have been caused by the extra practice sessions this week*, since ③ *that was the only thing they did differently.* ④ *They used the same starting lineup* ⑤ *they ran the same plays*, and ⑥ *their coach was the same.*

The inference indicator *since* signals that claim ③ supports claim ②. But what role do the other claims play, if any? Claim ① contains the resulting event, so it is an additional premise for claim ②. Thus far, the main argument consists of a conclusion and two premises. Notice that the conclusion is a causal claim, and the premises identify the resulting event and the precipitating event.

$$\frac{① + ③}{②}$$
$$\downarrow$$

What about the three remaining claims? Are they part of the argument? Yes, they comprise the specific evidence supporting premise ③ that singles out the precipitating event—namely, that the extra practice sessions are the only difference between the occurrence of the resulting event and its nonoccurrence. So claims ④, ⑤, and ⑥ are premises for claim ③. That means this argument has a subargument.

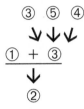

Now, we can easily put together the Formal Analysis of the causal argument with the resulting event, precipitating event, and method of causal reasoning identified.

P1: The Roadrunners used their usual starting lineup in their game against the Bulldogs.

P2: The Roadrunners ran their usual plays in their game against the Bulldogs.

P3: The Roadrunners used their usual coach in their game against the Bulldogs.

∴ Holding extra practice sessions last week is the only thing that the Roadrunners did differently to prepare for their game against the Bulldogs.

P1: The Roadrunners beat the Bulldogs last night.

P2: Holding extra practice sessions last week is the only thing that the Roadrunners did differently to prepare for their game against the Bulldogs.

∴ The Roadrunners' holding extra practice sessions caused their victory against the Bulldogs last night.

Issue: Whether the Roadrunners' holding extra practice sessions caused their victory against the Bulldogs last night.

R: beating the Bulldogs

P: holding extra practice sessions

M: difference

EXERCISE 10.4

Your Turn! Provide a Formal Analysis and diagram of the causal argument about multitasking that began this chapter. Then identify the resulting event, precipitating event, and method of causal reasoning.

Clinical studies use causal arguments in a particular way. They conclude that some causal claim is true by conducting experiments involving two groups, an experimental group and a control group. The difference between them is that only the experimental group experiences the precipitating event. When the resulting event occurs more often in the experimental group than in the control group, the researchers conclude that the two events are causally related. Then the researchers generalize from the sample (the experimental and control groups) that participated in the study to an appropriate target population. Thus, in clinical studies the causal argument serves only as a subargument supporting an inductive generalization.

Here's an example of such use of a causal argument.

Toothbrushing after each meal helps prevent cavities. A study in New Mexico found that 25% of a group of 40 young people who brushed their teeth after each meal had no cavities compared to 10% of the 35 young people who brushed only in the morning and at night. The only difference between the two groups was the number of times they brushed each day.

EXERCISE 10.5

Your Turn!   Identify the experimental group and the control group in this clinical study.

To reveal the structure of the argument, let's diagram it. First, underline and number each claim in the passage.

① *Toothbrushing after each meal helps prevent cavities.* ② *A study in New Mexico found that 25% of a group of 40 young people who brushed their teeth after each meal had no cavities compared to 10% of the 35 young people who brushed only in the morning and at night.* ③ *The only difference between the two groups was the number of times they brushed each day.*
④ Brushing teeth after each meal helped prevent cavities in the young people who took part in this New Mexico study.

The first claim is the main conclusion of the argument. Notice that it is a causal claim about toothbrushing preventing cavities, but it's not a causal claim about the young people actually observed. Instead, it generalizes from that sample group to the target of all young people. Therefore, since the conclusion is a general claim, the argument is an inductive generalization. The information in the claims about the study, claim

②, and claim ③ actually implies a conclusion. To diagram the argument, then, you must supply this missing conclusion as claim ④. It serves as both the conclusion of the subargument and a premise in the main argument.

Here is the entire argument set out in a Formal Analysis.

P1: A study in New Mexico found that 25% of a group of 40 young people who brushed their teeth after each meal had no cavities compared to 10% of the 35 young people who brushed only in the morning and at night.

P2: The only difference between the two groups in the New Mexico study was the number of times they brushed each day.

∴ Brushing teeth after each meal helped prevent cavities in the young people who took part in this New Mexico study.

P1: Brushing teeth after each meal helped prevent cavities in the young people who took part in this New Mexico study.

∴ Toothbrushing after each meal helps prevent cavities.

Issue: Whether toothbrushing after each meal helps prevent cavities

From the Formal Analysis of the subargument, we can identify the resulting event, precipitating event, and method of reasoning used in the argument.

R: having fewer cavities
P: brushing teeth
M: difference

You can recognize this causal argument as a clinical study because of two things: First, it has two groups that illustrate the occurrence of the precipitating event and the nonoccurrence of that event. Second, the causal claim in the conclusion is a general claim. That is, the researchers generalized from the two groups of young people (the sample) to the entire group of people (the target).

 EXERCISE 10.6

Provide a Formal Analysis and diagram of each of the following passages. Then identify the resulting event, precipitating event, and method of reasoning.

1. An inadequate job of soil compaction for the Rancho Estates housing development must be causing the cracking of the concrete sidewalks and driveways. This is because the sidewalks and driveways have started cracking in Rancho Estates and compacting of the soil is the only difference between the work done there and that done in the nearby Prairie View development, where no cracking occurred. The concrete work for both developments was performed by the same contractor.

2. Beginning this week, my sister started sneezing the minute she walked in my door. Given that the only thing that is different in my apartment is that I got a kitten, she must be allergic to the cat. I don't have any flowers in the house, the house is not dustier than usual, and I don't use air fresheners or other deodorizers.

3. Traffic is heavier on Milton Avenue since the beginning of the month. Since the road department finished widening the road right about that time, it's probably responsible for the extra traffic.

4. My three siblings and I are all adopted, and yet we all are unusually meticulous about keeping our apartments clean and extremely tidy. Given that we were all raised in the same household, we must have learned that behavior from observing our adoptive parents, who were also very meticulous and tidy.

5. An outbreak of salmonella poisoning occurred at the hospital. It must have been caused by eating eggs from a shipment that had gone bad because the only thing the patients had in common was eating custard pudding (which has eggs in it) for dessert. One of the patients had tuna salad, another had soup, and the third had meat loaf and mashed potatoes.

6. In three major metropolitan areas in the Northeast, mandatory waiting periods for handgun purchases were signed into law last year. Since then, homicide rates dropped by an average of 15%. It is reasonable to conclude that waiting periods for handgun purchases reduce homicides.

7. People who have big smiles live longer. Researchers examined the smiles from photos of 230 baseball players who began playing professional baseball prior to 1950. The smiles were rated for intensity, and then compared with data from deaths that occurred between 2006 and 2009. Some players lived an average of 72.9 years while others lived an average of 79.9 years. Given that the only thing that differentiates those players who lived longer from those who did not is their smiles, their longer lives must have been caused by their larger smiles.—*Psychological Science*

8. HIV is thought to have evolved from a simian virus found in African chimpanzees in the early 1930s. However, the virus spread very slowly until the middle of the 1950s, when it began to spread rapidly. One important change took place about that time—namely, the smallpox vaccine was withdrawn. It could have been helping to prevent the spread of the virus.

9. That old Native American cure for poison oak—covering the blistered area in a paste made from soaked and cooked acorns—is clearly effective. While hiking yesterday, you brushed up against some poison oak, and your blisters have shrunk considerably since you began putting on the acorn paste.

10. Since Andy Pettitte was sidelined two weeks ago with a sprained ankle, the Yankees have fallen from first place, losing five of their last eight games. The only difference in the lineup is Pettitte. They have the same exact infield and outfield from the previous month when they were winning 60% of their games. Also, the pitchers are all healthy and rotating as usual. This just shows that Pettitte is the one who makes the Yankees win.

Evaluating Causal Arguments

Since causal arguments are inductive, they are evaluated using the terms appropriate to inductive arguments. As you should remember, an inductive argument is strong when its premises, if true, would probably make the conclusion true. So judgments about a causal argument's structure will be made in terms of the argument's strength.

To determine whether or not a causal argument is strong, you must focus on how well the arguer demonstrates that the precipitating event is *the only reasonable cause* of the resulting event. For causal arguments that utilize the method of agreement, this means that you will evaluate the evidence that the precipitating event is *the only common* event that could cause the resulting event. And for causal arguments that utilize the method of difference, you will evaluate the evidence that the precipitating event is *the only different* event that could cause the resulting event.

> **Hint!**
>
> Many of the causal arguments you encounter in your life involve situations in which multiple precipitating events serve as contributing factors to the resulting event or in which the full range of contributing factors is unknown. In this chapter's exercises, you do not need to distinguish between precipitating events that may produce a particular resulting event on their own and those that are only part of a more complex causal process.

When an arguer presents a causal argument without offering any evidence that there is a causal relationship between the precipitating event and the resulting event, the argument is known as a **post hoc ergo propter hoc** (post hoc, for short) **fallacy**. The name is Latin for "after this, therefore, because of this." Fallacies occur when a mistake is made in reasoning, and the mistake in this case is that the arguer concludes that one event was caused by another simply because one preceded the other. However, without considering whether the order of events is simply coincidence, whether both

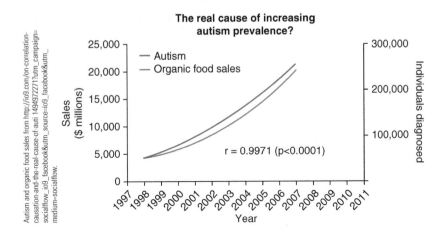

Autism and organic food sales from http://io9.com/on-correlation-causation-and-the-real-cause-of-auti 1494972271?utm_campaign=socialflow_io9_facebook&utm_source-io9_facebook&utm_medium=socialflow.

This graph suggests that there is a relationship between autism and organic food sales. Is this a causal relationship? Why or why not?

the resulting and the precipitating events are a result of some other event, or whether there is another event that could be more reasonably considered the cause, the arguer has unjustifiably jumped to a conclusion. All fallacies, including this one, are extremely weak arguments.

Here is an example of a post hoc causal argument.

> *The coffee this morning tasted terrible. It must have been caused by using tap water, since that was different from the way I usually make coffee.*

To evaluate this argument, first analyze it.

P1: The coffee this morning tasted terrible.

P2: Using tap water was different from the way I usually make coffee.

∴ The cause of this morning's coffee tasting terrible must have been using tap water.

Issue: Whether the cause of this morning's coffee tasting terrible must have been using tap water

R: tasting terrible

P: brewing with tap water

M: difference

Of course, it is *logically* possible that using tap water to make coffee causes the coffee to taste terrible. Notice, however, that the arguer neither claims nor provides evidence that using tap water is the only reasonable cause of the bad taste. Instead, he or she shows only that one event preceded the other. Perhaps the bad taste is a result of using stale coffee beans, or using a dirty coffee pot, or drinking from a plastic cup that has affected the flavor of the coffee. Without any evidence that the two events are causally related, the arguer has not given us good reasons to accept the conclusion that the coffee tasting terrible is caused by brewing the coffee with tap water.

Let's now look at a better version of that argument.

> *The coffee this morning tasted terrible. It must have been caused by using tap water, since that was the only difference from the way I usually make coffee.*

Again, the first step is a Formal Analysis.

P1: The coffee this morning tasted terrible.

P2: Using tap water was the only difference from the way I usually make coffee.

∴ The cause of this morning's coffee tasting terrible must have been using tap water.

Issue: Whether the cause of this morning's coffee tasting terrible must have been using tap water

R: tasting terrible

P: brewing with tap water

M: difference

Notice that what has changed in this version of the argument is the second premise. In the post hoc version, the arguer identifies using tap water as *a* difference from the way he or she usually makes coffee, whereas in the second version the arguer identifies using tap water as the *only* difference from the way he or she usually makes coffee. This second argument is stronger than the previous one because, if the premises are true—that the coffee tasted terrible and that the tap water was the only thing different—then the conclusion is likely to be true.

Finally, let's consider an even stronger version of the argument. This one does not simply assert that the only difference is that tap water was used to make the coffee; it also contains a subargument with premises to support that claim.

> *The coffee this morning tasted terrible. It must have been caused by using tap water, since that was the only difference from the way I usually make coffee. I used the same beans, the same coffee maker, and the same filter.*

Here's the Formal Analysis.

P1:   I used the same beans as usual to make today's coffee.

P2:   I used the same coffee maker as usual to make today's coffee.

P3:   I used the same filter as usual to make today's coffee.

∴   Tap water was the only difference from the way I usually make coffee.

P1:   The coffee this morning tasted terrible.

P2:   Using tap water was the only difference from the way I usually make coffee.

∴   The cause of the terrible-tasting coffee must have been using tap water.

Issue: Whether the cause of the terrible-tasting coffee must have been using tap water

R: tasting terrible

P: brewing with tap water

M: difference

Notice that this analysis begins with the subargument that provides *evidence* for the claim that using the tap water was the only difference between this morning's coffee and that of other mornings. This evidence rules out three other possible precipitating events, any one of which could reasonably be considered the cause of the resulting event. Since this third version of the argument provides evidence supporting the causal connection between the precipitating event and the resulting event, it is stronger than both of the previous arguments.

EXERCISE 10.7

For each of the following pairs of causal arguments, determine which version of the argument, A or B, is stronger. Briefly explain why.

1. **A.** Your pack has a huge hole in it. It must be the scissors that caused it, since they are the only sharp things inside.
   B. Your pack has a huge hole in it. It must be the scissors that caused it, since they are sharp.

2. **A.** The pizzas from Big John's have always been hot when they are delivered. However, the last two times they were barely warm when we got them. The new driver must not know his way around town.
   B. The pizzas from Big John's have always been hot when they are delivered. However, the last two times they were barely warm when we got them. The only thing different is that they have a new driver, and he must not know his way around town. I was in the restaurant the other day, and they certainly aren't busier than usual.

3. **A.** Four of the swimmers avoided the flu that was going around this summer. All four had the flu shots given out by the campus clinic, and that was the only preventative step they had in common. Three had been exposed to someone who was sick; two of them took vitamin C, but the other two didn't; and only one of them eats a healthy diet.
   B. Four of the swimmers avoided the flu that was going around this summer. All four had the flu shots given out by the campus clinic, and that was the only preventative step they had in common.

4. **A.** Why did I do so badly on the midterm? The answer is simple. Yesterday I broke a mirror, and that means seven years of bad luck. So it's obvious that my poor grade resulted from that broken mirror.
   B. Why did I do so badly on the midterm? The answer is simple. Yesterday I broke a mirror, and that means seven years of bad luck. I studied just as hard as I did for the previous exam, got a good night's sleep, and thought I really knew the material. So it's obvious that my poor grade resulted from that broken mirror.

5. **A.** Many people reported seeing flashing lights in the sky last night. Apparently, the sightings were caused by the car lot grand opening, since the only possible difference was that the business was shining searchlights all night long. No airport is nearby, no fireworks were set off, and we're too far south for the aurora borealis.
   B. Many people reported seeing flashing lights in the sky last night. Apparently, the sightings were caused by the car lot grand opening, since the business was shining searchlights all night long.

6. **A.** Did you hear that a former *Ink Master* employee is suing Spike TV? The employee was fired after reporting to her supervisor that Oliver Peck and Chris Núñez were sexually harassing her. Her dismissal must have been a result of her complaint.
   B. Did you hear that a former *Ink Master* employee is suing Spike TV? The employee was fired after reporting to her supervisor that Oliver Peck and Chris Núñez were sexually harassing her. Her dismissal must have been a result of her complaint since she had no job performance problems.

7. **A.** India has experienced below-normal rainfall during the monsoon season for the last three years. Each time, the surface temperature of the Pacific Ocean off the coast of Latin America has been warmer than usual. Thus, the warmer ocean water off Latin America probably caused those occasions of below-normal rainfall in India during the monsoon season.

   B. India has experienced below-normal rainfall during the monsoon season for the last three years. Each time, the only relevant common characteristic is that the surface temperature of the Pacific Ocean off the coast of Latin America has been warmer than usual. Thus, the warmer ocean water off Latin America probably caused those occasions of below-normal rainfall in India during the monsoon season.

8. **A.** The residence hall suffered a serious fire last night. During the investigation of the tragedy, detectives found a short in the electrical system. Therefore, the fire was probably caused by a short in the new electrical system. The investigation ruled out other possible causes. There was no sign of arson, the heater was working fine, and smoking is not allowed in the building.

   B. The residence hall suffered a serious fire last night. During the investigation of the tragedy, detectives found a short in the electrical system. Therefore, the fire was probably caused by a short in the new electrical system. The investigation ruled out other possible causes.

9. **A.** Several children have recently visited the clinic complaining of severe headaches. They all live in apartments with chipped lead paint on the walls. We believe that the lead paint is causing their headaches.

   B. Several children have recently visited the clinic complaining of severe headaches. The only commonality with them is that they all live in apartments with chipped lead paint on the walls. We believe that the lead paint is causing their headaches.

10. **A.** Johnson won the sales award two times in the past year. The only event that preceded each of his wins was attending a seminar on promoting teamwork—otherwise, he had contacted his usual clients and done his usual follow-up calls. Apparently, these seminars work.

    B. Johnson won the sales award two times in the past year. The only event that preceded each of his wins was attending a seminar on promoting teamwork—otherwise, he had contacted his usual clients, attended the usual sales meetings, and done his usual follow-up calls. Apparently, these seminars work.

EXERCISE 10.8

For each of the following causal arguments, consider whether each of the listed adjustments to the argument would strengthen, weaken, or result in no change to the strength of the original argument. Briefly explain why.

1. Three members of the golf team have set personal records during the last month. Each of them has been spending extra hours at the putting green this month, so the extra work is likely to be the cause of their improved performances.

a. Suppose each member had begun working out in the weight room this month, too.

b. Suppose only two of the members had been spending extra hours at the putting green this month.

c. Suppose the extra hours at the putting green constitute the only common precipitating event for the three of them.

d. Suppose each of the members of the golf team has a different coach.

2. My younger brothers recently realized they could actually remember a couple of events that happened before they were born. Both of them were recently hypnotized, so that must be the cause of their newfound memories.

a. Suppose being hypnotized is the only thing that has recently happened to both of them.

b. Suppose they both also underwent psychoanalysis.

c. Suppose false memories, psychoanalysis, and hallucinations were all ruled out as possible precipitating events.

d. Suppose they each recently started learning French.

3. My car's battery was dead this morning. Since the only difference from when the battery was okay was having a car radio installed yesterday afternoon, the car radio installation must have caused the battery to die.

a. Suppose it rained today but yesterday it was sunny.

b. Suppose the interior lights were not left on last night.

c. Suppose the car also had a new alternator installed yesterday.

d. Suppose the car also had a new alternator installed two weeks ago.

4. It's likely that the clam chowder caused my two friends and me to get sick last night. This is because we all got sick after eating dinner together and we all ate clam chowder.

a. Suppose the only food we ate in common was the clam chowder.

b. Suppose we all had different beverages with our meals.

c. Suppose, before we went to dinner, we visited a friend in the hospital.

d. Suppose we all used the same salt shaker to flavor our clam chowder.

5. Last year the county saw a reduction of 24% in the amount of solid waste material that was put into the county landfill. This means that the curbside recycling program, just instituted this year, is working.

a. Suppose in the past 10 months the county reduced garbage pickup to one can per week.

b. Suppose the county no longer accepts solid waste material from neighboring counties.

c. Suppose the population of the county has decreased by 10%.

d. Suppose the population of the county has remained stable over the past year.

PUTTING IT ALL TOGETHER: Writing a Critical Précis of a Causal Argument

You learned how to recognize and analyze arguments in Chapters 2, 3, and 4. In Chapter 5, you learned how to distinguish among different kinds of arguments. Now that you can evaluate causal arguments, you can put all of these skills together by adding causal argument evaluation to your Critical Précis assignments.

> ### Directions for a Critical Précis of a Causal Argument
>
> In *paragraph form*, use complete sentences and proper English grammar and spelling to do the following:
>
> **Step 1**: Identify the passage.
> ▸ Completely and correctly identify the author and the source (whenever such information is given).
> ▸ If the passage contains an argument, identify it as such. Then move to Step 2.
> ▸ If the passage does not contain an argument, identify it as a nonargument. Then specify which feature of an argument is lacking.
>
> **Step 2**: Analyze the argument.
> ▸ Clearly and completely identify the issue, conclusion, and premise or premises *in that order*.
> ▸ If the passage is a *multiple argument*, write *separate paragraphs* to analyze each separate argument.
>
> **Step 3**: Diagram the argument.
> ▸ Verify that the diagram is consistent with your Critical Précis.
>
> **Step 4**: Identify the kind of argument.
> ▸ If the argument is deductive, identify it as a categorical argument or a truth-functional argument.
> ▸ If the argument is inductive, identify it is an inductive generalization, an analogical argument, or a causal argument.
>
> **Step 5**: Evaluate the argument.
> ▸ If the argument is a causal argument, evaluate its strength by judging how well the arguer demonstrates that the precipitating event is *the only reasonable cause* of the resulting event.

Here are some samples of a Critical Précis for a causal argument. After seeing how these are done, you will try some on your own.

> *Wolf populations in the mountains of the western United States have increased in the last two decades. This result is most likely caused by the two decades of prohibition against hunting wolves, since that is the only significant difference between conditions now and conditions prior to the last two decades.—A conservationist*

First, identify the passage as an argument or a nonargument. This passage is an argument because it is trying to convince the reader that the wolf population increase was caused by the restrictions on hunting. Since the phrase *is most likely* indicates that the argument utilizes inductive reasoning and the conclusion is a causal claim, we can recognize the argument as an inductive causal argument. Thus, we will analyze and evaluate the argument in this manner.

> ① **Wolf populations in the mountains of the western United States have increased in the last two decades.** ② **This result is most likely caused by the two decades of prohibition against hunting wolves, since**

③ **_that is the only significant difference between conditions now and_**
conditions prior to the last two decades.

This passage from a conservationist contains an argument.
The issue is whether the increased populations of wolves in the
western United States are caused by the two decades of prohibition
against hunting wolves. The conclusion is that the increased
populations of wolves in the western United States are caused
by the two decades of prohibition against hunting wolves. The
premises are that wolf populations in the mountains of the western
United States have increased in the last two decades and that
the prohibition against hunting is the only significant difference
between conditions now and conditions prior to the last two
decades.

This argument is an inductive causal argument. It is a fairly
strong argument because it states that the ban on hunting is the
only reasonable cause of the increased wolf population.

Let's consider another example, this time one that is a clinical study. As discussed earlier in the chapter, clinical studies are chain arguments consisting of two different types of inductive argument. The main one is an inductive generalization, and the subargument is causal. When you evaluate these arguments, you do so as you would any chain argument—by evaluating the main argument only. Thus, in the case of clinical studies, you evaluate the inductive generalization, not the causal argument. You should refer to Chapter 8 for details on how to evaluate inductive generalizations.

> *In a university study, 42 college students described themselves as regular*
> *binge drinkers and 53 students stated that they do not drink alcohol*
> *regularly. Of these two groups, the binge drinkers performed significantly*
> *worse on a memory test while sober. For men, binge drinking is defined*
> *as having five or more alcoholic drinks during a two-hour period. For*
> *women, that number is four or more in that period of time. Researchers*
> *concluded that binge drinking may impair the brains of binge drinkers*
> *even when they are not drinking.—Alcoholism: Clinical and Experimental*
> *Research*

The final sentence of the passage is the conclusion, with the other claims intending to convince the reader of the truth of the conclusion. Thus, the passage is an argument. Since the main conclusion is not about the causal effects on the college students in the study, but rather about the causal effect on the target (all people) of which the college students are a sample, this is a clinical study; the main argument will be an inductive generalization, whereas the causal argument is a subargument. Here are the analysis and evaluation.

> ① *In a university study, 42 college students described themselves as regular binge drinkers and 53 students stated that they do not drink alcohol regularly.* ② *Of these two groups, the binge drinkers performed significantly worse on a memory test while sober.* ③ *For men, binge drinking is defined as having five or more alcoholic drinks during a two-hour period.* ④ *For women, that number is four or more in that period of time.* Researchers concluded that ⑤ *binge drinking may impair the brains of binge drinkers even when they are not drinking.*
> ⑥ **Binge drinking impaired the brains of the 42 students in the study who described themselves as regular binge drinkers.**

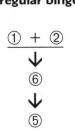

This passage from *Alcoholism: Clinical and Experimental Research* contains an argument. The issue is whether binge drinking may impair the brains of binge drinkers even when they are not drinking. The conclusion is that binge drinking may impair the brains of binge drinkers even when they are not drinking. The premise is that binge drinking impaired the brains of the 42 students in the study who described themselves as regular binge drinkers.

This argument contains a subargument. The intermediate conclusion is that binge drinking impaired the brains of the 42 students in the study who described themselves as regular binge drinkers. The first premise is that 42 college students described themselves as regular binge drinkers and 53 students stated that they do not drink alcohol regularly. The second premise is that the binge drinkers performed significantly worse on a memory test while sober than the nondrinkers.

The main argument is an inductive generalization. The argument is somewhat strong, since the sample size of 95 students is reasonably large. The argument does not identify how the participants were selected or their gender percentages; thus, we cannot determine how well the sample represented the target.

Notice that the causal argument is not evaluated because it is not the main argument. Also, claims ③ and ④—defining what is meant by binge drinking for men and for women—are extra claims, so they are not included in the analysis. This is because these claims are neither premises nor conclusions; they only clarify what qualifies as binge drinking.

EXERCISE 10.9

Write a Critical Précis for the following passages. Include an argument diagram, and identify the argument type when appropriate. Additionally, evaluate the strength of any causal arguments, and justify your evaluation.

1. Recently researchers compared 286 depressed workers with 193 others who were not depressed. Since only the depressed workers had such problems as fatigue, lack of motivation, and trouble managing their usual workload, researchers concluded that depression was the cause of their problems at work.—*American Journal of Health Promotion*

2. The theory of evolution is truly scientific, because we can think of experiments and observations that would support it or render it incorrect. And any time we can do that, the theory is truly scientific.—Wicander and Monroe, *Historical Geology: Evolution of Earth and Life Through Time.*

3. In 2010, a mudslide in Germany killed three people. Investigators discovered that a top-secret underground chemical facility used by the Nazis in World War II had collapsed directly underneath the site. It is believed, then, that the collapse of this facility triggered the disaster.—*Xenophilia (True Strange Stuff)*

4. If the demands of justice can be assessed only with the help of public reasoning, and if public reasoning is constitutively related to the idea of democracy, then there is an intimate connection between justice and democracy.—Amartya Sen, *The Idea of Justice*

5. Shows like *Survivor* are alluring precisely because they mirror the ancient struggles within our minds and among our peers.—Christakis and Fowler, *Connected*

6. Middle-aged and older women who have migraines and who experience auras (e.g., flashing lights that might signal the onset of pain) appear to have a higher risk of strokes and heart attacks than their migraine-free peers, a new study suggests. The study looked at 27,798 female health professionals ages 45 and older, including 3,568 who had migraines. It showed that women with weekly migraines with auras were four times as likely to have had a stroke during the 12-year study as women without migraines.—*Neurology*

7. Once the superego emerges, children will feel guilty or ashamed of their unethical conduct due to the fact that they will recognize their own transgressions. And if this is the case, the superego can be called an internal sensor. So the superego is truly an internal censor.—Schaffer and Kipp, *Developmental Psychology: Children and Adolescents*

8. Much of the water worldwide is privatized, commodified, and put on the open market. As a result, very little is left for those who need it but cannot pay for it. In a similar way, what is called the "genetic commons" is becoming privatized, commodified, and put on the open market. Thus we can expect that the genetic commons, the building blocks of life on earth, will only be available to those who pay for it, not for everyone who needs it.—Winston and Edelbach, *Society, Ethics, and Technology.*

9. There's good evidence to suggest that a new non-police program successfully reduced Chicago area crime rates last year. Violent crime arrests dropped by 44 percent after the city instituted a program called "BAM — Sports Edition," which provides 7th–10th grade boys with small group instruction in

social and life skills in school, and sports programming after school.
—*The Washington Post*

10. The death of one adult and the sickening of seven others resulted from eating cheese with *Listeria*. The Maryland victims all ate semi-soft Hispanic-style cheese bought from different locations of the same grocery store chain. *Listeria* was later detected in a sample of the cheese curd.—Centers for Disease Control and Prevention

CHAPTER REVIEW QUESTIONS

1. How do you identify the precipitating event and the resulting event in a causal argument?
2. How do you determine which method of causal reasoning is used in a causal argument?
3. How does a clinical study utilize causal reasoning?
4. What goes wrong in a post hoc ergo propter hoc causal argument?
5. How do you determine whether a causal argument is strong?
6. How do you write a Critical Précis of a causal argument?

ONE STEP FURTHER

Since the beginning of the twenty-first century, politicians, scientists, and other public figures have debated the nature, causes, and consequences of global warming. Are increased global temperatures within normal climatic variations, or are they a result of human activities? In reviewing the debate, you may encounter both causal arguments and causal explanations. In the case of a causal *argument*, the speaker is attempting to convince others that some causal claim is true, whereas in a causal *explanation*, the speaker is explaining how or why some accepted fact is true. Compare, for example, the following two passages.

How do we know the increase in CO_2 is human caused? There is an isotopic signature, like a fingerprint. CO_2 that comes from natural sources has a low carbon-14 ratio. The pre-industrial atmospheric levels of CO_2 were around 280ppm (parts per million). As of 2010 the amount is 390ppm. The extra 100ppm does not have the carbon-14 signature. The only other possible source that can account for the extra 100ppm is human industrial emissions of fossil fuels.—Open Source Systems, Science, Solutions Foundation

What is the cause of global warming? Global warming is occurring because humans use unprecedented amounts of carbon-based energy sources such as coal, gasoline, and natural gas.—Amy Farrar, *Global Warming*

1. Which of the passages is a causal argument, and which is a causal explanation? How can you tell?
2. In a causal argument, the conclusion can be questioned because it is the claim at issue. But in an explanation, the claim being explained is assumed to be true.

Since there is no conclusion to question in a causal explanation, what can you question?

3. Browse the information regarding climate-change science presented on the U.S. Environmental Protection Agency website: http://www.epa.gov/climatechange. Find an example of a causal argument and a causal explanation.

Satellite images from NASA's Earth Observatory show Tanzania's Mount Kilimanjaro on February 17, 1993 (top), and February 21, 2000. What conclusion, if any, can you infer from this pair of images?

Detecting Fallacies

We started this book with a discussion about whether to support the Smoke-Free Campus Initiative. Among the arguments presented is one we identified as committing a fallacy.

Veronica says Are we living in a fascist state now??? The only people who would support this are uptight nonsmokers who want to take away my freedom to express myself and enjoy life. I know smoking is bad for me, but it's my choice!

© istockphoto.com/Andrew Rich

When you first read this argument in Chapter 1, you may have realized that something isn't quite right with it. In this chapter, you will learn exactly what has gone wrong with this argument, as well as several other arguments that commit fallacies. A **fallacy** is a mistake in reasoning of some sort that is rhetorically persuasive, but on closer inspection, it is seen to be a bad argument. Learning to detect fallacious reasoning is an important part of critical thinking because such mistakes are notoriously common and easily overlooked.

If you completed the chapters on inductive reasoning, you have already encountered several fallacies: hasty generalization and biased generalization in Chapter 8, faulty analogy in Chapter 9, and post hoc ergo propter hoc in Chapter 10. In this chapter, you will learn about six additional fallacies. While there are many different ways that an argument can go wrong (with dozens of corresponding fallacy names to sort them), we will focus on six of the most common ones you are likely to encounter.

> **Hint!**
> Fallacies are often sorted into two main types: formal and informal. A formal fallacy is a mistake in the logical structure of an argument that renders it invalid. An informal fallacy is a mistake arising from the content rather than the structure of the argument. Frequently, such mistakes are due to the use of ambiguous language or irrelevant premises. The six fallacies introduced in this chapter are all informal fallacies.

LEARNING OUTCOMES

In this chapter, you will learn how to detect fallacies by:

- ▶ Recognizing the begging the question fallacy,
- ▶ Recognizing the appeal to ignorance fallacy,
- ▶ Recognizing the appeal to illegitimate authority fallacy,
- ▶ Recognizing the ad hominem fallacy,
- ▶ Recognizing the strawman fallacy,
- ▶ Recognizing the red herring fallacy, and
- ▶ Writing a Critical Précis of a fallacious argument.

Begging the Question

The fallacy of **begging the question** occurs when the conclusion of an argument is assumed by the argument's premises. Although technically the conclusion of such an argument must follow if the premises are true (after all, the conclusion is in the premises), an argument that begs the question isn't much of an argument at all. It states, in effect, that "some claim is true because that claim is true." This kind of argument is fallacious because it offers no evidence for its conclusion. The premise doesn't offer a reason to accept the truth of the conclusion; it merely restates it.

Consider this example.

> *Health-care reform in the United States will not work, since our health-care system simply cannot be reformed.*

Using the skills you learned from Chapter 3, let's take a closer look at this argument using a Formal Analysis.

> **P:**　　The U.S. health-care system cannot be reformed.
> **∴**　　Health-care reform in the United States will not work.
> **Issue:** Whether health-care reform in the United States will work

Notice that the premise does not offer a reason to accept that the conclusion is true. Instead, it offers a restatement of the conclusion in a different sentence. To say that the U.S. health-care system cannot be reformed is just another way of saying that health-care reform in the United States will not work. The mistake in this argument is particularly clear if you attempt to diagram it.

① *Healthcare reform in the United States will not work* since ① *our health-care system simply cannot be reformed.*

Recall from Chapter 2 that an argument is a set of claims, one of which is supported by the other, and that different sentences can express the same claim. Given that the two sentences in this passage express the same claim, this passage contains only one claim. This means that it doesn't really qualify as an argument at all.

> **Hint!**
> You may be familiar with the phrase *begs the question* from everyday speech. Often when someone says, "That begs the question...," he or she means that there is some unanswered question that needs to be addressed. This should not be confused with the fallacy of begging the question.

Although sometimes it is easy to spot arguments that beg the question, most cases of question begging are not as obvious as in the previous example. Arguers may disguise the conclusion in a premise by using synonyms for terms used in the conclusion.

Consider this example.

I just can't believe it! Nick Newman can't be guilty of murder, since there's no way Mr. Newman could kill someone.

Let's first present a Formal Analysis of the argument.

P: There is no way Mr. Newman could kill someone.

∴ Mr. Newman is not guilty of murder.

Issue: Whether Mr. Newman is guilty of murder

In this passage, the defense attorney wants to convince the jury that Nick Newman is not guilty of murder and offers as a premise the claim that Nick Newman couldn't be a killer. However, since the issue is *whether* Nick Newman is guilty of killing someone, the premise assumes that the issue has been resolved. The arguer commits the fallacy of begging the question by substituting the term *kill* for *murder*. As it stands, this is not an argument. There are no reasons offered for accepting the claim that Mr. Newman is not guilty of murder. Instead, the defense attorney simply restates the conclusion in a different sentence.

 EXERCISE 11.1

Your Turn! Why are arguments that beg the question bad arguments?

✎ **EXERCISE 11.2**

For each of the following, complete a Formal Analysis of the argument. Then determine whether the argument commits the fallacy of begging the question.

1. It's clear that smoking is bad for you because it is so harmful to your health.
2. Smoking is bad for you because it causes lung cancer, heart disease, stroke, and other cardiovascular diseases.
3. No, I do *not* believe that serial killers ought to be allowed to live. They have forfeited their right to live because anyone who kills lots of people has lost that right.
4. We need to apply the death penalty for all violent murderers. This is because death is the only way to make sure that these dangerous criminals never hurt another person.
5. James is a murderer because he wrongfully killed someone.
6. James is a murderer because he has been shown to have motive, opportunity, and no alibi for the time when the murder took place. Besides, his fingerprints are all over the murder weapon.
7. Adultery cannot be justified. The reason is that it is simply never acceptable for a married person to have sex with someone who is not his or her spouse.
8. Adultery is always wrong. This is because it breaks a promise made to one's spouse at the time of marriage. It also undermines the nuclear family, which is the foundation of our civilization.
9. A psychology course should be required of all college students because every university student should have to take at least one course in psychology.
10. An anatomy course should be required of all college students because every university student should know how the body works.

Appeal to Ignorance

The appeal to ignorance fallacy is committed when the arguer illegitimately shifts the burden of proof. An appeal to ignorance argument states, in effect, "I am right because no one has proven otherwise." This kind of argument is fallacious because it offers no evidence for its conclusion. The fact that your conclusion hasn't been proven false does not establish that it is true. To convince someone that your conclusion is true, you must offer reasons for that conclusion; otherwise, you won't convince anyone of anything.

Consider this example.

Clearly, God exists. After all, atheists have never proven that there is no God.

Here is the argument presented formally.

P: Atheists have not proven that God does not exist.
∴ God exists.
Issue: Whether God exists

Notice that we could easily provide a comparable argument for the opposite conclusion.

No one has ever proven that God exists; therefore, God does not exist.

Here is the argument presented formally.

P: <u>No one has ever proven that God exists.</u>

∴ God does not exist.

Issue: Whether God exists

The first argument concludes that God exists, and the second concludes that God does not exist. Notice that both of these arguments deal with the same issue—namely, whether God exists. Also notice that neither of these arguments is a good argument; neither offers reasons to support its conclusion. Instead, they both illegitimately shift the **burden of proof**—that is, the responsibility for providing the evidence—to those on the other side of the issue. Thus, they are both examples of a fallacious appeal to ignorance. If you want to prove that some claim is true, you must supply evidence for it.

Identifying who has the burden of proof with regard to an issue is the first step in determining whether the argument commits the appeal to ignorance fallacy. This can sometimes be tricky. Generally speaking, anyone trying to establish the truth of a claim has the responsibility to offer reasons for that claim. This burden of proof is placed on the arguer, even when the arguer's conclusion is a true claim. Consider the case of Galileo, the famous philosopher, astronomer, and mathematician. When he offered support for the *heliocentric* view of the universe (the view that Earth orbited around the sun), Galileo had the burden of proof. At the time, almost every other philosopher and astronomer, as well as the powerful Catholic Church, accepted the *geocentric* view of the universe (the view that the sun orbited around Earth). To establish his claim that Earth orbited the sun, and not the other way around, Galileo had to offer evidence (which he did in his *Dialogue Concerning the Two Chief World Systems*, published in 1632). Imagine if, instead of offering reasons to support his view, Galileo had given the following argument.

> *There should be no doubt that our glorious Earth, full of life, encircles the blazing sun, perched at the center. After all, no astronomer has ever adequately established the contrary.*

 EXERCISE 11.3

Your Turn! Complete a Formal Analysis of the previous argument.

Even though this conclusion is true, the argument commits a fallacious appeal to ignorance. The failure of an opponent to prove that your belief is wrong is no evidence that you are right. If you want your reader to accept your conclusion, you must offer reasons to do so.

There are some cases in which an argument resembling an appeal to ignorance does not commit a fallacy. (That is why we say that the appeal to ignorance fallacy occurs when the arguer *illegitimately* shifts the burden of proof.) When the burden of proof does not lie with the arguer, the fallacy is not committed.

Consider, for example, this courtroom speech.

Ladies and gentlemen, the district attorney has not provided a shred of evidence of my client's guilt. Therefore, you must declare the defendant "not guilty" of the charges.

In this example, the arguer claims that the defendant is "not guilty" of the charges on the basis that the defendant's guilt has not been established. Let's examine the argument formally.

P: The district attorney has not proven that the defendant is guilty.

∴ The defendant should be declared not guilty.

Issue: Whether the defendant should be declared guilty

Although the arguer is saying, in effect, "You should accept my conclusion as true because it hasn't been proven false," this argument does not commit a fallacy. This is because in criminal proceedings all defendants are presumed innocent until proven guilty; the burden of proof always lies with the prosecution. In this way, when we say that a defendant should be declared "not guilty," what we mean is that his or her guilt has not been proven, not that he or she is innocent.

 EXERCISE 11.4

Your Turn! When is an argument that shifts the burden of proof to the other side not a fallacy?

 EXERCISE 11.5

For each of the following, complete a Formal Analysis of the argument. Then determine whether the arguer has committed the fallacy of appeal to ignorance.

1. Of course you should buy a life insurance policy! Why shouldn't you?
2. Women shouldn't be in a big hurry to enter the military at this time. Why not? Because no plan is yet in place to ensure that all troops are safe from sexual assault.
3. Look, you can't prove that extraterrestrials don't exist. So that means that they are real!
4. Should the Ten Commandments be engraved onto the courthouse? Certainly. Why shouldn't they?
5. Angelina Jolie and Brad Pitt are having marital problems. After all, they haven't publicly denounced the magazine reports about their fights.
6. Every Christmas Eve, the cookies and milk we leave for Santa are eaten, and packages are under the tree that weren't there when we went to bed. It's clear, then, that Santa Claus exists.

7. No one has shown evidence that headphones promote healthy ears. Thus, listening to music on headphones is harmful to your hearing.
8. The governor is clearly guilty of lying to his constituents about not providing high-paying government jobs for his cronies. Not once has he shown that he was telling the truth.
9. Ghosts don't exist because, if they did, they would exist outside the boundaries of the universe science describes, and nothing can live outside those boundaries.
10. We know that phrenology—the ability to determine a person's personality traits by feeling the bumps on his or her skull—is reliable, since no one has ever demonstrated that it isn't.

The fallacies of begging the question and appeal to ignorance are closely related. They both fail to do what arguments should do—namely, offer reasons in support of a conclusion. Arguments that commit the fallacy of begging the question fail to offer reasons by simply restating the conclusion, typically in a disguised fashion. Arguments that commit the fallacy of appeal to ignorance fail to offer reasons by illegitimately shifting the burden of proof. The templates for these fallacies are described below, using C to symbolize the claim that is offered as the conclusion and the symbol ~ to represent the rejection of a claim.

Begging the Question	**Appeal to Ignorance**
P: $\dfrac{C}{C}$	**P:** $\dfrac{\sim C \text{ hasn't been proven}}{C}$
∴	∴
Issue: Whether C is true	**Issue:** Whether C is true

 EXERCISE 11.6

For each of the following, complete a Formal Analysis of the argument. Then determine whether the argument commits the fallacy of begging the question, the fallacy of appeal to ignorance, or no fallacy at all.

1. It would be bad for the government to let the deficit get any higher. Therefore, the government should not let it rise.
2. Occupational therapy is a profession that should have more men in it because it currently has too many women.
3. Australian shepherds must be the easiest dogs to train because no one has ever shown that training another kind of dog is easier.
4. Learning by memorization is an extremely effective way to learn. Has anyone ever shown a better way? The answer is no.
5. Quarantining those who contract the flu has never been disproven as the best means of keeping the disease from spreading. Thus, people with cases of the flu should be kept in quarantine.

6. It's clear that my child is smart because he is so intelligent.
7. My child scored above average on the IQ test last year. He is clearly smart enough to do well in school.
8. The senator must be taking illegal campaign contributions from wealthy donors because he has never disclosed documents to show that his campaign donations are legal.
9. You should believe what the palm reader tells you. No one has ever shown that her readings aren't accurate.
10. We must place some limit on the amount of money a candidate can be allowed to spend in a political campaign, since unlimited spending by political candidates must be stopped.

Appeal to Illegitimate Authority

Since it is impossible for any one person to have knowledge about every subject, we commonly appeal to authorities to confirm or disconfirm claims or to determine the best course of action. For example, when your car is not running properly, you rely on the expertise of a mechanic to diagnose the problem and return your car to working order. When you disagree with your housemate about the year that the Treaty of Versailles was signed, you rely on the authority of your history textbook or perhaps the *Internet Encyclopedia of History*. Any argument that appeals to authority states, in effect, "You should accept this claim because an expert said that it was true." Notice that your best bet is to trust someone who is an expert on the subject in question. You do not ask your history professor about auto repair, and you do not ask your auto mechanic for a lesson in European history. Whenever the referenced authority is not an authority on the subject in question, the argument commits the fallacy of **appeal to illegitimate authority**.

The use of illegitimate authorities is notoriously prevalent in advertising. Famous athletes, musicians, and other celebrities regularly endorse products and political campaigns about which they have no expert knowledge. Consider this famous 1986 example featuring actor Peter Bergman, well-known to audiences for playing Dr. Cliff Warner in the daytime drama *All My Children*.

> *I'm not a doctor, but I play one on TV. If your child had a cough, she would get just what the doctor ordered. But for your cough, you play doctor at home, even playing doctor with the medicine you bought for your child. You need one of the adult formulas from Vicks, for the coughs that adults get, with the strength adults need. Formula 44 for coughs. Formula 44D for coughs with congestion. Formula 44M for coughs with congestion and a raw, irritated throat. The adult formulas. You can't buy anything more effective.*

Now, imagine you are talking with your grandmother on the phone and after hearing you cough, your grandmother offers the following argument using Peter Bergman as an authority.

> *Honey, you should use Vicks Formula 44, since that handsome fella who plays Dr. Warner says it's the best.*

Let's examine the argument formally.

P1: Peter Bergman says that Vicks Formula 44 is the best treatment for a cough.

P2: Peter Bergman performs the role of a doctor on a TV show.

∴ Vicks Formula 44 is the best treatment for your cough.

Issue: Whether Vicks Formula 44 is the best treatment for your cough

This is a clear example of an argument that commits the fallacy of appeal to illegitimate authority. Although it is appropriate for someone to rely on a physician's expertise when choosing medicine to treat his or her illness, it would be foolish to rely on the testimony of an actor, even one who plays the role of a doctor. Of course, even legitimate experts can be wrong, and they often disagree with each other. But if someone has no more expertise than you do on a particular issue, his or her word is not a good enough reason to accept his or her conclusion.

Note that, in arguments that appeal to authority, the authority's testimony substitutes for reasons in support of the conclusion. This means that the credibility of the authority is essential to the argument. If the authority is in fact an expert on the subject in question and is likely to be unbiased, then his or her testimony is credible. However, if the cited authority is not an expert on the subject in question, then his or her testimony is not credible, and the argument commits the fallacy.

Compare the previous fallacious argument from your grandmother to this legitimate appeal to authority from your mother.

> *That cough of yours sounds really bad. You should take Vicks Formula 44, since that's what your primary care physician recommends.*

 EXERCISE 11.7

Your Turn! Provide a Formal Analysis of the previous argument.

Although arguments that appeal to an illegitimate authority are fallacious, this does not mean that all arguments given by nonexperts are fallacies. Consider this example from a commercial against a 2008 Washington State ballot measure.

> *Initiative 1000 is a dangerous idea that could be imposed on the poor, disabled, and most vulnerable in our society. Initiative 1000 tells doctors that it's ok to give a lethal drug overdose to a seriously ill person even if they are suffering from depression. Additionally, your spouse could die by assisted suicide and you wouldn't have to be told. People who are ill need real medical care and compassion, not lethal drugs. Vote "no" on Initiative 1000. –Martin Sheen*

Like your grandmother's argument for using Vicks, this argument involves a celebrity endorsement—namely, one provided by an actor who played a U.S. President. However, when you perform a Formal Analysis on Martin Sheen's argument, you can see an important difference between the two arguments.

P1: Initiative 1000 could be imposed on the poor, disabled, and most vulnerable in our society.

P2: Initiative 1000 allows doctors to give a lethal drug overdose to seriously ill persons even if they are suffering from depression.

P3: Initiative 1000 allows a person to die by assisted suicide without informing his or her spouse.

∴ You should not vote for Initiative 1000.

Issue: Whether you should vote for Initiative 1000

Unlike your grandmother's Vicks argument, this argument does not appeal to authority. Although a famous actor, Martin Sheen, is the speaker, he does not use his testimony as a substitute for reasons in support of a conclusion. Instead, he provides reasons that support his conclusion.

EXERCISE 11.8

Your Turn! Does an argument given by a person who is not an authority on the subject in question commit the fallacy of illegitimate authority? Justify your answer.

Actor Martin Sheen is well known for his role as President of the United States on *The West Wing* television series.

© NBC/courtesy Everett Collection

Hint!
On many important issues, those who are experts on the subject in question disagree. Take, for example, the topic of genetically modified crops. There has been considerable debate in the U.S. media over whether the use of genetically modified food poses a danger to human health and the environment. Given that science experts have weighed in on both sides of the issue, it is all the more important that reasons be given to support conclusions rather than relying on appeals to authority.

EXERCISE 11.9

For each of the following, complete a Formal Analysis of the argument. Then determine whether the argument commits the fallacy of appeal to illegitimate authority.

1. Vitamin water must be a great, healthy alternative to sodas. I saw award-winning rapper 50 Cent drinking it in a commercial, and he said it's great.
2. Harald zur Hausen, winner of the 2008 Nobel Prize in Medicine, says that because the human papilloma virus (HPV) is the leading cause of cervical cancer, all women should be screened for HPV. So you should get tested for HPV during your annual gynecological exam.
3. Dow Constantine, who is running for King County executive in this November's election, was publicly endorsed by the rock band Pearl Jam. Therefore, Mr. Constantine must be the best candidate for the job.
4. Dr. Bradshaw, our family physician, has stated that the creation of muonic atoms of deuterium and tritium holds the key to producing a sustained nuclear fusion reaction at room temperature. In view of Dr. Bradshaw's expertise as a physician, we can conclude that this is indeed true.
5. According to the Centers for Disease Control and Prevention (CDC), every person should receive an annual vaccination against the influenza virus. Sounds to me like a good reason to get vaccinated! After all, they are the experts!
6. Aldous Huxley, the celebrated author of *Brave New World*, was convinced that wearing eyeglasses actually makes the eyes weaker. Therefore, we should not get corrective glasses to improve our sight.
7. According to the American Dental Association, the largest dental association in the United States, both children and adults should floss after meals to prevent cavities. Therefore, you should floss your teeth every day.
8. You really ought to try out for the basketball team because the park groundskeeper, Willie, says you have real potential.
9. There's nothing wrong with downloading pirated copies of movies because my roommate, Jerry, said that it's not cheating anyone.
10. Drew Brees, quarterback for the New Orleans Saints, says that NyQuil is the best medicine to relieve cold symptoms. Sounds like a good reason to use NyQuil to me!

Ad Hominem

The Latin term *ad hominem* translates as "toward the person," and so the ad hominem fallacy is also known as a fallacious argument against a person. The ad hominem fallacy occurs when an arguer rejects his or her opponent's conclusion on the basis of some characteristic of that person, typically his or her circumstances, social position, history, or personal associations. This kind of argument is fallacious because *who* gives the argument is irrelevant to whether or not the argument is a good one. Bad people can give great arguments, just as good people can give terrible arguments. When evaluating an argument, you should examine the truth of the premises and the logical connection between the premises and conclusion, not the source of the argument.

> **Hint!**
> In an appeal to authority, whether legitimate or not, the conclusion is supported by the authority being appealed to. Thus, whether that person is a legitimate authority is relevant to whether we should accept the argument. In an ad hominem fallacy, however, the person attacked has given an *argument*, and the ad hominem fallaciously criticizes the arguer instead of the premises of his or her argument.

There are three common ways that fallacious ad hominem arguments are constructed. A person may be attacked because of his or her perceived bias, because of inconsistency in his or her words and deeds, or because of his or her psychological make-up. Some critical thinking instructors differentiate among these different types of ad hominem arguments as ad hominem abusive, ad hominem circumstantial, and ad hominem tu quoque, respectively. Although it can be helpful to recognize these different ways of attacking a person, the important lesson is that these are all fallacious attacks against the person rather than the argument itself. If you want to show that someone's argument is flawed, you must find errors in his or her reasoning. Attacking the person may sometimes be rhetorically persuasive, but it does not qualify as critical thinking.

Consider this example.

> *Jack argues that we should abolish capital punishment because it has no proven deterrent effect and it has a severely negative psychological impact on the prison staff involved in executions. But did you know that Jack's younger brother is on death row right now? When you consider Jack's special interest in the matter, you can see that he is wrong.*

Notice that the passage contains two arguments that must not be confused. One of these is the view that the arguer opposes, and the other is the one the arguer defends. Recall from Chapter 3 that when you analyze an argument, a passage may contain extra claims that provide background information to motivate the argument. Therefore, when you analyze this passage, you should treat the argument opposed by the arguer—that is, the motivation for the argument being defended—as extra claims.

EXERCISE 11.10

Your Turn!   In the argument above, which conclusion does the speaker reject? Which does he or she defend? How can you tell which is which?

Moreover, since these arguments are in conversation with each other, they are engaging the same issue—in this case, whether we should abolish capital punishment. You should keep this in mind when you identify the conclusion of the argument. It would be a mistake to simply identify the conclusion as "He is wrong." Why? Because your task is to determine exactly what claim the arguer is trying to convince you is true. When the arguer writes, "He is wrong," what exactly is he or she trying to prove? Since "he" refers to Jack and Jack argues that we should abolish capital punishment, the conclusion advanced by the author of the passage must be that we should *not* abolish capital punishment. The Formal Analysis of the passage can then be presented as follows:

> **P1:**   Jack argues that we should abolish capital punishment.
>
> **P2:**   Jack's younger brother is currently on death row.
>
> ∴   We should not abolish capital punishment.
>
> **Issue:** Whether we should abolish capital punishment

In this case, the arguer commits the ad hominem fallacy. Rather than finding a flaw in Jack's argument, the author attacks Jack himself as biased. However, the fact that someone may have a personal stake in an issue does not mean that his or her argument is bad. You must examine the reasons, not his or her motivations.

Let's consider another example.

> *Bill has argued that you shouldn't smoke cigarettes. Ha! There's no reason to listen to him; I saw him smoking at a party last weekend.*

As in the previous example, this passage refers to two arguments. One is the argument that is opposed by the author of the passage, and the other is the argument advocated by the author of the passage. Although the arguer does not provide Bill's premises, the use of the word *argued* signals that Bill elsewhere gives an argument for the conclusion "You shouldn't smoke cigarettes." So, again, this is an example of the ad hominem fallacy. Moreover, when analyzing the argument advanced by the speaker, do not simply identify the conclusion as "There's no reason to listen to him." You must determine not only who "he" is, but also what it is that he said to accurately identify the conclusion.

EXERCISE 11.11

Your Turn!   Present a Formal Analysis of the previous argument.

Rather than finding a flaw in Bill's argument, the speaker attacks the source of the argument, this time by pointing to Bill's hypocrisy. However, the fact that Bill does not follow his own advice does not mean that Bill's argument is flawed. His argument stands or falls on its own merits.

Technically, not every argument that attacks a person is fallacious. To distinguish between arguments that commit the ad hominem fallacy and those that legitimately criticize a person, you must pay careful attention to the issue. If the issue is about the person, then the criticism is relevant. If it is not, then focusing on the person is irrelevant to the conclusion of the argument. Consider the use of statements in a court case. When a witness gives a statement under oath, that person's credibility is crucial to whether or not the jury accepts his or her claims. This does not mean that the jury should simply accept the reports of all credible witnesses, since credible sources can lie or misinform, just as unreliable sources can be truthful. It does, however, mean that whether a person is credible or not is deeply relevant to whether the jury should accept his or her deposition. In any situation in which all you have to go on is a person's word, you can regard the argument as one involving an issue about the person.

Consider this example.

Jack Masters testified that there's no way the defendant could have committed murder. But did you know that the defendant is Jack's younger brother? Given his strong incentive to help his brother avoid prison time, we should question his impartiality.

In the earlier example about capital punishment, Jack gave evidence for his conclusion. Here, however, the only evidence given is his word, and the issue concerns whether we should trust his word. Notice the difference in the Formal Analysis of the argument.

P1: Jack testifies that the defendant is not capable of murder.

P2: Jack's testimony is biased.

∴ We should not accept Jack's testimony.

Issue: Whether we should accept Jack's testimony

Whenever a source is not credible, we lack sufficient reason to accept the person's claims. This, of course, does not mean that his or her claims are false. Indeed, the witness may be telling the truth. However, since the only evidence that is offered is his or her statements given on the witness stand, we cannot accept the claims as convincing when the person is biased. Therefore, the conclusion of the argument is "We should not accept Jack's testimony," not "The defendant is capable of murder."

Other arguments that legitimately focus on a person are ones in which the person's character is what is at issue. Consider this one.

We should not hire John Greene for the position of chief accountant, the person responsible for managing all of our company's accounts. This is because he has been convicted of embezzling funds from his last two employers.

Here is the argument analyzed formally.

P: John Greene has been convicted of embezzling funds from his last two employers.

∴   We should not hire John Greene for the position of chief accountant.

Issue: Whether we should hire John Greene for the position of chief accountant

Although this argument does attack a person, it is not an example of the ad hominem fallacy. John Greene's past workplace behavior is highly relevant to whether he should be hired. Since his character is what is at issue, the focus on him is legitimate.

 EXERCISE 11.12

Your Turn!   How do you decide whether an ad hominem argument is a fallacy or a legitimate argument?

 EXERCISE 11.13

For each of the following, complete a Formal Analysis of the argument. Then determine whether the argument commits the ad hominem fallacy.

1. Samuel argues that extraterrestrial creatures exist. He cites the 1965 UFO crash in Roswell, New Mexico; the inexplicable crop circle phenomenon; and the hundreds of stories of abduction from people across the globe. But this can't be believed. Did you know that he has been diagnosed with schizophrenia?
2. Samuel told me that he was abducted by "little green men" and subjected to "experiments" when he was 12. But this can't be believed. Did you know that he has been diagnosed with schizophrenia?
3. Mr. Johnson's argument that the oil deposits in Warren County will last another 100 years must be discounted. Didn't you realize that he is the president of Lone Star Oil Company?
4. The manager of the local baseball team should be fired immediately. He doesn't motivate the players, and he has a terrible work ethic. Besides that, he's not honest with the fans.
5. Professor Hardy has argued that Suzy's Law will not prevent suicides. We can ignore his argument because he is always looking for attention.
6. The economist John Flamingo may have given some pretty good reasons why we should all invest in the stock market. I, for one, don't accept that conclusion because he hasn't invested any of his money in the stock market.
7. Becky's argument that we should pay nurses higher salaries can't be accepted. After all, her own husband just graduated from nursing school.
8. Don't pick Frank's Landscaping Service because they do terrible work. The last time they trimmed my trees, they killed five of them.

9. Frank has argued that planting trees near your home will reduce summertime energy use. But don't listen to him. He owns Frank's Landscaping Service and is just looking to increase his business.
10. William Shakespeare could not possibly have written all the plays that are attributed to him. He was only an illiterate, slow-witted actor who spent most of his time drunk. Also, he could never have had the life experiences necessary to write a play like *Hamlet* or *Julius Caesar*.

The fallacies of appeal to illegitimate authority and ad hominem have similar features in that they both refer in their premises to what someone else says. Arguments that appeal to illegitimate authority are fallacious because the source referenced is not a genuine authority on the issue. This means that when the source is a legitimate authority, the argument does not commit the fallacy. Ad hominem arguments are fallacious because they reject a person's argument based on features of that person rather than the reasons the person offers for his or her conclusion. If the referenced person instead makes claims we are expected to believe rather than an argument, the attack would not commit the ad hominem fallacy because the issue would be about his or her credibility.

To distinguish between these two fallacies, you must pay close attention to whether the person referenced in the premises asserts a claim or offers an argument. When someone merely *asserts a claim*, all we have to go by is his or her reliability as a good source of information. But when someone *offers an argument*, he or she provides us with reasons that can be assessed, so the source of the argument is irrelevant. The templates for these fallacies are described below, using C to symbolize the claim that is offered as the conclusion, P to symbolize the person referred to in the argument, and the symbol ~ to represent the rejection of a claim.

Appeal to Illegitimate Authority	Ad Hominem
P1: P says C	**P1:** P argues for C
P2: P is an authority on a subject unrelated to C.	**P2:** P is untrustworthy
∴ C	∴ ~ C
Issue: Whether C is true	**Issue:** Whether C is true

EXERCISE 11.14

For each of the following, complete a Formal Analysis of the argument. Then determine whether the argument commits the appeal to illegitimate authority fallacy, the ad hominem fallacy, or no fallacy at all.

1. You argue that I should not eat so much red meat. That's clearly unconvincing, since you're no vegetarian yourself.
2. My dad's accountant says that I will have to declare my Las Vegas winnings on my income taxes. I guess I'll just have to bite the bullet and do so.

3. The Chinese government has been arguing that the United States should give more support to developing countries. But we should urge our legislators to discount this argument. Since when did the Chinese government provide substantial aid to developing countries?

4. The Russian government recently argued that the West should not set up a missile defense system in eastern Europe. We should not give weight to that argument because Russia is still locked into a Cold War mentality.

5. Former Secretary of State Henry Kissinger has urged the United States to maintain close ties with the state of Israel. Since he has so much experience in foreign relations, we should do as he says.

6. The National Dairy Board's argument that milk producers must be granted subsidies is completely wrongheaded. The dairy board just wants its members to make more money, while you pay more for groceries.

7. Claire should not be promoted to the vice president of sales position at corporate headquarters. She does not have an MBA, she is not committed to the future of the company, and the people who currently work under her complain about unfairness and favoritism. She's not a good choice.

8. Since the quarterback of our university's football team says that athlete's foot can be cured by not washing your feet more than twice a week, it must be true. He's an athlete, after all.

9. Mr. Waterstone may be a nice guy, but he should not be promoted to district manager. This is because he has a poor performance record, he tries to undermine others in the office, and he spreads lies about his coworkers.

10. Rihanna, the pop star who won a Grammy for her "Umbrella" song, has endorsed the Totes Isotoner umbrella. Therefore, the Totes Isotoner umbrella is the best umbrella on the market.

Strawman

The **strawman** fallacy occurs when an arguer misrepresents the conclusion of an opposing view and then attacks that view in its misrepresented form. This fallacy is committed in an effort to make an opponent's view seem ridiculous or patently false—and, hence, easy to reject. Although this strategy may be rhetorically persuasive to those who are inclined to disagree with the opposing view, it does nothing to show that the opponent's view is actually wrong. To show that someone's conclusion is mistaken requires that an accurate representation of that conclusion be refuted.

Like the ad hominem fallacy, arguments that commit the strawman fallacy are accompanied by a second argument—namely, the one that is rejected by the author of the passage. In the case of the strawman fallacy, the mistake is that the speaker misrepresents the other person's position by exaggerating the claims offered, by presenting an extremist version of the position as representative of the general position, or by taking claims out of context. In each of these cases, the arguer substitutes a distorted version of the opposing conclusion.

Consider this example.

> *There is a growing movement for the recognition of a right to pray in public schools. But we should not require every child to recite the Lord's Prayer at mealtimes. Protestants and Catholics say the prayer differently. Some children don't even know the prayer. And the parents of non-Christians might not want their children to learn it.*

Notice that the passage contains two different conclusions—one is associated with the original argument being opposed, and the other is the strawman, or distorted, version. Therefore, you must carefully determine what exactly is at issue. In this case, the issue being debated is given in the first sentence: whether we should recognize a right to pray in public schools. The Formal Analysis of the argument is as follows:

> **P1:**   Protestants and Catholics say the Lord's Prayer differently.
>
> **P2:**   Some children don't even know the Lord's Prayer.
>
> **P3:**   The parents of non-Christians might not want their children to learn the Lord's Prayer.
>
> ∴   We should not require every child to recite the Lord's Prayer at mealtimes.
>
> **Issue:** Whether we should recognize a right to pray in public schools

When you compare the issue to the conclusion, the distortion becomes apparent. Instead of addressing the issue of whether we should recognize a right to pray in public schools, the speaker provides reasons to support the claim "We should not require every child to recite the Lord's Prayer at mealtimes." But this conclusion does not counter the opposition's conclusion "We should recognize a right to pray in public schools." The arguer distorts the other view by treating the right to pray as if it were a requirement to pray.

Here's another example.

> *Colin Powell, former Secretary of State and Chairman of the Joint Chiefs, has argued that the United States should never engage in torture. It's clear that Powell thinks we shouldn't even be allowed to ask dangerous terrorists simple questions. Such a "hands off" attitude will be a disastrous foreign policy, and it will lead to more brazen attacks against the United States. I think Powell is really wrong on this one.*

 EXERCISE 11.15

> **Your Turn!**   What is Powell's conclusion? What, then, is the issue up for debate?

Once you have the issue identified—the one from Colin Powell's argument—the Formal Analysis of the argument reveals the distortion of his conclusion.

> **P1:**   Not being allowed to ask dangerous terrorists simple questions will be a disastrous foreign policy.
>
> **P2:**   Not being allowed to ask dangerous terrorists simple questions will lead to more brazen attacks against the United States.
>
> ∴   The United States should be able to ask dangerous terrorists simple questions.
>
> **Issue:** Whether the United States should engage in torture

This argument commits the strawman fallacy. The arguer provides reasons to support the claim "The United States should be able to ask dangerous terrorists simple questions." However, this claim is not the rejection of the opposing view; instead, it is a rejection of a distortion of Powell's conclusion. Asking dangerous terrorists simple questions is not the same thing as engaging in torture. The arguer thus does not address what's at issue, yet acts as if he or she has done so when claiming "Powell is really wrong on this one."

EXERCISE 11.16

For each of the following, complete a Formal Analysis of the argument. Then determine whether the argument commits the strawman fallacy. When the fallacy is committed, explain how the arguer distorts his or her opponent's conclusion.

1. Look, maybe you think it's okay to legalize tribal casinos, but I don't. Letting every random group of people in the country open a casino is a ridiculous idea because it is bound to cause trouble.

2. Look, maybe you think it's okay to legalize tribal casinos, but I don't. More casinos mean more gambling, and more gambling means more gambling addicts. Also, organized crime is never far away from casinos, and that's the last group we need to subsidize. I say, let's stop the casinos on the reservations.

3. Anti-abortion groups have given a number of reasons why they oppose abortions. But what these groups really want to do is outlaw every form of birth control, and that is clearly a bad idea. Not everyone can afford to have a child, and legal birth control allows families to plan their pregnancies. Clearly, we should oppose the anti-abortion conclusion.

4. My academic advisor has been encouraging me to apply for a summer internship offered by a local attorney. She says it will make me more attractive to good law schools in the future. I completely disagree. Internships seldom pay wages, they often amount to nothing more than "gofer" work, and a summer internship will prevent me from returning to Alaska to visit my family.

5. Old-school soccer fans argue that using instant-replay technology to resolve questionable referee calls will ruin the game. But this isn't true. Teams could be limited to one challenge per half, and many challenges would involve disputed goals, when play is already stopped.

6. I know that education experts argue that a multicultural curriculum in elementary school will lead to more tolerance and fewer biases toward those perceived as "different." But we should reject teaching nothing but multicultural dogma. It would leave our students deficient in the basic skills they need to learn such as math, reading, and science.

7. A local pastor argued that people who are wealthy should donate a percentage of their income to help those who are hungry and homeless. Well, it's unfortunate that this leader wants wealthy people to give away all of their income to help strangers. If the wealthy did this, then they would become poor. How does that help anyone?

8. Psychologists claim that the Rorschach inkblot test reveals a person's unconscious motivations and drives, and for that reason, they want to test children who are disruptive in school. But psychoanalyzing everyone in the country would be foolish. It would be too invasive and expensive for a nation like ours.

9. Some employers argue that they have the right to monitor employee Internet use. I completely disagree. Why should employers be allowed to spy on the private lives of their employees and learn everything about them? No one supports such an intrusion by Big Brother.
10. Senator Jones argues in favor of legalizing marijuana for medical use. But how can we allow everyone in the country to get high all of the time? No one would go to work or take care of their kids. And everyone would be driving under the influence.

Red Herring

The **red herring** fallacy is a fallacy in which the arguer provides premises that do not support the conclusion the arguer claims to support; instead, the arguer deliberately attempts to distract you by providing reasons that are irrelevant to the issue in question. Determining whether a passage commits the red herring fallacy requires that you first identify the conclusion. Once you have the conclusion identified, you can ask whether the premises provided are actually relevant to it.

> **Hint!**
> The term *red herring* comes from the practice of taking a fish that has been cured in brine or heavily smoked and dragging it across a trail to throw tracking dogs off the scent of the person or animal they are pursuing.

Occasionally, arguments that commit the red herring fallacy contain premises that are obviously irrelevant. However, in most cases the fallacy is not so blatant. These arguments often involve topics that evoke a strong emotional response, and it is this response that may distract you from the issue and trick you into accepting the conclusion.
Consider this argument.

> *Environmentalists argue that the construction of 30 new dairies in Tippecanoe County will endanger public health, worsen our air quality, and contaminate the ground and surface water. However, the fact of the matter is that each new dairy will create hundreds of new jobs for our county's residents, and the property taxes paid by the dairies will provide us with the revenue needed to fund important programs for our community. When you consider the benefits to come, it's clear that the environmentalists are wrong.*

Notice that, as in the ad hominem and strawman fallacies, there are two different views presented in the passage. The arguer begins by stating the view of his or her opponent. You must be sure that you do not confuse the opponent's argument with that of the author of the passage. At the end of the passage, the arguer states that the environmentalists are wrong. But what exactly are they wrong about? The environmentalists contend that the proposed dairies will endanger public health, worsen air quality, and contaminate the water. Since the arguer disagrees with the environmentalists, the conclusion of the argument, then, is that the proposed dairies will *not* endanger public health, worsen air quality, and contaminate the water supply. Let's present the argument formally.

P1: Each new dairy will create hundreds of new jobs for the residents of Tippecanoe County.

P2: Each new dairy will provide property tax revenue needed to fund important community programs.

∴ The new dairies will not endanger public health, worsen air quality, and contaminate the water supply.

Issue: Whether the new dairies will endanger public health, worsen air quality, and contaminate the water supply

Once you have the conclusion identified, it is much easier to determine whether the premises are relevant or irrelevant. Although these premises may be good reasons to support the construction of the dairies, they do not establish that the dairies will not have harmful effects on public health, air quality, and water supplies. The argument thus commits the red herring fallacy because it provides premises that distract the reader from the issue in question.

Let's consider one more example.

Immediately after the Freedom Industries chemical spill, the governor of West Virginia warned residents that their tap water was contaminated. But it couldn't be. Tap water in nearly every city across the country has been fluoridated to promote dental health. And, besides, using tap water instead of bottled water saves you hundreds of dollars each year and reduces household waste.

EXERCISE 11.17

Your Turn!   What conclusion is being opposed by the author of this passage? What, then, is the issue up for debate?

AP Images/Steve Helber, File

In January 2014, the drinking water for over 300,000 West Virginians was contaminated by a Freedom Industries plant's chemical spill.

Once you have the issue identified, you can then identify the conclusion of the argument and determine whether or not the premises are relevant to it. The Formal Analysis of the argument is as follows:

> **P1:** Tap water in nearly every city across the country has been fluoridated to promote dental health.
>
> **P2:** Using tap water instead of bottled water saves you hundreds of dollars each year.
>
> **P3:** <u>Using tap water instead of bottled water reduces household waste.</u>
>
> ∴ The tap water in West Virginia was not contaminated.
>
> **Issue:** Whether the tap water in West Virginia was contaminated

In analyzing the argument, you can see that the premises do not support the conclusion the arguer purports to defend. Instead of supporting the claim "The tap water in West Virginia was not contaminated," the premises distract the listener by listing the general benefits of using tap water. The argument, then, commits the red herring fallacy.

 EXERCISE 11.18

For each of the following, complete a Formal Analysis of the argument. Then determine whether the argument commits the red herring fallacy.

1. Opponents of increased oil drilling offshore contend that more drilling will be dangerous to the marine environment. This isn't true. Offshore drilling will provide hundreds of local jobs, improve the local economy, and decrease our reliance on energy importation. So you must agree that increased drilling offshore will not be dangerous to the marine environment.

2. Environmentalists blamed pollution from local industries for a massive fish kill in Bayou Chaland earlier this month. But they're wrong. The fish kill was caused by a low tide. The low tide prevented the flow of water between the bayou and the Gulf of Mexico, and the fish simply lacked sufficient oxygen to survive.

3. A recent Highway Patrol report maintained that texting while driving is as dangerous as drinking and driving. I completely disagree. Texting is a great way to stay in touch with family and friends. You can send someone a message whenever you want. What's more, it's fun! It's plain that this author is completely misguided about texting.

4. The nurses at the local hospital contend that they should get a pay raise. But many people in this world don't even have jobs. They get by on handouts, charity, and what little they can earn through day labor. The hospital administration should say "no" to this raise.

5. Lots of political commentators say that the first piece of business for the new Congress should be to pass income tax reform that helps the very poorest people in this country. I agree for several reasons. First, the people on the bottom of the economic ladder suffer tremendously from sales taxes. Second, these overworked, overtaxed people lose much of their pitifully small income to federal income tax. Also, many are so poorly educated that they can't find legal means to protect their hard-earned dollars.

6. A recent study showed that learning to play the piano helps children do better at math. However, this just isn't true. Pianos cost a lot of money, lessons are difficult to arrange, and most people lack sufficient room for such a large instrument.

7. In your editorial, you argued that the graduates of our social work program are not prepared for jobs in the private sector. This is simply false. The private sector is a wonderful place to work, and many jobs are being created in the private sector each year. Small- and medium-sized businesses create more than their share of jobs, and the pay is above average for the field.

8. Have you seen the ad that claims that going through a three-month job training program prepares you for employment better than a university does? This is nonsense. Employers care about their future employees being able to think critically, write clearly, and possess knowledge about a number of different subjects. And that kind of training happens only at a university.

9. A popular American history text used in college courses argues that nationalism was a volatile force in the mid-nineteenth century. But this can't be supported. Without nations, we would be living in tribal groups, fighting with other tribes over hunting territories. It is nationalism that has allowed the human race to make progress in combating disease, malnutrition, superstition, and many other evils people experience in tribal culture.

10. In 1998, the Arizona Supreme Court ruled that declaring English as the state's official language deprives people of their fundamental First Amendment right to access government. These judges are clearly wrong, since the majority of the population of Arizona speaks English. To be successful in school and in one's career, speaking English is a must.

The strawman and red herring fallacies can be difficult to distinguish. Both arguments that commit the strawman fallacy and those that commit the red herring fallacy refer to the opposing view as the motivation for their arguments. Strawman arguments are fallacious because, rather than offering premises that support rejecting the opponent's conclusion, they offer reasons to reject a *distorted* version of the opponent's conclusion. In this way, the argument does not address the issue up for debate. Red herring arguments are fallacious because the arguer distracts the reader from what's at issue by providing premises that are irrelevant to the conclusion they are intended to support. The templates for these fallacies are illustrated below, using C to symbolize the claim that is offered as the conclusion and the symbol ~ to represent the rejection of a claim.

Strawman	**Red Herring**
P: Premise(s)	**P:** Premises (irrelevant)
∴ ~ C (distorted)	∴ C
Issue: Whether C is true	**Issue:** Whether C is true

✒ **EXERCISE 11.19**

For each of the following, complete a Formal Analysis of the argument. Then determine whether the argument commits the strawman fallacy, the red herring fallacy, or no fallacy at all.

1. A bunch of fanatics have been clamoring for restrictions on alcohol use by pregnant women to prevent fetal alcohol syndrome. They forget that alcohol is a perfectly normal part of society. It can help people relax in social situations and make people feel happy. Why, virtually every culture on Earth has used alcohol for a relaxant.

2. The governor has argued that the state could save much-needed funds through the early release of nonviolent offenders who have served at least 90% of their sentences. Why does the governor want people who commit crimes to escape all punishment? Letting these dangerous felons loose in the streets will just lead to more crime and endanger more lives.

3. The head of our employees' union contends that the new contract should include a raise that keeps employee wages in line with inflation. But using all the company savings just to enrich the employees is a bad idea. Why, we need to pay for additional inventory, pay our suppliers, and put money away for a rainy day. I urge the board to resist the union's demand for raises.

4. I've heard statistics used to show that wearing seatbelts in a moving vehicle saves lives. But this is ridiculous. Cars provide us with a relatively cheap and easy way to travel quickly across great distances. If it weren't for cars, we'd be stuck walking or riding horses to work every day.

5. Some people argue that the death penalty is no more of a deterrent to crime than life in prison without parole. But I disagree. What's to stop convicted murderers from killing prison guards and other prisoners while they're incarcerated?

6. You have probably heard arguments against suspending athletes who use performance enhancers. How can the integrity of sports be maintained if we just let them off with no penalties at all? Competition is unfair if athletes are allowed to cheat without consequences. Therefore, we must penalize athletes who cheat if we want to ensure the quality of sports.

7. You may be aware of the recent proposal to create a pub on campus that would sell beer and wine to adult students. Having the entire campus drunk day and night is a bad idea and one we all should oppose. It will only lead to violence, destruction of property, and a dramatic decline in academic performance.

8. Recently, animal rights supporters charged that horse racing can cause life-threatening injuries to young animals. This doesn't make sense. Not only is horse racing an important source of jobs for thousands of people, but also it provides thrilling entertainment for untold numbers of spectators and bettors across the country.

9. Horse racing is a popular sport all across the country. But did you realize that racing a horse before it is fully mature can result in life-threatening leg injuries? This is because the leg bones of young horses are not very strong, and if the leg bones are not strong, then injury can easily result.

10. I've heard complaints that the current tax laws are unfair to small businesses because small businesses are taxed on a higher share of their income than larger businesses. I completely disagree with that because taxes are a normal part of life as a citizen of the United States. Also, when you pay taxes, you are helping strengthen our country, and anytime you do that, you show yourself to be a patriot. Therefore, current tax laws are not unfair to small businesses.

PUTTING IT ALL TOGETHER: Writing a Critical Précis of a Fallacious Argument

At this point in the book, not only have you learned how to recognize, analyze, and evaluate many different kinds of arguments, but also you have learned how to identify six common mistakes in reasoning. Now, you can put all of these skills together by adding fallacy detection to your Critical Précis assignments.

Directions for a Critical Précis of a Fallacious Argument

In *paragraph form*, use complete sentences and proper English grammar and spelling to do the following:

Step 1: Identify the passage.

▸ Completely and correctly identify the author and the source (whenever such information is given).

▸ If the passage contains an argument, identify it as such. Then move to Step 2.

▸ If the passage does not contain an argument, identify it as a nonargument. Then specify which feature of an argument is lacking.

Step 2: Analyze the argument.

▸ Clearly and completely identify the issue, conclusion, and premise or premises in that order.

▸ If the passage is a multiple argument, write separate paragraphs to analyze each separate argument.

Step 3: Detect fallacious reasoning.

▸ If the argument commits a fallacy, write a separate paragraph identifying the fallacy and describing how that fallacy is committed.

Let's work through one example before you try some on your own. Consider this one.

> *My dental school instructor claims that I should advocate for the Rolling Stroke Method, since it is quite effective for maintaining healthy gums. But I think she's wrong. There's no way she spends two full minutes every morning and every night carefully grooming her teeth.*—Pascual, dental student

First, you should notice that this passage contains two arguments, one by the dental school instructor and one by the dental student. Remember that when analyzing and evaluating an argument, your focus should always be on the argument advanced by the author of the passage. Because he disagrees with his instructor, we can readily identify the issue—namely, whether Pascual should advocate for the Rolling Stroke Method. The dental school instructor argues that Pascual should advocate for this method. And when Pascual says, "I think she's wrong," he concludes that "I should not advocate for the Rolling Stroke Method." Next, what premises does Pascual offer to support his conclusion? When he states, "There's no way she spends two full minutes every morning and every night carefully grooming her teeth," Pascual isn't actually offering reasons to not advocate for the Rolling Stroke Method. Instead, he is effectively accusing the instructor of hypocrisy—of some inconsistency between the instructor's recommendation and her own dental care habits. But of course, even if the instructor doesn't follow her own advice, this does not mean that the advice is not supported by the reasons she provides. If Pascual wishes to demonstrate that the Rolling Stroke Method should not be advocated, he must provide reasons, not attack his instructor.

Here is the Critical Précis of the argument.

> **This passage by Pascual, a dental student, contains an argument. The issue is whether I should advocate for the Rolling Stroke Method. The conclusion is that I should not advocate for the Rolling Stroke Method. The first premise is that my dental school instructor argues that I should advocate for the Rolling Stroke Method. The second premise is that there's no way my dental school instructor spends two full minutes every morning and every night carefully grooming her teeth.**
>
> **This argument commits the ad hominem fallacy. The arguer attacks the dental school instructor for an inconsistency between her words and her deeds instead of addressing the reasons she provides for her conclusion.**

Notice how the analysis of the argument reflects the template for the ad hominem fallacy presented earlier in the chapter. There are two premises presented: One identifies the dental school instructor's conclusion, and the other identifies how the arguer attacks her. Also notice that in the second paragraph the fallacy is identified and how the fallacy is committed is also explained.

 EXERCISE 11.20

Write a Critical Précis for the following passages. For any fallacious arguments, identify the fallacy committed, and explain how the mistake in reasoning occurred.

1. If you don't eat your meat, you can't have any pudding. Because, how can you have any pudding, if you don't eat your meat?—Pink Floyd, "Another Brick in the Wall"

2. For over 50 years, massive amounts of radioactive waste have been piling up at nuclear power plants. The U.S. Congress proposed to store 70,000 tons of the waste in Yucca Mountain, a site 90 miles northwest of Las Vegas. Oscar Goodman, mayor of Las Vegas, opposes the plan because it will be dangerous to transport the materials across the country, including railways and highways that pass through Las Vegas. But we shouldn't listen to Goodman. He is just trying to make sure he gets reelected next year.

3. Many have applauded the success of welfare reform because many have made the transition from welfare to employment. However, welfare reform has often done more harm than good. First, the employment found by former welfare recipients does not pay well enough to support a family. Second, parents who are unable to afford child care costs routinely leave their children at home to fend for themselves. And, finally, the jobs obtained by former welfare recipients rarely include health-care benefits.—Lester Spence, political science professor at Johns Hopkins University

4. Richard Nixon has to be one of the worst presidents in the history of this country. Look at his record: lies, corruption, and scandal. Plus, he is the only president forced to resign the office.—Political blogger

5. No one has ever demonstrated that Iraq didn't have weapons of mass destruction. In the absence of such evidence, isn't it reasonable to conclude that they did have them?

6. Some people claim that the elementary and high school teachers in this country deserve our respect, as they have to work very hard. But I think it's clearly ridiculous to worship teachers like they are enlightened beings. Teachers make mistakes, some of them are lazy and incompetent, and worshipping any human is irreligious. I think it's clear that teachers don't deserve our respect.

7. A team of engineers found that Hurricane Katrina damaged the structural integrity of the Lake Pontchartrain bridge. Therefore, the bridge should be closed until its safety can be assured.

8. Peter Singer argues that the treatment of chickens in factory farms is inhumane. But Singer is just plain wrong. Chicken is a great source of protein and is significantly healthier than beef or pork.

9. Some people argue that we should increase foreign aid to Pakistan. But this is a terrible idea! Pakistan is currently too unstable, and its regime is corrupt. Furthermore, Pakistan may use the money to attack neighboring countries like India.

10. I've heard rumors that a newly discovered meteor is dangerously close to hitting Earth. But I'm not worried about it, and you shouldn't be either. A team of astronomers from the Griffith Observatory reassured the public that the meteor will not come near Earth's orbit, so the rumors aren't true.—Museum docent

CHAPTER REVIEW QUESTIONS

1. Define *fallacy*.
2. What does it mean to say that an argument begs the question?
3. How do you determine who has the burden of proof?
4. How do you know whether an authority is legitimate or not?
5. When is an argument that attacks a person not an ad hominem fallacy?
6. What mistake does an arguer make when committing the strawman fallacy?
7. What is the error in reasoning when an arguer commits the red herring fallacy?
8. How do you write a Critical Précis of a fallacious argument?

ONE STEP FURTHER

In this chapter, you have learned how to identify a handful of the many possible ways in which an argument can go wrong. The examples you have encountered are highly stylized to facilitate your ability to recognize these six common mistakes in reasoning. The truth is, however, that when reasoning goes awry, there are often many mistakes that occur simultaneously and differentiating them may be very difficult or impossible. But even when it is clear what the mistake is, even when you are able to identify an argument as committing one of the fallacies you have learned, what is your next step?

While you may be tempted to declare victory over your interlocutor and move on with your day, we believe that there is more work to be done. If you are able to identify a fallacy in another person's argument, it is likely that the argument's author will revise his or her argument by offering reasons that do not commit that fallacy. After all, he or she believes the argument's conclusion and wants to convince you that you should, too. In that case, you will need to return to your argument analysis and evaluation skills to respond to the revised argument. Another possibility is that you could provide assistance in repairing the fallacious argument. This strategy is particularly useful in cases in which you agree with the conclusion, but for different (and hopefully better!) reasons. Knowing how the fallacious argument has failed provides you with a starting point for revising it.

1. Look back at the argument by Veronica presented at the start of this chapter. What mistake (or mistakes!) in reasoning have occurred?
2. How might you revise Veronica's argument to avoid fallacious reasoning? Compare your revised argument to those of your peers.
3. A fun resource for learning about fallacies is Ali Almossawi's *An Illustrated Book of Bad Arguments*, also found at https://bookofbadarguments.com. Try illustrating your own example of fallacious reasoning at http://www.makebeliefscomix.com/. Or, better yet, illustrate how to repair a fallacious argument!

Truth and reconciliation commissions, such as the one pictured here, use arguments collaboratively to foster agreement and cooperation between opposing groups.

Oryx Media Archive/Gallo Images/Getty Images

CHAPTER
12

Constructing Arguments

A t some point during your college studies, an instructor will give you an assign-ment to write an argumentative essay. Let's suppose that, while trying to think of an appropriate topic, you come across a Facebook entry about a movement aiming to make your campus smoke-free, not unlike the one presented at the beginning of this book.

© Pressmaster/Shutterstock.com

Sara says Hey people! Check out this link! We should definitely start this campaign on our campus...

Smoke-Free Campus The Smoke-Free Campus Initiative aims to promote a clean, safe, and healthy campus environment by eliminating smoking from college campuses...

© Mark William Richardson/Shutterstock.com

You think that this issue is certainly controversial and also something about which you have a strong opinion. In fact, you are tempted to participate in the debate online. Choosing this topic for your essay will allow you to think through the issue in a more organized fashion, create an essay for your assignment, and contribute to the online debate. But how should you go about developing an argument?

The overarching skills you have practiced and learned in this book—recognizing, analyzing, and evaluating arguments—will help you develop good arguments of your own, whether you want to join in an online debate, support your position in a con-versation with friends or classmates, or successfully write an argumentative essay.

Even though the arguments you construct in these three contexts most likely will differ in style and length, each requires the same foundational critical thinking tools that you have acquired in the preceding chapters. However, instead of identifying an argument's premises and conclusions and judging how well the conclusion is supported, you will be defending a conclusion of your own by providing relevant premises that support it. To use the formal terms from Bloom's Taxonomy, you will be creating rather than analyzing and evaluating.

Good writing is a process that typically requires prewriting, writing, and revising. In this chapter, we do not provide instructions for improving your writing skills. Instead, we help you use the critical thinking skills that you have learned in this text in order to produce a logically convincing argument or argumentative essay. Even though an argumentative essay is generally longer and more formal than arguments you might post online or present to friends or classmates, the basic steps you will learn in this chapter can be applied to a wide range of argumentative writing formats.

LEARNING OUTCOMES

In this chapter, you will learn how to write an argumentative essay by:

▸ Formulating an argument,
▸ Introducing the argument,
▸ Supporting the conclusion,
▸ Considering objections,
▸ Summarizing the argument, and
▸ Citing sources.

Formulating Your Argument

In your writing or composition classes, you may have learned some prewriting techniques to help you generate ideas about your topic. One that may be useful for your argumentative essay is brainstorming. When you **brainstorm**, you write down as many ideas as you can that relate to the issue you have chosen to write about. Just think about the issue, and write down any ideas that might be relevant to your argument. Don't worry about the form of the ideas or how well they might work for your essay. The purpose of the exercise is simply to engage your mind and start collecting ideas you may have.

 EXERCISE 12.1

Your Turn! Brainstorm at least five ideas for and five ideas against a campus-wide smoking ban.

Once you have generated some ideas through prewriting, you will need to examine them to decide which will be most convincing in your essay. Remember, as you learned in Chapter 2, an argument's purpose is to persuade the reader or listener to accept the truth of your conclusion, so you must be sure that you understand the issue, that your conclusion is clearly stated and completely addresses the issue, and that your premises support your conclusion as unmistakably and forcefully as possible. When your reader needs convincing, you cannot expect that he or she will readily agree with you; instead, you should construct your argument as if the reader's opinion opposes your own. What will convince him or her? Only clearly stated reasons relevant to the conclusion you are putting forward will be convincing.

Let's suppose that you have decided to argue in favor of the Smoke-Free Campus Initiative. What reasons can you offer to support this view? In determining how to best convince someone who is not already inclined to accept your position, make sure that you do not utilize fallacious reasoning.

First, when offering a premise, do not give a claim that simply restates the conclusion, as in the following example.

> *We should ban smoking on campus because smoking on campus should be prohibited.*

As you learned in Chapter 11, to say that "some claim is true because that claim is true" is to commit the fallacy of begging the question. No one who didn't already accept the conclusion would accept this premise.

Common Fallacies

Hasty generalization	The arguer uses a sample which is too small to offer even minimal support for the conclusion.
Biased generalization	The arguer uses a sample which misrepresents the target.
Faulty analogy	The arguer refers to similarities between the sample and target that are irrelevant to the feature.
Post hoc ergo propter hoc	The arguer concludes that one event was caused by another simply because one preceded the other.
Begging the question	The conclusion of an argument is assumed by the argument's premises.
Appeal to ignorance	The arguer illegitimately shifts the burden of proof to his or her opponent.
Appeal to illegitimate authority	The arguer uses a source that is not an authority on the subject in question to support a conclusion.
Ad hominem	The arguer rejects an opposing argument based on the characteristics of its author.
Strawman	The arguer mischaracterizes the conclusion of his or her opponent's argument and then attacks the argument in its distorted form.
Red herring	The arguer distracts the reader from the issue by using irrelevant premises.

Second, do not shift the burden of proof, as in the following example.

We should ban smoking on campus. This is because no one has given a good reason to believe that we shouldn't.

This argument commits the fallacy of appeal to ignorance because, rather than offering reasons to accept the conclusion, the arguer illegitimately shifts the burden of proof to his or her opponent. If you want to convince someone that your conclusion is true, you must provide reasons for that conclusion rather than expecting your opponent to do all the work.

Finally, make sure that the premises you provide are relevant to the conclusion they are intended to support. Consider the following example.

We should ban smoking on campus. After all, tobacco companies use deceptive marketing tactics targeted to young people in order to manipulate them into becoming lifelong smokers. And for what? Pure profit!

Although the premises in this argument may support penalizing tobacco companies for their social irresponsibility, they do not support the stated conclusion—namely, that we should ban smoking on campus. In this way, the argument comes dangerously close to committing the red herring fallacy.

What *good* reasons can you provide for supporting a campus-wide ban on smoking? Let's suppose that you agree with the Smoke-Free Campus Initiative because it will make for a cleaner, safer, and healthier campus. You can use a Formal Analysis to outline your argument.

> **P1:**   Cleaner campus.
> **P2:**   Safer campus.
> **P3:**   <u>Healthier campus.</u>
> ∴   Ban smoking.
>
> **Issue:** Smoking on campus

 EXERCISE 12.2

Your Turn!   What has gone wrong in the Formal Analysis above?

You should be able to recognize two problems with the Formal Analysis that was just stated. First, the premises and conclusion are not stated as claims. Recall from Chapter 2 that you can determine whether a sentence is a claim by placing the phrase *it is true that* ... in front of it. You wouldn't say "It is true that cleaner campus" or "It is true that ban smoking." These need to be reformulated as claims that are clear and specific.

The second problem with this Formal Analysis is that the issue is not properly identified. "Smoking on campus" is a topic, not an issue. Recall from Chapter 3 that every issue begins with the word *whether*. Once you have formulated your conclusion as a claim, place *whether* in front of it, and the result will be the issue. Notice how the following Formal Analysis clearly presents the premises and conclusion as claims and properly identifies the issue.

> **P1:** Cigarette butts are a significant source of litter on campus.
>
> **P2:** Secondhand smoke is hazardous to both smokers and nonsmokers.
>
> **P3:** <u>Banning smoking supports those students who want to quit smoking.</u>
>
> ∴ We should ban smoking on campus.
>
> **Issue:** Whether we should ban smoking on campus

 EXERCISE 12.3

Your Turn! Write a Formal Analysis containing three premises supporting a conclusion on the other side of this issue.

Introducing Your Argument

An argumentative essay typically consists of four to six well-developed paragraphs comprising three main parts: an introduction, a body, and a conclusion. Since the purpose of an argument, and thus an argumentative essay, is to convince the reader of something, an inviting and compelling introduction is vital. Within this paragraph, you must grab the reader's attention, identify the issue and show its importance, and make clear what main point you intend to support in the body of the paper.

In an attempt to gain reader interest, writers commonly construct ineffective introductions, as in the following example.

> *Since the beginning of time, some people have believed that they are allowed to do whatever they want, even if it endangers others. The case of the so-called rights of smokers to foul the public air with their secondhand smoke is a current example of this problem. Students on this campus are trying to ban all cigarette smoking, and I completely agree with them. In this paper, I intend to prove beyond a shadow of a doubt that my conclusion is the only possible correct one.*

In trying to catch the reader's attention, this introduction commits a common mistake by giving an overly simplified generalization that is factually inaccurate.

> *Since the beginning of time, some people have believed that they are allowed to do whatever they want, even if it endangers others.*

The problem of people endangering others hasn't occurred since the "beginning of time," if for no other reason than that people haven't existed since the beginning of time. It also misstates what the issue is by claiming that people want to do "whatever they want." The issue is whether cigarette smoking should be banned on campus, a much more specific issue.

The second sentence continues the theme of trying to be dramatic as a way of getting the reader to pay attention.

> *The case of the so-called rights of smokers to foul the public air with their secondhand smoke is a current example of this problem.*

Smokers may harm or annoy others, but doing so is not their primary motivation. To suggest otherwise mischaracterizes the position of smokers' rights advocates, a mistake you should recognize as a strawman fallacy. Furthermore, smoking outdoors certainly leads to less exposure to secondhand smoke than smoking indoors.

In the third sentence, the writer is attempting to present his or her main point. Although the reader might be able to figure out the writer's position on the issue, it would be better if the conclusion was explicitly stated. When you are attempting to convince a reader of the truth of your conclusion, you want that conclusion to be easily understood.

Finally, the last sentence in the introduction overreaches.

> *In this paper, I intend to prove beyond a shadow of a doubt that my conclusion is the only possible correct one.*

Here the writer has substituted not-so-subtle rhetoric—"prove beyond a shadow of a doubt" and "my conclusion is the only possible correct one"—for good argumentation. When analyzing an argument, you should leave such rhetorical flourish out of the analysis of the argument because the conclusion is not more likely to be true just because the author claims that it is "proven." Also, the task in the paper is to give a good argument, not prove something beyond any possible doubt.

So how could this paragraph be improved? Consider the following example.

> *Many states not only prohibit smoking in designated areas, but have banned smoking entirely in workplaces and other public spaces. This movement has extended to college campuses. According to the American Nonsmokers' Rights Foundation, 1,343 U.S. college campuses have enacted smoke-free campus policies ("Smokefree and Tobacco-Free U.S. and Tribal Colleges and Universities"). Many people disagree about whether smoking should be completely prohibited on college campuses. In this essay, I will argue that our university should completely prohibit smoking across campus because doing so will make our campus cleaner, safer, and healthier.*

In this introduction, the author presents a clear context for the debate over banning smoking on campus. The initial sentence is still general, but much more in line with what most of us would acknowledge to be the case—that fewer and fewer public places, such as offices and restaurants, allow people to smoke. The context as the author has developed it in the first two sentences begins quite generally, but by the third sentence, the author has narrowed it to the debate on campus. This is sometimes referred to as a funnel introduction. With this kind of context development, the author gives evidence that the issue is important, and if the issue is important, the essay arguing about that issue is important, too. Note, also, that the source of the information from the American Nonsmokers' Rights Foundation is cited in parentheses. Finally, the fifth sentence in the paragraph presents the exact conclusion that will be supported in this essay and summarizes the reasons to support that conclusion. This is sometimes referred to as the thesis of the essay. Notice that, as you learned in Chapter 3, the issue and conclusion should be consistent. The issue stated in the fourth sentence employs almost identical terms to those used to identify the conclusion supported by the arguer.

EXERCISE 12.4

> **Your Turn!** Write an effective introduction to the argument you outlined in
> Exercise 12.3.

Supporting Your Conclusion

In the body of the essay, you will take each of your premises that support the main
conclusion and make them the focus of an individual paragraph. Thus, in the first paragraph of the body of the essay, you will restate your first premise and give additional
evidence as well as examples as needed to clarify and support that premise. In other
words, each paragraph should present a subargument in support of one of the premises
in your main argument. Depending on the assignment, you may need to offer support
from reliable outside sources, or you may just offer support based on your own careful
thinking. Again, since the reader cannot be expected to already be on your side in this
matter, you must give the best subarguments you can and be clear about how all of this
contributes to the support of each premise.

We have chosen to give an argument with three premises, but you could construct an argument with a different number of premises. Three or four solid reasons
often provide substantive support for an argument, while remaining a small enough
number to not overwhelm the reader. As you build each subargument, remember to
state clearly each intermediate conclusion and its supporting premises as claims. To
help the reader differentiate the premises for the main conclusion from the premises
for the intermediate conclusion, use inference indicators generously. Also, if you utilize
sources to support your claims, make sure that the sources are ones that your reader
will find credible.

Let's start with the first premise, "Cigarette butts are a significant source of litter on campus." What reasons can you offer that support this claim? Suppose that you
are disgusted by the number of cigarette butts littering the areas surrounding building
entrances. You write the following paragraph to reflect your feelings.

> *First, cigarette butts are a significant source of litter on campus. Who
> likes to see that? It's gross. Stop using the campus as an ashtray!*

You may remember from Chapter 3 the difficulty of identifying claims that are implied
by rhetorical questions and commands like the ones used in this passage. Although
they can be interpreted as implying premises, this is usually a poor argument technique.
Using rhetorical questions and commands rests on the reader's ability to figure out what
claims you intend as support. Therefore, if you want to convince the reader to accept
your conclusion, you will be more successful if you clearly state your reasons rather
than hoping that the reader will be able to figure out what you mean.

In the following example, the author presents the subargument with each claim
explicitly stated. Notice the use of inference indicators to help the reader distinguish
the intermediate conclusion (serving here as a topic sentence) from the premises that
support it.

> *First, cigarette butts are a significant source of litter on campus. This
> is because, although courteous smokers use designated cigarette waste*

receptacles, many smokers extinguish their cigarettes on the ground or in other unsuitable places, leaving the smoldering butts behind. Since so many smokers refuse to responsibly dispose of their cigarette waste, the campus has a serious litter problem.

Now it is clear that the second and third claims are premises of the subargument that are meant to support the first premise of the main argument. Notice also that the fourth claim is a restatement of the first. To develop the paragraph further, you can explain how litter is a problem or give examples of problem areas on campus associated with smokers. Just make sure that the reasons you offer in your subargument are clearly stated and relevant to the conclusion they are supporting.

Now, let's turn to the second premise of the main argument—namely, "Secondhand smoke is hazardous to both smokers and nonsmokers." Although you might think it is common knowledge that secondhand smoke is a health hazard, your argument will be stronger if you provide evidence that this is true. Suppose this passage is what you come up with.

The second reason for banning smoking on campus is that secondhand smoke is hazardous to both smokers and nonsmokers. According to Americans for Nonsmokers' Rights, secondhand smoke kills over 50,000 people each year ("Secondhand Smoke"). Eliminating smoke on campus will lessen the number of people on campus who are exposed to these toxic fumes.

Although the statistic that secondhand smoke kills over 50,000 people each year, if true, would add a lot of power to your argument, you must remember that you are trying to convince a potentially skeptical reader. That means that whatever sources you use must be ones that your reader will find credible.

Hint!
Any time you use another's ideas or words, you must cite the source. We have used Modern Language Association (MLA) formatting, and the full bibliographic information appears later in the chapter in the "Works Cited" list at the end of the essay. See the section "Citing Your Sources."

What makes a source credible? A credible source is one that is *knowledgeable* about the subject and one that readers can trust to be *honest*. After all, a source is hardly to be believed if he or she is ignorant of the subject. And a source can't be trusted if he or she is likely to be biased, dishonest, or trying somehow to take advantage of the reader. As you should remember from Chapter 11, when you reference an authority that is not knowledgeable about the subject in question, you commit a fallacy of illegitimate authority. Moreover, if the source you reference is an advocate for one side of the debate, your reader is unlikely to trust that source. Although what the advocate says may be true, the source is unlikely to convince your reader. You are better off citing sources that are considered objective.

The second reason for banning smoking on campus is that secondhand smoke is hazardous to both smokers and nonsmokers.

According to the Centers for Disease Control and Prevention, smoking not only causes heart disease and lung cancer in smokers, but also causes heart disease and cancer in adults who have never smoked. Nonsmokers who are exposed to secondhand smoke at home or at work increase their risk of developing heart disease by 25–30% and increase their risk of developing lung cancer by 20–30% ("Health Effects of Secondhand Smoke"). Since secondhand smoke poses a health hazard to nonsmokers, we should ban smoking to protect the health of everyone on campus.

This argument is more likely to convince a skeptical reader, since it references a source, the Centers for Disease Control and Prevention, that is both knowledgeable about the subject and commonly regarded as objective.

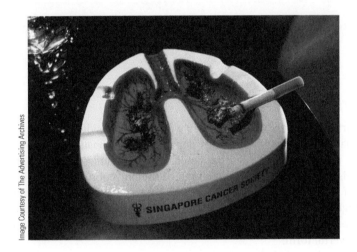

Image Courtesy of The Advertising Archives

Is this an effective image for an anti-smoking campaign? Why or why not?

Finally, let's turn to the third premise of the main argument, "Banning smoking supports those students who want to quit smoking." Suppose you provide the following support for this premise.

The final reason to ban smoking on campus is that banning smoking supports those students who want to quit. For example, when I moved to California in 2000, I was finally able to quit smoking, in part, because smoking was prohibited in enclosed public spaces. So, banning smoking on campus will likely help others do the same.

Using examples is a great way to support your claims. However, notice that with only this one example, the argument is rather weak. You learned in Chapter 8 that arguments that generalize from a very small sample size to a larger population are mistakes in reasoning called hasty generalizations. The argument would be stronger with more evidence.

Consider this example.

The final reason to ban smoking on campus is that banning smoking supports those students who want to quit. This is demonstrated by a 2007 study comparing the effects of having strong (a complete smoking ban) to weak (all other "no smoking" restrictions) smoking regulations for restaurants in 351 Massachusetts towns. Researchers randomly interviewed 1,712 adult smokers, and found that living in a town with a strong regulation was associated with a threefold increase in the odds of making a quit attempt (Albers et al.). Therefore, complete smoking bans encourage people to quit smoking.

Notice how much stronger the evidence is in the second version. A study with a sample size of 1,712 people is much stronger than the previous anecdotal evidence with a sample size of 1.

 EXERCISE 12.5

Your Turn! Develop effective subarguments to support the premises of the argument you introduced in Exercise 12.4.

Considering Objections

The last part of the body of the essay is where you consider an objection that would likely be made by someone who does not accept your position. Although it might be tempting to present an objection that you can easily dismiss or disarm, the strength of your essay is proportionate to the strength of the objection you are able to refute. You can think of it like the scoring in an Olympic diving competition—the more difficult the dive, the higher your score if you perform it successfully. So, for this section, choose the objection you believe most forcefully opposes your position, and state it clearly and in its most powerful form.

Suppose that you believe the strongest reason not to support the smoking ban is that it infringes on an individual's right to choose how to live. Present this objection as clearly and forcefully as you can.

> *Many people who object to banning smoking on college campuses claim that doing so violates an individual's right to choose how to live his or her life. They claim that the only legitimate reason to limit a person's freedom is to prevent harm to others, and if smokers want to risk their health, it should be their choice. Besides, nonsmokers can choose whether or not to be around smoke. If they don't want to risk breathing secondhand smoke, they can just avoid designated smoking areas.*

Next, you should reply to the objection. If you can show that there is a major flaw in the argument's premises or that the objection can be overcome by your argument, your position on the issue will be more convincing. However, be careful not to claim too much, as is done in the following example.

> *However, we should reject this argument because it's clear that anyone who supports so-called smokers' rights is himself or herself a smoker.*

This reply isn't very effective. As you learned in Chapter 11, arguments that attack the arguer instead of the argument commit the ad hominem fallacy. In fact, that is what has happened here. Although smokers are likely to be advocates of smokers' rights, that they have a vested interest in their position does not mean that they have given a poor argument. To show that their conclusion is false, you must respond to their argument, not attack them.

Most controversial issues have good reasons for and against supporting them, and you should acknowledge a good objection if one exists. So, instead of pretending that a good objection is easily dismissed, you should honestly appraise the point and concede what needs to be conceded. This reply to the objection, for example, is more effective than the first version.

> *This argument makes a good point. Any ban on smoking does limit the freedom of those individuals who would choose to smoke, so it is not something that should be taken lightly. However, on many occasions, as in the case of seatbelt or helmet laws, the public safety benefits outweigh the loss of freedom to the individual. Besides, nonsmokers shouldn't have their freedom restricted in order to avoid health hazards. Let the smokers be the ones to move.*

Rather than misrepresenting the opponent's viewpoint, this reply acknowledges the strength of the objection. However, it proposes that, even in spite of the strength of the objection, the reasons for the other side of the argument are more compelling.

 EXERCISE 12.6

Your Turn!   Present the strongest objection you can think of to your argument against the Smoke-Free Campus Initiative, and write an effective response to it.

Summarizing Your Argument

Your final paragraph is your last chance to convince the reader to accept your side of the issue. The most effective strategy is to briefly restate the major points of your argument—namely, the conclusion and premises of your main argument. If handled poorly, a conclusion can actually leave the reader with less inclination to be convinced rather than with more. Let's consider one example.

> *Smoking is an unhealthy, disgusting, and expensive habit that does not belong on a college campus. We must ban smoking wherever we find it. Won't you please join me in eliminating this scourge from our campus community?*

Although this conclusion may be passionate, it is not effective, and it does not follow the guidelines for a successful concluding paragraph. First, this paragraph is clear about which side of the issue is defended, but it doesn't restate the main points of the essay. The second sentence goes beyond the conclusion argued for in the premise by urging a universal ban on smoking. Finally, the essay ends on a weak plea for help, one that is not likely to win any converts to the cause.

tter way of concluding the essay.

ave argued that we should ban smoking on campus.
onclusion with three lines of reasoning. First, banning
on campus. Second, banning smoking will reduce
ndhand smoke. And, third, banning smoking will
o quit. Although banning smoking on campus will
of individuals, the benefits of doing so greatly
of having to leave campus to smoke. In order to
cts of cigarette smoking, we next need to work
smoke-free campus.

the main points of the argument in somewhat
ws the importance of your argument. By suggesting
.. accepting the conclusion, you connect the argument to its

EXERCISE 12.7

Your Turn!   Develop an effective conclusion for your argumentative essay.

Citing Your Sources

Whenever you use the ideas or words of another person, you must acknowledge doing so and utilize proper citation techniques. Otherwise, whether done deliberately or accidentally, you commit **plagiarism**, the presentation of another person's ideas or words as if they are your own. In the example essay we constructed, we have utilized MLA formatting. However, this is not the only way to properly cite sources; the formats developed by the American Psychological Association (APA) and the University of Chicago are also commonly used in academic writing. Be sure to check with your instructor to find out which citation style he or she requires for essays.

At the end of your essay, you should include a list of "Works Cited." It is very important that you provide the information about your sources in the proper format so that your reader can verify the evidence you provide in your argument. If your citations do not match, the reader will likely find you unreliable and will not be convinced by your argument (or, worse, your essay will be penalized!).

Works Cited

Albers, Alison B., et al. "Effect of Smoking Regulations in Local Restaurants on Smokers' Anti-Smoking Attitudes and Quitting Behaviours." *Tobacco Control* 16.2 (2007): 101–6. Print.

"Health Effects of Secondhand Smoke." *Centers for Disease Control and Prevention*. 5 Mar 2014. Web. 26 June 2014.

"Secondhand Smoke." *Americans for Nonsmokers' Rights*. 4 Feb. 2014. Web. 26 June 2014.

"Smokefree and Tobacco-Free U.S. and Tribal Colleges and Universities." *American Nonsmokers' Rights Foundation*. 29 Apr. 2014. Web. 26 June 2014.

reviewed (handwritten)

see back (handwritten)

Each of the four references to sources that we used in this chapter (including source we deemed not credible) and that we included in parentheses has a co ing entry in the "Works Cited" list.

 EXERCISE 12.8

Your Turn!   Write a "Works Cited" page for any sources you utilize in developing your argument.

compose short essay (200-400 words) by following 6 steps (handwritten)

Hint!
Reread and revise your essay to make sure that the argument is clear and that you have not committed any grammatical or spelling mistakes. **Peer review—** having a classmate or friend critically evaluate your paper—is an effective means of improving the quality of your essay. Another set of eyes (hopefully, *before* your instructor's) can spot errors in logic or grammar that you have overlooked.

Writing an Argumentative Essay

Step 1: Outline your argument.
▸ Match the conclusion with the issue.
▸ State the premises and conclusion as claims.
▸ Choose premises that are clearly relevant to the conclusion.

Step 2: Introduce your argument.
▸ Grab the reader's attention.
▸ Identify the issue, and set out the context.
▸ Clearly state your conclusion.
▸ Summarize your premises.

Step 3: Support your conclusion.
▸ Identify each of the main premises, and state each as a claim.
▸ Provide reasons, evidence, and/or examples that support each premise.

Step 4: Consider objections.
▸ Accurately represent the strongest point(s) against your view.
▸ Honestly appraise how your argument accommodates the objection(s).

Step 5: Summarize your argument.
▸ Repeat your main conclusion.
▸ Restate your main premises in the same order in which they appear, but using different language.
▸ Suggest one important larger implication of your argument.

Step 6: Cite your sources.
▸ Choose credible sources.
▸ Give full and detailed credit for others' ideas to avoid plagiarism.

EXERCISE 12.9

As a class or on your own, choose an issue from the following list, and use it to write an argumentative essay. Alternatively, your instructor may assign the entire class to work on a single issue.

1. Issue: Whether the U.S. government should reinstitute a military draft
2. Issue: Whether juveniles who commit violent crimes should be treated as adults in the criminal justice system
3. Issue: Whether euthanasia should be permitted so that a terminally ill person can end his or her extreme suffering
4. Issue: Whether using cell phones while driving should be banned
5. Issue: Whether health care should be free for all citizens
6. Issue: Whether torture is ever acceptable
7. Issue: Whether animals should be used for scientific research
8. Issue: Whether English should be the official language of the United States
9. Issue: Whether same-sex couples should be allowed to marry
10. Issue: Whether marijuana should be legalized

CHAPTER REVIEW QUESTIONS

1. How does brainstorming help you formulate your argument?
2. What goes in the first paragraph of an argumentative essay?
3. How should you provide support for your conclusion in an argumentative essay?
4. What are the two features of a credible source?
5. Why must you respond to the strongest objection to your position when writing an argumentative essay?
6. What goes in the summary of an argumentative essay?
7. How can you successfully avoid plagiarism in your argumentative essays?

ONE STEP FURTHER

The five-paragraph essay, long a staple of university courses, may strike you as something you will leave behind as soon as you graduate. If so, you might be in for a surprise. You can use your argument construction skills to help you in your career. For example, a letter of application, whether it is for a job, a promotion, or admission to graduate school, should be an argument. But instead of giving support for some side of a controversial issue, your letter should include evidence to convince someone that you are the best person for the opportunity you seek. Moreover, strong argument construction skills can help you convince your boss that your ideas should be adopted, convince your clients that your services are in their best interest, or convince your co-workers that your solution to a problem will be effective. You may even be expected to put such arguments in writing.

Jeff Bezos, the founder and CEO of Amazon and recent purchaser of *The Washington Post*, is reported to require essays from his executives.

Don Graham, the former owner of the *Post*, explained that Mr. Bezos's dedication to the essay was one reason he decided to sell the venerable newspaper to him:

When Jeff holds meetings at Amazon he asks people not to use Powerpoints but to write an essay about their product or program or what the meeting is to be about. For the first 10 or 15 minutes everyone sits and reads the essay. His point is that if you write at length, you have to think first, and he feels the quality of thought you have to do to write at length is greater than the quality of thought to put a Powerpoint together.

Fortunately, you now have skills that will leave you better prepared for the writing that you may have to do for and in your career.

1. Do you agree that writing out an argument improves the quality of your thinking in ways that preparing a PowerPoint presentation does not? Why or why not?
2. Write an argumentative essay in the form of a letter of application for a new job, a promotion at your current job, an internship, a scholarship, or a leadership position within a student or community organization. Format your letter using the structure outlined in the image below. Note that it differs slightly from the argumentative essay format in that you will not include an issue in the first paragraph, and will not consider an objection to your position in paragraph five.
3. Exchange letters with one or more classmates. Write a Formal Analysis of your peer's argument. Does he or she provide three reasons to select him or her for the position? Does he or she provide evidence for each of those reasons? Make one suggestion for how the letter can be improved.

Application Letter

Introduction
- Clearly state the purpose of your letter (i.e., your conclusion).
- Summarize the reasons (i.e., premises) demonstrating that you should be selected.

Body
- Provide evidence (educational background, examples of your past success, credible references, etc.) to prove that each of your premises is true.

Conclusion
- Restate your conclusion and premises.
- Provide your contact information.
- Thank the reader.

Supplement to Chapter 6: Evaluating Categorical Arguments

In Chapter 6, you learned how to use Venn diagrams to evaluate categorical arguments. In this chapter, you will learn a second method for evaluating categorical arguments—namely, how to use the rules of validity. When you know how to properly draw Venn diagrams and the rules of validity, you can employ the two methods to check your work. When your diagram shows the argument is invalid, you can use the list of rules to determine how the argument went wrong. And when the argument is valid, you can verify your work by making sure that none of the rules is broken. When applied properly, an evaluation using a Venn diagram and an evaluation using the rule procedures will always concur.

Using Rules to Determine Validity

Five rules must be satisfied in order for a categorical syllogism to be valid. If an argument breaks any of the rules, it is invalid. All valid arguments satisfy each of the rules. To understand the rules of validity, it helps to recall the four standard form claims and the Venn diagrams that correspond to each of the claims shown in the Four Standard Forms figure. As we discuss each of the five rules, we will frequently refer to these four standard form claims.

The rules of validity are not difficult to learn, but since two of the rules involve the concept of distribution, that term must first be explained. A subject or predicate term is **distributed** if the categorical claim refers to every member of the group. Each of the four standard form claims has a unique distribution pattern. In the following examples, the distributed terms are *underlined*.

A claim: All S̲ are P.

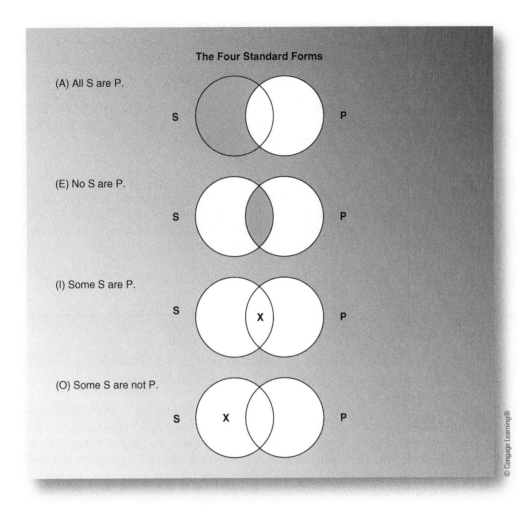

The Four Standard Forms

(A) All S are P.

S   P

(E) No S are P.

S   P

(I) Some S are P.

S   X   P

(O) Some S are not P.

S   X   P

© Cengage Learning®

In an A claim, the claim is that *all S* are something, so the claim is about every member of the S group. Thus, subject terms of A claims are distributed. The predicate term is not distributed in an A claim because the claim does not concern every member of that set. You can see this readily in the Venn diagram for an A claim. The S circle is shaded except where it overlaps with the P circle. All of the S's are in the P circle because there is nowhere else for them to be. The P circle, however, is not shaded at all. So P's could be in S or P's could be outside of S. No mention is made in this claim about the P category except where S's fit with it.

Hint!
Distribution of terms depends solely on the kind of claim and position within the claim (subject or predicate position). Therefore, the subject term in an A claim is distributed whether the claim is a premise or a conclusion.

E claim: No S̲ are P̲.

Every E claim distributes both the S and the P terms. Since the claim is universal, it should be clear that it refers to *all* of something. But the distribution pattern is clearest in the Venn diagram for an E claim. When the middle part is shaded, the two sets, S and P, have no common members. That is, *all* of the S are outside of *all* of the P. This explains why E claims can be read in either direction—"No S are P" or "No P are S." Since both terms are distributed, either version is correct.

I claim: Some S are P.

It should be apparent that a particular claim does not include every member of the S group. Nor is it making any claim about each and every member of the P group. All it is claiming is that at least one S is also a P. Nothing is said about what happens with the other members of S or P. Therefore, neither term is distributed.

 EXERCISE 13.1

Your Turn!   I claims can also be read in either direction. Explain why.

O claim: Some S are not P̲.

Again, the S term cannot be distributed. But what about the P term? The answer can be most effectively seen in the Venn diagram. Notice that the X is placed *in* S, but *outside of the entire circle* of P. The claim is about all of P—the X must be outside of the entire set. Therefore, particular negatives distribute the predicate term, but not the subject.

The result is four unique distribution patterns.

Type of Claim	Distribution Pattern
A claim	subject term only
E claim	both terms
I claim	neither term
O claim	predicate term only

 EXERCISE 13.2

Your Turn!   Find the patterns for term distribution.

Both universal *claims distribute* _____ *terms.*
Neither particular *claim distributes* _____ *terms.*
Both negative *claims distribute* _____ *terms.*
Neither affirmative *claim distributes* _____ *terms.*

EXERCISE 13.3

Translate all claims into standard form, and underline all distributed claims.

1. All M are P.
2. Some P are M.
3. Some M are not S.
4. No S are M.
5. All economics majors are intelligent students.
6. Some kangaroo rats are members of an endangered species.
7. No felons are voters.
8. Only voters are participants.
9. The only good ice cream is chocolate ice cream.
10. Not every lizard is a reptile.

Now that you understand the concept of distribution and can determine which claims in a categorical syllogism are distributed and which are not, we can introduce the five rules a valid categorical syllogism must satisfy. The first two rules relate to *distribution*, the second two rules relate to the *quality* of the claims, and the final rule involves the *quantity* of the claims.

Rules for Valid Syllogisms
▶ The middle term must be distributed at least once.
▶ Any term that is distributed in the conclusion must be distributed in a premise.
▶ If a premise is negative, the conclusion must be negative, and vice versa.
▶ A valid argument cannot have two negative premises.
▶ A valid argument cannot have two universal premises when the conclusion is particular.

The first rule concerning the distribution of terms in the argument is that *the middle term must be distributed at least once*. The middle term, you remember, is the term in each of the premises that is not in the conclusion. If the middle term is not distributed in at least one premise, then the argument is invalid. In a categorical syllogism, the conclusion asserts a relationship between the major and minor terms. In order for that conclusion to follow from the premises, at least one of those two terms must be related to every member of the middle term. That is why the rules for a valid syllogism state that the middle term must be distributed at least once in the premises. Any argument that fails to distribute the middle term is invalid and can be said to commit what is called the **fallacy of undistributed middle**.

Hint!
A fallacy is a mistake in reasoning. Since categorical logic is considered a formal system of logic (because it's the form of the argument that determines validity), the fallacy of undistributed middle is considered a formal fallacy.

EXERCISE 13.4

Identify the syllogisms that commit the fallacy of undistributed middle.

1. All M are P.
   <u>All S are M.</u>
   All S are P.

2. All P are M.
   <u>All M are S.</u>
   Some S are P.

3. No P are M.
   <u>No S are M.</u>
   No S are P.

4. All P are M.
   <u>Some S are M.</u>
   Some S are P.

5. All P are M.
   <u>Some S are not M.</u>
   No S are P.

6. All great scientists are college graduates. Some professional athletes are college graduates. Therefore, some professional athletes are great scientists.
7. Only a masochist enjoys pain. You're a masochist, so it's clear that you must enjoy pain.
8. Some maple trees are not tropical plants. Therefore, some tropical plants are not fruit trees, since no fruit trees are maple trees.
9. Because all minds are in our heads, it follows that nothing in our heads are brains, since no brains are minds.
10. Some athletes are not college students, and some college students are not handball players. Therefore, some athletes are not handball players.

The second rule concerning the distribution of terms in the argument is that *any term that is distributed in the conclusion must be distributed in a premise.* Look first to see if any terms are distributed in the conclusion. If a subject or predicate term is distributed in the conclusion, that term must also be distributed in a premise. A valid argument cannot draw a conclusion about every member of some group unless it asserts something about every member of that group in a premise. Take care not to get this rule backwards. An argument can be valid if the premise is about all members of a class and the conclusion is about fewer members of that class. Put another way, it is not a problem to distribute a term in the premise and not distribute that same term in the conclusion.

The first rule relating to the quality of the claims is that *if a premise is negative, the conclusion must be negative, and vice versa.* Two kinds of claims are negative—E claims and O claims. If one of the premises is an E or an O, the conclusion must be an E or an O. This rule works both ways—if the conclusion is negative, then a premise must be negative.

The second rule relating to the quality of the claims is that *a valid argument cannot have two negative premises*. Regardless of whether the conclusion is negative or affirmative, a valid argument cannot contain two negative premises.

The final rule, concerning the quantity of the claims, is that *a valid argument cannot have two universal premises when the conclusion is particular*. The explanation of the problem with this combination of claims is fairly technical—at least more technical than our chapter will allow. Considering the Venn diagram of such an argument will allow you to see how the rule is broken. If the premises are both universal, they will contribute only shading to the Venn diagram of the argument. If the conclusion is particular, it will need an X to satisfy it. Since neither premise required placing an X in the Venn diagram, then the conclusion is not already pictured. Therefore, the argument is invalid.

 EXERCISE 13.5

Determine whether the following arguments are valid or invalid using the rules for valid syllogisms. For all invalid arguments, state which rule or rules are violated.

1. All S are M.
   All M are P.
   All S are P.

2. All M are S.
   No P are M.
   No S are P.

3. Some P are M.
   Some M are S.
   Some S are P.

4. No M are S.
   Some P are not M.
   Some S are not P.

5. No M are P.
   All S are M.
   No S are P.

6. No caterpillars are ants.
   All ants are insects.
   Some caterpillars are insects.

7. Some jaywalkers are not felons.
   All jaywalkers are circus performers.
   Some felons are circus performers.

8. All executives are workaholics.
   No workaholics can relax.
   No executives can relax.

9. All carrots are nutritious snacks.
   <u>No fast food is a carrot.</u>
   No fast food is a nutritious snack.

10. All quintuplets are hungry mouths to feed.
    <u>All hungry mouths to feed are things to be avoided.</u>
    All quintuplets are things to be avoided.

EXERCISE 13.6

Determine whether the following arguments are valid or invalid using the rules for valid syllogisms. For all invalid arguments, state the rule or rules that are violated.

1. Some lizards are poisonous.
   <u>Anything that is poisonous should be avoided.</u>
   Some lizards should be avoided.

2. All vine-ripened tomatoes require extra care at the store.
   <u>Some things that require extra care at the store need to be expensive.</u>
   Some vine-ripened tomatoes need to be expensive.

3. Some squirrels are not animals.
   <u>Some penguins are not animals.</u>
   No squirrels are penguins.

4. All squirrels are animals.
   <u>No penguins are animals.</u>
   No penguins are squirrels.

5. All kangaroos are Australian.
   <u>Some turtles are not Australian.</u>
   Some turtles are not kangaroos.

6. All kangaroos are Australian.
   <u>Some turtles are not kangaroos.</u>
   Some turtles are not Australian.

7. Some Danes speak English.
   <u>All Northern Europeans speak English.</u>
   All Northern Europeans are Danes.

8. No principals are teachers.
   <u>No teachers are fifth-graders.</u>
   No principals are fifth-graders.

9. Some students take critical thinking, and some students are math majors. So some people who take critical thinking are math majors.

10. Anyone who reads philosophy books will immediately get smarter. Some people who get smarter will become President of the United States. So anyone who reads philosophy books will become President of the United States.
11. Some squash are not pumpkins, and some pumpkins are legumes. Accordingly, no squash are legumes.
12. All soccer players are baseball players. And no baseball players are accordion players. Consequently, some soccer players are accordion players.
13. All kites are flying toys, since all flying toys are model airplanes and some model airplanes are not kites.
14. People who live in Minnesota endure severely cold winters and thus should be treated with respect because people who endure severely cold winters should all be treated with respect.
15. Since all sociologists are social scientists, it follows that no theologian is a social scientist, since no sociologists are theologians.

Using Rules to Complete Categorical Arguments

Sometimes categorical arguments are presented with an unstated premise or conclusion. Such an argument is called an **enthymeme**. Finding the missing premise or conclusion of an enthymeme is a great way to master the rules of valid syllogisms. To show how this works, let's begin with a sample argument.

> *Some dogs are celebrities, for some dogs are movie stars.*

The task with this example, and with any enthymeme, is to supply the missing piece that makes the argument *valid*. That means that the completed syllogism must not break any of the rules for a valid syllogism. If it is impossible for all the rules to be followed, then the enthymeme cannot be completed. For our purposes, every enthymeme in this chapter can be made valid.

The first task is to determine whether the missing part is a premise or a conclusion. In this example, the word *for* indicates that the first claim is the conclusion and the second claim is the premise. Set it out in standard form like this.

> Some dogs are movie stars.
> _____
> Some dogs are celebrities.

Next, we must identify which two terms will be in that missing premise. We know that all three terms must be used exactly twice. So, since *dogs* is already included twice in the argument (in a premise and in the conclusion), the missing premise must contain the terms *celebrities* and *movie stars*.

 EXERCISE 13.7

Your Turn!   Which term is the middle term of this enthymeme?

The next step is to determine whether the premise will be affirmative or negative. Since the conclusion is affirmative, the missing premise must be affirmative, too. That means that the missing premise must be either an A claim or an I claim.

EXERCISE 13.8

Your Turn!   What rule would be broken if we made the premise negative?

Now, distribution must be considered. The middle term must be distributed, so you must determine whether the middle term is already distributed or not. Since *dogs* and *celebrities* are in the conclusion, *movie stars* has to be the middle term, and it is not distributed already. That means that the middle term must be distributed in the missing premise.

    EXERCISE 13.9

Your Turn!   How do you know the middle term isn't already distributed?

If the middle term needs to be distributed, then the premise must be an A claim, since an I claim will not distribute any terms. Furthermore, since the subject term is the only term distributed in an A claim, *movie stars* must be the subject term.

Distribution also might occur in the conclusion. Are any terms distributed in the conclusion of this enthymeme? If so, they would need to be distributed in a premise. But since the conclusion is an I claim and I claims do not distribute either term, no term is distributed in the conclusion. Thus, we can determine that the missing premise is an A claim with *movie stars* as the subject term.

The completed valid argument should look like this.

> All movie stars are celebrities.
> Some dogs are movie stars.
> Some dogs are celebrities.

As you can see, the missing premise is discovered by a process of elimination using the rules for valid syllogisms. You go through the rules until the answer satisfies each of the rules. Once you have the completed syllogism, the final step is to check the completed argument against the rules to verify that it is valid. It's also a good idea to draw a Venn diagram just to make sure you've done everything right.

How to Complete Enthymemes

Step 1: Determine whether the missing claim is a premise or a conclusion.

Step 2: Identify which two terms are in the missing claim.

Step 3: Determine whether the claim will be affirmative or negative.

Step 4: Make sure that terms are properly distributed.

Step 5: Verify that all rules for valid syllogisms are followed.

EXERCISE 13.10

Turn the following enthymemes into valid categorical syllogisms. All syllogisms need to be presented in standard form.

1. <u>No S are M.</u>
   No S are P.

2. <u>No P are M.</u>
   Some S are M.

3. <u>All X are Y.</u>
   All X are Z.

4. Some J are T because all R are J.
5. Some P are not M. Thus, some S are not M.
6. No mature lobsters are good things to eat, since all good things to eat are low in calories.
7. Offshore oil fields are environmentally sensitive areas, so they should be protected.
8. Because every metaphor is a trope, all schemes are tropes.
9. All elephants are herbivores, so some herbivores are not domesticated.
10. Some birds are not chickens, and every Bantam is a chicken.
11. Australian shepherds make good guard dogs, given that they are alert for danger.
12. Only pirates are true sailors, so a few tank commanders are pirates.
13. Enthymemes are not syllogisms, and valid arguments are enthymemes.
14. Not all snakes are poisonous reptiles; thus, not every animal is a poisonous reptile.
15. Since plants won't grow in the shade, some places the sun shines aren't places plants will grow.

CHAPTER
14

Supplement to Chapter 7: Evaluating Truth-Functional Arguments

In Chapter 7, you learned how to determine whether a truth-functional argument is valid or invalid using the Truth Table Method. In this chapter, you will learn a second method for evaluating truth-functional arguments, the Short-Cut Method (sometimes called an indirect truth table). Why might you want to learn this other method? For one thing, you can use the Short-Cut Method to verify that your truth table is correct. But, more compellingly, the Short-Cut Method is often a faster way to determine whether a truth-functional argument is valid or invalid. Recall the fact that, when you use the Truth Table Method, the number of rows in your table doubles for each additional simple claim in the argument. This can get overwhelming very quickly. Just imagine completing a truth table for an argument with five simple claims ($2^5 = 32$) or more! Luckily, there is a shortcut.

To understand this Short-Cut Method, think about how much information you ignore when completing the last step of the Truth Table Method. Once all the possible truth-value assignments are determined, you look only for cases in which all the premises are true and yet the conclusion is false. If there is even one line with all true premises and a false conclusion, the argument is invalid. And if there are no such lines, then the argument is valid. The Short-Cut Method is a way of searching for the same conditions without having to sort through the other information you normally disregard. But how? The Short-Cut Method begins by determining what the truth-value of each simple claim must be for the argument to turn out invalid. That is, if it is possible for the argument to have all true premises and a false conclusion, the argument is invalid. If those conditions are impossible, the argument must be valid.

Using the Short-Cut Method to Determine Validity

Just as with the Truth Table Method, the Short-Cut Method relies on your knowledge of the **truth-functional definitions** for negation, conjunction, disjunction, and conditional operators. Recall that these definitions specify when a particular compound claim is true and when it is false. Here they are again for your quick reference.

~ X	X • Y	X ∨ Y	X ⊃ Y
F T	T T T	T T F	T T T
T F	T F F	T T F	T F F
	F F T	F T T	F T T
	F F F	F F F	F T F

Notice that for each of these definitions, there is one row that is unique. For negation, there is only one instance in which the compound claim is true and only one instance in which the compound claim is false. For conjunction, there is only one instance in which the compound claim is true—namely, when both conjuncts are true; otherwise, the claim is false. For disjunction, there is only one instance in which the compound claim is false—namely, when both disjuncts are false; otherwise, the claim is true. And for conditional, there is only one instance in which the compound claim is false—namely, when the antecedent is true and the consequent is false; otherwise, the claim is true. It is these unique values that are most important when using the Short-Cut Method.

As with the Truth Table Method, we begin by translating the argument into symbolic form and writing it out utilizing the symbol / to signal the start of a new premise and // to signal the conclusion. Let's start with an example from Chapter 7.

$$C \vee {\sim}R / C // R$$

Now, remember the aim of the Short-Cut Method: to show that the argument is invalid. We must try, therefore, to make all the premises true and the conclusion false. To remind yourself of this goal, write it below the main operator of each premise and conclusion.

$$\underline{C \vee {\sim}R / C // R}$$

T   T   F

In order to prove that each premise can be true while the conclusion is false, we must assign particular truth-values to each simple claim. When doing so, it is important to assign truth-values to the simple claims only when there is exactly one possible truth-value assignment to achieve our goal. In this argument, although the first premise has three possible assignments that would result in the disjunction being true, the second premise and the conclusion each have exactly one possible truth-value assignment that would make all the premises true and the conclusion false. In order to have a true second premise, C must be true, and in order to have a false conclusion, R must be false.

We should insert these truth-values into the table each time that the simple claim occurs in the argument.

$$\underline{C \lor \sim R \,/\, C \,//\, R}$$

T		F	**T**	**F**
T			T	F

Now that we have all the values of the simple claims assigned throughout the argument, we can apply the remaining operators—in this case, the operators in the first premise. Since false is assigned to R, ~ R will be true. Now, we can determine the truth-value of the first premise, the disjunction C ∨ ~ R.

$$\underline{C \lor \sim R \,/\, C \,//\, R}$$

T	**T**	T	F	**T**	**F**
T				T	F

As you can see, it is possible for all the premises to be true while the conclusion is false. Thus, we have shown that the argument is invalid.

 EXERCISE 14.1

Your Turn! Complete a truth table for the argument above. In what row do you find the evidence that the argument is invalid? Compare that row to the table created above using the Short-Cut Method.

Now, let's see what happens when an argument is valid. Consider this one.

$$\underline{P \supset Q \,/\, \sim R \,/\, P \,//\, Q \lor R}$$

	T		T		T		F

In this argument, there are three possible places to begin. The second premise, the third premise, and the conclusion all have exactly one possible truth-value assignment that would allow the premises to be true and the conclusion to be false. Once you have determined the values that must be assigned for particular simple claims, insert those values throughout the argument.

Let's start with the third premise, since it is already a simple claim. In order for the third premise to turn out true, P must be true. So we can assign true to every instance of P in the argument.

$$\underline{P \supset Q \,/\, \sim R \,/\, P \,//\, Q \lor R}$$

T				**T**		
T		T		T		F

There are several options for your next move. Since you know the value of P, you can determine what truth-value must be assigned to Q so that the first premise turns out true. Or you can determine the value that must be assigned to R so that the second premise turns out true. Or you can determine the values that must be assigned to Q and R so that the conclusion turns out false. Any of these options would work. Let's examine the second premise, since it contains only one simple claim. In order for ~ R to turn out true, R must be false. So we can assign false to every instance of R in the argument.

$$P \supset Q / {\sim} R / P /\!/ Q \lor R$$

T		**T** **F**	**T**		F
T		T	T		F

The only simple claim remaining is Q. We can determine what value to assign to Q by making the first premise true or by making the conclusion false. Either option works. Let's examine the first premise. We have assigned true to P. What value must we assign to Q so that the first premise turns out true? Since the first premise is a conditional and the antecedent (P) is true, the consequent (Q) must also be true; otherwise, the conditional will turn out false. So we must assign true to every instance of Q.

$$P \supset Q / {\sim} R / P /\!/ Q \lor R$$

T **T** **T**	**T** **F**	**T**	**T** **T** **F**
T	T	T	F

But notice what has happened to the conclusion. Since Q is true and R is false, the conclusion must be true. But we were aiming to show that the conclusion is false when all the premises are true. Since this has turned out to be impossible, that means that the argument is valid.

> **Hint!**
> It is important to remember that you must not randomly assign truth-values to the simple claims. Instead, assign only those values that would make the premises true and the conclusion false.

EXERCISE 14.2

> **Your Turn!** Suppose that, instead of examining the first premise, you had chosen to assign the truth-value for Q that would make the conclusion false. Would you still conclude that the argument is valid? Why or why not?

Occasionally, you may find that the truth-value of a particular simple claim will not make a difference in the truth-value of the premise or conclusion. Do not assign truth-values to claims like these because it may make a difference later on in the table. Consider this example.

$$P \supset Q / {\sim} (P \bullet R) /\!/ {\sim} Q \lor {\sim} R$$

T	T		F

Since both of the premises can be made true in more than one way, we'll begin with the conclusion. What values must be assigned to Q and R to achieve a false conclusion? Insert them into the truth table.

$$P \supset Q\ /\ \sim(P \cdot R)\ //\ \sim Q \vee \sim R$$

T			T		F	T F F T
T	T					F

Now, let's look at the first premise. Since the consequent is true, what value must we assign to P? It doesn't matter! When the consequent is true, the conditional will be true regardless of whether the antecedent is true or false.

$$P \supset Q\ /\ \sim(P \cdot R)\ //\ \sim Q \vee \sim R$$

?T T   T   F T F F T

T   T   F

It is very important to not arbitrarily assign a value to P in that first premise! Since P occurs elsewhere in the argument, later on it may matter what value is assigned to it. So let's leave the P in the first premise as an unknown truth-value and move on to the second premise. What value must we assign to P here to end up with a true second premise? Because the main operator is negation, the conjunction must turn out false so that when it is negated, the premise is true. Since R is true, the conjunction will be false only when P is false.

$$P \supset Q\ /\ \sim(P \cdot R)\ //\ \sim Q \vee \sim R$$

?T T   T F F T   F T F F T

T   T   F

What we have discovered, then, is that if we had assigned true to P in the first premise, we would not have shown the second premise to be true. As a result, we would have mistakenly concluded that the argument is valid when in fact it is invalid. Thus, you must be sure to assign a truth-value to a simple claim only when there is exactly one possible assignment that would achieve the desired outcome—namely, all true premises and a false conclusion.

How to Determine Validity Using the Short-Cut Method

Step 1: Translate the argument into symbolic form.

Step 2: Write the argument horizontally, using / to separate premises and // in front of the conclusion.

Step 3: Write out the goal truth-values for each premise and conclusion (i.e., all true premises and a false conclusion).

Step 4: Assign the truth-values to simple claims for which there is only one possible truth-value assignment that would result in a true premise or false conclusion.

Step 5: Insert truth-values throughout the argument for any simple claim whose value was determined in Step 4.

Step 6: Determine the truth-values of any remaining premise or conclusion.

Step 7: Evaluate whether the argument is valid or invalid by checking whether the truth-values of the premises and the conclusion achieve the goal of all true premises and a false conclusion. If they do, then the argument is invalid. If they do not, then the argument is valid.

 EXERCISE 14.3

Determine whether each argument is valid using the Short-Cut Method.

1. $A \supset B$
   $\underline{B}$
   $\therefore A$

2. $C \lor \sim D$
   $\underline{\sim D}$
   $\therefore C$

3. $G \supset J$
   $\underline{\sim J \supset I}$
   $\therefore \sim I \supset G$

4. $\sim (M \lor N)$
   $\underline{O \supset M}$
   $\therefore \sim O$

5. $S \lor \sim T$
   $\underline{U \supset T}$
   $\therefore S \supset \sim U$

6. $\sim A \supset (B \lor C)$
   $\underline{\sim B}$
   $\therefore C \supset A$

7. $R \supset (S \bullet T)$
   $U \supset (V \bullet R)$
   $\underline{W \bullet U}$
   $\therefore W \bullet T$

8. $A \supset (B \lor C)$
   $B \supset D$
   $\underline{A}$
   $\therefore \sim C \supset D$

9. $\sim A \supset B$
   $C \supset A$
   $\underline{C \supset \sim B}$
   $\therefore A \lor \sim B$

10. $X \supset Y$
    $Y \supset Z$
    $\sim W \supset X$
    $\underline{\sim Z}$
    $\therefore W$

 EXERCISE 14.4

Translate each argument into symbolic form, and then determine whether the argument is valid or invalid using the Short-Cut Method.

1. Qualified employees will be passed over if racial quotas are adopted for promoting employees, but prior discrimination will go unaddressed if racial quotas are not adopted for promoting employees. Therefore, either qualified employees will be passed over, or prior discrimination will go unaddressed.

2. History should not be considered a social science unless historians collect data and that data can be quantified. Since history is not considered a social science, it must not be the case that historians collect data.

3. If we want to avoid further catastrophic bridge collapses like the I-35 Mississippi River bridge collapse in Minnesota in 2007, then Congress needs to authorize massive spending for retrofitting the aging bridges in this country.

Why? Because Congress will either authorize more funding for retrofitting, or it will be responsible for the loss of life in future bridge collapses. And if Congress is responsible for the loss of life in future bridge collapses, the American voters will be outraged. We can trust that Congress will not do something to outrage the voters.

4. If the Drug Abuse Resistance Education (D.A.R.E.) program is instituted in city schools, then many children will learn about the dangers of drugs. If children don't learn about the dangers of drugs, then they are likely to get into trouble with the law. Unfortunately, the D.A.R.E. program is being dropped from the city school budget. Thus, it is not the case that children will learn about the dangers of drugs and they will get in trouble with the law.

5. Why isn't Pluto classified as a planet? Well, Pluto is classified as a planet if it is in orbit around the sun, has sufficient mass to form a round shape, and has "cleared the neighborhood" around its orbit. Since Pluto is in orbit around the sun and has sufficient mass to form a round shape, it must not have "cleared the neighborhood" around its orbit given that it is not classified as a planet.

6. If your car won't start, then either it is either out of gas, or the battery is dead. But your car can't be out of gas, in that you filled the tank this morning. Thus, either the car will start, or the battery is dead.

7. Business owners either look out for their own interests or try to help others. And we all know that business owners look out for their own interests, for their businesses are profit-making enterprises. Accordingly, business owners do not try to help others.

8. Either vitamins need to be regulated, or they should be available only by prescription. I say this because vitamins are not always safely manufactured, and either vitamins should be always safely manufactured, or they should be regulated. Also, if vitamins can pose a health risk, then they should be available only by prescription. Finally, if vitamins are not always safely manufactured, then they can pose a health risk.

9. If Proposition 8 is a constitutional revision, then it is either quantitatively broad or qualitatively deep. Proposition 8 was improperly introduced if it is a constitutional revision, and if it was improperly introduced, then it is an invalid law. Since Proposition 8 is neither quantitatively broad nor qualitatively deep, it must not be an invalid law.

10. Either video games enhance the cognitive capacities of users, or video games deaden the brains of users and decrease their motivation to think. Given that it's not true that video games deaden the brains of users and decrease their motivation to think, we can conclude that video games do enhance users' cognitive capacities. Besides, if video games enhance the cognitive capacities of users, then either video games are addictive, or they are habit forming, and it's clear that video games are either addictive or habit forming.

Glossary

A

Ad hominem: a fallacious argument in which an opposing argument is rejected based on the characteristics of its arguer.

Analogical argument: an inductive argument that uses an analogy to conclude that, because one case has some feature, the other case should, too.

Analogues: the things that are compared in an analogy.

Analogy: a comparison of two (or more) things.

Analyze: to break something down into its most elementary parts; in the case of an argument, to identify the issue, conclusion, and premise(s).

Antecedent: the part of a conditional claim that is a sufficient condition for the consequent to be true; normally, this is the part of the claim following the word *if*.

Appeal to ignorance: a fallacious argument in which the arguer illegitimately shifts the burden of proof to his or her opponent.

Appeal to illegitimate authority: a fallacious argument in which a source who is not an authority on the subject in question is relied on to support a conclusion.

Argument: a set of claims that offers reasons as evidence for the truth of one of its claims.

Argument diagram: a visual representation of an argument's structure.

Argument with multiple conclusions: two or more arguments that share the same premise(s).

B

Begging the question: a fallacious argument in which the conclusion is assumed by the premise(s).

Biased generalization: an inductive generalization in which the sample misrepresents the target.

Brainstorm: a prewriting tool for generating ideas; in argument construction, you list as many ideas as you can that relate to the issue you have chosen to write about.

Burden of proof: a phrase indicating who has the responsibility of providing reasons to support his or her conclusion.

C

Categorical argument: a deductive argument that contains categorical claims.

Categorical claim: a claim that relates two categories of things.

Categorical syllogism: a common type of categorical argument, containing two premises and a conclusion.

Causal argument: an inductive argument that provides evidence that a causal claim is true.

Causal claim: a claim indicating a causal relationship between one event and another.

Chain argument: two or more arguments constituting a chain of reasoning, in which the conclusion of one argument is the premise of another.

Claim: a statement that has truth-value.

Cogent inductive argument: an inductive argument that is strong and has all true premises.

Compound claim: a truth-functional claim in which one or more simple claims are combined with a logical operator.

Conclusion: the claim being supported in an argument.

Conclusion indicator: a word or phrase signaling that the claim following it is a conclusion.

Conditional: (also called a *conditional claim, hypothetical claim, implication,* or *material implication*) a compound claim that combines two other claims (called the *antecedent* and the *consequent*) using the phrase *if . . . then . . .* or its equivalent.

Conditional claim: *see* **Conditional**.

Conjunct: one of the two claims combined in a conjunction.

Conjunction: a compound claim that combines two claims (called *conjuncts*) using the word *and* or its equivalent.

Consequent: the part of a conditional claim that is a necessary condition for the antecedent to be true; normally, this is the part of the claim following the word *then*.

Convergent premises: two or more premises that each provide independent support for the same conclusion.

Copula: in a categorical claim, the verb linking the subject and predicate terms.

Critical Précis: a critical thinking tool that demonstrates in paragraph form the recognition, analysis, and evaluation of arguments and other forms of discourse.

Critical thinking: thinking that uses reason to decide what to do and what to believe.

D

Deductive argument: an argument in which the arguer attempts to demonstrate that the truth of the conclusion *necessarily* follows from the premises.

DeMorgan's Law: a rule in truth-functional logic used to change the negation of a conjunction into a disjunction or the negation of a disjunction into a conjunction.

Descriptive claim: a claim that describes a situation.

Diagram: *see* **Argument diagram** or **Venn diagram**.

Disjunct: one of the two claims combined in a disjunction.

Disjunction (or *disjunctive claim*): a compound claim that combines two claims (called *disjuncts*) using the phrase *either . . . or* or its equivalent.

Disjunctive claim: *see* **Disjunction**.

Distributed term: in a categorical claim, a subject or predicate term that refers to every member of the group that the subject or predicate term represents.

Dogmatic assertion: a judgment presented without providing reasons or justification for its truth.

E

Enthymeme: a deductive categorical argument in which a premise or conclusion is unstated.

Evaluate: to judge the quality of something; in the case of an argument, a judgment that an argument's conclusion does or does not follow from its premise(s).

Evaluative claim: a claim that evaluates, or makes a judgment about, whether something is good or bad, right or wrong, useful or useless, beautiful or ugly, or the like.

Exclusive disjunction: a disjunction in which, in order for the compound claim to be true, exactly one of the disjuncts is true.

Explanation: a set of claims, one of which offers an account of how or why some given claim is true.

Extended argument: a chain argument that contains several subarguments.

Extra claim: a claim that is neither a conclusion nor a premise, but that accompanies an argument.

F

Fallacy: a common mistake in reasoning that is often rhetorically persuasive.

Faulty analogy: in an analogical argument, a mistake in reasoning in which the arguer refers to similarities between the sample and the target that are irrelevant to the feature.

Feature: in an inductive generalization, the characteristic of the sample that the arguer is trying to prove is also true of the target; in an analogical argument, the characteristic of the source that the arguer is trying to prove is also true of the target.

Formal Analysis: a method for presenting the analysis of an argument in which the premises are listed above a line and the conclusion is stated under it.

G

General claim: a claim that makes a statement about all, most, or many members of a group or set.

General form: in an inductive generalization, analogical argument, and causal argument, the formal analysis of the argument showing its universal pattern.

H

Hasty generalization: in an inductive generalization, a mistake in reasoning in which the sample is too small to offer even minimal support for the conclusion.

Hypothetical claim: *see* **Conditional**.

I

Implication: *see* **Conditional**.

Implied claim: a conclusion or premise of an argument that is implied by a non-claim—typically, a command or rhetorical question.

Inclusive disjunction: a disjunction in which, in order for the compound claim to be true, at least one of the disjuncts is true.

Indirect truth table method: *see* **Short-Cut Method**.

Inductive argument: an argument in which the arguer attempts to demonstrate that the truth of the conclusion *probably* follows from the premises.

Inductive generalization: an inductive argument that concludes that some, most, or all of a particular group have some feature based on evidence that a portion of that group has the feature.

Inference indicator: word or phrase that signals the structure of an argument.

Intermediate conclusion: in a chain argument, a claim that serves as both the conclusion of a subargument and a premise of the main argument.

Issue: the matter that is up for debate or being questioned.

L

Linked premises: premises that depend on each other to support a conclusion.

Logical operator: *see* **Operator**.

M

Main operator: the operator that applies to an entire truth-functional claim.

Major term: in a categorical syllogism, the predicate term of the conclusion, which is also present in one of the premises.

Material implication: *see* **Conditional**.

Method of agreement: in a causal argument, a method of reasoning in which the arguer concludes that an event in common among every known instance of the resulting event is the cause of that event.

Method of difference: in a causal argument, a method of reasoning in which the arguer concludes that the factor that is different between the occurrence and nonoccurrence of the resulting event is the cause of that event.

Middle term: in a categorical syllogism, the term that occurs in both premises but is absent from the conclusion.

Minor term: in a categorical syllogism, the subject term of the conclusion, which is also present in one of the premises.

Multiple argument: either a chain argument or an argument with multiple conclusions, so called because it may seem to violate the rule that an argument has only one conclusion.

N

Necessary condition: in a true conditional claim, the part (*consequent*) that must be true for the other part (*antecedent*) to be true.

Negation: a compound claim that combines a claim with the word *not* or its equivalent.

O

Operator: a word or phrase combined with one or more truth-functional claims to create a new, compound claim.

P

Particular affirmative: a type of categorical claim expressing an inclusive relation between a portion of a category of things and another category of things.

Particular negative: a type of categorical claim expressing an exclusive relation between a portion of a category of things and another category of things.

Peer review: having a classmate or friend read your paper to provide advice for improvement.

Plagiarism: using the ideas or words of another person without providing a proper citation.

Post hoc ergo propter hoc: in a causal argument, a mistake in reasoning in which the arguer concludes that one event was caused by another simply because one preceded the other.

Precipitating event: in a causal argument, the event that an arguer knows has occurred prior to the resulting event and that he or she suspects is the cause of that resulting event.

Predicate term: in a standard form categorical claim, the second plural noun identifying a class, group, or set.

Premise: a claim intended as support for an argument's conclusion.

Premise indicator: a word or phrase signaling that the claim following it is a premise.

Q

Quality: a feature of a categorical claim, which is determined by whether the members of the subject class are included or excluded from the predicate class.

Quantifier: the term beginning a standard form categorical claim that indicates the quantity and quality of the claim.

Quantity: a feature of a categorical claim, which is determined by whether all or some members of the subject class are referred to by the claim.

R

Random sample: in an inductive generalization, a sample that accurately represents the target because all members of the target had an equal opportunity to be part of the sample.

Red herring: a fallacious argument in which the arguer distracts the reader from the main issue by using irrelevant premises.

Resulting event: in a causal argument, the event that the arguer knows has occurred and for which he or she infers a cause.

S

Sample: in an inductive generalization, a portion of an entire class or group referred to in the premise.

Short-Cut Method: a method to determine whether a deductive argument is valid or invalid by considering only the conditions under which the argument would be invalid without determining all possible truth conditions.

Simple claim: a truth-functional claim that does not contain any other claim as a component.

Sound deductive argument: a deductive argument that is valid and has all true premises.

Source: in an analogical argument, the analogue given only among the premises.

Standard form: the form of presenting categorical claims following the formal rules of their expression.

Strawman: a fallacious argument that mischaracterizes the conclusion of an opponent's argument and then attacks the argument in its distorted form.

Strong inductive argument: an inductive argument in which if the premises are true, the conclusion is probably true.

Subargument: in a chain argument, the intermediate conclusion and the premise or premises that support it.

Subject term: in a standard form categorical claim, the first plural noun identifying a class, group, or set.

Sufficient condition: in a true conditional claim, the part (*antecedent*) that, when true, guarantees that the other part (*consequent*) is true.

Syllogism: a deductive argument containing two premises and a conclusion.

T

Target: in an inductive generalization, the entire group or class represented by the sample and found in the conclusion; in an analogical argument, the analogue about which the arguer is drawing a conclusion.

Truth-functional argument: a deductive argument that contains truth-functional claims.

Truth-functional claim: a claim that is either a simple claim or a compound claim.

Truth-functional definitions: a table listing all the conditions under which a compound claim is true or false.

Truth Table Method: a method to determine whether a deductive argument is valid or invalid by listing all possible truth-values for the claims in the argument.

Truth-value: the truth or falsity of a claim.

U

Undistributed middle: a formal fallacy that occurs when the middle term of a categorical syllogism is not distributed.

Universal affirmative: a type of categorical claim expressing an inclusive relation between an entire category of things and another category of things.

Universal negative: a type of categorical claim expressing an exclusive relation between an entire category of things and another category of things.

V

Valid deductive argument: a deductive argument in which, if the premises are true, the conclusion must be true.

Venn diagram: a diagram of overlapping circles used to represent the relationship between categorical claims.

Answers to Selected Exercises

Chapter 1

EXERCISE 1.5

3. c
6. c
9. b

EXERCISE 1.7

Student answers will vary.

EXERCISE 1.9

3. In this passage, a defense attorney is trying to convince the jury to acquit his or her client. Whether the client would ever steal money from a church is relevant to the verdict, but the attorney doesn't give any evidence that this is true. Instead, the attorney appeals to the emotions of the jurors by trying to make them feel sorry for the client.

EXERCISE 1.12

3. This passage is likely spoken by an athletics coach who is emphasizing winning as the only goal for the players.

Chapter 2

EXERCISE 2.3

3. Claim
6. Claim
9. Claim
12. Claim
15. Claim
18. Claim

EXERCISE 2.9

3. There are three claims: (1) Last weekend I saw *Machete*; (2) *Machete* is a film directed by Richard Rodriguez; and (3) I wonder if the sequel to *Machete* will be as enjoyable as the first movie.
6. There are two claims: (1) Lowering payroll taxes may provide people with bigger paychecks; and (2) Lowering payroll taxes will reduce Louisiana's ability to fund higher education.
9. There are three claims: (1) Weevils are in the flour; (2) We are out of salt; and (3) The milk has turned sour.
12. There are two claims: (1) The economy is awful; and (2) There's little hope that the economy will improve anytime soon. Be frugal with your paycheck is a command, not a claim.
15. There are two claims: (1) The holiday shopping season now begins in October; and (2) Busy retailers will most likely hire part-time employees for two months instead of one.
18. There are two claims: (1) Jim works at the Guitar Center; and (2) Jim doesn't know how to play a guitar.

EXERCISE 2.12

3. This passage is not an argument. Neither claim offers a reason for the other.
6. Dolores is good at playing the violin.
9. Chocolate contains sugar.
12. A good dictionary is useful in every university course.
15. The Bible says that killing is always wrong.
18. This passage is not an argument. There is only one claim.

EXERCISE 2.13

3. I saw a new guy picking up a uniform at the personnel office yesterday. This passage is an argument because

the reason provides evidence to prove that we hired another member for the night shift.
6. My professor constantly makes fun of me in front of the other students. This passage is an argument because the reason provides evidence to prove that my professor hates me.
9. The defendant used the weapon to kill the victim. This passage is not an argument because the reason explains how the defendant's fingerprints got on the weapon.

EXERCISE 2.16

3. Argument
6. Nonargument
9. Nonargument
12. Argument
15. Nonargument
18. Nonargument

EXERCISE 2.18

3.   This passage from *Nutrition: Concepts and Controversies* by Frances Sizer and Ellie Whitney contains an argument.
6.   This passage from *I Was Wrong: The Meaning of Apologies* by Nick Smith contains an argument.
9.   This passage from the *Chicago Tribune* is not an argument. It contains only one claim, and arguments require at least two claims.

Chapter 3

EXERCISE 3.3

3. Since <u>premise</u>, <u>conclusion</u>.
6. <u>Premise</u>. In conclusion, <u>conclusion</u>.
9. <u>Premise</u>. As a result, <u>conclusion</u> inasmuch as <u>premise</u>.
12. <u>Premise</u> and <u>premise</u>. This shows that <u>conclusion</u>.
15. <u>Conclusion</u> in that <u>premise</u> and <u>premise</u>.
18. <u>Conclusion</u> may be derived from <u>premise</u>.
21. <u>Premise</u>. This demonstrates that <u>conclusion</u>.
24. <u>Conclusion</u>, as <u>premise</u> and <u>premise</u>.

EXERCISE 3.5

3. **P:** <u>Many stores are not restocking their shelves this year.</u>
∴ You should get your holiday shopping done early.

   Issue: Whether you should get your holiday shopping done early

6. **P1:** Video piracy has reached unprecedented levels.
P2: The cost to make a Hollywood movie continues to <u>escalate.</u>
∴ Studios will be increasingly hesitant to invest in films that are unlikely to be box office hits.

   Issue: Whether studios will be increasingly hesitant to invest in films that are unlikely to be box office hits

9. **P1:** The majority of students who responded to a campus survey said our fraternity would have been their number one pick.
P2: The students who responded to the campus <u>survey in favor of our fraternity cannot be wrong.</u>
∴ Our fraternity is the best on campus.

   Issue: Whether our fraternity is the best on campus

EXERCISE 3.10

3. **P:** <u>Conrad is a visionary.</u>
∴ You should vote for Conrad.

   Issue: Whether you should vote for Conrad

6. **P1:** Increasing troop levels puts more of our troops at risk.
P2: Increasing troop levels increases the possibility of <u>civilian casualties.</u>
∴ An increase in troop levels is not the best means for fighting an insurgency.

   Issue: Whether an increase in troop levels is the best means for fighting an insurgency

9. **P:** <u>Tropical oceans are warming.</u>
∴ This year will be rainier than most.

   Issue: Whether this year will be rainier than most

EXERCISE 3.13

3. **P:** <u>The best man for the job is a woman.</u>
∴ You should vote for Councilwoman Hagen for mayor.

   Issue: Whether you should vote for Councilwoman Hagen for mayor

6. **P:** <u>The university is trying to encourage all students to apply at the same time as it is limiting enrollment.</u>
∴ The university is sending a mixed message to the community.

   Issue: Whether the university is sending a mixed message to the community

9. **P:** No amount of money will make up for a boring, unsatisfying career.

∴ You should choose the program that will make you happiest over the long haul.

Issue: Whether you should choose the program that will make you happiest over the long haul

EXERCISE 3.14

3. **P:** You may need to use a cell phone to report a drunk driver on the highway.

∴ We should not ban all cell-phone use when driving.

Issue: Whether we should ban all cell-phone use when driving

6. **P:** Driving over the speed limit will lead you to break other laws.

∴ You should not drive over the speed limit.

Issue: Whether you should drive over the speed limit

9. **P:** You wouldn't want someone to disparage your race.

∴ We must pass laws to curtail hate speech.

Issue: Whether we must pass laws to curtail hate speech

12. **P1:** You have seen blood before.
P2: You're wearing gloves.

∴ You should stop being so squeamish.

Issue: Whether you should stop being so squeamish

15. **P:** Staying up late studying is ruining your health.

∴ You should stop staying up late studying.

Issue: Whether you should stop staying up late studying

18. **P:** Dizziness is not a medical emergency.

∴ You should stop whining.

Issue: Whether you should stop whining

EXERCISE 3.18

3. Chain argument

P: Maria tore up all her credit cards.

∴ Maria will again be living within her means.

P: Maria will again be living within her means.

∴ Maria should be able to earn back an excellent credit rating.

Issue: Whether Maria should be able to earn back an excellent credit rating

6. Argument with multiple conclusions

P: Prohibition of alcohol didn't work.

∴ It's pointless to try to prohibit recreational drug use.

Issue: Whether it's pointless to try to prohibit recreational drug use

P: Prohibition of alcohol didn't work.

∴ It's pointless to try to prohibit steroids and other performance enhancers.

Issue: Whether it's pointless to try to prohibit steroids and other performance enhancers

9. Chain argument

P: You and your family have paid a great deal of money for your college education.

∴ You really must take your studies more seriously.

P: You really must take your studies more seriously.

∴ You should quit working 40 hours a week.

Issue: Whether you should quit working 40 hours a week

12. Argument with multiple conclusions

P1: The economy is awful.
P2: There's little hope for economic improvement anytime soon.

∴ You should be frugal with your paycheck.

Issue: Whether you should be frugal with your paycheck

P1: The economy is awful.
P2: There's little hope for economic improvement anytime soon.

∴ You should put more money in savings.

Issue: Whether you should put more money in savings

15. Argument with multiple conclusions

P1: The military has had an increasingly difficult time meeting recruitment goals.
P2: Veteran soldiers are retiring at an unusually high rate.

∴ The military will soon be much smaller than it was five years ago.

Issue: Whether the military will soon be much smaller than it was five years ago

P1: The military has had an increasingly difficult time meeting recruitment goals.
P2: <u>Veteran soldiers are retiring at an unusually high rate.</u>
∴ The military will remain smaller for years to come.

Issue: Whether the military will remain smaller for years to come

18. Chain argument

P1: The city zoo is heavily in debt.
P2: <u>The city zoo is poorly managed.</u>
∴ Extreme measures must be taken.

P: <u>Extreme measures must be taken.</u>
∴ The town council should take charge of the zoo right away.

Issue: Whether the town council should take charge of the zoo right away

EXERCISE 3.22

3.   This passage from the U.S. Supreme Court ruling in *Santa Fe v. Doe* (2000) contains an argument. The issue is whether school sponsorship of a religious message is permissible. The conclusion is that school sponsorship of a religious message is impermissible. The first premise is that school sponsorship of a religious message sends the ancillary message to members of the audience who are nonadherents that they are outsiders, not full members of the political community. The second premise is that school sponsorship of a religious message sends an accompanying message to adherents that they are insiders, favored members of the political community.

6.   This passage from *Popular Science* contains an argument. The issue is whether you should always click Eject. The conclusion is that you should always click Eject. The first premise is that disconnecting a USB drive before ejecting it can destroy data. The second premise is that it is better to be safe than sorry.

9.   This passage from *Parade* by Margaret Cho contains an argument. The issue is whether *Drop Dead Diva* is a great show for women. The conclusion is that *Drop Dead Diva* is a great show for women. The first premise is that *Drop Dead Diva* promotes beautiful images of different kinds of women. The second premise is that *Drop Dead Diva* has a great heroine who really doesn't have to sell herself short in any way.

   This passage from *Parade* by Margaret Cho contains another argument. The issue is whether *Drop Dead Diva* is a great show for women to watch with their daughters. The conclusion is that *Drop Dead Diva* is a great show for women to watch with their daughters. The first premise is that *Drop Dead Diva* promotes beautiful images of different kinds of women. The second premise is that *Drop Dead Diva* has a great heroine who really doesn't have to sell herself short in any way.

Chapter 4

EXERCISE 4.7

3. ①
   ↓
   ②

6. ①
   ↓
   ②

9. ① + ②   ①   ②
      ↓   ↘ ↙
      ③   ③

EXERCISE 4.11

3. ① <u>You should get your holiday shopping done early</u> because ② <u>many stores are not restocking their shelves this year.</u>

   ②
   ↓
   ①

6. ① <u>Tomlin would make the best mayor.</u> ② <u>She is honest,</u> and ③ <u>she knows how to work with people who disagree with her.</u>

   ②   ③
     ↘ ↙
     ①

9. ① You clearly have a case of the fungal infection called ringworm. ② You have a red, elevated, ring-like sore on your arm, and ③ only ringworm causes sores like those.

12. ① The recent outbreak of food poisoning among CSUB students was caused by corndogs served at the Club Fair yesterday. ① The corndogs must have been the problem because ② corndogs were served at the Club Fair and ③ all of the students who became ill ate lunch at the Club Fair yesterday.

15. ① No Republicans are Democrats, so ② no Republicans are big spenders, since ③ all big spenders are Democrats.

18. ① Young children have increasingly large amounts of money to spend, and ② they exert an ever larger influence on their parents' buying. Accordingly, ③ marketers will spend even more money in the coming years attempting to attract young consumers.

EXERCISE 4.14

3. ① Francisco is most likely good at math because ② he has an analytical mind.

6. ① All sailboats are expensive to buy, and ② a Hobie Cat is a sailboat. ③ You know what that means about Hobie Cats, right?
③ A Hobie Cat is expensive to buy.

9. ① There is clearly a health-care crisis in the United States. ② If there were people in need of health care who can't afford it, then the United States would have a health-care crisis. And ③ aren't there lots of people who need health care, but can't afford it?
③ There are lots of people who need health care, but can't afford it.

12. ① We hope you agree that our fraternity is the best on campus. ② The majority of students who responded to a campus survey said our fraternity would be their number one pick. ③ How could they be wrong?
③ The students who responded in favor of our fraternity cannot be wrong.

15. ① Video game players shouldn't become surgeons. ② Haven't you seen how many gamers have jittery nerves?
② Many gamers have jittery nerves.

18. ① Which charity should you donate to? The one that supports projects in your community. This is because ② you will be able to see the benefits directly.

① You should donate to the charity that supports projects in your community.

$$② \\ \downarrow \\ ①$$

EXERCISE 4.17

3.
$$① \\ \downarrow \\ ② \\ \downarrow \\ ③$$

6.
$$②\quad③\quad④ \qquad ②+③\quad④ \\ \searrow \downarrow \swarrow \qquad\quad \searrow \swarrow \\ ① \qquad\qquad\quad ①$$

9.
$$③\quad② \qquad ③+② \\ \searrow\swarrow \qquad\quad \downarrow \\ ① \qquad\qquad ① \\ \downarrow \qquad\qquad \downarrow \\ ④ \qquad\qquad ④$$

EXERCISE 4.18

3. ① It is important for university students to use their education to help people who never had the opportunity to go to school, since ② they have benefited from others who came before them. Also, ③ making their community better will help students develop the wisdom necessary to apply their knowledge.

$$②\quad③ \\ \searrow\swarrow \\ ①$$

6. ① You should move to Arizona, since ② it is much warmer. Therefore, ③ you should give two weeks' notice at your office.

$$②\\ \downarrow\\①\\ \downarrow\\③$$

9. ① Prohibition of alcohol didn't work, so ② it's pointless to try to prohibit drug use, and ③ it's equally pointless to try to prohibit steroids and other performance enhancers.

$$①\\ \swarrow\searrow\\②\quad③$$

12. ① Horatio took little care of his teeth when he was a teenager, so ② he will probably have dental problems when he gets older. Consequently, ③ he should always buy dental insurance.

$$①\\ \downarrow\\②\\ \downarrow\\③$$

15. ① Anderson will soon be getting a raise. This is because ② she is likely to get a promotion, since ③ she was so successful on the Hamer project.

$$③\\ \downarrow\\②\\ \downarrow\\①$$

18. ① I got the new job! That means that ② I will be able to afford my mortgage payments and ③ I can start replenishing my savings account.

$$①\\ \swarrow\searrow\\②\quad③$$

EXERCISE 4.30

3. ① <u>You won't graduate this year unless you complete</u> <u>senior seminar</u>. Accordingly, ② <u>you won't graduate,</u> since ③ <u>you can't complete senior seminar</u>. After all, ④ <u>you didn't even enroll in it!</u>

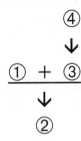

6. Look, Leila. Since ① <u>you want to save more money,</u> ② <u>you should open a money market account at the</u> <u>bank</u>, and ③ <u>you should cancel all of your credit cards.</u>

9. Given that ① <u>clowns perform in rodeos</u>, we can con-clude that ② <u>they get paid</u>. This is because ③ <u>anyone</u> <u>who performs in a rodeo gets paid</u>. This means that ④ <u>clowns should pay taxes</u>, in view of the fact that, ⑤ <u>if clowns get paid, we should make them pay taxes.</u>

$$
\frac{① + ③}{↓}
$$
$$
\frac{② + ⑤}{↓}
$$
$$
④
$$

12. ① <u>All self-employed workers are professionals</u>. ② <u>Beauticians are self-employed</u>; hence, ③ <u>they are pro-fessionals</u>. Now, ④ <u>all professionals need licenses</u>. This proves that ⑤ <u>beauticians need a license.</u>

$$
\frac{① + ②}{↓}
$$
$$
\frac{③ + ④}{↓}
$$
$$
⑤
$$

15. Since ① <u>Europeans were divided in the 1930s</u> and ② <u>any time Europeans are divided it will become a</u> "dishonest decade," we can conclude that ③ <u>the</u> <u>1930s were a dishonest decade</u>. And ④ <u>a dishonest</u> <u>decade is liable to cause trouble in the long run</u>. Thus, ⑤ <u>the results of the 1930s are obvious.</u>
⑤ The 1930s will cause trouble in the long run.

$$
\frac{① + ②}{↓}
$$
$$
\frac{③ + ④}{↓}
$$
$$
⑤
$$

18. ① <u>If meteorites are the rarest materials found</u> <u>on Earth, then they are the oldest things humans</u> <u>have touched</u>. ② <u>Either meteorites are the rarest</u> <u>materials found on Earth or flawless diamonds are</u> <u>the rarest</u>, and ③ <u>diamonds aren't the rarest</u> <u>things found on Earth</u>. Therefore, ④ <u>meteorites</u> <u>are the rarest things found on Earth</u> and consequently ⑤ <u>are the oldest things humans have touched.</u>

$$
\frac{② + ③}{↓}
$$
$$
\frac{④ + ①}{↓}
$$
$$
⑤
$$

EXERCISE 4.31

3. ① <u>Tyrone won't be happy unless Jesse Ventura</u> <u>is elected</u>. But ② <u>Ventura won't get elected,</u> since ③ <u>he is not on the ballot</u>, so ④ <u>you can</u> <u>see for yourself what will follow from that</u>. Now, ⑤ <u>if Tyrone is unhappy, then Grace will be</u> <u>unhappy, too</u>. Thus, it is clear that ⑥ <u>Grace will</u> <u>be unhappy.</u>
④ Tyrone won't be happy.

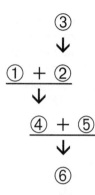

6. ① If art is something that any person can learn to appreciate, then art must be able to be judged by an objective measure. Now ② it's unlikely that art can be judged by an objective measure, given that ③ what is called art varies so widely, so ④ art must not be something that any person can learn to appreciate. Besides, ⑤ if merely a few people get an emotional feeling from art, then art must not be something that people can learn to appreciate, and ⑥ only a few people can get an emotional feeling from art.

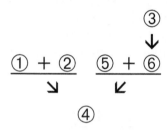

9. Good afternoon, ladies and gentlemen of the jury. It is evident that ① my client, Janie Jacobson, is not guilty of kidnapping Baby Zack. Since ② Baby Zack was taken from his mansion in the Hamptons on December 20, 2010, ③ Ms. Jacobson could not be guilty of kidnapping him if she was in Las Vegas at that time. And ④ she was in Las Vegas on that day, as ⑤ is evidenced by the casino surveillance footage.
⑤ Casino surveillance footage shows that Janie Jacobson was in Las Vegas on December 20, 2010.

```
   ②        ⑤
   ↓         ↓
   ③   +    ④
        ↓
        ①
```

12. ① If your children watch a lot of television, then they are more likely to believe in racial and gender stereotypes. ② You don't want your children to believe these harmful stereotypes, so ③ you should turn off the television more often. Besides, ④ if you limit the amount of television your children watch, then they are more likely to engage in constructive activities, and I know ⑤ you want your children to engage in more constructive activities.

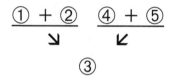

15. Who ate the last slice of cheesecake from the office workroom? Well, there's no doubt that ① it had to be one of the office workers, since ② only they have keys to the workroom. But ③ it couldn't have been any of the secretaries. After all, ④ they are all on low-fat diets. ⑤ It also couldn't have been any of the custodians because ⑥ they are on vacation this week. This all proves that ⑦ the last slice of cheesecake must have been eaten by one of the members of the management team—CEO Saner or President Gamboa. But ⑧ there's no way President Gamboa would have eaten the cheesecake, since ⑨ he's diabetic. We can conclude that ⑩ it had to be CEO Saner.

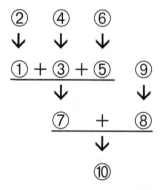

EXERCISE 4.32

3. ① Physics is *the* fundamental science. ② It explains how the universe behaves and ③ gives us an extraordinary power over the world. ④ Professor Richard Wolfson's lectures introduce you to scores of fundamental ideas related to Newtonian mechanics, oscillations and waves, thermodynamics, electricity and magnetism, optics quantum theory, and more.—Ad for *Physics and Our Universe: How It All Works*

This passage from an ad for *Physics and Our Universe: How It All Works* contains an argument. The issue is whether physics is the fundamental science. The conclusion is that physics is the fundamental science. The first premise is that physics explains how the universe behaves. The second premise is that physics gives us an extraordinary power over the world.

6. ① Energy-drink consumption is a rising public health problem. ② More than 20,000 people were admitted to emergency rooms in 2011 with anxiety, rapid heartbeat, seizures, or heart attacks after downing energy drinks. In addition, ③ many consumers combine the drinks with alcohol or prescription drugs, ④ making the drinks even more dangerous.—U.S. Food and Drug Administration

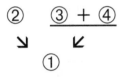

This passage from the U.S. Food and Drug Administration contains an argument. The issue is whether energy-drink consumption is a rising public health problem. The conclusion is that energy-drink consumption is a rising public health problem. The first premise is that more than 20,000 people were admitted to emergency rooms in 2011 with anxiety, rapid heartbeat, seizures, or heart attacks after downing energy drinks. The second premise is that many energy-drink consumers combine the drinks with alcohol or prescription drugs. The third premise is that combining energy-drinks with alcohol or prescription drugs makes the drinks even more dangerous.

9. ① Violence as a way of achieving racial justice is impractical. ① It is impractical because ② it is a descending spiral ending in destruction for all. ③ The old law of an eye for an eye leaves everybody blind.—Martin Luther King, Jr.

This passage from Martin Luther King, Jr. contains an argument. The issue is whether violence as a way of achieving racial justice is impractical. The conclusion is that violence as a way of achieving racial justice is impractical. The premise is that violence as a way of achieving racial justice is a descending spiral ending in destruction for all.

This passage contains a subargument. The intermediate conclusion is that violence as a way of achieving racial justice is a descending spiral ending in destruction for all. The premise is that the old law of an eye for an eye leaves everybody blind.

Chapter 5

EXERCISE 5.5

3. Deductive argument
   P1: Mitchell's roommate has seen the *Lord of the Rings* trilogy four times.
   P2: Rita has never seen the *Lord of the Rings* trilogy.
   ∴ Rita cannot be Mitchell's roommate.

   Issue: Whether Rita can be Mitchell's roommate

6. Deductive argument
   P: Jackman was born four months later than Waterman.
   ∴ Waterman is not older than Jackman.

   P1: Either Waterman is older than Jackman or he's older than Bootman.
   P2: Waterman is not older than Jackman.
   ∴ Waterman is older than Bootman.

   Issue: Whether Waterman is older than Bootman

9. Deductive argument
   P1: The airbag in Jose's car failed to deploy when he crashed.
   P2: Anyone whose airbag fails to deploy in an accident gets hurt.
   ∴ Jose is hurt.

   Issue: Whether Jose is hurt

12. Inductive argument
    P1: *The Adventures of Tom Sawyer* and *Huckleberry Finn* were written by the same author.
    P2: *The Adventures of Tom Sawyer* and *Huckleberry Finn* have similar stories.
    P3: *Huckleberry Finn* won the Nobel Prize for Literature.
    ∴ *The Adventures of Tom Sawyer* won the Nobel Prize for Literature.

    Issue: Whether *The Adventures of Tom Sawyer* won the Nobel Prize for Literature

15. Deductive argument

   P1: <u>You work every afternoon.</u>

   ∴   You can't attend soccer practice every afternoon.

   P1: If you join the soccer team, you will have to attend practice every afternoon.

   P2: <u>You can't attend soccer practice every afternoon.</u>

   ∴   You won't be joining the soccer team.

   Issue: Whether you will be joining the soccer team

EXERCISE 5.8

3. Truth-functional claim
6. Categorical claim
9. Truth-functional claim

EXERCISE 5.11

3. Truth-functional argument. Disjunction (Either Naomi goes bowling or Miguel studies) and conditional (If Miguel does not study, then Naomi goes bowling).
6. Truth-functional argument. Conditionals (If you passed geology, then you passed a science class; If you passed a science class, then you have qualified for honors; and If you passed geology, then you have qualified for honors).
9. Truth-functional argument. Conditional (A defendant is guilty of murder only if he intended to kill the victim).

EXERCISE 5.15

3. Causal claim
6. General claim
9. Analogical claim

EXERCISE 5.19

3. Inductive generalization. General claim (All members of the IT department are really bright).
6. Inductive generalization. General claim (All of my classes here will be in large lecture halls).
9. Inductive generalization. General claim (All poets smoke cigarettes).
12. Analogical argument. Analogy (Senator Brown and the two Democratic senators are alike).
15. Causal argument. Implied causal claim (Poverty causes crime).

EXERCISE 5.20

3. Causal argument
6. Truth-functional argument
9. Analogical argument

12. Truth-functional argument
15. Analogical argument
18. Inductive generalization

EXERCISE 5.23

3. c

EXERCISE 5.26

3. c

EXERCISE 5.28

3.   This passage from the Associated Press does not contain an argument. Although there are at least two claims, none of the claims offers a reason for another claim, as is necessary in arguments.

6. ① <u>Why wouldn't a woman consider herself a feminist?</u> ② <u>Even my husband calls himself a feminist.</u> ③ <u>If he can call himself that, then every woman should be able to call herself that.</u>—Mary Elizabeth Winstead
① Every woman should consider herself a feminist.

   This passage from Mary Elizabeth Winstead contains an argument. The issue is whether every woman should consider herself a feminist. The implied conclusion is that every woman should consider herself a feminist. The first premise is that my husband calls himself a feminist. The second premise is that if my husband considers himself a feminist, then every woman should consider herself a feminist.

   This is a deductive, truth-functional argument.

9. ① <u>Some sediment-laden rivers do not have a broad continental shelf to provide a platform for sediment to accumulate,</u> and ② <u>all deltas require a broad continental shelf to provide a platform for sediment to accumulate.</u> As a result, ③ <u>some sediment-laden rivers do not have deltas.</u>—Tom Garrison, *Oceanography*

   This passage from Tom Garrison's book *Oceanography* contains an argument. The issue is whether all sediment-laden rivers have deltas. The conclusion is that some sediment-laden rivers do not have deltas. The first premise is that some sediment-laden rivers do not have a broad continental shelf to provide a platform for sediment to accumulate. The second premise is that all deltas require a broad continental shelf to provide a platform for sediment to accumulate.

This is a deductive, categorical argument.

Chapter 6

EXERCISE 6.2

3. Some S are P.
6. Some S are P.
9. Some rhinos are not pterodactyls.

EXERCISE 6.5

3. Some violins are expensive instruments.
6. All physicians are people in the military.
9. In standard form.
12. All stagehands are people in the cast.
15. In standard form.

EXERCISE 6.7

3. All people identical to Theodore Roosevelt are people who fought in the Spanish-American War.
6. All people who die young are good people.
9. Some pigeons are not dirty birds.
12. All mammals are cows.
15. All people who enter the movie theater are people over the age of 17.

EXERCISE 6.8

3. Some bears are not mammals.
6. All objects made of wood are flammable objects.
9. No children are people in class.
12. All places there is a bull are places there is a cow.
15. All universal tools are duct tapes.
18. No interns are people who are paid.
21. Some shirts are clothes.
24. Some calves are not Holsteins.

EXERCISE 6.10

3. Major: barn owls
   Minor: animals
   Middle: pets

6. Major: people who can relax
   Minor: executives
   Middle: workaholics
9. Major: bread slices
   Minor: crusts
   Middle: heels

EXERCISE 6.12

3. ① Jack-o-lanterns are pumpkins, for ② jack-o-lanterns are Halloween objects, and ③ some Halloween objects are pumpkins.

All jack-o-lanterns are Halloween objects.
Some Halloween objects are pumpkins.
All jack-o-lanterns are pumpkins.

6. ① Not every metaphysician is a rationalist. Since ② every rationalist is a Platonist, ③ some metaphysicians are not Platonists.

Some metaphysicians are not rationalists.
All rationalists are Platonists.
Some metaphysicians are not Platonists.

9. ① All languages that are not spoken regularly are dead languages, and ② Latin is not spoken regularly. Consequently, ③ Latin is a dead language. Given that ④ Greek is also a dead language, ⑤ Greek is Latin.

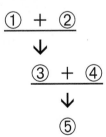

All languages identical to Latin are dead languages.
All languages identical to Greek are dead languages.
All languages identical to Greek are languages identical to Latin.

EXERCISE 6.16

3.

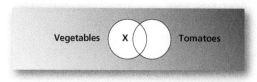

6.

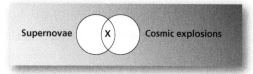

9.

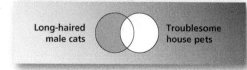

EXERCISE 6.19

3. Valid

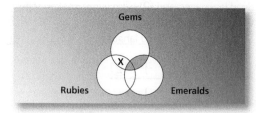

6. Valid

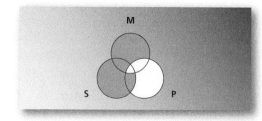

9. Invalid

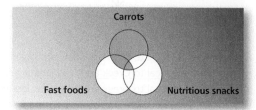

12. Invalid

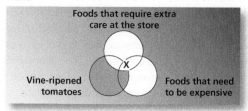

15. Valid

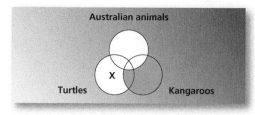

18. Invalid

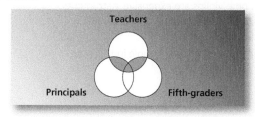

EXERCISE 6.20

3. Invalid

All athletes are baseball players.
No baseball players are soccer players.
All soccer players are athletes.

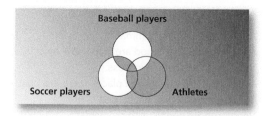

6. Valid

All people who passed geology are people who passed a science class.
All people who passed a science class are people qualified for honors.

All people who passed geology are people qualified for honors.

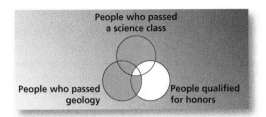

9. Invalid

All senators are corruptible people.
Some liars are corruptible people.
No senators are liars.

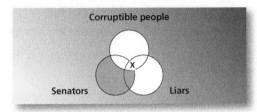

12. Invalid

All animals allowed in the gym are mascots.
All animals allowed in the gym are nuisances.
All nuisances are mascots.

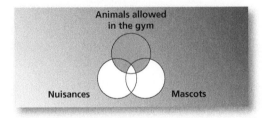

15. Valid

All war crimes are crimes that demean innocent humans.
All crimes that demean innocent humans are events beyond any kind of moral justification.
All war crimes are events beyond any kind of moral justification.

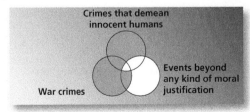

18. Invalid

All avatars are sacred figures.
All shamans are sacred figures.
All avatars are shamans.

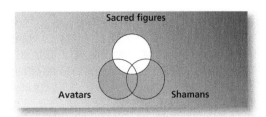

EXERCISE 6.22

3. ① You can be certain that some assignments that reinforce writing skills involve laboratory experiments. This is because ② some of the homework assignments in physics reinforce writing skills, and ③ some homework assignments in physics involve laboratory experiments.—Physics instructor

This passage from a physics instructor contains an argument. The issue is whether some assignments that reinforce writing skills involve laboratory experiments. The conclusion is that some assignments that reinforce writing skills involve laboratory experiments. The first premise is that some of the homework assignments in physics reinforce writing skills. The second premise is that some homework assignments in physics involve laboratory experiments.

This argument is a deductive, categorical argument. The standard form of the argument is as follows:

Some of the homework assignments in physics are assignments that reinforce writing skills.
Some of the homework assignments in physics are assignments that involve laboratory experiments.
Some of the assignments that reinforce writing skills are assignments that involve laboratory experiments.

The following Venn diagram demonstrates that the argument is invalid.

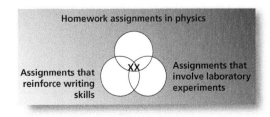

6. The authors of *The Bell Curve* argue that ① there are basic inherited differences in intelligence between races. ② We reject that argument. ③ If there are no scientifically valid racial differences, the basic argument of *The Bell Curve* falls apart. And ④ there are no scientifically valid racial differences, for ⑤ the vast majority of anthropologists and sociologists reject the idea of separate races as biological entities. Thus, ② *the basic argument of The Bell Curve* falls apart.—Walker, Spohn, and DeLeone, *The Color of Justice*
② There are no basic inherited differences in intelligence between races.

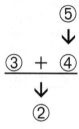

This passage from Walker, Spohn, and DeLeone's book *The Color of Justice* contains an argument. The issue is whether there are basic inherited differences in intelligence between races. The conclusion is that there are no basic inherited differences in intelligence between races. The first premise is that if there are no scientifically valid racial differences, the basic argument of *The Bell Curve* falls apart. The second premise is that there are no scientifically valid racial differences.

This passage contains a subargument. The intermediate conclusion is that there are no scientifically valid racial differences. The premise is that the vast majority of anthropologists and sociologists reject the idea of separate races as biological entities.

This argument is a deductive, truth-functional argument.

9. ① Defenders of advertising claim that, despite criticisms, advertising enjoys protection under the First Amendment as a form of speech. But ② this doesn't mean that all advertising should be allowed. Indeed, ③ some advertising should *not* be allowed because ④ no allowable speech has bad social consequences, and ⑤ some advertising has bad social consequences.—Shaw and Berry, *Moral Issues in Business*

This passage from Shaw and Berry's book, *Moral Issues in Business*, contains an argument. The issue is whether all advertising should be allowed. The conclusion is that some advertising should *not* be allowed. The first premise is that no allowable speech has bad social consequences. The second premise is that some advertising has bad social consequences.

This argument is a deductive, categorical argument. The standard form of the argument is as follows:

No allowable forms of speech are forms of speech having bad social consequences.
Some advertisements are forms of speech having bad social consequences.
Some advertisements are not allowable forms of speech.

The following Venn diagram demonstrates that the argument is valid.

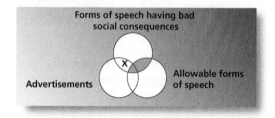

Chapter 7

EXERCISE 7.6

3. I • D
   I = The player on the field appears to be injured.
   D = The team doctor has been called to the scene.

6. C • T
   C = Loose clothing is more comfortable in hot weather.
   T = I have trouble finding loose clothing that is attractive.

9. B ⊃ C
   B = A bear is in the house.
   C = A crocodile is in the yard.

12. ~ B
   B = You definitely have a bronchial infection.

15. H ⊃ P
   H = Primroses are hearty in our climate.
   P = Primroses are protected from the gophers.

18. S ⊃ F
   S = The regiment is split into two battalions.
   F = The regiment will be more flexible.

EXERCISE 7.10

3. Disjunction
6. Conditional
9. Conjunction

EXERCISE 7.11

3. Conditional ~ C ⊃ D
   C = The pet owner is extremely consistent.
   D = Housebreaking a new kitten can be difficult.

6. Conditional ~ P ⊃ ~ R
   R = You can register your car.
   P = You pass the smog inspection.

9. Conditional O ⊃ (D ∨ M)
   D = We can go out to dinner.
   M = We can go to the movies.
   O = You want to go out tonight.

12. Negation ~ (E ⊃ H)
    E = Lawyers are ethical.
    H = Lawyers' firms are highly regulated.

15. Disjunction L ∨ (H • I)
    L = Limits must be placed on health-care costs.
    H = Health care will become more expensive.
    I = Insurance premiums will rise.

EXERCISE 7.13

3. The conjunction is false.
   A = Africa is a country.
   K = Ketchup is a vegetable.
   A • K
   F **F** F

6. The negation is true.
   A = Apples are purple.
   C = Carrots are green.
   ~ (A ∨ C)
   T F F F

9. The disjunction is false.
   A = Africa is a country.
   L = Lima is the capital of Peru.
   A ∨ ~ L
   F **F** F T

12. The negation is true.
    H = Horses have hooves.
    P = Puppies can fly.
    ~ (H • P)
    T T F F

15. The disjunction is true.
    G = Golf is a sport.
    S = Cowboys wear ballet slippers.
    C = Christmas is in July.
    (S ⊃ G) ∨ C
    F T T **T** F

18. The conditional is true.
    Q = Queen Latifah has visited the Grand Canyon.
    A = Africa is a country.
    Q ⊃ ~ A
    ? **T** T F

EXERCISE 7.20

3. The argument is invalid.
   S ⊃ C / ~ S // ~ C

T	**T** T	**F** T		**F** T
T	**F** F	**F** T		**T** F
F	T T	**T** F		**F** T
F	T F	**T** F		**T** F

6. The argument is valid.
   ~ A ⊃ B / ~ A // B

F	T **T** T	**F** T	**T**
F	T **T** F	**F** T	**F**
T	F **T** T	**T** F	**T**
T	F **F** F	**T** F	**F**

9. The argument is invalid.
   Q / P ⊃ Q // P

T	T **T** T	**T**	
T	F **T** T	**F**	
F	T **F** F	**T**	
F	F **T** F	**F**	

12. The argument is invalid.
    C ∨ D / C // ~ D

T **T** T	**T**	**F** T	
T **T** F	**T**	**T** F	
F **T** T	**F**	**F** T	
F **F** F	**F**	**T** F	

15. The argument is valid.
    K ∨ L / K ⊃ M / L ⊃ M // M

T **T** T	T **T** T	T **T** T	**T**
T **T** T	T **F** F	T **F** F	**F**
T **T** F	T **T** T	F **T** T	**T**
T **T** F	T **F** F	F **T** F	**F**
F **T** T	F **T** T	T **T** T	**T**
F **T** T	F **T** F	T **F** F	**F**
F **F** F	F **T** T	F **T** T	**T**
F **F** F	F **T** F	F **T** F	**F**

18. The argument is invalid.

S ⊃ (T • R) / ~ S // ~ (T • R)

T	**T**	T T T	**F** T	**F** T T T
T	**F**	T F F	**F** T	**T** T F F
T	**F**	F F T	**F** T	**T** F F T
T	**F**	F F F	**F** T	**T** F F F
F	**T**	T T T	**T** F	**F** T T T
F	**T**	T F F	**T** F	**T** T F F
F	**T**	F F T	**T** F	**T** F F T
F	**T**	F F F	**T** F	**T** F F F

EXERCISE 7.21

3. The argument is invalid.
Anis's mother said that ① he will go to Disneyland only if he finishes all his homework. I guess ② he's going to Disneyland, then, because ③ he finished all his homework.

D = Anis will go to Disneyland.
F = Anis finishes his homework.

D ⊃ F / F // D

T	**T**	T	**T**	**T**
T	**F**	F	**F**	**T**
F	**T**	T	**T**	**F**
F	**T**	F	**F**	**F**

6. The argument is valid.
① Gay marriage? Why not? ② If we allow infertile heterosexual couples to marry, then we should allow same-sex couples to marry, and, of course, ③ we should allow infertile heterosexual couples to marry. ① Gay marriage should be allowed.

I = We allow infertile heterosexual couples to marry.
G = We allow same-sex couples to marry.

I ⊃ G / I // G

T	**T**	T	**T**	**T**
T	**F**	F	**T**	**F**
F	**T**	T	**F**	**T**
F	**T**	F	**F**	**F**

9. The argument is valid.
① If Paula is a grandmother, then either her son or her daughter has a child. ② Paula is not a grandmother, since ③ neither her son nor her daughter has a child.

P = Paula is a grandmother.
S = Paula's son has a child.
D = Paula's daughter has a child.

P ⊃ (S ∨ D) / ~ (S ∨ D) // ~ P

T	**T**	T T T	**F** T T T	**F** T
T	**T**	T T F	**F** T T F	**F** T
T	**T**	F T T	**F** F T T	**F** T
T	**F**	F F F	**T** F F F	**F** T
F	**T**	T T T	**F** T T T	**T** F
F	**T**	T T F	**F** T T F	**T** F
F	**T**	F T T	**F** F T T	**T** F
F	**T**	F F F	**T** F F F	**T** F

12. The argument is valid.
① Those strawberries are labeled "certified organic" only if they are grown without the use of pesticides. Since ② either the strawberries are labeled "certified organic" or they are grown with the use of pesticides, that means that, ③ if they are grown without the use of pesticides, then they will be labeled "certified organic."

L = Those strawberries are labeled "certified organic."
P = Those strawberries are grown with the use of pesticides.

L ⊃ ~ P / L ∨ P // ~ P ⊃ L

T	**F** F T	**T** T T	**F** T T T
T	**T** T F	**T** T F	**T** F T T
F	**T** F T	**F** T T	**F** T T F
F	**T** T F	**F** F F	**T** F F F

15. The argument is valid.
① There will be more traffic accidents unless people stop using their cell phones while driving. But ② people won't stop using their cell phones while driving because

③ <u>they do not realize how dangerous it is</u>. As a result,
④ <u>traffic accidents will increase</u>.

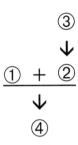

M = There will be more traffic accidents.
S = People stop using their cell phones while driving.

M ∨ S	/	~ S	//	M
T **T** T		**F** T		**T**
T **T** F		**T** F		**T**
F **T** T		**F** T		**F**
F **F** F		**T** F		**F**

18. The argument is invalid.
① <u>Cinderella can go to the royal ball if she finishes all</u>
<u>of her chores and finds something suitable to wear.</u>
Given that ② <u>her stepsisters will sabotage her efforts,</u>
③ <u>neither will Cinderella finish all of her chores, nor</u>
<u>will she have something suitable to wear.</u> Therefore,
④ <u>Cinderella won't go to the ball.</u>

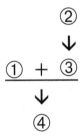

G = Cinderella goes to the royal ball.
C = Cinderella finishes all of her chores.
W = Cinderella finds something suitable to wear.

(C • W) ⊃ G	/	~ C • ~ W	//	~ G
T T T **T** T		**F** T **F** F T		**F** T
T T T **F** F		**F** T **F** F T		**T** F
T F F **T** T		**F** T **F** T F		**F** T
T F F **T** F		**F** T **F** T F		**T** F
F F T **T** T		**T** F **F** F T		**F** T
F F T **T** F		**T** F **F** F T		**T** F
F F F **T** T		**T** F **T** T F		**F** T
F F F **T** F		**T** F **T** T F		**T** F

EXERCISE 7.22

3. Which physics laws should be taught first? ① <u>We</u>
<u>can either teach the correct, but unfamiliar, law or we</u>
<u>can teach the approximate, but familiar law.</u> ② <u>We</u>
<u>shouldn't teach the unfamiliar law first</u> since ③ <u>it can't</u>
<u>be understood unless the student knows the familiar</u>
<u>law.</u> So, ④ <u>it is with the familiar law that physics instruc-</u>
<u>tion should begin.</u>—Richard Feynman, *Six Easy Pieces*

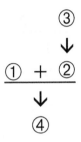

This passage from *Six Easy Pieces* by Richard
Feynman contains an argument. The issue is whether
physics instruction should begin with the familiar law.
The conclusion is that physics instruction should begin
with the familiar law. The first premise is that we can
either teach the correct, but unfamiliar, law or we can
teach the approximate, but familiar law. The second
premise is that we shouldn't teach the unfamiliar law first.

This passage contains a subargument. The
intermediate conclusion is that we shouldn't teach the
unfamiliar law first. The premise is that the unfamiliar
law can't be understood unless the student knows the
familiar law.

This is a deductive, truth-functional argument. The
truth table below demonstrates that the argument is
valid because it is impossible for the conclusion to be
false when both premises are true.

C = We can teach the correct, but unfamiliar law.
A = We can teach the approximate, but familiar law.

C ∨ A	/	~ C	//	A
T **T** T		**F** T		**T**
T **T** F		**F** T		**F**
F **T** T		**T** F		**T**
F **F** F		**T** F		**F**

6. This passage from Kaibara Ekken does not contain
an argument. It contains only one claim, and arguments
require at least two claims.

9. ① <u>If student researchers want to interview, survey,</u>
<u>systematically observe, or collect other data from</u>
<u>human subjects, the project must be authorized by the</u>

University's Institutional Review Board (IRB). Moreover, ② in order to get authorization from the IRB, all key personnel in the research project must be certified in Human Subjects Protection Training (HSPT). Therefore, ③ if student researchers want to interview, survey, systematically observe, or collect other data from human subjects, all key personnel in the research project must be certified in HSPT.—University policy on human subject research

This passage from the University policy on human subject research contains an argument. The issue is whether, if student researchers want to interview, survey, systematically observe, or collect other data from human subjects, all key personnel in the research project must be certified in HSPT. The conclusion is that, if student researchers want to interview, survey, systematically observe, or collect other data from human subjects, all key personnel in the research project must be certified in HSPT. The first premise is that, if student researchers want to interview, survey, systematically observe, or collect other data from human subjects, the project must be authorized by the University's Institutional Review Board (IRB). The second premise is that, if student researchers want to get authorization from the IRB, all key personnel in the research project must be certified in Human Subjects Protection Training (HSPT).

This is a deductive, truth-functional argument. The truth table below demonstrates that the argument is valid because it is impossible for the conclusion to be false when both conclusions are true.

I = Student researchers want to interview, survey, systematically observe, or collect other data from human subjects.
A = The project must be authorized by the University's Institutional Review Board (IRB).
C = All key personnel in the research project must be certified in Human Subjects Protection Training (HSPT).

I ⊃ A / A ⊃ C // I ⊃ C

T **T** T	T **T** T	T **T** T
T **T** T	T **F** F	T **F** F
T **F** F	F **T** T	T **T** T
T **F** F	F **T** F	T **F** F
F **T** T	T **T** T	F **T** T

F **T** T   T **F** F   F **T** F
F **T** F   F **T** T   F **T** T
F **T** F   F **T** F   F **T** F

Chapter 8

EXERCISE 8.2

3. **P:** When 30,000 people in an online survey of English usage conducted by Professor Bert Vaux of Harvard University were asked how they addressed a group of two or more people, the largest number (42.5%) said they used *you guys*.

∴ Most Americans refer to a group of two or more people as *you guys*.

Issue: Whether most Americans refer to a group of two or more people as *you guys*

How do most Americans refer to a group of two or more people? ① They use the words *you guys*. ② This is the conclusion of an online survey of English usage conducted by Professor Bert Vaux of Harvard University that has had over 30,000 participants. ③ When people were asked how they addressed a group of two or more people, the largest number (42.5%) said they used *you guys*. Interestingly, ④ *y'all* was given by 14% of the respondents.

S: 30,000 respondents to an online survey of English pronunciation conducted by Professor Bert Vaux of Harvard University
T: all Americans
F: refer to a group of two or more people as *you guys*

6. **P:** The cognitive skills required for computer programming, playing a musical instrument, and playing chess are acquired only after diligent and consistent practice.

∴ All cognitive skills are acquired only after diligent and consistent practice.

Issue: Whether good cognitive skills are acquired only after diligent and consistent practice

① You sometimes hear it said that people who have good cognitive skills are just born with them.

I disagree. Given that the cognitive skills required for computer programming, playing a musical instrument, and playing chess are acquired only after diligent and consistent practice, all cognitive skills must be acquired by the same means.

↓

S: the cognitive skills required for computer programming, playing a musical instrument, and playing chess

T: all cognitive skills

F: acquired only after diligent and consistent practice

9. **P:** Five of the hunting implements found at the previously undiscovered Native American campsite in Michigan were shown by carbon dating to be over 2,000 years old.

∴ The vast majority of the hunting implements that were discovered at the Native American campsite in Michigan are a couple of thousand years old.

Issue: Whether the vast majority of the hunting implements that were discovered at the Native American campsite in Michigan are a couple of thousand years old

① Recently a team of archaeologists found a previously undiscovered Native American campsite in Michigan that contained hundreds of hunting implements. ② Five of the several hundred arrowheads and other hunting implements found at the site were carbon-dated. ③ They were shown to be over 2,000 years old. So it's likely that ④ the vast majority of those tools that were discovered at the site are a couple of thousand years old.

↓

S: five of the hunting implements found at the Native American campsite in Michigan

T: all of the hunting implements that were discovered at the Native American campsite in Michigan

F: a couple of thousand years old

EXERCISE 8.5

3. B is stronger. A has a sample of 3 oranges, and B has a sample of 10 oranges, so the sample in B is larger.

EXERCISE 8.7

3. A is stronger. A has a sample of over 30,000 people, and B has a sample of 30 people, so the sample in A is larger. Additionally, the sample in B is biased.

EXERCISE 8.8

3. a. Stronger because, although this sample is no more representative of the target than the sample in the original argument, this sample is less likely to have the feature
   b. Stronger because the sample is more representative of the target
   c. Stronger because the sample is more representative of the target
   d. Weaker because the sample is biased toward the feature

6. a. Stronger because the sample size is larger
   b. Weaker because the sample is self-selected
   c. Weaker because the sample is biased toward the feature
   d. Weaker because the sample is biased toward the feature

9. a. Stronger because the sample size is more varied
   b. Weaker because the sample is biased toward the feature
   c. No change because the additional question concerns a different country
   d. Weaker because the sample is less representative of the target

EXERCISE 8.9

3. ① In 2008, several universities participated in a study in which 80 randomly selected new high school graduates were compared to another 82 students who served as the control group. ② The students who attended the summer programs were more likely to attend a four-year school (41% compared to 26% in the control group). This proves that ③ the participants in the study are much more likely to enroll in college as a result of their participation in summer programs. Therefore, ④ most students will benefit from summer programs run by their high schools that provide them with the information, skills, and support they need to succeed in college.—Karen Arnold, *Thought and Action*

This passage from Karen Arnold in *Thought and Action* contains an argument. The issue is whether most students will benefit from summer programs run by their high schools that provide them with the information, skills, and support they need to succeed in college. The conclusion is that most students will benefit from summer programs run by their high schools that provide them with the information, skills, and support they need to succeed in college. The premise is that the participants in a 2008 study were more likely to enroll in college as a result of their participation in summer programs.

This passage contains a subargument. The intermediate conclusion is that the participants in a 2008 study were more likely to enroll in college as a result of their participation in summer programs. The premise is that the students in a 2008 study who attended the summer programs were more likely to attend a four-year school (41% compared to 26% in the control group).

This is an inductive generalization. It is strong because, although the sample size is small, the sample is random.

6. ① <u>The high cost of private golf clubs prevents minorities and women from joining</u>. This is because ② <u>few women and minorities belong to private clubs</u>, and ③ <u>prices have remained high for years even though other barriers to membership have disappeared</u>.—Kaser and Brooks, *Sports and Entertainment Management*

This passage from Kaser and Brooks' *Sports and Entertainment Management* contains an argument. The issue is whether the high cost of private golf clubs prevents minorities and women from joining. The conclusion is that the high cost of private golf clubs prevents

minorities and women from joining. The first premise is that few women and minorities belong to private clubs. The second premise is that prices have remained high for years even though other barriers to membership have disappeared.

This is an inductive, causal argument.

9. This passage from Coffin and Stacey's *Western Civilizations* does not contain an argument. It has at least two claims, one of which offers a reason for the other, but the reason does not attempt to prove that the other claim is true.

Chapter 9

EXERCISE 9.2

3. **P1:** Beefsteak tomatoes are very juicy.
   P2: <u>Roma tomatoes are like Beefsteak tomatoes.</u>
   ∴ Roma tomatoes are juicy.

   Issue: Whether Roma tomatoes are juicy

   S: Beefsteak tomatoes
   T: Roma tomatoes
   F: being very juicy

6. **P1:** The second chemistry exam is similar to the first chemistry exam.
   P2: <u>You did well on the first chemistry exam.</u>
   ∴ You will do well on the second chemistry exam.

   Issue: Whether you will do well on the second chemistry exam

   S: the first chemistry exam
   T: the second chemistry exam
   F: you performed well

9. **P1:** The Hudson River is like the James River.
   P2: The James River is less polluted than it was a <u>couple of decades ago.</u>
   ∴ The Hudson River is less polluted than it was a couple of decades ago.

   Issue: Whether the Hudson River is less polluted than it was a couple of decades ago

   S: the James River
   T: the Hudson River
   F: less polluted than it was a couple of decades ago

EXERCISE 9.5

3. **P1:** A prince is the child of a king.
   P2: A princess is the child of a king.
   ∴   A prince is like a princess.

   P1: A prince is like a princess.
   P2: A princess leads a sheltered life.
   ∴   A prince leads a sheltered life.

   Issue: Whether a prince leads a sheltered life

   S: a princess
   T: a prince
   F: leads a sheltered life

   ① A prince is the child of a king. ② A princess, too, is the child of a king. So ③ a prince is like a princess. Also, ④ a princess leads a sheltered life. Thus, ⑤ a prince most likely leads a sheltered life.

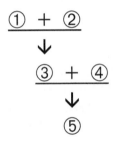

6. **P1:** Astrology studies the stars and has been around for hundreds of years.
   P2: Astronomy studies the stars and has been around for hundreds of years.
   ∴   Astrology is like astronomy.

   P1: Astrology is like astronomy.
   P2: Astronomy is worthy of being called a science.
   ∴   Astrology is worthy of being called a science.

   Issue: Whether astrology is worthy of being called a science

   S: astronomy
   T: astrology
   F: worthy of being called a science

   ① Astrology studies the stars and has been around for hundreds of years. ② Astronomy also studies the stars and has been around for hundreds of years. We know that ③ astronomy is worthy of being called a science. Therefore, ④ astrology is likewise worthy of being called a science. ⑤ Astrology is like astronomy.

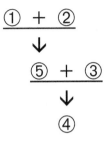

9. **P1:** The Nile River is a body of fresh water.
   P2: The Mississippi River, the Potomac River, and the Hudson River are all bodies of fresh water.
   ∴   The Nile River is like the Mississippi, Potomac, and Hudson Rivers.

   P1: The Nile River is like the Mississippi, Potomac, and Hudson Rivers.
   P2: The Mississippi River, the Potomac River, and the Hudson River all flow toward the ocean.
   ∴   The Nile River flows toward the ocean.

   Issue: Whether the Nile River flows toward the ocean

   S: the Mississippi River, the Potomac River, and the Hudson River
   T: the Nile River
   F: flows toward the ocean

   ① The Mississippi River, the Potomac River, and the Hudson River are all bodies of fresh water ② that flow toward the ocean. So ③ the Nile River probably flows toward the ocean, since ④ it, too, is a body of fresh water. ⑤ The Nile River is like the Mississippi, Potomac, and Hudson Rivers.

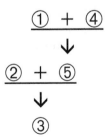

12. **P1:** Utah is dry, mountainous, and dependent on water from other states.
    P2: California is dry, mountainous, and dependent on water from other states.
    ∴   Utah is like California.

P1: Utah is like California.
P2: California has profited from large-scale drip irrigation of agricultural land.
∴   Utah would profit from large-scale drip irrigation of agricultural land.

Issue: Whether Utah would profit from large-scale drip irrigation of agricultural land

S: California
T: Utah
F: profit from large-scale drip irrigation of agricultural land

We can infer that ① <u>Utah is much like California</u> because ② <u>Utah is dry, mountainous, and dependent on water from other states</u> and ③ <u>California is dry, mountainous, and dependent on water from other states</u>. Because ④ <u>California has profited from large-scale drip irrigation of agricultural land</u>, ⑤ <u>Utah would probably also profit from large-scale drip irrigation of agricultural land</u>.

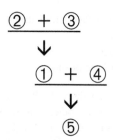

15. **P:** Comedies and musicals are both theatrical performances.
    ∴ Comedies are like musicals.

    P1: Comedies are like musicals.
    P2: Musicals incorporate dancing.
    ∴   Comedies incorporate dancing.

    Issue: Whether comedies incorporate dancing

    S: musicals
    T: comedies
    F: incorporate dancing

    ① <u>Comedies and musicals are both theatrical performances</u>. Given that ② <u>musicals incorporate dancing</u>, ③ <u>comedies are likely to incorporate dancing</u> also.
    ④ Comedies are like musicals.

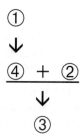

EXERCISE 9.7

3. B is stronger. A lists 2 similarities, while B lists 3, so B has more similarities.
6. A is stronger. A lists 4 similarities, while B lists 3 similarities, so A has more similarities.
9. B is stronger. A lists 2 similarities, while B lists 3 similarities, so B has more similarities.

EXERCISE 9.9

3. The similarity (directed by Tim Burton) is relevant to the feature (stars Johnny Depp).

    S: *Charlie and the Chocolate Factory, Corpse Bride, Sweeney Todd,* and *Alice in Wonderland*
    T: *Maleficent*
    F: stars Johnny Depp

EXERCISE 9.10

3. a. Stronger because sample is larger
   b. Weaker because difference is relevant
   c. Weaker because difference is possibly relevant
   d. No change because difference is irrelevant

EXERCISE 9.12

3. Just as ① <u>the leader of an athletic team must have a management style that facilitates the group working together</u>, so too ② <u>the manager of a business must be able to help his or her employees to work well together</u>. This is because ③ <u>a manager of a business is like an athletic team coach</u> given that ④ <u>each has to work well with people of all different backgrounds and personalities</u>.—Les R. Deblay, James L. Burrow, and Brad A. Kleindl, *Principles of Business.*

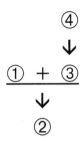

This passage from Les R. Deblay, James L. Burrow, and Brad A. Kleindl's book, *Principles of Business*, contains an argument. The issue is whether the manager of a business must be able to help his or her employees to work well together. The conclusion is that the manager of a business must be able to help his or her employees to work well together. The first premise is that a manager of a business is like an athletic team coach. The second premise is that the leader of an athletic team must have a management style that facilitates the group working together.

The passage contains a subargument. The intermediate conclusion is that a manager of business is like an athletic team coach. The premise is that both a manager of business and an athletic team coach have to work well with people of all different backgrounds and personalities.

This is an inductive, analogical argument. There is one analogy presented, there is one similarity supporting the analogy, and the similarity is relevant to the feature, so this is a strong argument.

6. ① A Web poll reveals that the top feature iPod users would want on the next generation of the popular music player is an FM radio tuner. ② A recent online survey of more than 25,000 participants by Detroit-based rock radio consultants, Jacobs Media, found a full 43% of iPod owners want an FM radio integrated into the next version of the iPod. ③ These participants are more than likely listeners to rock stations on the radio. ④ Participation was solicited on 69 different rock radio stations.—*Infosyncworld.com*

This passage from *Infosyncworld.com* contains an argument. The issue is whether the top feature iPod users would want on the next generation of the popular music player is an FM radio tuner. The conclusion is that the top feature iPod users would want on the next generation of the popular music player is an FM radio tuner. The premise is that 43% of iPod owners who responded to a recent Web poll want an FM radio integrated into the next version of the iPod.

This is an inductive generalization.

9. This passage from CBS News is not an argument. There are two claims, but neither provides a reason for the other, as is necessary in an argument.

Chapter 10

EXERCISE 10.2

3. **P1:** The bugs that were eating the spinach in my garden have disappeared.
   P2: I surrounded my garden with marigolds.
   ∴ The bugs disappearing was caused by my surrounding my garden with marigolds.

   Issue: Whether the bugs disappearing was caused by my surrounding my garden with marigolds

   R: disappearing
   P: being surrounded by marigolds

6. **P1:** My two friends and I got sick after eating dinner together.
   P2: My two friends and I ate the clam chowder.
   ∴ My two friends and I getting sick last night was caused by our eating the clam chowder.

   Issue: Whether my two friends and I getting sick last night was caused by our eating the clam chowder

   R: getting sick
   P: eating clam chowder

9. **P1:** The IRS reported a higher-than-usual number of people not paying their taxes last year.
   P2: Last year was the first year in a decade that taxes were increased.
   ∴ An increased number of scofflaws who don't pay taxes was caused by taxes being increased last year.

   Issue: Whether an increased number of scofflaws who don't pay taxes was caused by taxes being increased last year

   R: increase in scofflaws who don't pay taxes
   P: increase in taxes

EXERCISE 10.6

3. **P1:** Traffic is heavier on Milton Avenue since the beginning of the month.
   P2: The road department finished widening Milton Avenue at the beginning of the month.
   ∴ The road being widened caused the traffic to become heavier on Milton Avenue.

   Issue: Whether the road being widened caused the traffic to become heavier on Milton Avenue

   R: an increase in traffic
   P: widening the road
   M: difference

   ① Traffic is heavier on Milton Avenue since the beginning of the month. Since ② the road department finished widening the road right about that time, ③ it's probably responsible for the extra traffic.

6. **P1:** In three major metropolitan areas in the Northeast, mandatory waiting periods for handgun purchases were signed into law last year.
   P2: Homicide rates in three major metropolitan areas in the Northeast dropped by an average of 15% last year.
   ∴ The homicide rates in three major metropolitan areas in the Northeast dropping by an average of 15% was caused by mandatory waiting periods for handgun purchases being signed into law.

   P: The homicide rates in three major metropolitan areas in the Northeast dropping by an average of 15% was caused by mandatory waiting periods for handgun purchases being signed into law.
   ∴ Waiting periods for handgun purchases reduce homicides in any city.

   Issue: Whether waiting periods for handgun purchases reduce homicides in any city

   R: dropping homicide rates
   P: mandatory waiting periods
   M: difference
   ① In three major metropolitan areas in the Northeast, mandatory waiting periods for handgun purchases were signed into law last year. ② Since then, homicide rates dropped by an average of 15%. It is reasonable to conclude that ③ waiting periods for handgun purchases reduce homicides.
   ④ The homicide rates in three major metropolitan areas in the Northeast dropping by an average of 15% was caused by mandatory waiting periods for handgun purchases being signed into law.

9. **P1:** While hiking yesterday, you brushed up against some poison oak.
   P2: Your blisters have shrunk considerably since you began putting on the acorn paste.
   ∴ Your blisters shrinking was caused by using acorn paste.

   P: Your blisters shrinking was caused by using acorn paste.
   ∴ Covering the blistered area in a paste made from soaked and cooked acorns is an effective treatment for poison oak.

   Issue: Whether covering the blistered area in a paste made from soaked and cooked acorns is an effective treatment for poison oak

   R: shrinking blisters
   P: using acorn paste
   M: difference

   ① That old Native American cure for poison oak—covering the blistered area in a paste made from soaked and cooked acorns—is clearly effective. ② While hiking yesterday, you brushed up against some poison oak, and ③ your blisters have shrunk considerably since you began putting on the acorn paste.
   ④ Your blisters shrinking was caused by using acorn paste.

   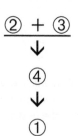

EXERCISE 10.7

3. A is stronger. Unlike B, A provides evidence that the flu shots were the only possible cause.
6. B is stronger. Unlike A, B states that advertisers' complaints are the only possible cause.
9. B is stronger. Unlike A, B states that chipped lead paint is the only possible cause.

EXERCISE 10.8

3. a. Weaker because another difference is introduced
   b. Stronger because it provides evidence that the installation is the only difference
   c. Weaker because another difference is introduced
   d. No change because the new difference is not a reasonable cause of the resulting event

EXERCISE 10.9

3. ① In 2010, a mudslide in Germany killed three people. ② Investigators discovered that a top-secret underground chemical facility used by the Nazis in World War II had collapsed directly underneath the site. It is believed, then, that ③ the collapse of this facility triggered the disaster.— *Xenophilia (True Strange Stuff)*

This passage from *Xenophilia (True Strange Stuff)* contains an argument. The issue is whether the collapse of a top-secret underground chemical facility used by the Nazis in World War II triggered a mudslide that killed three people in Germany. The conclusion is that the collapse of a top-secret underground chemical facility used by the Nazis in World War II triggered a mudslide that killed three people in Germany. The first premise is that in 2010, a mudslide in Germany killed three people. The second premise is that investigators discovered that a top-secret underground chemical facility used by the Nazis in World War II had collapsed directly underneath the site of a deadly 2010 German mudslide.

This argument is an inductive, causal argument. The argument is relatively strong because it suggests that the suspected cause is the only relevant difference between the time when the hillside was stable and the time of the mudslide.

6. ① Middle-aged and older women who have migraines and who experience auras (e.g., flashing lights that might signal the onset of pain) appear to have a higher risk of strokes and heart attacks than their migraine-free peers, a new study suggests. ② The study looked at 27,798 female health professionals ages 45 and older, including 3,568 who had migraines. ③ It showed that women with weekly migraines with auras were four times as likely to have had a stroke during the 12-year study as women without migraines.—*Neurology*

This passage from *Neurology* contains an argument. The issue is whether middle-aged and older women who have migraines and who experience auras (e.g., flashing lights that might signal the onset of pain) have a higher risk of strokes and heart attacks than their migraine-free peers. The conclusion is that middle-aged and older women who have migraines and who experience auras (e.g., flashing lights that might signal the onset of pain) have a higher risk of strokes and heart attacks than their migraine-free peers. The premise is that a study of 27,798 female health professions showed that women with weekly migraines with auras were four times as likely to have had a stroke during the 12-year study as women without migraines.

This argument is an inductive generalization.

9. There's good evidence to suggest that ① a new non-police program successfully reduced Chicago area crime rates last year. ② Violent crime arrests dropped by 44 percent after the city instituted a program called "BAM—Sports Edition," ③ which provides 7th–10th grade boys with small group instruction in social and life skills in school, and sports programming after school.—*The Washington Post*

The passage from *The Washington Post* contains an argument. The issue is whether the BAM—Sports Edition program successfully reduced Chicago area crime rates last year. The conclusion is that the BAM—Sports Edition program successfully reduced Chicago area crime rates last year. The premise is that violent crime arrests dropped by 44 percent after the city instituted a program called "BAM—Sports Edition."

This argument is an inductive, causal argument. The argument is weak because the arguer concludes that one event was caused by another simply because one preceded the other. There is no evidence that the program was the only reasonable cause of the drop in crime rates.

Chapter 11

EXERCISE 11.2

3. Begging the question
   P: <u>Anyone who kills lots of people has lost the right to live.</u>
   ∴ Serial killers have forfeited their right to live.

   Issue: Whether serial killers have forfeited their right to live

6. Not a fallacy
   P1: James had a motive for murder.
   P2: James had an opportunity for murder.
   P3: James had no alibi for the time when the murder took place.
   ∴ James is a murder.

   Issue: Whether James is a murderer

9. Begging the question
   P: Every university student should have to take at least one course in psychology.
   ∴ A psychology course should be required of all college students.

   Issue: Whether a psychology course should be required of all college students

EXERCISE 11.5

3. Appeal to ignorance
   P: <u>You can't prove that extraterrestrials don't exist.</u>
   ∴ Extraterrestrials are real.

   Issue: Whether extraterrestrials are real

6. Not a fallacy. The arguer does not shift the burden of proof.
   P1: Every Christmas Eve, the cookies and milk we leave for Santa are eaten.
   P2: Every Christmas Eve, packages are under the tree that weren't there when we went to bed.
   ∴ Santa Claus exists.

   Issue: Whether Santa Claus exists

9. Not a fallacy. The arguer does not shift the burden of proof.
   P1: If ghosts exist, they would exist outside the boundaries of the universe science describes.
   P2: Nothing can live outside the boundaries of the universe science describes.
   ∴ Ghosts don't exist.

   Issue: Whether ghosts exist

EXERCISE 11.6

3. Appeal to ignorance
   P: No one has ever shown that another kind of dog is easier to train than an Australian shepherd.
   ∴ Australian shepherds are the easiest dogs to train.

   Issue: Whether Australian shepherds are the easiest dogs to train

6. Begging the question
   P: <u>My child is so intelligent.</u>
   ∴ My child is smart.

   Issue: Whether my child is smart

9. Appeal to ignorance
   P: No one has ever shown that the palm reader's readings aren't accurate.
   ∴ You should believe what the palm reader tells you.

   Issue: Whether you should believe what the palm reader tells you

EXERCISE 11.9

3. Appeal to illegitimate authority
   P1: Dow Constantine was publicly endorsed by Pearl Jam.
   P2: Pearl Jam is a famous rock band.
   ∴ Mr. Constantine must be the best candidate for the job of King County executive.

   Issue: Whether Mr. Constantine must be the best candidate for the job of King County executive

6. Appeal to illegitimate authority
   P1: Aldous Huxley was convinced that wearing eyeglasses actually makes the eyes weaker.
   P2: Aldous Huxley is the celebrated author of *Brave New World*.
   ∴ We should not get corrective glasses to improve our sight.

   Issue: Whether we should get corrective glasses to improve our sight

9. Appeal to illegitimate authority
   P1: Jerry said that downloading pirated copies of movies is not cheating anyone.
   P2: Jerry is my roommate.
   ∴ There's nothing wrong with downloading pirated copies of movies.

   Issue: Whether there's anything wrong with downloading pirated copies of movies

EXERCISE 11.13

3. Ad hominem
   P1: Mr. Johnson argues that oil deposits in Warren County will last another 100 years.
   P2: Mr. Johnson is the president of Lone Star Oil Company.
   ∴ The oil deposits in Warren County will not last another 100 years.

   Issue: Whether the oil deposits in Warren County will last another 100 years

6. Ad hominem
   P1: The economist John Flamingo argues that we should all invest in the stock market.
   P2: The economist John Flamingo hasn't invested any of his money in the stock market.
   ∴ We should not invest in the stock market.

   Issue: Whether we should all invest in the stock market

9. Ad hominem
   P1: Frank has argued that planting trees near your home will reduce summertime energy use.
   P2: Frank is just looking to increase his landscaping business.
   ∴ Planting trees near your home will not reduce summertime energy use.

   Issue: Whether planting trees near your home will reduce summertime energy use

EXERCISE 11.14

3. Ad hominem
   P1: The Chinese government argues that the United States should give more support to developing countries.
   P2: The Chinese government does not provide substantial aid to developing countries.
   ∴ The United States should not give more support to developing countries.

   Issue: Whether the United States should give more support to developing countries

6. Ad hominem
   P1: The National Dairy Board argues that milk producers must be granted subsidies.
   P2: The dairy board just wants its members to make more money, while you pay more for groceries.
   ∴ Milk producers should not be granted subsidies.

   Issue: Whether milk producers should be granted subsidies

9. Not a fallacy.
   P1: Mr. Waterstone has a poor performance record.
   P2: Mr. Waterstone tries to undermine others in the office.
   P3: Mr. Waterstone spreads lies about his co-workers.
   ∴ Mr. Waterstone should not be promoted to district manager.

   Issue: Whether Mr. Waterstone should be promoted to district manager

EXERCISE 11.16

3. This argument commits the strawman fallacy. The conclusion extends the issue to every form of birth control, rather than addressing abortion only.
   P1: Not everyone can afford to have a child.
   P2: Legal birth control allows families to plan their pregnancies.
   ∴ Outlawing every form of birth control is a bad idea.

   Issue: Whether abortion should be opposed

6. This argument commits the strawman fallacy. The conclusion pretends that the issue restricts elementary education to a multicultural curriculum only, rather than including a multicultural curriculum along with other educational content.
   P: Teaching nothing but multicultural dogma will leave our students deficient in the basic skills they need to learn such as math, reading, and science.
   ∴ We should reject teaching nothing but multicultural dogma.

   Issue: Whether a multicultural curriculum in elementary school will lead to more tolerance and fewer biases toward those perceived as "different"

9. This argument commits the strawman fallacy. The conclusion extends the issue to include comprehensive spying on employees, not just to employee Internet usage.

P: No one supports Big Brother spying on employees' private lives to learn everything about them

∴ Employers should not be allowed to spy on the private lives of their employees and learn everything about them.

Issue: Whether employers have the right to monitor employee Internet use

EXERCISE 11.18

3. Red herring fallacy
P1: Texting is a great way to stay in touch with family and friends.
P2: Texting allows you to send someone a message whenever you want.
P3: Texting is fun.
∴ Texting while driving is not as dangerous as drinking and driving.

Issue: Whether texting while driving is as dangerous as drinking and driving

6. Red herring fallacy
P1: Pianos cost a lot of money.
P2: Piano lessons are difficult to arrange.
P3: Most people lack sufficient room for such a large instrument as a piano.
∴ Learning to play the piano does not help children do better at math.

Issue: Whether learning to play the piano helps children do better at math

9. Red herring fallacy
P1: Without nations, we would be living in tribal groups, fighting with other tribes over hunting territories.
P2: Nationalism has allowed the human race to make progress in combating disease, malnutrition, superstition, and many other evils people experience in tribal culture.
∴ Nationalism was not a volatile force in the mid-nineteenth century.

Issue: Whether nationalism was a volatile force in the mid-nineteenth century

EXERCISE 11.19

3. Strawman fallacy
P1: We need to pay for additional inventory.
P2: We need to pay our suppliers.

P3: We need to put money away for a rainy day.
∴ Using all the company savings just to enrich the employees is a bad idea.

Issue: Whether the new contract should include a raise that keeps employee wages in line with inflation

6. Strawman fallacy
P: Competition is unfair if athletes are allowed to cheat without consequences.
∴ We must penalize athletes who cheat if we want to ensure the quality of sports.

Issue: Whether we should suspend athletes who use performance enhancers

9. No fallacy
P1: The leg bones of young horses are not very strong.
P2: If the leg bones of young horses are not strong, then injury can easily result.
∴ Racing a horse before it is fully mature can result in life-threatening leg injuries.

Issue: Whether racing a horse before it is fully mature can result in life-threatening leg injuries

EXERCISE 11.20

3. ① Many have applauded the success of welfare reform because ② many have made the transition from welfare to employment. However, ③ welfare reform has often done more harm than good. First, ④ the employment found by former welfare recipients does not pay well enough to support a family. Second, ⑤ parents who are unable to afford child care costs routinely leave their children at home to fend for themselves. And, finally, ⑥ the jobs obtained by former welfare recipients rarely include healthcare benefits.—Lester Spence, political science professor at Johns Hopkins University.

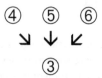

This passage from Lester Spence, a political science professor at Johns Hopkins University, contains an argument. The issue is whether welfare reform has often done more harm than good. The conclusion is that welfare reform has often done more harm than good. The first premise is that the employment found by former welfare recipients does not pay well enough to support a family. The second premise is that parents who are unable to afford child-care costs routinely leave their children at home to fend for themselves. The third premise is that the jobs obtained by former welfare recipients rarely include health-care benefits.

6. This passage contains an argument. The issue is whether the elementary and high school teachers in this country deserve our respect. The conclusion is that we should not worship teachers like they are enlightened beings. The first premise is that teachers make mistakes. The second premise is that some teachers are lazy and incompetent. The third premise is that worshipping any human is irreligious.

This passage commits the strawman fallacy because the author misrepresents the conclusion of the opponent's argument and then attacks that view in its misrepresented form.

9. ① Some people argue that we should increase foreign aid to Pakistan. But ② this is a terrible idea! ③ Pakistan is currently too unstable and ④ their regime is corrupt. Furthermore, ⑤ they may use the money to attack neighboring countries like India.

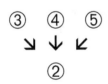

This passage contains an argument. The issue is whether we should increase foreign aid to Pakistan. The conclusion is that we should not increase foreign aid to Pakistan. The first premise is that Pakistan is currently too unstable. The second premise is that Pakistan's regime is corrupt. The third premise is that Pakistan may use the money to attack neighboring countries like India.

Chapter 12

EXERCISE 12.9

Student answers will vary.

Chapter 13

EXERCISE 13.3

3. Some M are not S̲.

6. Some kangaroo rats are members of an endangered species.
9. All good ice creams are chocolate ice creams.

EXERCISE 13.4

3. Does not commit the fallacy.
6. Commits the fallacy of undistributed middle.
9. Does not commit the fallacy.

EXERCISE 13.5

3. Invalid. The middle term is not distributed.
6. Invalid. A valid argument cannot have two universal premises and a particular conclusion; if a premise is negative, the conclusion must be negative.
9. Invalid. A term (*nutritious snacks*) is distributed in the conclusion, but not in a premise.

EXERCISE 13.6

3. Invalid. A valid argument cannot have two negative premises; a term (*penguins*) is distributed in the conclusion, but not in a premise.
6. Invalid. A term (*Australian animals*) is distributed in the conclusion, but not in a premise.
9. Invalid. The middle term is not distributed.
12. Invalid. A valid argument cannot have two universal premises and a particular conclusion; if a premise is negative, the conclusion must be negative.
15. Invalid. A term (*social scientists*) is distributed in the conclusion, but not in a premise.

EXERCISE 13.10

3. *All Y are Z.
   All X are Y.
   All X are Z.
6. All good things to eat are things low in calories.
   *No things low in calories are mature lobsters.
   No mature lobsters are good things to eat.
9. *Some elephants are not domesticated.
   All elephants are herbivores.
   Some herbivores are not domesticated.
12. All true sailors are pirates.
   *Some true sailors are tank commanders.
   Some tank commanders are pirates.
15. *Some places the sun shines are places in the shade.
   No places plants will grow are places in the shade.
   Some places the sun shines aren't places plants will grow.

Chapter 14

EXERCISE 14.3

3. The argument is invalid.

$$G \supset I \,/\, {\sim} J \supset I \,/\!/\, {\sim} I \supset G$$
F T T   F T T F   T F F F

6. The argument is invalid.

$${\sim}A \supset (B \lor C) \,/\, {\sim}B \,/\!/\, C \supset A$$
T F T   F T T   T F   T F F

9. The argument is invalid.

$${\sim}A \supset B \,/\, C \supset A \,/\, C \supset {\sim}B \,/\!/\, A \lor {\sim}B$$
T F T T   F T F   F T F T   F F F T

EXERCISE 14.4

3. The argument is valid.
A = We will avoid further catastrophic bridge collapses like the I-35 Mississippi River bridge collapse in Minnesota in 2007.
S = Congress will authorize massive spending for retrofitting the aging bridges in this country.
R = Congress will be responsible for the loss of life in future bridge collapses.
O = Congress will do something to outrage the voters.

$$S \lor R \,/\, R \supset O \,/\, {\sim}O \,/\!/\, A \supset S$$
F F F   F T F   T F   T F F

OR

$$S \lor R \,/\, R \supset O \,/\, {\sim}O \,/\!/\, A \supset S$$
F T T   T F F   **T** F   T F F

OR

$$S \lor R \,/\, R \supset O \,/\, {\sim}O \,/\!/\, A \supset S$$
F T T   T T T   F T   T F F

6. The argument is valid.
S = Your car will start.
O = Your car is out of gas.
B = Your car's battery is dead.

$${\sim}S \supset (O \lor B) \,/\, {\sim}O \,/\!/\, S \lor B$$
T F F   F F F   T F   F F F

OR

$${\sim}S \supset (O \lor B) \,/\, {\sim}O \,/\!/\, S \lor B$$
T F T   T T F   **F** T   F F F

9. The argument is invalid.
R = Proposition 8 is a constitutional revision.
B = Proposition 8 is quantitatively broad.
D = Proposition 8 is qualitatively deep.
P = Proposition 8 was properly introduced.
V = Proposition 8 is a valid law.

$$R \supset (B \lor D) \,/\, (R \supset {\sim}P) \cdot ({\sim}P \supset {\sim}V) \,/\, {\sim}B \cdot {\sim}D \,/\!/\, V$$
F T   F F F   F T ?   **T** ?   T T F   T F T T F   **F**

Index